MACMILLAN / McGRAW-HILL

Mathematics in Action

Audrey L. Jackson   Martin L. Johnson   Steven J. Leinwand
Richard D. Lodholz   Gary L. Musser   Walter G. Secada

MACMILLAN/McGRAW-HILL SCHOOL PUBLISHING COMPANY
New York   Columbus

CONSULTANTS

MULTICULTURAL AND EDUCATIONAL CONSULTANTS

Rim An

Marcia Ascher

Elsie Babcock

Vicki Chan

Dr. Alejandro Gallard

Zelda Gold

Jerilyn Grignon

Earlene Hall

Susan Lair

Dr. Barbara Merino

Carol Mitchell

James R. Murphy

Gail Lowe Parrino

Yolanda Rodriguez

Claudia Zaslavsky

ASSESSMENT CONSULTANT

Michael Priestley

COOPERATIVE LEARNING CONSULTANT

Liana Nan Graves

ACKNOWLEDGMENTS

The publisher gratefully acknowledges permission to reprint the following copyrighted material:

"Average Mass of Adult Animals," adapted from COMPARISONS, The Diagram Group. Copyright © 1980. Published by St. Martin's Press and used with their permission.

"Normal Monthly Temperatures in U.S. Cities," from THE WORLD ALMANAC, 1988. Copyright © Newspaper Enterprise Association. New York, N.Y. 10166. Used by permission.

"There's a Hole in the Bucket," from MUSIC AND YOU, Gr. 3, Barbara Staton and Merrill Staton, Senior Authors. Copyright © 1988 Macmillan Publishing Company.

COVER DESIGN Designframe Inc. **COVER PHOTOGRAPHY** Pete McArthur

ILLUSTRATION Rick Berlin; 126, 156, 157 • Hal Brooks; 64, 230, 231 • Patrick Chapin; 34, 35, 142, 143 • Circa 86, Inc.; 293, 298, 337, 338, 407, 410 • Eva Cockrille; 348, 349, 360 • William Colrus; 148, 149 • Margaret Cusack; 312, 313 • Jim Deigan; 3, 346, 347 • Daniel DelValle; 32, 33, 124, 128, 158, 222, 342 • Nancy Didion; 28, 29, 430A, 490, 491 • Eldon Doty; 18, 19, 78, 79, 97, 422F • Kathleen Dunne; 4, 5, 238, 454, 455, 494, 495 • Barbara Friedman; 57, 66, 196 • Don Gambino; 249 • Kate Gartner; 266, 267, 344A, 345 • Rick Geary; 354, 355 • Myron Grossman; 388, 389 • Marika Hahn; 460, 461 • Gary Halgren; 426, 427 • Meryl Henderson; 107 • Julie Hodd; 272, 273 • Pamela Johnson; 268 • Dave Joly; 16, 17, 394, 395, 396, 397 • Terry Kovalcik; 146, 147, 280 • Lions Gate; 8, 9 • Loretta Lustig; 316, 317, 488, 489 • Benton Mahan; 181 • Ginidir Marshall; 414, 502 • Mas Mayamoto; 72, 73 • Richard McNeel; 194, 195 • Patrick Merrell; 198, 199 • MKR Design; Handmade props • Leo Monahan; 1 • Hima Pamoedjo; 83, 265, 286, 382A, 416A, B, C, 428, 438, 516 • Cathy Pavia; 224, 225, 380, 381 • Deborah Pinkney; 382, 383 • Susan Pizzo; 6, 7 • Scott Pollack; 26, 27 • Mary Power; 364 • Chris Reed; 502 • Doug Roy; 278, 279, 288 • Margaret San Filippo; 108, 200, 201, 226, 227, 343 • Roz Schanzer; 76, 77, 150, 151, 276, 277 • S.D. Schindler; 411, 515 • Terry Sirrell; 112, 113 • Jerry Smath; 100, 101 • April Blair Stewart; 320, 424, 425, 456 • Susan Swan; 116, 117 • George Ulrich; 211, 229 • Bruce VanPatter; 464, 465 • Vantage Art, Inc.; 217, 377 • Anna Walker; 70, 71 • Linda Weller; 307, 468 • Josie Yee; 500 • Lane Yerkes; 160, 161, 188, 189 • Rusty Zabransky; 36, 168, 204, 234, 242, 246, 285, 286, 287, 324A, 325, 398, 470 • Ron Zalme; 190, 191, 232, 233, 418, 419, 434, 435 • Maggie Zanders; 312, 313, 325, 486 • Jerry Zimmerman; 118, 119, 152, 153, 184, 185, 384 • **CONTENTS:** Don Baker

PHOTOGRAPHY Allstock/Patricia Woeber, 378 • © American Museum of Natural History/© Craig Chesek, 484C, 485BR; Denis Finnin, 98T; R.P. Sheridan, 99T • Art Resource, 341 • The British Museum, 50L, 51BL, BR • Bruce Coleman Inc./E.R. Degginger, 327B; Keith Gunnar, 206T; M.P. Kahl, 170T; Hans Reinhard, 37B, 287 • Comstock, 354-355 bkgnd • Bob Daemmrich, 122, 123; © Michael Thompson, 485BL • DDB Stock Photo/John Curtis, 99B • FPG International, 328T; B.A. Mikesell, 472T • Folio, Inc./Greg Pease, 416 • David R. Frazier, 357 • Frederic V. Granfeld Collection, 379C • Scott Harvey for MMSD, 31TR, 58T, 60TR, 386C • Grant Heilman Photography/Alan Pitcairn; 128B; Runk Schoenberger, 364R • Richard Haynes, Jr., 20, 21, 66, 67 • Michal Heron, 86BR, 162, 239, 243, 302, 303, 308, 322, 323, 358, 359, 393 • © 1992 The Huntington Library, Art Collections and Botanical Gardens, 300-301 • Ice Capades, 120 • The Image Bank, 234T; Cliff Feulner, 274T; Larry Dale Gordon, 30-31; Al Hamdan, 301; © Janeart Ltd., 192L; Benn Mitchell, 471MR; Guido Alberto Rossi, 218-219; Al Satterwhite, 274B; Michael Skott, 327M; Marc Soloman, 86TL; H. Wendler, 182-183; Eric L. Wheater, 10-11; Frank Whitney, 126B • The Image Works/Bob Daemmrich, 128T, 144 • Index/Stock International/Jack Gescheidt, 105; Tom Ross, 472B • Interarts Ltd., © 1992 GLA Kurtor AB, 50-51 • International Stock Photography Ltd./Brent Winebrenner, 38 • Ken Karp for MMSD, 24C, 25T • Shinen Kan Collection, Los Angeles County Museum of Art/Watanabe Nangaku (1767-1813) Edo Period, late 18th Century Kakemono, ink & slight color on paper 84¼ × 27¾, 260R • © 1987 Lawrence Migdale, 193T • Minden Pictures/© Frans Lanting, 484T • National Museum of the American Indian, 485C, T • Nawrocki Stock Photo/Wm. S. Nawrocki, 300-301R, 300B, L; © Larry Stevens, 50R; Steve Vidler, 378-379, 378BL inset • Michael Nelson, 328B • Northwind Picture Archives, 300C • Stephen Ogilvy, 15, 66TR, 104, 171, 187, 204, 205, 236, 237, 249, 262, 263, 285, 286, 304, 305, 306, 326, 327, 350, 364, 365, 399, 439, 473 • Omni-Photo Communications, Inc./Ken Karp, 12, 13, 22, 28, 36, 53, 55, 87, 154, 163, 166, 167, 168, 169, 220, 221, 392, 401, 436, 437; John Lei, 14, 16, 39, 52, 102, 103, 114, 115, 129, 154, 155, 242, 314, 315, 363, 364, 414, 415, 458, 459, 471, 473, 498, 499, 505 • Mark Philbrick for MMSD, 413R • Photo Researchers/Marc and Evelyne Bernheim, 248; John Bova, 183T; Ray Coleman, 234MB; F.B. Grunzweig, 467L; Richard Hutchings, 467R; Jacana, 234MR; Jacana/R. Konig, 126L; Steven J. Krasemann, 400; Ann Purcell, 219C; © Art Twomey, 484-485 bkgnd; Jerome Wexler, 234BL, 234BR • © Carl Purcell; 11B, 218T • The Picture Cube/© Glasheen Graphics, 51C • ProFiles West/Allen Russell; 148L, 412-413, 413L • Rainbow/Coco McCoy, 327TR • Research Plus, 206B; Franklin Avery, 141, 169, 341, 365; Laurence Bartone, 11, 37TL, 99, 127, 183, 205, 287, 379, 399, 413, 439, 453, 471, 503; Lawrence Migdale, 219, 247; H. Armstrong Roberts Inc./Camerique, 274M; Jeff Rotman, 127B, 287 • Joseph Sachs, 37TR, 207, 247, 329, 502 • J. Gerard Smith, 108, 206, 365 • from the Phillip Stern Estate, 260-261B • Stock Boston/Jacques Charles, 110; Bob Daemmrich, 192 • The Stock Market/Connie Hansen, 471BR; Brownie Harris, 504; Roy Morsch, 503; Claudia Parks, 452-453; Alese & Mort Pechter, 127T; Pete Salontos, 388-389, 450-451; Stephanie Stokes, 170B • Stock South, Walter Lewis, 300-301R, top • Taurus Photos, Inc./Alec Duncan, 236 • Third Coast Stock Source/© MacDonald Photography, 319T • Tom Stack & Associates/D.G. Barker, 182T • Uniphoto/© D. Pictor & J. Heaton, 340T, L; © Bob Shafer, 318L • Viesti Associates, Inc./Dab Barba, 165, 466; Skye Mason, 164, 202R, 203, 270; Ginny Ganong Nichols, 70L, 74, 75, 282, 310, 390, 391, 420, 432, 433, 462; Ken Ross, 30C, 31, 62, 63, 202L, 241, 271, 283, 311, 352, 356, 387, 463, 492C, 493, 496, 497; Joe Viesti, 111, 421, 492L • WestLight/© M. Angelo, 341C strip; Lawrence Manning, 453L; Robert Young Pelton, 464-465; © H.D. Thorean, 340 • Woodfin Camp & Associates/Marc & Evelyne Bernheim, 453B; Robert Frerck, 98-99; Michal Heron, 440; Loren McIntyre, 98M, L • **CONTENTS:** Bob Daemmrich, xT • Michal Heron, viiT • Ken Karp, viiB • John Lei, ivB, vB • Stephen Ogilvy, vi, viii, ix • Ginny Ganong Nichols, Viesti Associates, Inc., iiiT, ivB, v

Macmillan/McGraw-Hill School Division
10 Union Square East
New York, New York 10003

Printed in the United States of America
ISBN 0-02-109264-8 / 3
3 4 5 6 7 8 9 RRW 99 98 97 96 95

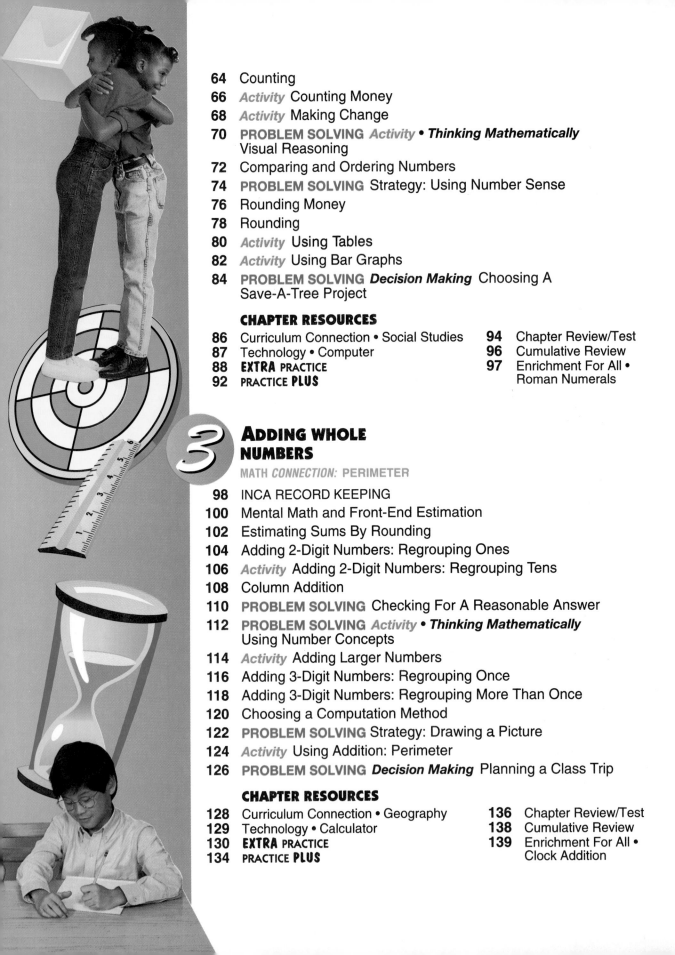

3 ADDING WHOLE NUMBERS

MATH *CONNECTION:* PERIMETER

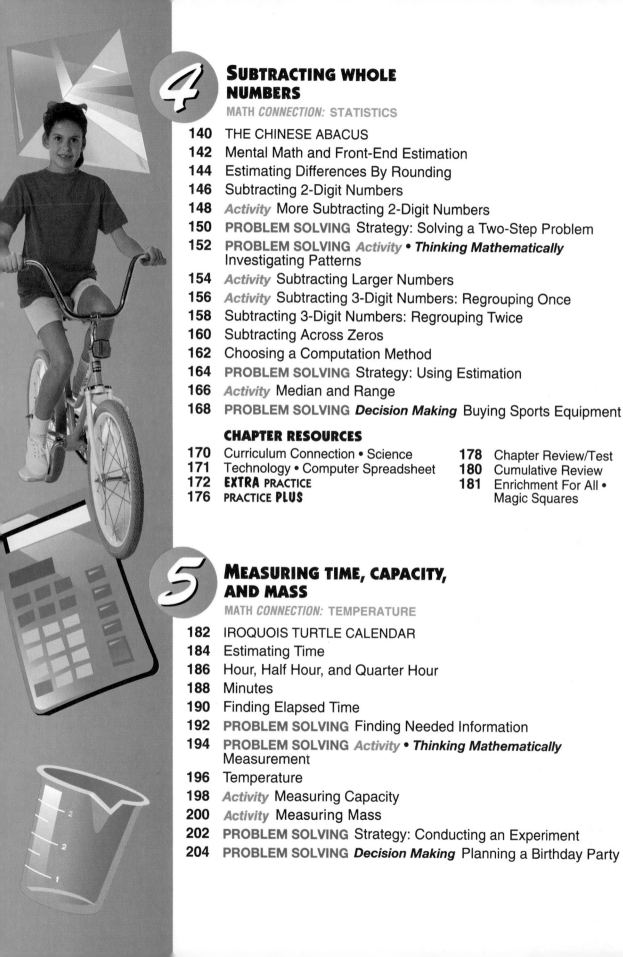

V

6 MULTIPLICATION FACTS

MATH *CONNECTIONS:* ALGEBRA • AREA

7 DIVISION FACTS

MATH *CONNECTIONS:* ALGEBRA • STATISTICS

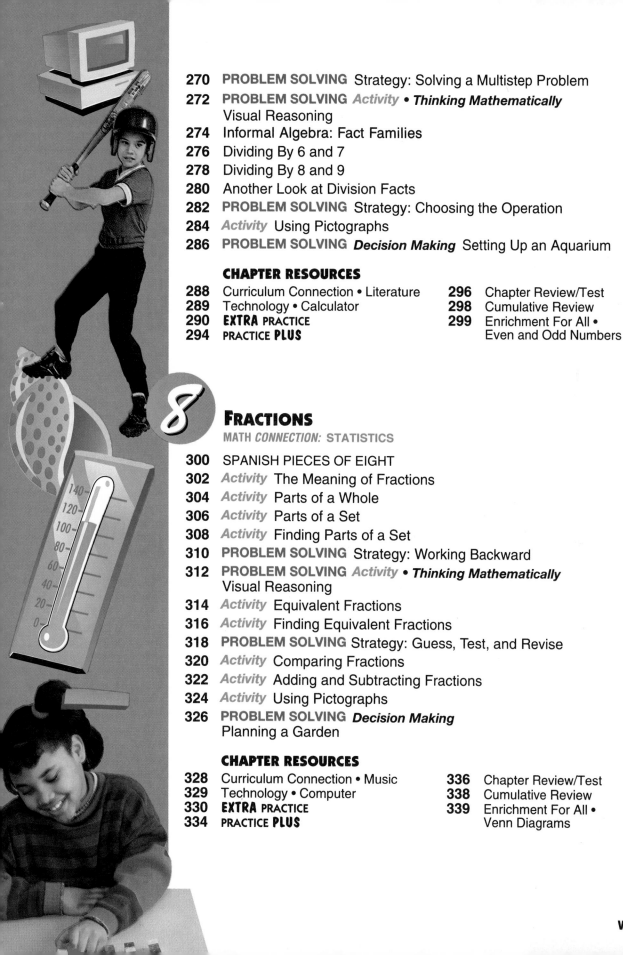

8 FRACTIONS

MATH *CONNECTION:* STATISTICS

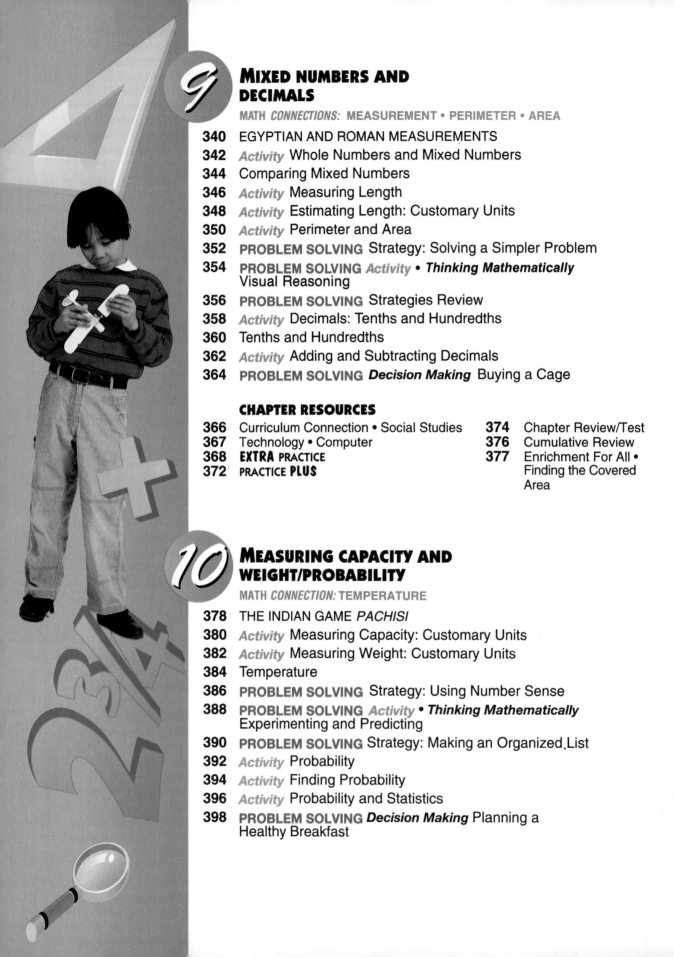

11 GEOMETRY

MATH *CONNECTIONS:* ALGEBRA • VOLUME

12 MULTIPLYING WHOLE NUMBERS

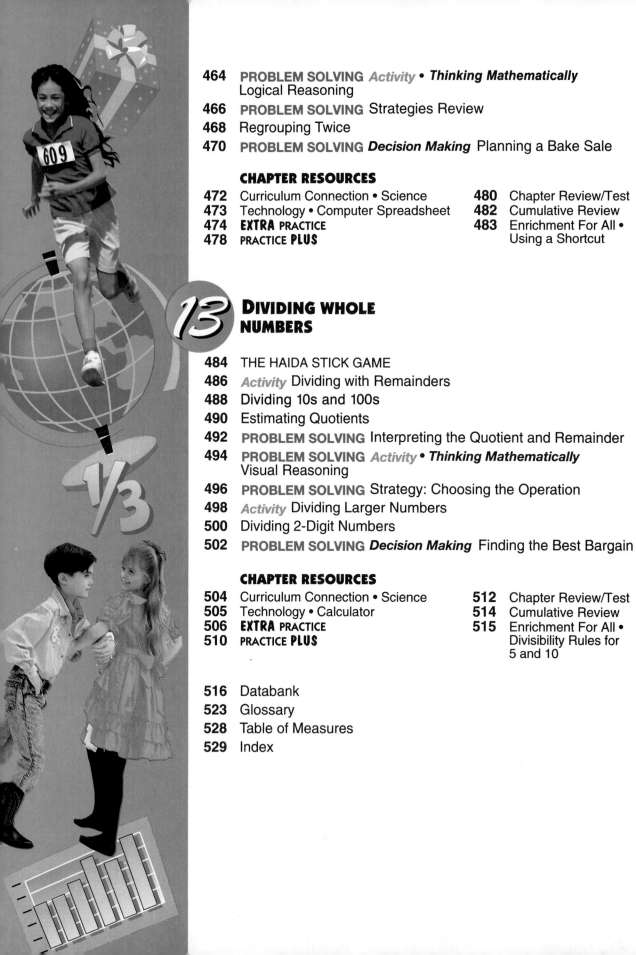

13 DIVIDING WHOLE NUMBERS

GETTING STARTED

THINKING MATHEMATICALLY

Look around you. There are numbers and shapes everywhere. What will you do today? Think about how many times you will use mathematics. Mathematics is very important. Do you ever wonder why?

On the next few pages, you will find some interesting puzzles and games to try. They are all different, but they all use mathematics in some way. For each, you will be "thinking mathematically." What does it mean to "think mathematically"? Finish the pages, and you will begin to understand.

Audrey Jackson

Martin Johnson

Richard Lodholz

Steve Leinwand

Gary L. Musser

Walter G. Secada

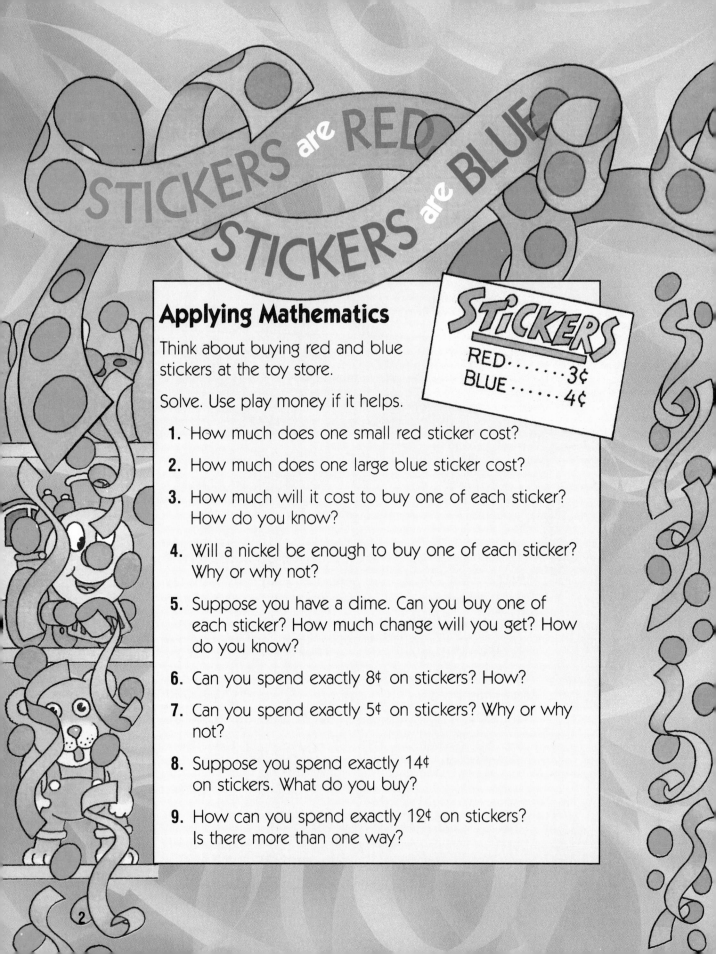

STICKERS are RED
STICKERS are BLUE

Applying Mathematics

Think about buying red and blue stickers at the toy store.

Solve. Use play money if it helps.

STICKERS
RED . . . . . . 3¢
BLUE . . . . . . 4¢

1. How much does one small red sticker cost?

2. How much does one large blue sticker cost?

3. How much will it cost to buy one of each sticker? How do you know?

4. Will a nickel be enough to buy one of each sticker? Why or why not?

5. Suppose you have a dime. Can you buy one of each sticker? How much change will you get? How do you know?

6. Can you spend exactly 8¢ on stickers? How?

7. Can you spend exactly 5¢ on stickers? Why or why not?

8. Suppose you spend exactly 14¢ on stickers. What do you buy?

9. How can you spend exactly 12¢ on stickers? Is there more than one way?

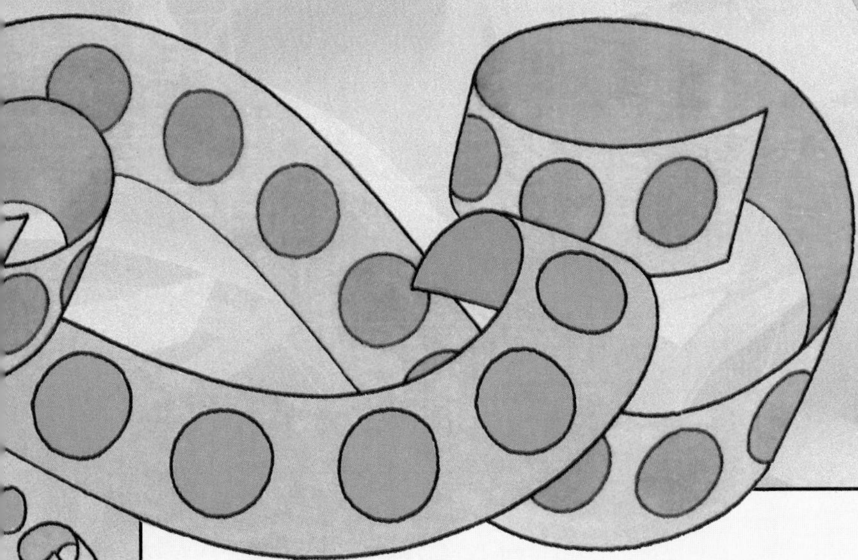

The toy store has a new rule. The owner put this sign in the window:

> # NO MORE THAN
> ## 2 OF EACH TYPE OF
> ### STICKER
> ## TO A CUSTOMER.

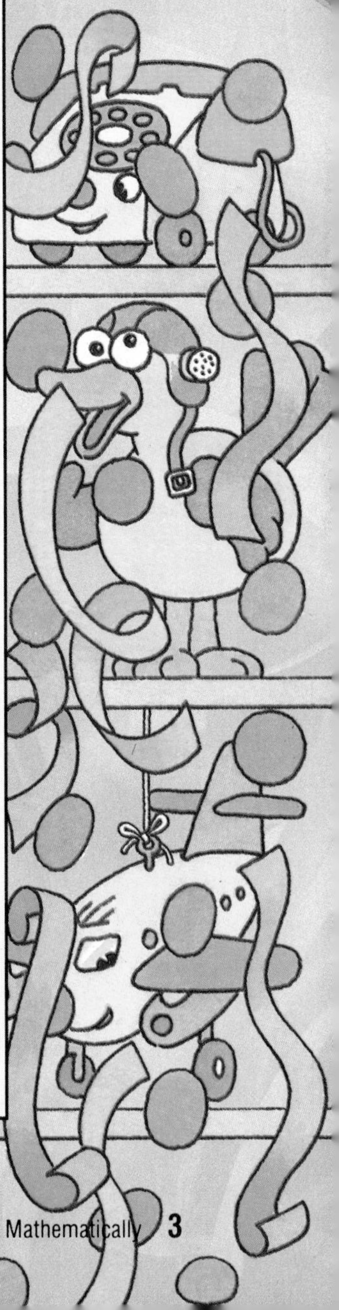

10. Can you spend exactly 11¢ on stickers? How?

11. Can you spend exactly 12¢ on stickers now? Why or why not?

12. What is the greatest amount you can spend on stickers now? Explain how you found your answer.

13. Which amounts between 1¢ and 15¢ can you spend on stickers with the new rule?

14. *Write a problem* about buying stickers that can be solved using addition.

15. *Write a problem* about buying stickers that can be solved using subtraction.

Using Number Concepts

Make a set of 9 playing cards. Use blank cards or cut sheets of paper into pieces of the same size. Write one of the numbers from 1 to 9 on each card. Work with a partner. Play these games.

A. Use 2 cards. Find different ways to make sums of 13. For example:

$$9 + 4 = 13$$

Be careful, $\boxed{4} + \boxed{9} = 13$ is not a different way.

1. Make a list of all the 2-card ways to make sums of 13.

2. How many different ways did you find?

3. How do you know you found all the 2-card ways?

B. Use 3 cards. Find different ways to make sums of 13. For example:

$$9 + 3 + 1 = 13$$

4. Make a list of all the 3-card ways to make sums of 13.

5. How many different ways did you find?

C. Use as many cards as you wish. Find all the other ways to make sums of 13.

6. Make a list of the ways.

7. How many ways did you find this time? How many 5-card ways did you find?

8. Look at your answers for games A, B, and C. How many ways did you find in all?

9. How do you know that you found all the possible ways?

10. Try the games again for ways to make sums of 14. Do you think the number of ways will be greater or less than the 13 game? Try it and see what happens.

Visual Reasoning

Look at the triangle at the right. It is drawn on dot paper. This triangle touches 8 dots. Count them.

Work with a partner. Use dot paper. Join the dots carefully. A straightedge will help you.

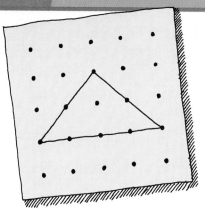

1. Draw some other triangles that touch exactly 8 dots. How many different triangles can you find?

2. There is one dot inside the triangle shown above. Can you draw an 8-dot triangle with no inside dots? with two inside dots?

Now try some 6-dot triangles.

3. Can you draw a 6-dot triangle with no inside dots?

4. Can you draw a 6-dot triangle with one inside dot? with two inside dots?

5. Make up your own dot-paper triangle puzzle. Be sure you have the answer. Then exchange puzzles with another student.

My Desk Is As Long As???

Measuring

There are many ways to measure the length of your desk. Pick a unit of measure. You could use this textbook. You could use one of your fingers. You could even use a ruler.

Complete the chart. First think about each of the objects shown. Estimate the length of your desk in each of the units. Then use each object to find an actual measurement.

LENGTH OF MY DESK

Measuring Unit	Estimated Length	Actual Length
Textbook		
Pointer finger		
Paper clip		
Pencil		
Hand		

1. Which object did you need the most of? Why?

2. Which object did you need the fewest of? Why?

3. How close were your estimates to the actual length? Were the estimates closer for some objects than for others? Why do you think this is so?

4. Why are these objects not usually used to measure the length of your desk?

5. What units of measurement are most likely to be used to measure the length of your desk?

THE
SUPER
SHOELACE
Search

Collecting and Interpreting Data

GETTING STARTED

Some people in your classroom are wearing shoelaces and some are not.

1. Do you think that more girls than boys are wearing shoelaces? Why or why not?

2. Do you think that more students than teachers are wearing shoelaces? Why or why not?

3. Do you think the people with shoelaces are wearing sneakers or shoes?

COLLECTING AND DISPLAYING DATA

A better way to answer these questions is to collect some actual data. Copy the chart and fill it out for 10 people.

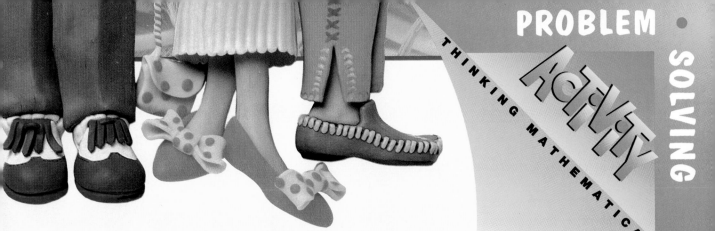

Name	Girl or Boy Man or Woman	Sneakers or Shoes	Laces or No Laces
1.			
2.			
3.			
4.			
5.			
6.			
7.			
8.			
9.			
10.			

ANALYZING DATA

4. Did you learn anything about whether more boys or more girls wear shoelaces? What did you learn?

5. Did you learn anything about whether more children or more adults wear shoelaces? What did you learn?

6. Did you learn whether people with shoelaces are more likely to be wearing sneakers or shoes? What did you learn?

7. Were you surprised by any of the things you learned? Why or why not?

8. *What if* you sell shoelaces? How could you use what you learn from this survey to sell more shoelaces?

KAMBA
FINGER COUNTING

one *(Imye)*

two *(Ili)*

three *(Itatu)*

four *(Inya)*

five *(Itaano)*

six *(Thanthatu)*

seven *(Muonza)*

eight *(Nyaanya)*

nine *(Ikenda)*

ten *(Ikumi)*

ADDITION AND SUBTRACTION FACTS

A market in the East African country of Kenya is often a noisy and colorful place. Among the many things people buy and sell are all kinds of foods.

Rodah passes the market on her way home from school. She sees a pile of bright oranges. Rodah wants to buy some oranges for herself and her sisters. She points to the oranges and says *nyaanya*. This is the word for 8 in the Kamba language spoken by many people in this part of Kenya. Rodah also shows the Kamba hand sign for 8 to tell the seller how many oranges she wants.

AFRICA
Kenya

1 How did Rodah show eight using her fingers?

2 Look at the Kamba hand signs for numbers. What patterns do you see?

3 How might you use your fingers to show numbers?

Informal Algebra: Meaning of Addition and Subtraction

You can use cubes to explore addition and subtraction.

WORKING TOGETHER

Count out 9 red cubes and 9 blue cubes and put them in separate bags.

1. Pull out some of the red cubes and snap them together. Write the number.

2. Pull out some of the blue cubes and snap them together. Write the number.

3. Join the blue and red cubes to make one train. How many cubes do you have in all?

4. Write a number sentence to show what you have done. Use the chart to help you.

Number of red cubes	plus	Number of blue cubes	equals	Total number of cubes
■	+	■	=	■
↑ addend		↑ addend		↑ sum

5. Take away the red cubes from the train you made. Write the number of cubes that you took away.

6. Write the number of blue cubes that are left.

7. Write a number sentence to show what you have done.

8. Put the cubes back in the bags and repeat the activity. Compare your number sentences with those of others.

Total number of cubes	minus	Number of cubes taken away	equals	Number of cubes left
■	−	■	=	■
				↑ difference

Complete the tables. Use cubes to help you.

	Number of red cubes		Number of blue cubes		Total number of cubes
9.	4	+	6	=	■
	6	+	4	=	■
11.	0	+	9	=	■
	9	+	0	=	■

	Total number of cubes		Number of cubes taken away		Number of cubes left
10.	10	−	6	=	■
	10	−	4	=	■
12.	9	−	0	=	■
	9	−	9	=	■

SHARING IDEAS

13. Talk about how the tables show that addition and subtraction are opposites. Give an example.

14. If you add numbers in a different order, does their sum change? Give an example.

15. What happens when 0 is added to a number? when 0 is subtracted from a number?

16. What happens when you subtract a number from itself?

ON YOUR OWN

17. *Make a list* of five ways you use addition or subtraction at home. Share your list with other students.

18. Cut out pictures from magazines. Write addition or subtraction sentences that describe the pictures.

Solve. Use cubes to help you. Tell whether you added or subtracted.

19. Li has 6 colored pens. He needs 8 pens in all. How many more pens must Li buy?

20. Melody has 4 pens. Jan has 8 pencils. How many pens and pencils do they have?

Mental Math: Addition, Subtraction Facts

Dom and Belinda are working on a math paper. They use mental math to find sums and differences.

A. Dom uses **counting on** to add 2 + 5.

1. Add 3 + 7 by counting on. What do you know about the order of addends that would make adding these two numbers easier?

B. Belinda uses **counting back** to subtract 6 − 4.

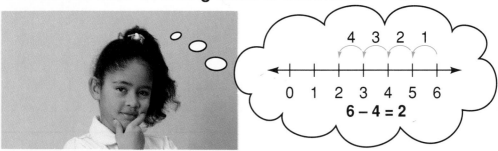

2. Subtract 8 − 5 by counting back. What is the difference?

TRY OUT Find the sum or difference. Use mental math.

3. 5 + 4 = ▪

4. 6 + 5 = ▪

5. 9 − 3 = ▪

6. 8 − 1 = ▪

PRACTICE

Find the sum or difference. Use mental math.

7. 8
    $+ 1$

8. 0
    $+ 7$

9. 7
    $+ 1$

10. 2
    $+ 9$

11. 0
    $+ 6$

12. 1
    $+ 5$

13. 8
    $- 6$

14. 9
    $- 8$

15. 10
    $- 1$

16. 6
    $- 5$

17. 13
    $- 8$

18. 13
    $- 4$

19. 1
    $+ 8$

20. 8
    $- 8$

21. 9
    $+ 9$

22. 15
    $- 7$

23. 1
    $+ 7$

24. 11
    $- 9$

25. $7 + 2 =$ ___

26. $7 - 6 =$ ___

27. $2 + 8 =$ ___

28. $9 - 7 =$ ___

29. $10 - 7 =$ ___

30. $3 + 6 =$ ___

Mixed Applications

31. Dom has 4 books. Belinda buys him 1 more book. How many books does Dom have now?

32. Ida has 8 toys. She gives 3 of them to Jon. How many toys does Ida have now?

33. Andre has 4 bags of marbles. Rosco has 8 bags of marbles. How many more bags of marbles does Rosco have?

34. Crystal has 8 large marbles. Sasha gives her 5 more. How many large marbles does Crystal have now?

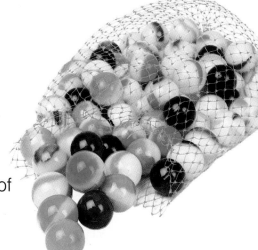

Mixed Review

Complete.

35. 9
    $+ 1$

36. 8
    $- 7$

37. 3
    $+ 5$

38. 10
    $- 2$

39. 3
    $+ 1$

40. 7
    $+ 2$

Sums and Differences Through 10

A. Chip sees some new models in the hobby store. He sees 5 new model trucks and 4 new model cars. How many new models does he see?

Chip knows two ways to use **doubles** to help him add mentally.

$5 + 4 = \blacksquare$
I know $4 + 4 = 8$.
5 is 1 more than 4.
$4 + 4 + 1 = 9$

So $5 + 4 = 9$.

$5 + 4 = \blacksquare$
I know $5 + 5 = 10$.
4 is 1 less than 5.
$5 + 5 - 1 = 9$

So $5 + 4 = 9$.

Chip sees 9 new models.

1. Chip used the doubles $4 + 4$ and $5 + 5$. What other doubles do you know?

2. How can you use doubles to add $2 + 3$?

B. You can use addition facts to subtract mentally.

$\begin{array}{r} 10 \\ -\ 5 \\ \hline \end{array}$ ***Think:*** Since $5 + 5 = 10$, then $10 - 5 = 5$.

$\begin{array}{r} 9 \\ -\ 3 \\ \hline \end{array}$ ***Think:*** Since $3 + 6 = 9$, then $9 - 3 = 6$.

3. How can you use an addition fact to find $10 - 7$?

TRY OUT Write the letter of the correct answer.

4. $3 + 4$ **a.** 5   **b.** 6   **c.** 7   **d.** 8

5. $4 + 5$ **a.** 6   **b.** 9   **c.** 10   **d.** 11

6. $10 - 8$ **a.** 1   **b.** 2   **c.** 3   **d.** 18

7. $8 - 5$ **a.** 2   **b.** 3   **c.** 5   **d.** 13

PRACTICE

Add or subtract.

| **8.** | 1
+ 1 | **9.** | 3
+ 3 | **10.** | 3
+ 7 | **11.** | 2
+ 1 | **12.** | 1
+ 2 | **13.** | 6
+ 0 |

| **14.** | 8
− 4 | **15.** | 10
− 6 | **16.** | 7
− 4 | **17.** | 6
− 2 | **18.** | 9
− 9 | **19.** | 5
− 4 |

| **20.** | 9
+ 1 | **21.** | 5
− 5 | **22.** | 2
+ 7 | **23.** | 10
− 9 | **24.** | 7
− 0 | **25.** | 4
+ 4 |

26. 2 + 4 = ■   **27.** 7 − 5 = ■   **28.** 9 − 4 = ■

29. 8 + 0 = ■   **30.** 5 + 1 = ■   **31.** 10 − 4 = ■

32. 6 + 7 = ■   **33.** 10 − 6 = ■   **34.** 5 + 5 = ■

Use the rule to complete.

35. Rule: Subtract 2.

10	9	8	7	6	5	4	3	2
■	■	■	■	■	■	■	■	■

36. Rule: Add 3.

0	1	2	3	4	5	6	7
■	■	■	■	■	■	■	■

Mixed Applications

37. Jean has 4 more models than Ling has. Ling has 6 models. How many models does Jean have?

38. Yana has 7 stuffed dolls. Zelda has 3 more dolls than Yana. How many dolls does Zelda have?

39. Bonnie had 7 car stickers. She gave some to Al. Now she has 3 stickers. How many stickers did she give to Al?

40. Dolph has 8 model trucks. He paints 7 of them blue. How many model trucks are not blue?

Sums Through 18

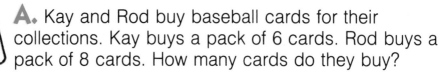

A. Kay and Rod buy baseball cards for their collections. Kay buys a pack of 6 cards. Rod buys a pack of 8 cards. How many cards do they buy?

Kay and Rod use **doubles** to add mentally.

6 + 8 = ▪️

Kay thinks: 6 + 6 = 12.

I know 8 is 2 more than 6.

6 + 6 + 2 = 14

So 6 + 8 = 14.

Rod thinks: 8 + 8 = 16.

I know 6 is 2 less than 8.

8 + 8 − 2 = 14

So 6 + 8 = 14.

They buy 14 baseball cards.

1. If 6 + 8 = 14, what is the sum of 8 + 6? How do you know?

2. Tell how you would use doubles to add 7 + 5.

B. Kay buys 9 more baseball cards. How many cards does she have now?

Another way to add mentally is to **make a 10.**

$$\begin{array}{r} 9 \\ + 6 \end{array}$$ Kay thinks: I add 1 to 9 to make 10.
I take away 1 from 6 to make 5. $$\begin{array}{r} 10 \\ + 5 \\ \hline 15 \end{array}$$

Since 10 + 5 = 15, Kay knows that 9 + 6 = 15.

Kay now has 15 baseball cards.

3. Why is making a 10 an easy way to add two addends?

TRY OUT Add.

4. $2 + 9 = $ <u>   </u>
       5. $8 + 5 = $ <u>   </u>
       6. $6 + 6 = $ <u>   </u>

PRACTICE

Add. Use mental math.

7. $\begin{array}{r} 4 \\ +\,4 \\ \hline \end{array}$	**8.** $\begin{array}{r} 7 \\ +\,0 \\ \hline \end{array}$	**9.** $\begin{array}{r} 6 \\ +\,1 \\ \hline \end{array}$	**10.** $\begin{array}{r} 2 \\ +\,8 \\ \hline \end{array}$	**11.** $\begin{array}{r} 0 \\ +\,0 \\ \hline \end{array}$	**12.** $\begin{array}{r} 3 \\ +\,2 \\ \hline \end{array}$
13. $\begin{array}{r} 8 \\ +\,8 \\ \hline \end{array}$	**14.** $\begin{array}{r} 6 \\ +\,2 \\ \hline \end{array}$	**15.** $\begin{array}{r} 9 \\ +\,2 \\ \hline \end{array}$	**16.** $\begin{array}{r} 8 \\ +\,7 \\ \hline \end{array}$	**17.** $\begin{array}{r} 9 \\ +\,5 \\ \hline \end{array}$	**18.** $\begin{array}{r} 8 \\ +\,9 \\ \hline \end{array}$
19. $\begin{array}{r} 3 \\ +\,5 \\ \hline \end{array}$	**20.** $\begin{array}{r} 5 \\ +\,5 \\ \hline \end{array}$	**21.** $\begin{array}{r} 0 \\ +\,4 \\ \hline \end{array}$	**22.** $\begin{array}{r} 1 \\ +\,6 \\ \hline \end{array}$	**23.** $\begin{array}{r} 9 \\ +\,9 \\ \hline \end{array}$	**24.** $\begin{array}{r} 8 \\ +\,5 \\ \hline \end{array}$

25. $7 + 8 = $ <u>   </u>
   26. $1 + 4 = $ <u>   </u>
   27. $0 + 4 = $ <u>   </u>

28. $5 + 8 = $ <u>   </u>
   29. $5 + 2 = $ <u>   </u>
   30. $3 + 9 = $ <u>   </u>

31. $8 + 4 = $ <u>   </u>
   32. $6 + 3 = $ <u>   </u>
   33. $4 + 2 = $ <u>   </u>

Critical Thinking

34. Tom adds $8 + 5$ mentally. He thinks: $10 + 3 = 13$, so $8 + 5 = 13$. Talk about how Tom changed the numbers to make it easier for him to add mentally.

Mixed Applications

35. Rod gives 4 baseball cards to Kay. He has 9 cards left. How many cards did he have to start with?

36. Gustavo has 3 more baseball caps than T-shirts. He has 8 T-shirts. How many caps does he have?

37. On Tuesday, 10 pennants were sold. That was 8 more than were sold on Monday. How many were sold on Monday?

38. *Write a problem* using addition. Ask others to solve it and then change it to a subtraction problem.

Differences Through 18

A. Flo bought a collection of 15 glass cats. When she got home she found that 6 were broken. How many cats are left?

Patterns can help you subtract mentally.

$$
\begin{array}{cccc}
12 & 13 & 14 & 15 \\
-\ 3 & -\ 4 & -\ 5 & -\ 6 \\
\hline
9 & 9 & 9 &
\end{array}
$$

Think: When the bottom digit is one more than the top digit, the difference is always 9.

So $15 - 6 = 9$.
There are 9 glass cats left.

1. What other subtraction facts can you write that follow this pattern?

B. There are other patterns that can help you remember subtraction facts.

$$
\begin{array}{ccc}
16 & 17 & 18 \\
-\ 9 & -\ 9 & -\ 9 \\
\hline
7 & 8 & 9
\end{array}
$$

Think: When you subtract 9, the difference is one more than the digit in the ones place of the top number.

2. What other subtraction facts can you write that follow this pattern?

C. You can also subtract from 10, then add.

Subtract: $14 - 8$

Think:
$$
\begin{array}{rcl}
14 & = & 10 + 4 \\
-\ 8 & & -\ 8 \\
\hline
& & 2 + 4 = 6
\end{array}
$$

3. Complete to show how you can use this method to subtract 5 from 12.

$$
\begin{array}{rcl}
12 & = & 10 + \rule{0.5cm}{0.15cm} \\
-\ 5 & & -\ 5 \\
\hline
& & 5 + \rule{0.5cm}{0.15cm} = \rule{0.5cm}{0.15cm}
\end{array}
$$

TRY OUT Subtract. Use mental math.

4. 13
      − 8

5. 14
      − 9

6. 13
      − 7

7. 11
      − 2

8. 12
      − 9

9. 13
      − 6

PRACTICE

Subtract. Use mental math.

10. 12
       − 4

11. 14
       − 6

12. 12
       − 3

13. 17
       − 9

14. 10
       − 4

15. 13
       − 9

16. 13
       − 5

17. 12
       − 8

18. 15
       − 9

19. 16
       − 8

20. 15
       − 6

21. 14
       − 8

22. 10 − 5 = ■

23. 11 − 4 = ■

24. 18 − 9 = ■

25. 17 − 8 = ■

26. 16 − ■ = 9

27. 14 − ■ = 5

28. 9 − ■ = 9

29. ■ − 4 = 0

30. 12 − ■ = 6

Mixed Applications

31. Jason has 15 model horses. He gives 8 of them to Jan. How many model horses does he have now?

32. Ann has $13.00. She spends $8.00 on glass animals. How much money does she have left?

33. Clara has 7 big glass birds. She also has 9 little birds. How many birds does she have in all?

34. Mara has 8 models of pintos and 7 models of mustangs. How many models in all?

Mixed Review

Complete.

35. 8 + 0 = ■

36. 12 − 6 = ■

37. 10 − 5 = ■

Informal Algebra: Fact Families

A. Ben and Jerry are playing a game with counters. Ben puts 5 of his counters on the table and keeps the rest covered. He tells Jerry that he has 12 counters in all. How many counters are covered?

Jerry says he can add to find the answer.

1. What addition sentences can you write that have 12 as a sum and 5 as an addend?

2. What is the missing addend? How many counters are covered?

3. How can Jerry find the answer another way? Write a number sentence to show how.

4. Can you write another number sentence using these numbers? If so, write it.

B. Number sentences that use the same numbers are **related.** They belong to the same **fact family.**

Here is the fact family for 5, 6, and 11.

$$5 + 6 = 11 \qquad 6 + 5 = 11$$
$$11 - 6 = 5 \qquad 11 - 5 = 6$$

5. Write the fact family for 4, 4, and 8. How is this family different from the family for 5, 6, and 11?

TRY OUT Write the letter of the correct answer.

Find the missing addend.

6. $7 + \blacksquare = 14$ **a.** 0   **b.** 14   **c.** 21   **d.** 7

7. $\blacksquare + 6 = 13$ **a.** 7   **b.** 6   **c.** 13   **d.** 19

PRACTICE

Find the missing addend.

8. $3 + \blacksquare = 10$

9. $\blacksquare + 5 = 11$

10. $7 + \blacksquare = 13$

11. $9 + \blacksquare = 17$

12. $6 + \blacksquare = 14$

13. $8 + \blacksquare = 16$

14. $9 + \blacksquare = 12$

15. $\blacksquare + 4 = 13$

16. $\blacksquare + 4 = 11$

17.
$$\begin{array}{r} 8 \\ + \blacksquare \\ \hline 14 \end{array}$$

18.
$$\begin{array}{r} 9 \\ + \blacksquare \\ \hline 13 \end{array}$$

19.
$$\begin{array}{r} 8 \\ + \blacksquare \\ \hline 15 \end{array}$$

20.
$$\begin{array}{r} 7 \\ + \blacksquare \\ \hline 14 \end{array}$$

21.
$$\begin{array}{r} 6 \\ + \blacksquare \\ \hline 12 \end{array}$$

22.
$$\begin{array}{r} 8 \\ + \blacksquare \\ \hline 12 \end{array}$$

Complete the fact family.

23. 5, 7, 12

$\blacksquare + 5 = 12$
$5 + 7 = \blacksquare$
$12 - \blacksquare = 5$
$12 - 5 = \blacksquare$

24. 7, 9, 16

$9 + 7 = \blacksquare$
$7 + \blacksquare = 16$
$16 - 9 = \blacksquare$
$\blacksquare - 7 = 9$

25. 3, 8, 11

$11 - 8 = \blacksquare$
$11 - 3 = \blacksquare$
$8 + 3 = \blacksquare$
$\blacksquare + \blacksquare = \blacksquare$

26. 6, 9, 15

$\blacksquare + 9 = 15$
$9 + 6 = \blacksquare$
$\blacksquare - 6 = 9$
$15 - \blacksquare = 6$

27. 5, 8, 13

$5 + 8 = \blacksquare$
$8 + \blacksquare = \blacksquare$
$13 - \blacksquare = 8$
$\blacksquare - \blacksquare = \blacksquare$

28. 9, 9, 18

$\blacksquare + \blacksquare = \blacksquare$
$\blacksquare - \blacksquare = \blacksquare$

Mixed Applications

29. Sue buys 9 goldfish and 6 guppies. How many more goldfish than guppies does she buy? Did you add or subtract?

30. Jen throws 12 jacks on a table. She picks up some of them. There are 9 jacks left on the table. How many did she pick up?

31. Walter hides some counters from Ben. Ben knows that there are 16 counters in all. He sees that there are 7 counters left. How many counters are hidden?

32. Describe what a fact family is. How do you think it got its name?

PROBLEM SOLVING

Using the Five-Step Process

Sammy Fawaz and Terry Saad have $5 to spend on food for a picnic. Foods from the Middle East, where their families lived before coming to the United States, will be served. They want to buy chickpeas for $.99 and pita bread for $1.89. Do Sammy and Terry have enough money?

Study how the five-step process is used to solve this problem.

UNDERSTAND	
What do I know?	Sammy and Terry have $5. The items they want to buy cost $.99 and $1.89.
What do I need to find out?	I need to find out whether Sammy and Terry have enough money to buy the items.
PLAN	
What can I do?	I can estimate the total cost.
TRY	***Think:*** $.99 is about $1.
Let me try my plan.	$1.89 is about $2.
	$1 + $2 = $3
	The total is less than $5. They have enough money.
CHECK	
Have I answered the question?	Yes. They have enough money.
Does my answer make sense?	Yes. When I estimated, I used prices greater than the real costs.
EXTEND	
What have I learned?	I learned that I can solve some problems by estimating.

PRACTICE

Apply what you have learned about the five-step process to solve the problem.

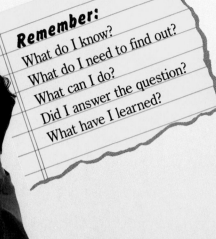

Remember:
What do I know?
What do I need to find out?
What can I do?
Did I answer the question?
What have I learned?

1. Terry's brother Khalid makes a salad for the picnic. He uses 4 tomatoes and 5 cucumbers. How many vegetables does he use in all?

2. Sammy and Terry need cans of juice for the lunch. Sammy brings 5 cans, and Terry brings 7 cans. How many cans of juice do they bring in all?

3. Terry invites 6 friends to the picnic. Sammy invites 9 friends. How many more friends does Sammy invite?

4. Terry wants to buy a bag of oranges that costs $3.89 and a roll of film for $4.98. Will $10 be enough for these items?

5. Pita bread comes in packages of 8. Slices of cheese come in packages of 12. How many more slices of cheese than pita bread are there in a package?

6. Barbara brings cakes called "birds' nests" to the picnic. She brings 18 cakes. Her sister brings 9 cakes. How many more cakes than her sister does Barbara bring?

IT ALL ADDS UP

Using Number Concepts

A. Calculators can help you find answers.

You know that 2 + 6 = 8. Can you use a calculator to show that you are right? Try pressing these keys:

[2] [+] [6] [=].

What does the calculator show?

1. How would you add 58, 256, and 745 on a calculator? What is the sum?

2. If you make a mistake, do you have to start all over again?
   Suppose you want to add 46 and 85, but you make a mistake. You enter:
   [4] [6] [+] [8] [2].

   Now press the [C] key once. What happens?

   The 46 in the display means that you have erased the 82. The calculator has not erased the first number, 46.
   To continue, press [+] [8] [5] [=].
   What does the display show?

   Press the [C] key once when you want to erase only the last number entered.

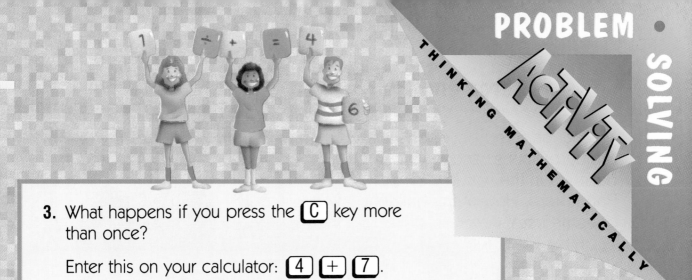

3. What happens if you press the C key more than once?

Enter this on your calculator: 4 + 7 .

Now press the C key twice.

You will see a 0 in the display.
You have erased everything you entered.
When you press it more than once, the C key erases everything.
You must start again.

B. Calculators can help you subtract, too.
Try entering this problem:

8 − 5 = .

What does the calculator show?

4. Find the difference between 486 and 179 with your calculator.

5. Does the C key work the same way with subtraction? Experiment with your calculator to find out.

6. Here's a calculator puzzle:
Imagine that you have a broken calculator.

Only these four keys work: 1 0 + = .

Can you get the calculator to show 67? You can use only the working keys. What keys will you press?
How many keystrokes will you use in all?
Can you think of another way to solve the puzzle that is quicker?

ACTIVITY
Three and Four Addends

Mel hangs 6 red balloons, 3 blue balloons, and 4 yellow balloons in the window of the Party Store. How many balloons does he use?

WORKING TOGETHER

1. Use red, blue, and yellow cubes to show how many balloons Mel uses. Group the red and blue cubes. Then combine them with the yellow cubes.

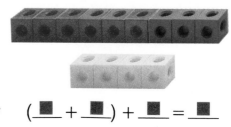

2. Complete the addition sentence to show how you combined the cubes.

(■ + ■) + ■ = ■

3. How many cubes are there in all? How many balloons does Mel use?

> *Hint:* You always do what is in the **parentheses** ( ) first.

4. Separate the cubes by color. Group the blue and yellow cubes. Then combine them with the red cubes.

5. Complete the addition sentence to show how you combined the cubes.

■ + (■ + ■) = ■

You can sometimes reorder the addends to help you add mentally.

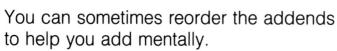

6. Separate the cubes by color. Group the red and yellow cubes. Then combine them with the blue cubes.

7. Rewrite the addition sentence.

(■ + ■) + ■ = ■

8. Add. Use ( ) to show how you grouped the addends. You may wish to reorder them to help you add mentally.

2 + 7 + 8 = ■

6 + 3 + 6 = ■

SHARING IDEAS

9. What happens to the sum when you change the order of the grouping of the addends?

10. How does grouping or reordering the addends help you to add mentally?

PRACTICE

Add.

11.	12.	13.	14.	15.	16.
4	3	6	6	7	4
7	4	8	4	9	8
+ 1	+ 5	+ 0	+ 5	+ 1	+ 4

17.	18.	19.	20.	21.	22.
7	6	2	8	9	8
2	5	1	2	3	5
+ 3	+ 4	4	3	1	5
		+ 2	+ 2	+ 3	+ 2

Find the missing number.

23. 6 + 6 + 1 = ___

24. 5 + 7 + 2 = ___

25. 9 + 0 + 1 + 4 = ___

26. 9 + (7 + 3) = ___

27. (3 + 3) + 8 = ___

28. (5 + 2) + (1 + 9) = ___

29. 9 + 3 + 1 = 3 + 1 + ___

30. 3 + 4 + 7 = 3 + ___ + 4

Mixed Applications

31. Mel buys 6 hats, 7 horns, and 3 streamers. How many things does he buy?

32. Gail buys 8 plates, 8 cups, and 1 tablecloth. How many things does she buy?

33. Jorge brings 12 burritos to the party. The children eat 8 of them. How many burritos have not been eaten?

34. Tina needs 9 birthday cards. She has already picked 4 cards. How many more cards does she need?

PROBLEM SOLVING

Strategy: Choosing the Operation

A. María Fernandez and Gigi Juste are neighbors. Their grandmothers are neighbors, too. María's grandmother lives in the Dominican Republic. Gigi's grandmother lives in Haiti. Both the Dominican Republic and Haiti are countries on the island of Hispaniola in the Caribbean Sea.

Gigi is having a party for María before she goes to visit the Dominican Republic. There are 7 girls and 6 boys at the party. How many children are at the party?

Gigi knows that there are two groups. She plans to **combine** the group of boys with the group of girls.

1. What can she do to find the number of children who are at the party?   **6 + 7 = ___**

2. How many children are at the party?

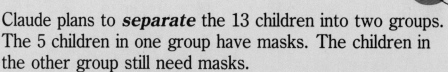

B. Claude and Ray are making masks for everyone. They have made 5 masks. How many more masks must the boys make?

Claude plans to **separate** the 13 children into two groups. The 5 children in one group have masks. The children in the other group still need masks.

3. What can Claude do to find the number of children who still need masks?   **13 − 5 = ___**

4. How many children still need masks?

5. Which operation should you use when you combine two groups?

6. Which operation should you use when you separate a group into two parts?

PRACTICE

**Decide which operation to use.
Then solve the problem.**

7. There are 14 children at the party but only 9 chairs. How many more chairs does Gigi need?

8. Ray has made 8 red party hats and 6 blue party hats. How many hats are there in all?

9. A plate has 12 pieces of fruit. If 5 pieces are pineapple, how many pieces are not pineapple pieces?

10. Gigi has 9 cups of juice left on the tray. Only 4 of the children have taken their cups. How many cups of juice did Gigi have?

Strategies and Skills Review

11. Ray put 7 ginger cookies and 4 peanut butter cookies on the table. How many cookies did he put on the table?

12. Alicia bought a costume for $4 and a mask for $2. How much did she pay?

13. Gigi knows 13 Spanish words. María taught her 8 of the words. How many of the words did María not teach Gigi?

14. There are 15 red balloons and blue balloons at the party. If 6 balloons are red, how many are blue?

15. María brought a box of candles to use on a cake. She uses 8 candles. There are 4 candles left. How many candles were in the box?

16. *Write a problem* that can be solved by addition or subtraction. Solve the problem. Ask others to solve your problem.

EXTRA PRACTICE, page 42

AcTiViTy

Measuring Length

Use a mix of large and small paper clips to measure this pencil.

1. The pencil is about ⬛ paper clips long.

A **centimeter (cm)** is a metric unit of length used to measure small objects.

To measure to the nearest centimeter:

Step 1 Line up the left end of the model car with the left end of the scale.

Step 2 Look at the other end of the car. Find the closest centimeter mark.

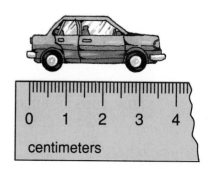

The model car is about 4 centimeters long.

2. Use your ruler to measure the length of the pencil to the nearest centimeter.

SHARING IDEAS

3. How did your measurement using paper clips compare with those of other students? Why do you think this is so?

4. How did your measurement using centimeters compare with those of other students? Why do you think this is so?

5. Why is it better to use centimeters than paper clips to measure the length of small objects?

PRACTICE

Use your centimeter ruler. Measure to the nearest centimeter.

6.

■

7.

■

8.

■

9.

■

Use your centimeter ruler. Draw a line for each length.

10. 7 cm　　　**11.** 1 cm　　　**12.** 9 cm　　　**13.** 11 cm　　　**14.** 19 cm

Mixed Applications

15. Mr. Case puts labels on boxes. A box is 8 cm long. A label is 5 cm long. How much longer is the box than the label?

16. Rita has a piece of yarn 15 cm long. She cuts it into two pieces. One is 6 cm long. How long is the other piece?

17. Una has stacks of coins that are 2 cm, 3 cm, and 8 cm high. She puts them all in one stack. How high is the stack?

18. Jeb has 5 colored pencils. Ken has 9 colored pencils. How many colored pencils do Jeb and Ken have in all?

LOGICAL REASONING

Look at these shapes.

1. Sort the shapes. Tell how you did it.

2. Compare what you did with what others did. Can you think of other ways to sort the shapes?

Estimating Length: Metric Units

Decimeter (dm), **meter (m)**, and **kilometer (km)**
are other metric units of length.

A **decimeter** is about the height of a soup can.

A **meter** is about the width of your teacher's desk.

A **kilometer** is about how far a person
can walk in 20 minutes.

WORKING TOGETHER

1. Choose a unit of length
to use to measure these
objects.

> **10 centimeters (cm) = 1 decimeter (dm)**
> **10 decimeters (dm) = 1 meter (m)**
> **1,000 meters (m) = 1 kilometer (km)**

2. Estimate. Then find the objects in your room.
Measure each one to the nearest unit you chose.

a.    **b.**   **c.**   **d.**

e.   **f.**   **g.**    **h.**

SHARING IDEAS

3. For which things did you choose centimeters?
decimeters? meters? kilometers? Why?

4. For which metric units of measure were your
estimates closest? Why do you think that happened?

PRACTICE

Complete the chart. Use the units given.

Object	Estimate		Actual	
Bookshelf (m)	5.	■	6.	■
Width of hand (cm)	7.	■	8.	■
Lunchbox (dm)	9.	■	10.	■

11. Estimate and measure three more objects.

Write the letter of the best estimate.

12. length of a kitten   **a.** 1 cm   **b.** 1 dm   **c.** 1 m   **d.** 1 km

13. height of a bicycle   **a.** 1 cm   **b.** 1 dm   **c.** 1 m   **d.** 1 km

14. thickness of a magazine   **a.** 1 cm   **b.** 1 dm   **c.** 1 m   **d.** 1 km

15. long-distance race   **a.** 1 cm   **b.** 1 dm   **c.** 1 m   **d.** 1 km

Critical Thinking

16. Marie measured the length of a paintbrush as 20 centimeters. Jon said its length was 2 decimeters. Who is correct? Why?
(*Hint:* Look at a ruler marked in centimeters and decimeters.)

Mixed Applications

17. Beth has 10 toy cats. There are 3 white cats, and the rest are black. How many of the toy cats are black?

18. Jaime rides his bike to the mall. Does he ride 2 cm or 2 km to the mall?

19. Jack and the Bean Stalk Toy Store has shops in two different cities. What is the best metric unit to describe the distance between the two stores?

20. Micky sees several giant dinosaur models in a toy store window. There are 5 green dinosaurs, 3 blue, and 4 yellow. How many dinosaurs are in the window?

DECISION MAKING

Problem Solving: Buying Gifts

SITUATION

You want to give each of your three best friends a gift.
You have saved $18 to buy the gifts.

PROBLEM

How will you spend the $18 to buy gifts
for your three friends?

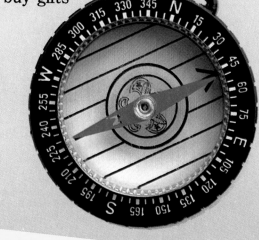

DATA

HARPER'S
DEPARTMENT STORE SALE!
GIFTS FOR UNDER $10

Goldfish and Bowl $6	Book of Funny Fads $5	Swim Cap $8
Sketch Pad $2	Baseball Mitt $9	Actor's Makeup Kit $6
Stamp Album $8	Scout Compass $4	Dance Leg Warmers $2

What my friends like to do.

Lisa – dancing, reading,
       stamp collecting

Bill – drawing, fish,
       baseball

Susan – scouting, acting,
        swimming

MAGYAR POSTA

USING THE DATA

Name the item with the lowest price that each friend would like.

1. Lisa   **2.** Bill   **3.** Susan

Name the item with the highest price that each friend would like.

4. Lisa   **5.** Bill   **6.** Susan

What is the total cost of these gifts?

7. stamp album
baseball mitt
swim cap

8. book
goldfish and bowl
actor's make-up kit

9. scout compass
sketch pad
dance leg warmers

MAKING DECISIONS

10. What other things do you need to think about when buying gifts for friends?

11. Can you buy the gifts that cost the most for each friend? Why or why not?

12. If you buy the least expensive gift for each friend, how much money will you have left over?

13. Why are the book, goldfish and bowl, and actor's make-up kit good choices for gifts?

14. *Write a list* of the things you would think about when buying gifts for your friends.

CURRICULUM CONNECTION

Math and Science

Snakes are reptiles, like lizards. Snakes have dry skin and scales. They breathe with lungs and have backbones.

Like all reptiles, snakes are cold-blooded. This means that their body temperature is about the same as the temperature around them.

There are about 2,700 different kinds of snakes. Only about 270 of them are harmful to humans.

Snakes come in many sizes. Some Pythons can be 30 feet long. A Carpet Python is only 13 feet long. Bull Snakes are about 6 feet long. A Garter Snake might not even be 1 foot long.

How much longer is a Carpet Python than a Bull Snake?

Think: Subtract $13 - 6 = 7$.

So the Carpet Python is 7 feet longer than the Bull Snake.

ACTIVITY

1. The Black Snake is 8 feet long. A King Cobra can be 17 feet long. The Grass Snake is only 3 feet long. Make a poster with a friend. Draw the snakes. Write and solve 2 word problems about the snakes.

Calculator: Find the Hidden Number

Tamla and Don are playing a calculator game using the memory keys. Tamla hides a number in the calculator's memory. She does not let Don see what she is doing.

She presses the keys below:

Calculator Display

[9] [M+]

| M | 9. |

Then she presses:

[on/c]

| M | 0. |

She hands the calculator to Don. He makes a guess and presses:

[5] [M+] to add 5 to the number in memory

| M | 5. |

Then he presses:

[MRC]

| M | 14. |

Don says, "I added 5 to the hidden number and got 14. The number is 9."

"You're correct," says Tamla. She presses [MRC] and [on/c] to clear the memory and the screen. Then they play the game again.

USING THE CALCULATOR

1. Play the game with a partner. Pick a number from 0 to 9. Press [M+] to enter it into the memory. Then press [on/c] to clear the screen. Hand the calculator to your partner who enters another number from 0 to 9, presses [M+], and presses [MRC]. Then your partner uses the number displayed to find the first number you entered. Take turns.

2. Play the game using the [M−] key instead. How does the game change?

EXTRA PRACTICE

Mental Math: Addition, Subtraction Facts, page 15 ....

Find the sum or difference. Use mental math.

1.	2.	3.	4.	5.	6.
6	0	5	6	0	1
+1	+4	+1	+6	+9	+3

7.	8.	9.	10.	11.	12.
6	9	12	8	11	15
−3	−9	−5	−1	−4	−8

13. 6 + 2 = ▪   **14.** 8 − 5 = ▪   **15.** 1 + 7 = ▪

Sums and Differences Through 10, page 17 ....

Add or subtract.

1.	2.	3.	4.	5.	6.
2	4	2	1	0	3
+2	+6	+5	+2	+7	+3

7.	8.	9.	10.	11.	12.
10	6	8	7	9	5
−4	−2	−6	−7	−8	−3

13. 3 + 4 = ▪   **14.** 11 − 7 = ▪   **15.** 10 − 8 = ▪

Sums Through 18, page 19 ....

Add. Use mental math.

1.	2.	3.	4.	5.	6.
3	8	4	1	0	2
+3	+0	+1	+7	+0	+5

7.	8.	9.	10.	11.	12.
8	9	8	7	5	4
+5	+7	+8	+6	+7	+4

13. 9 + 5 = ▪   **14.** 0 + 9 = ▪   **15.** 4 + 7 = ▪

16. 8 + 4 = ▪   **17.** 8 + 6 = ▪   **18.** 9 + 9 = ▪

40 Chapter 1

Differences Through 18,   page 21 ....

Subtract. Use mental math.

1. 13   **2.** 11   **3.** 10   **4.** 17   **5.** 15   **6.** 14
    − 9   − 7   − 3   − 8   − 9   − 7

7. $15 - \blacksquare = 8$ **8.** $16 - \blacksquare = 9$ **9.** $\blacksquare - 6 = 0$

Fact Families,   page 23 ....

Find the missing addend.

1. 7   **2.** 2   **3.** 8   **4.** 9   **5.** 3   **6.** 7
   + ■   + ■   + ■   + ■   + ■   + ■
   15   10   16   18   12   16

7. $6 + \blacksquare = 10$ **8.** $\blacksquare + 7 = 14$ **9.** $8 + \blacksquare = 17$

Complete the fact family.

10. 4, 7, 11   **11.** 5, 9, 14   **12.** 6, 13, 7
    $\blacksquare + 4 = 11$ $5 + 9 = \blacksquare$ $\blacksquare + 6 = 13$
    $4 + 7 = \blacksquare$ $9 + \blacksquare = 14$ $6 + 7 = \blacksquare$
    $11 - \blacksquare = 4$ $14 - 9 = \blacksquare$ $13 - 7 = \blacksquare$
    $11 - 4 = \blacksquare$ $\blacksquare - 5 = 9$ $13 - \blacksquare = 7$

Problem Solving: Using the Five-Step Process,   page 25 ....

Use the five-step process to solve the problem.

1. Ginger brought 8 pounds of pasta salad to the barbeque. Tyrone brought 7 pounds of potato salad. How many pounds of salad is that?

2. Emilio needs 15 bags of ice to fill the cooler. Juana brought 6 bags of ice. How many more bags of ice does he need to fill the cooler?

3. There are 9 buns on the grill. The grill can hold 12 buns. How many more buns can Mrs. Chavez put on the grill?

EXTRA PRACTICE

Three and Four Addends, page 29 ....

Add.

1.	2.	3.	4.	5.	6.
3	4	5	6	3	8
1	2	1	2	4	5
+2	+5	+3	+4	+5	+2

7.	8.	9.	10.	11.	12.
6	5	2	7	4	3
1	3	2	4	3	6
+1	+5	+4	+2	+7	+4

13.	14.	15.	16.	17.	18.
1	2	4	3	4	4
2	5	6	9	9	5
4	6	7	2	2	3
+5	+1	+2	+1	+3	+3

19. 2 + 3 + 4 = ▪____   20. 1 + 4 + 6 = ▪____

21. 4 + 3 + 3 = ▪____   22. 6 + 3 + 4 = ▪____

23. 8 + 6 + 4 = ▪____   24. 5 + 7 + 3 = ▪____

25. 8 + 0 + 9 + 2 = ▪____   26. 4 + 4 + 7 + 3 = ▪____

Problem Solving Strategy: Choosing the Operation, page 31 ....

Decide which operation to use. Then solve the problem.

1. Lynn puts 6 muffins on a plate. Her friends eat 4 muffins. How many muffins are left?

2. There are 9 pink hats and 8 white hats. How many hats are there all together?

3. Michael has 12 records. During the party he plays 8 of them. How many records have not yet been played?

4. There are 9 guests left. Only 3 of the guests have gone home. How many guests were there to start with?

Measuring Length, page 33 ....

Use your centimeter ruler. Measure to the nearest centimeter.

1.

        ■

2.

      ■

Use your centimeter ruler. Draw a line for each length.

3. 10 cm   **4.** 1 cm   **5.** 8 cm

6. 12 cm   **7.** 15 cm   **8.** 5 cm

Estimating Length: Metric Units, page 35 ....

Complete the chart. Use the units given.

Object	Estimate		Actual	
Desk top (m)	**1.**	■	**2.**	■
Length of foot (cm)	**3.**	■	**4.**	■
Textbook (cm)	**5.**	■	**6.**	■
Bulletin board (m)	**7.**	■	**8.**	■

9. Estimate and measure three more objects of your choice.

Write the letter of the best estimate.

10. long run   **a.** 2 cm   **b.** 2 dm   **c.** 2 m   **d.** 2 km

11. thickness of a notebook   **a.** 2 cm   **b.** 2 dm   **c.** 2 m   **d.** 2 km

12. height of a man   **a.** 2 cm   **b.** 2 dm   **c.** 2 m   **d.** 2 km

13. length of a puppy   **a.** 2 cm   **b.** 2 dm   **c.** 2 m   **d.** 2 km

Practice PLUS

KEY SKILL: Sums Through 18 (Use after page 19.)

Level A

Write the letter of the correct answer.

1. 3 + 3 = ___
   a. 6   **b.** 33

2. 4 + 1 = ___
   a. 5   **b.** 3

3. 5 + 2 = ___
   a. 52   **b.** 7

4. 2 + 2 = ___
   a. 4   **b.** 22

5. 6 + 3 = ___
   a. 10   **b.** 9

6. 5 + 5 = ___
   a. 10   **b.** 15

7. Rob has 6 baseball cards. Kit gives him 4 more. How many baseball cards does Rob have now?

Level B

Add. Use mental math.

8.	9.	10.	11.	12.	13.
6 + 6	3 + 8	7 + 3	2 + 9	7 + 5	2 + 8

14. 3 + 9 = ___   15. 8 + 4 = ___   16. 6 + 5 = ___

17. Risa has 4 pennants. Tom gives her 7 more. How many pennants does Risa have now?

Level C

Add. Use mental math.

18.	19.	20.	21.	22.	23.
7 + 7	8 + 5	5 + 9	9 + 7	6 + 9	9 + 8

24. 7 + 6 = ___   25. 6 + 8 = ___   26. 8 + 8 = ___

27. Jan gives 8 baseball caps to Ian. She has 9 caps left. How many baseball caps did Jan start with?

KEY SKILL: Differences Through 18 (Use after page 21.)

Level A
Write the letter of the correct answer.

1. $4 - 3 = $ ___
  a. 1 **b.** 7

2. $8 - 4 = $ ___
  a. 6 **b.** 4

3. $5 - 2 = $ ___
  a. 2 **b.** 3

4. $3 - 2 = $ ___
  a. 5 **b.** 1

5. $6 - 4 = $ ___
  a. 2 **b.** 10

6. $9 - 1 = $ ___
  a. 10 **b.** 8

7. Justin has 8 model cars. He gives 4 of them to Cassie. How many model cars does he have now?

Level B
Subtract. Use mental math.

8.	**9.**	**10.**	**11.**	**12.**	**13.**
10	11	13	12	14	11
− 3	− 7	− 4	− 6	− 5	− 4

14. $13 - 7 = $ ___

15. $10 - 5 = $ ___

16. $14 - 9 = $ ___

17. Tim has 17 stamps from England. He gives 8 of them to Pat. How many stamps does he have left?

Level C
Subtract. Use mental math.

18.	**19.**	**20.**	**21.**	**22.**	**23.**
16	10	18	14	15	12
− 7	− 8	− 9	− 8	− 9	− 7

24. $11 - 8 = $ ___

25. $14 - 9 = $ ___

26. $10 - 3 = $ ___

27. Lou has 16 books. He gives some to Dan, and has 9 left. How many books did he give to Dan?

CHAPTER REVIEW/TEST

LANGUAGE AND MATHEMATICS

Complete the sentences. Use the words in the chart.

VOCABULARY
sum
kilometer
centimeter
difference

1. In 40 minutes you can walk about one ▪__.

2. The answer in addition is called the ▪__.

3. The ▪__ between 4 and 9 is 5.

CONCEPTS AND SKILLS

Add or subtract.

4.	3 +9	5.	10 − 2	6.	16 − 9	7.	7 +8

8.	12 − 6	9.	9 +9	10.	14 − 7	11.	6 +4

12. $5 + 6 = $ ▪__

13. $15 - 8 = $ ▪__

14. $9 + 2 + 1 = $ ▪__

15. $4 + 3 + 6 + 2 = $ ▪__

Find the missing number.

16. $7 + $ ▪__ $ = 7$

17. $6 - $ ▪__ $ = 0$

18. $8 - $ ▪__ $ = 0$

19. $5 + 3 = $ ▪__ $ + 5$

Write the letter of the best estimate.

20. length of a small dog   **a.** 3 cm   **b.** 3 dm   **c.** 3 m   **d.** 3 km

21. height of a table   **a.** 1 cm   **b.** 1 dm   **c.** 1 m   **d.** 1 km

Use your centimeter ruler. Measure to the nearest centimeter.

22. _____

Critical Thinking

23. Hal adds two 1-digit numbers. His sum has a 3 in the tens place. Can his sum be correct? Why or why not?

Mixed Applications

24. Lee lives 3 km from town. Mayumi lives 7 km from town. How much closer to town does Lee live?

25. Kevin painted 2 shells blue and 8 shells red. How many shells did he paint in all?

PERFORMANCE ASSESSMENT

Work with your group to solve the problem.

Suppose your class went on a field trip to Red Canyon Campground on page 518 of the Databank. At the camp, the class was divided into 3 groups. One group hiked just one trail, one group hiked two trails, and one group hiked three trails. No group took the Adventure Walk. Work together with your group to make a poster of the nature trails. Mark on the poster the route that each group hiked.

1. *Think about:*
   - what kind of ruler to use
   - how to draw nature trails that are 1 km long, 5 km long, 9 km long, and 13 km long
   - how to decide what group hiked which trail

2. At the bottom of the poster, write how much longer or shorter each trail is than the other three trails. Also, write the total number of kilometers each group hiked.

CUMULATIVE REVIEW

Choose the letter of the correct answer.

1. $5 - 5 = $ ▪
   a. 0   **c.** 10
   b. 1   **d.** not given

2. $14 - $ ▪ $ = 5$
   a. 6   **c.** 9
   b. 11   **d.** not given

3. $1 + 5 + 4 = $ ▪
   a. 9   **c.** 154
   b. 11   **d.** not given

4. What is the best unit to measure a room?
   a. cm   **c.** km
   b. m   **d.** not given

5.   8
      $\underline{+9}$
   a. 16   **c.** 18
   b. 17   **d.** not given

6. $9 - 8 = $ ▪
   a. 1   **c.** 17
   b. 2   **d.** not given

7. Which sentence is related to $8 + 3 = 11$?
   a. $7 + 4 = 11$
   b. $6 + 5 + 11$
   c. $11 - 3 = 8$
   d. not given

8. $4 + 4 + 5 = $ ▪
   a. 12   **c.** 14
   b. 13   **d.** not given

9. $(4 + 6) + (8 + 1) = $ ▪
   a. 15   **c.** 17
   b. 16   **d.** not given

10. $11 - 7 = $ ▪
   a. 4   **c.** 18
   b. 5   **d.** not given

11.   9
       $\underline{+9}$
   a. 0   **c.** 18
   b. 17   **d.** not given

12.   14
        $\underline{- 8}$
   a. 6   **c.** 8
   b. 7   **d.** not given

13. $16 - $ ▪ $ = 9$
   a. 6   **c.** 8
   b. 7   **d.** not given

14. Which number represents the sum in the sentence $7 + 5 = 12$?
   a. 5   **c.** 12
   b. 7   **d.** not given

ESTIMATING THE LENGTH OF A CURVE

It is difficult to measure the actual length of a curve.
But you can estimate the length of a curve by using a ruler.

Follow these steps to estimate the length of a curve.

Step 1 Mark several points on the curve.

Step 2 Connect the points with line segments.

Step 3 Measure the line segments to the nearest centimeter.

Step 4 Find the sum of these lengths.

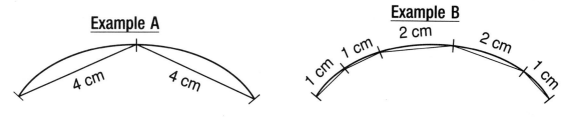

Example A

Example B

1. What is the sum of the lengths of Example A?

2. What is the estimated length of Example A?

3. What is the estimated length of Example B?

4. In which example is the estimated length of the
   curve closest to the actual length of the curve? Why?

5. How can you use a piece of string to check your estimate?

Estimate the length of the curve.

6.
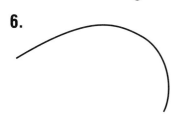

7.

8. Draw your own curve. Estimate its length.

You are probably used to seeing coins that are round and flat. But some very old coins look more like knives or dolphins than nickels or dimes. Some look like lumps of metal.

The oldest known coins are metal pieces with simple designs on them. These coins came from the ancient kingdom of Lydia about 2,600 years ago. Lydia was located in what is now the country of Turkey.

COINS FROM MANY

▲ Dolphin coin from Eastern Europe

◄ The oldest known coin

In ancient China, the first coins were shaped like tools. In Japan, some early coins looked like small gold bricks. Today, most countries have their own special coins. Which of these modern coins have you seen?

CHAPTER 2

UNDERSTANDING NUMBERS AND MONEY

MATH *CONNECTION*: Statistics

1 Compare the old coins with the modern ones. What changes do you notice? How are they the same?

2 What kinds of information do coins have on them? Look at some coins to find out.

PLACES

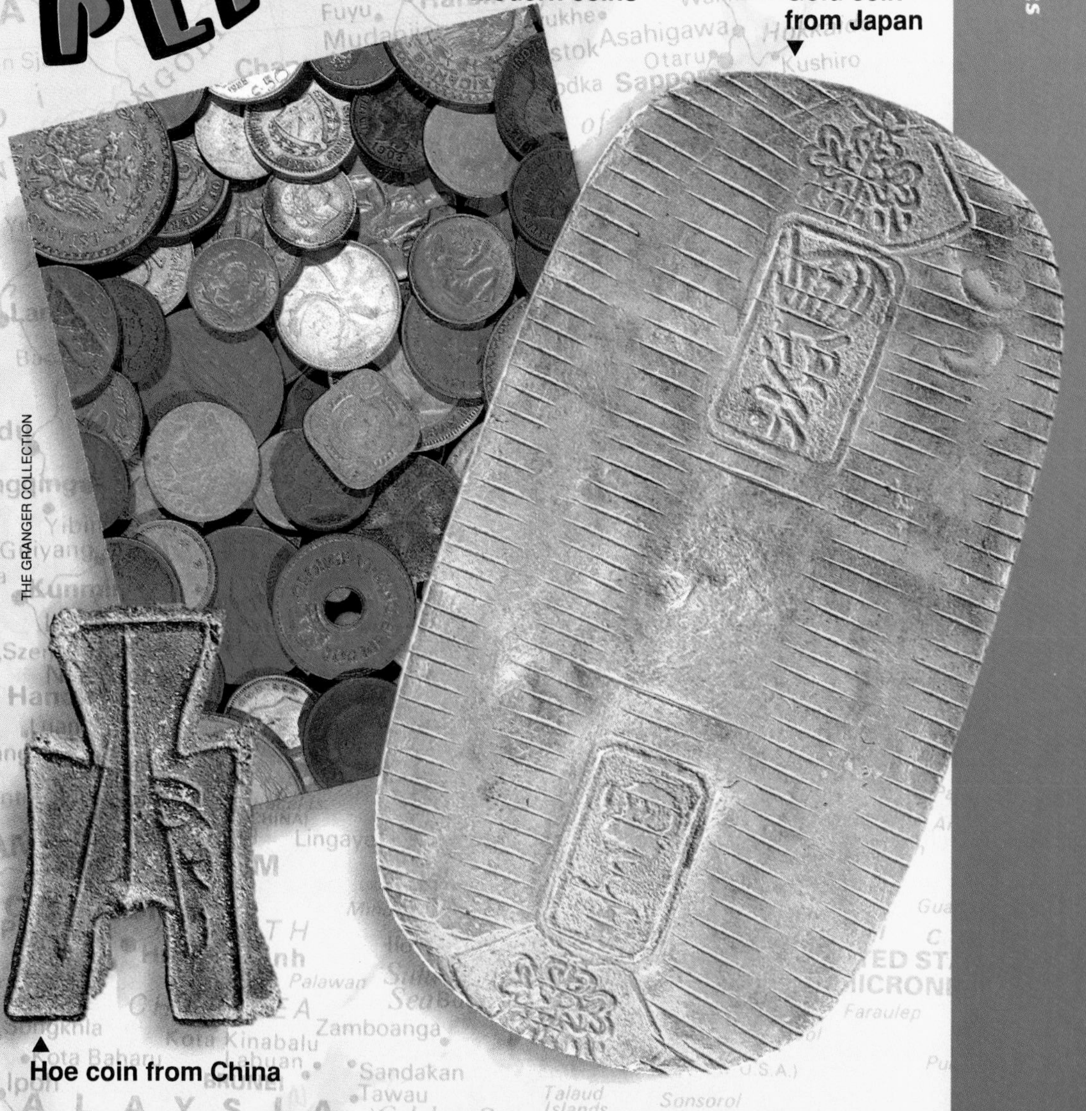

▼Modern coins

Gold coin from Japan ▼

▲ Hoe coin from China

THE GRANGER COLLECTION

ACTIVITY

Building Tens and Hundreds

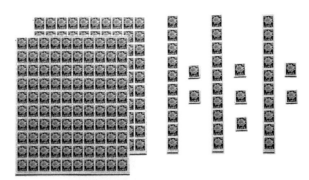

Jani went to the post office to buy stamps. The clerk gave her these stamps. How many stamps did she get?

WORKING TOGETHER

1. Use place-value models to show how many stamps Jani got. Arrange them on a chart like this.

2. Record on a place-value chart how many of each model you used.

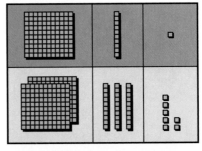

Hundreds	Tens	Ones
2	3	7

You can name this number in different ways.

Jani got 237 stamps.

2 hundreds 3 tens 7 ones
200 + 30 + 7
237
Two hundred thirty-seven

3. **What if** Jani bought 2 sheets and 7 strips of stamps? Build a model to show this. How many stamps would she get? Write the number.

4. **What if** Jani bought 2 sheets and 7 single stamps? Build a model to show this. How many stamps would she get? Write the number.

5. **What if** Jani bought 2 strips and 7 single stamps? Build a model to show this. How many stamps would she get? Write the number.

SHARING IDEAS

6. How many ones are in 1 ten? How many tens are in 1 hundred? What do you notice?

7. How do the place-value models and chart help you read and write numbers.

8. Which digit did you use to show that there are no tens or ones? Do you need to use this digit if there are no hundreds?

ON YOUR OWN

Choose one activity. You may wish to do more than one, or to do each more than once.

9. Pick any 3-digit number. Tell another student how to model the number. Have them build a model and name the number.

10. Use a 0 to 9 spinner. Spin it once for the number of hundreds, again for the number of tens, and a third time for the number of ones. Write the number and build a model for it. Challenge another student to build a different model for the same number.

Solve this number riddle.

11. I am thinking of a number that has the same number of ones, tens, and hundreds. The sum of the digits is 12. What is my number?
Make up your own number riddles. Challenge other students to name your number.

ACTIVITY

Regrouping Tens and Hundreds

A. Lauren buys these stamps for her stamp collection. She can fit 10 stamps on each page of her stamp albums. How many pages can she fill? How many stamps are left?

WORKING TOGETHER

1. Use place-value models to show how many stamps Lauren bought. Copy and complete the place-value chart.

Hundreds	Tens	Ones
0	0	■

Think: You can regroup 10 ones as 1 ten.

2. Regroup your models to show how many pages are filled. Write how many of each model you have now.

Hundreds	Tens	Ones
0	■	■

3. How many pages does Lauren fill? How many stamps are left?

B. Lauren had filled 16 pages of another album. She put 7 stamps on the last page. How many stamps are in the album?

4. Use your place-value models to show this. Copy and complete the place-value chart.

Hundreds	Tens	Ones
0	■	■

Think: You can regroup 10 tens as 1 hundred.

5. Regroup your models to show hundreds. Write how many of each model you have now.

Hundreds	Tens	Ones
■	■	■

6. How many stamps are in the album?

7. How can you regroup ones to make tens?

8. How can you regroup tens to make ones?

9. How is regrouping tens as hundreds like regrouping ones as tens?

10. How is regrouping hundreds to tens like regrouping tens to ones?

PRACTICE

Use place-value models. Regroup.

11.

____ hundreds ____ tens ____ ones

12.

____ hundreds ____ tens ____ ones

13.

Hundreds	Tens	Ones
2	10	4
■	■	4

14.

Hundreds	Tens	Ones
1	15	0
■	■	0

Use place-value models. Regroup once to make more ones.

15.

Hundreds	Tens	Ones
1	2	3
■	■	■

16.

Hundreds	Tens	Ones
5	2	0
■	■	■

17. 2 hundreds 4 tens 8 ones = ____ hundreds ____ tens ____ ones

Regroup.

18. 18 ones   **19.** 20 ones   **20.** 10 tens   **21.** 32 tens

ACTIVITY

Numbers to Thousands

Students at the Mill School are making a mosaic design. Tiles come in cartons of 100, boxes of 10, and as single tiles. The students used 12 cartons, 3 boxes, and 5 single tiles. How many tiles did they use?

WORKING TOGETHER

1. Use place-value models to show how many tiles they used. Record how many of each model you used on a place-value chart.

2. You can regroup 10 hundreds as 1 thousand. Regroup the hundreds. Record how many of each model on a place-value chart.

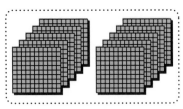 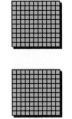 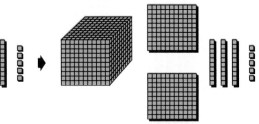

Hundreds	Tens	Ones
12	3	5

→

Thousands	Hundreds	Tens	Ones
1	2	3	5

Expanded Form: 1 thousand 2 hundreds 3 tens 5 ones
1,000 + 200 + 30 + 5

Standard Form: 1,235   A comma is used to separate thousands from hundreds.

Word Name: One thousand, two hundred thirty-five
The students used 1,235 tiles.

3. The value of the 2 in the hundreds place is 200. What is the place and value of the 3?

4. ***What if*** the students used 24 cartons and 9 single tiles? Build a model to show this. How many tiles would they have used? Write the number.

5. ***What if*** the students used 10 cartons and 5 boxes of tiles? Build a model to show this. How many tiles would they have used? Write the number.

SHARING IDEAS

6. How can you regroup hundreds to make thousands?

7. How is regrouping hundreds to thousands like regrouping tens to hundreds?

8. Explain the value of the digit 0 in the number 1,075.

PRACTICE

Write the number.

9. 6 tens 5 ones

10. 6 hundreds 5 tens 3 ones

11. 4,000 + 700 + 1

12. 6,000 + 50

13. 4 thousands 7 hundreds 3 tens 1 one

Write the word name.

14. 63

15. 102

16. 4,987

17. 1,005

What is the value of the digit 7 in the number?

18. 376

19. 87

20. 4,762

21. 7,809

Mixed Applications

22. Mr. Alvarez bought 16 cartons of tiles for his students. They used 8 cartons. How many cartons are left?

23. Pick any 4-digit number. Tell another student how to model it. Have the student build or draw the model and write the number.

Mixed Review

Solve.

24. 7 + 3 = ____

25. 15 − 6 = ____

26. 4 + 2 + 5 = ____

Numbers to Ten Thousands

A. Su-ki's family moved to New York City from Seoul, Korea when she was a baby. As part of a Social Studies project she learned that in 1992 there were about 21,600 people living in the city who were born in Korea.

You can think about this number in different ways.

Ten Thousands	Thousands	Hundreds	Tens	Ones
2	1	6	0	0

2 ten thousands 1 thousand 6 hundreds 0 tens 0 ones
Word Name: Twenty-one thousand, six hundred

1. What digit is in the ten thousands place? What is its value?

2. What digit is in the thousands place? What is its value?

3. What do the zeros mean in this number?

4. **What if** 10 more Koreans moved to New York? Which place on the chart would change? Write the new number.

5. **What if** 1,000 Koreans moved away from New York? How would the original number change? Write the new number.

B. Look at the place-value chart above.

6. How many hundreds are in 1,000? How many thousands are in 10,000? What pattern do you see as the numbers increase place by place on the chart?

TRY OUT

Write the place and value of the digit 4 in the number.

7. 463   **8.** 3,042   **9.** 54,317   **10.** 43,087

Write the number that is 1,000 more than the given number.

11. 46,309   **12.** 7,063   **13.** 20,348   **14.** 54,921

PRACTICE

Write the number.

15. 6 ten thousands 5 thousands 7 hundreds
3 tens 6 ones

16. thirty-four thousand, five hundred forty-two

17. ninety thousand, seventy-six

Write the place and value of the digit 6 in the number.

18. 45,698   **19.** 96,302   **20.** 68,031   **21.** 752,467

Copy and complete the table. Write the numbers that are 10,000 less, 1,000 less, 1,000 more, and 10,000 more than the given number.

	10,000 less	1,000 less	Number	1,000 more	10,000 more
22.			74,231		
23.			57,932		
24.			41,375		

Critical Thinking

25. What number is 1 greater than 34,999? In which place did the digits change? Why?

Numbers to Hundred Thousands

Heta wants to be a lawyer when she grows up so she can help her people on the Hopi reservation. She finds in an almanac that there are about 527,000 lawyers in the United States.

Look at this number on a place-value chart.

Thousands Period			Ones Period		
Hundred Thousands	Ten Thousands	Thousands	Hundreds	Tens	Ones
5	2	7	0	0	0

Word Name: Five hundred twenty-seven thousand

1. What digit is in the hundred thousands place? What is its value?

2. What do the zeros in this number mean?

3. **What if** the number of lawyers went up by 10,000? Which place on the chart would change? Write the new number.

4. How many ten thousands are in 100,000? How do you know?

TRY OUT Write the place and value of the digit 5 in the number.

5. 1,254

6. 51,136

7. 740,514

8. 516,386

Give the next number and describe the pattern.

9. 430,000; 420,000; 410,000; ■   10. 275,000; 285,000; 295,000; ■

PRACTICE

Write the number.

11. 4 hundred thousands 4 thousands 8 hundreds 2 tens 5 ones

12. three hundred sixty thousand, four hundred fifty-three

13. eighty-eight thousand, eight hundred eight

Write the place and value of the digit 2 in the number.

14. 7,235   **15.** 42,610   **16.** 251,764   **17.** 824,031

Give the next number and describe the pattern.

18. 340,000; 240,000; 140,000; ▪   **19.** 75,000; 85,000; 95,000; ▪

Mixed Applications

20. In Heta's class 7 girls want to be scientists. There are 5 boys who want to be scientists. How many more girls want to be scientists?

21. **Make a list** of some interesting facts that are given with large numbers in an almanac. Share your list with other students.

CHALLENGE

Ten hundred thousands is **one million** (1,000,000).

Suppose you wanted to store 1,000,000 cubes. Would they fit in your desk? a closet? a classroom?

Think: A small bag holds about 100 cubes.

1. How many bags hold about 1,000 cubes? Where could you store these bags?

2. How can you estimate where you can store 10,000 cubes? 100,000 cubes?

3. Estimate where you can store 1,000,000 cubes.

PROBLEM SOLVING

Identifying Extra Information

The Rojas family has a Cousins Club. Emily is the treasurer. One day Emily goes to the store to buy wrapping paper and ribbon to wrap presents for the club's party. She gives the cashier a $10 bill to pay for the two items. How much does she spend?

1. What information do you know?

2. What do you need to find out?

Some problems have more information than you need.

3. List all the information you need to solve the problem.

4. Name some information in the problem that you do not need.

5. How much does Emily spend?

6. Why is it important to know what information you need to solve a problem?

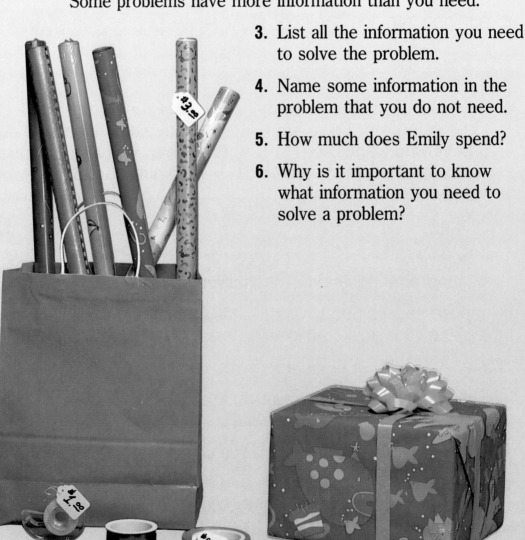

PRACTICE

Solve the problem. List the extra information.

7. The Cousins Club has $9 in the bank. Emily plans to deposit $3 this month and $4 next month. How much will Emily deposit in the next two months?

8. At one Cousins Club meeting, there were 5 boys, 3 girls, and 4 pets. How many children were at the meeting?

9. The Stamp Collectors Club has 15 members and meets 9 times a year. Of the members, 7 have not paid their dues. How many members have paid their dues?

10. The club is having a race. Of the 18 club members, 11 runners start the race, and 7 finish the race. How many runners do not finish the race?

Strategies and Skills Review

11. Last month 5 friends joined a swimming club. Now the club has 12 members. How many people were in the club before the friends joined?

12. One afternoon 16 cousins went to a ball game. Eight cousins took the bus and the rest went by car. How many cousins went by car?

13. The club members sold raffle tickets for charity. Bonnie sold 9 tickets. Derek sold 4 tickets. Reba sold $5 worth of tickets. How many tickets did Bonnie and Derek sell?

14. At a meeting 14 members voted for buying a table, 9 voted against it, and 3 did not vote. How many more people voted for buying the table than against buying it?

15. At the park 6 brothers, 3 sisters, and 4 friends play soccer. How many brothers and sisters play?

16. **Write a problem** that has extra information. Solve the problem. Ask others to solve your problem.

Counting

A. On the school bus Seth and Marta played a game in which they counted every other number.

You can show on a number line how Seth counted.

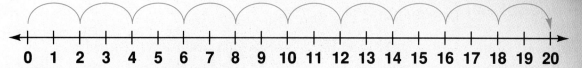

0 1 2 3 4 5 6 7 8 9 10 11 12 13 14 15 16 17 18 19 20

1. Which numbers did Seth call out?

Seth's numbers are **even numbers.**

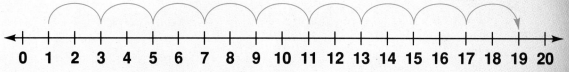

0 1 2 3 4 5 6 7 8 9 10 11 12 13 14 15 16 17 18 19 20

2. Marta started counting at 1. Count by 2s to name the numbers she called out.

Marta's numbers are **odd numbers.**

3. Look at both groups of numbers. Tell how you know if a number is even or odd.

B. You can also use **ordinal numbers** to show order.

Jill	Rod	Bella	Ashi	Sue	Martin	Lynn	Sal	Jody	Lee	Leah	José
12th	11th	10th	9th	8th	7th	6th	5th	4th	3rd	2nd	1st

4. Who is first in line?

5. Who is eighth in line?

6. What is Bella's place in line?

7. How many students are there in front of Jody?

TRY OUT

8. Count by 2s. Write each missing number.

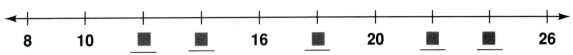

8   10   ■   ■   16   ■   20   ■   ■   26

9. What is the fifth number shown on the number line?

PRACTICE

10. Count by 2s. Write each missing number.

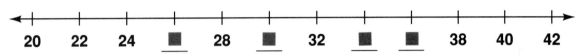

20   22   24   ■   28   ■   32   ■   ■   38   40   42

11. Count by 3s. Write each missing number.

33   36   ■   42   45   ■   51   ■   ■   60   63

12. Count by 4s. Write each missing number.

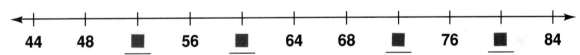

44   48   ■   56   ■   64   68   ■   76   ■   84

13. Count by 5s. Write each missing number.

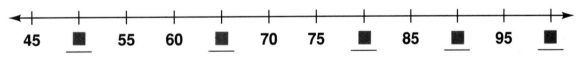

45   ■   55   60   ■   70   75   ■   85   ■   95   ■

14. Which of the counting patterns above show only even numbers? only odd numbers? both even and odd numbers?

Mixed Applications

15. Don is 40th in line. How many people are there in front of him?

16. Line *A* has 8 people. Line *B* has 12 people. How many more people are in line *B*?

17. Count from 0 to 100 by 10s. Then count from 0 to 1,000 by 100s. Compare the numbers you counted. Talk about the patterns you see.

ACTIVITY Counting Money

Maya earns money by recycling cans. She has earned 1 five-dollar bill, 3 one-dollar bills, 1 quarter, 3 dimes, 4 nickels, and 2 pennies. How much money does Maya have?

You can use what you know about sorting and skip-counting to find the amount.

WORKING TOGETHER

1. Use play money to show the bills and coins Maya has.

2. Sort the bills and coins.

3. Count the bills. Then count the coins.

4. How much money does Maya have?

5. What other bills and coins can you use to show this amount? What are the fewest bills and coins you can use?

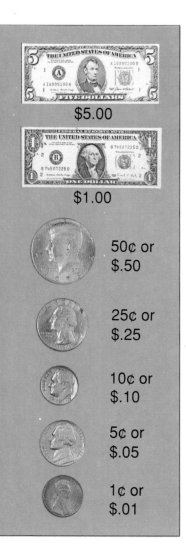

$5.00

$1.00

50¢ or $.50

25¢ or $.25

10¢ or $.10

5¢ or $.05

1¢ or $.01

SHARING IDEAS

6. How did you sort and count the bills and coins? Compare your method with those of others.

7. How do you know if you are using the fewest bills and coins to show an amount?

PRACTICE

Write the amount. Use a dollar sign ($) and a decimal point (.) in your answer.

8.

9.

10. 1 quarter, 2 nickels

11. 6 dimes, 3 pennies

12. 4 dollars and 37 cents

13. 11 dollars and 40 cents

14. twenty-two dollars and fifty cents

15. sixty dollars and three cents

Use play money to show the amount. Copy and complete the chart to record the number of bills and coins you use. Compare your chart to those of others.

	Amount	$5.00	$1.00	50¢	25¢	10¢	5¢	1¢
16.	$ .63	■	■	■	■	■	■	■
17.	$1.05	■	■	■	■	■	■	■
18.	$9.80	■	■	■	■	■	■	■

Critical Thinking

19. Carla has 2 bills and 4 coins. She has $6.16. What are the bills and coins she has?

Mixed Applications

20. Bob finds 3 quarters, 3 nickels, and 1 dime under his bed. How much money does he find?

21. Kai has 18 dimes. She gives 9 of them to Ralph. How many dimes does Kai have left?

ACTIVITY

Making Change

Carrie buys a small tree for Earth Day that costs $3.79. She gives the clerk $4.00. The clerk counts up from $3.79 as she gives Carrie her **change.** She gives Carrie a coin and counts "$3.80," another coin and counts, "$3.90," and another coin and counts, "$4.00". How much change did the clerk give Carrie?

You can count up using play money to find the answer.

WORKING TOGETHER

1. What amount did the clerk start counting from? Why?

$3.79 $3.80 $3.90 $4.00

2. What coin did the clerk use to get to $3.80? $3.90? $4.00? Use play money to show these coins.

3. Why did the clerk stop counting at $4.00?

4. How much change did the clerk give Carrie?

5. What other coins could the clerk have used to make this change?

6. **What if** Carrie had bought a pen for $1.35 and given the clerk a $5.00 bill, how could the clerk have counted the change? How much change would she have given Carrie?

7. What amount do you start counting from when you are making change? At what amount do you stop counting?

8. How do you know if you are using the fewest bills and coins to make change?

PRACTICE

Count up to find the correct change.

9. Amount given—$5.00

$3.45

Use play money to make the change. Copy and complete the chart to record the number of bills and coins you use. Compare your chart to those of others.

	Cost	Amount Given	1¢	5¢	10¢	25¢	50¢	$1.00	Total Change
10.	$2.75	$5.00	■	■	■	■	■	■	■
11.	$.39	$1.00	■	■	■	■	■	■	■
12.	$1.43	$5.00	■	■	■	■	■	■	■

Mixed Applications

13. Nadia buys a Save-a-Seal poster for $2.48. If she pays the exact amount, what bills and coins does she use?

14. *Write a problem* about buying food that costs less than $5.00. Give your problem to another student to solve.

Visual Reasoning

A. Gather a set of blocks like the ones shown.
Are any two blocks exactly the same?

1. How are these two blocks alike?

Are they the same shape?
Are they the same color?
Are they the same size?
These two blocks have the same *size*.
They have different *shapes* and *colors*.
They are the same in one way.
They are different in two ways.

2. How are these two shapes alike?
How are they different?

How many ways are these two
shapes the same?
How many ways are they different?

Difference?

B. Look at the train below. Each car can hold one block. You can make Difference Trains with your set of blocks.

3. First, put the small blue circle in the first car.
   Next, choose a block that is different in *one* way.
   Which blocks can you choose?
   Place your choice in the second car.
   Then, place the rest of the blocks.
   When each block has exactly one difference from its neighbors, you have made a One-Difference Train.

4. Now try to make a Two-Difference Train.
   Start with any block.
   Next, choose a block that is different in *two* ways.
   Can you complete this train?

Comparing and Ordering Numbers

A. Ms. Stein's class read 275 books during Readathon month. Mr. Sak's class read 283 books. Which class read more books?

You can use a number line to compare numbers.

270 271 272 273 274 275 276 277 278 279 280 281 282 283 284 285

Think: 275 comes **before** 283.
275 **is less than** 283.

Think: 283 comes **after** 275.
283 **is greater than** 275.

Write: 275 < 283

Write: 283 > 275

Hint: The "arrow" points to the lesser number.

Mr. Sak's class read more books.

B. You can compare and order numbers without a number line. Order 2,354; 454; and 2,534 from least to greatest.

Step 1	Step 2	Step 3
Line up the ones. Begin at the left and compare to find the first place where the digits are different.	Compare the other numbers.	Order the numbers from least to greatest.
454← The number with the fewest digits is the least. 2,354 2,534	2,354 2,534 *Think:* 300 < 500 So 2,354 < 2,534.	454; 2,354; 2,534

1. How would you order the numbers from greatest to least?

2. Which is the least: $1.29, $.87, or $2.49? Why?

TRY OUT

Compare. Use >, <, or =.

3. 14 ● 41   **4.** 290 ● 209

Order from least to greatest.

5. 476; 467; 697   **6.** $.85; $.76; $.58

PRACTICE

Compare. Use >, <, or =.

7. 27 ● 31   **8.** 98 ● 74   **9.** 11 ● 11   **10.** 30 ● 29   **11.** 45 ● 54

12. 790 ● 790   **13.** 235 ● 241   **14.** 707 ● 770   **15.** 1,010 ● 110

16. $.79 ● $.79   **17.** 4,305 ● 430   **18.** 999 ● 989   **19.** 990 ● 9,090

Order from least to greatest.

20. 365; 357; 589   **21.** 989; 1,001; 999   **22.** 2,178; 5,332; 1,985

23. $8.75; $.99; $3.25   **24.** 908; 890; 98   **25.** 99; 999; 98

Order from the greatest to the least.

26. 217; 96; 4,025   **27.** 54; 454; 4,545   **28.** 6,789; 5,432; 5,897

29. $.87; $3.19; $5.13   **30.** 78; 878; 88   **31.** $8.90; $8.09; $12.01

Mixed Applications

32. Belinda spends 2 quarters and 3 dimes. Ari spends 1 half dollar and 6 nickels. Who spends more?

33. Tawana reads 6 adventure books and 5 mystery books. How many books is that in all?

LOGICAL REASONING

Phyllis, Roy, Pat, and Peg are waiting in line to get their Reading pins. Peg is between Phyllis and Roy. Phyllis is not first in line. Pat is next to Phyllis. Roy is not second in line. Pat is last in line. In what order are they standing?

PROBLEM SOLVING

Strategy: Using Number Sense

José has $1 to spend. He wants to buy something he can use at school. José uses number sense to make a list of things he thinks cost about $1.

Items Costing About $1

notepad
eraser
pencil sharpener
12-inch ruler
10-pack of pencils
2 pens

Items Costing About $10

book bag
baseball bat
sweatshirt
calculator
volleyball
basketball

1. Look at José's list. Do you think he can buy a notepad for $1? Why or why not?

2. Make your own list of things you think cost about $1. Compare your list with those of others. How are they alike? How are they different?

3. **What if** José had $10 to spend? Do you think he could buy all the items on his $1 list? Why or why not? Could he buy all the items on your list?

4. José wants to buy a soccer ball. He thinks he can buy one for $10. Do you agree? Why or why not?

5. Make your own list of things you think you can buy for $10. Compare your list with those of others. How are they alike? How are they different?

6. How did you use what you know about numbers to help you make your $1 and $10 lists?

PRACTICE

Use number sense to solve the problem.

7. Pete wants to buy a new ten-speed bike. About how much money will he need?
   a. $1   b. $10   c. $100

8. Jane wants to buy a volleyball. About how much money will she need?
   a. $2   b. $10   c. $90

9. Rose wants to buy 2 pens. About how much money will she need?
   a. $.10   b. $1   c. $30

10. Marv wants to buy a baseball hat. About how much money will he need?
    a. $1   b. $10   c. $100

11. Kelly wants to buy a ten-pack of pencils and an eraser. About how much money will she need?
    a. $2   b. $20   c. $200

12. Fran has a notepad for each of her school subjects. About how many notepads does she have?
    a. 5   b. 50   c. 500

13. James wants to buy a sweatshirt and a bookbag. About how much will they cost?
    a. $2   b. $20   c. $200

14. Dee is saving money to buy her mother a purse. About how much money should she save?
    a. $1   b. $15   c. $750

15. Joe wants to give his brother 2 shirts for his birthday. About how much money will he need?
    a. $2   b. $20   c. $200

16. Bud wants to buy gifts for his brothers and sisters. How many gifts will he need?
    a. 3   b. 30   c. 300

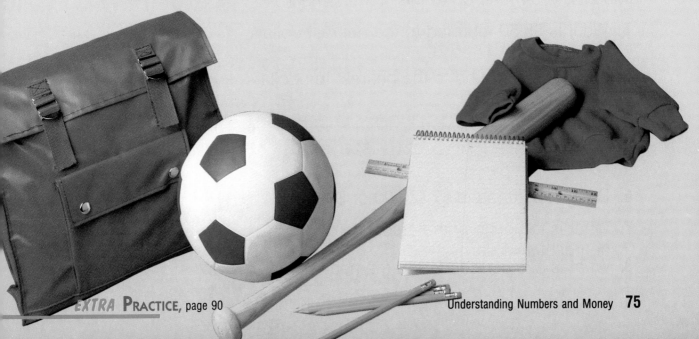

EXTRA PRACTICE, page 90

Rounding Money

Cassette Tape $5.70
Videotape $23.00
Calculator $26.99

A. Marilyn and Mitchell want to buy their father a cassette tape for his birthday. About how much money will they spend?

You **round** money amounts to tell about how much. You can use a number line to help you.

Round $5.70 to the nearest dollar.

$5.00 $5.10 $5.20 $5.30 $5.40 $5.50 $5.60 $5.70 $5.80 $5.90 $6.00

Think: $5.70 is between $5.00 and $6.00.

1. Is $5.70 nearer to $5.00 or to $6.00?

2. What is $5.70 rounded to the nearest dollar?

3. About how much will Marilyn and Mitchell spend?

4. What is $5.27 rounded to the nearest dollar? Why?

When an amount is exactly halfway between two dollar amounts, you round up to the higher amount.

5. What is $5.50 rounded to the nearest dollar?

B. You also can round to the nearest ten dollars.

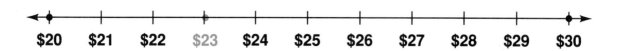

$20 $21 $22 $23 $24 $25 $26 $27 $28 $29 $30

6. Does $23.00 round to $20.00 or $30.00? Why?

7. What is the price of the calculator to the nearest ten dollars?

8. What is $25.00 rounded to the nearest ten dollars?

SHARING IDEAS

9. Do you need to look at the 9 when you are rounding $1.39 to the nearest dollar? Why or why not?

10. Do you need to look at the 7 when you are rounding $24.76 to the nearest $10.00? Why or why not?

11. Tell how you round money amounts. Compare your method with those of others.

PRACTICE

Round to the nearest dollar.

12. $2.32 **13.** $5.67 **14.** $6.90 **15.** $1.12 **16.** $9.45

17. $3.50 **18.** $7.19 **19.** $4.81 **20.** $9.45 **21.** $9.99

Round to the nearest ten dollars.

22. $87.65 **23.** $52.10 **24.** $89.50 **25.** $65.01 **26.** $14.95

27. $21.50 **28.** $49.49 **29.** $97.03 **30.** $45.00 **31.** $4.49

Critical Thinking

32. Bernie has $30.00. The price of a radio rounds down to $30.00. Can he buy it? Why or why not?

Mixed Applications

Solve. You will need to use the Databank on page 517.

33. Jo buys a calculator, a watch, and a silver heart pendant. Which item costs the most?

34. Dawn wants to buy a jewelry box. How many one-dollar bills will she need?

35. Sandy has a five-dollar bill, 3 quarters, 3 dimes, and 4 nickels. Can she buy a videocassette that costs $6.15?

36. Marc chooses to buy something from Silbey's catalog. He wants to spend about $60.00. Which item can he buy?

Rounding

A. Sam's Super Store is having a sale. About how many shirts have been sold? About how many slacks have been sold?

You can round numbers to estimate about how many. You can use a number line to help you.

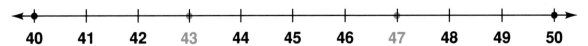

| 40 | 41 | 42 | 43 | 44 | 45 | 46 | 47 | 48 | 49 | 50 |

Round 43 to the nearest ten.

Think: 43 is closer to 40.
Round **down.**
43 to the nearest ten
rounds to 40.

About 40 shirts have been sold.

Round 47 to the nearest ten.

Think: 47 is closer to 50.
Round **up.**
47 to the nearest ten
rounds to 50.

About 50 slacks have been sold.

1. What is 42 rounded to the nearest ten?

When a number is halfway between two numbers, round up to the greater number.

2. About how many sweaters have been sold?

B. You can round numbers without using a number line.

Round 144 to the nearest hundred.

Step 1	Step 2	Step 3
Find the place to which you are rounding.	**Look at the digit to the right of that place.**	**If it is 5 or greater, round up. If it is less than 5, round down.**
		Think: $4 < 5$ Round down.
144	1**4**4	144 → 100

So 144 rounded to the nearest hundred is 100.

3. Round 83 to the nearest ten.

   a. 80 **b.** 85 **c.** 90 **d.** 100

4. Round 150 to the nearest hundred.

   a. 100 **b.** 150 **c.** 160 **d.** 200

PRACTICE

Round to the nearest ten.

5. 38	**6.** 61	**7.** 55	**8.** 86	**9.** 49
10. 65	**11.** 72	**12.** 92	**13.** 25	**14.** 9

Round to the nearest hundred.

15. 234	**16.** 365	**17.** 912	**18.** 375	**19.** 555
20. 432	**21.** 864	**22.** 650	**23.** 441	**24.** 105

25. Which number rounded to the nearest ten is 50?
   a. 42 **b.** 48 **c.** 55

Critical Thinking

26. What is 3,436 rounded to the nearest thousand? How do you know?

Mixed Applications

27. Sam's Super Store is 147 miles from the town of Reston, 262 miles from Burke, and 176 miles from Sterling. Which town is closest?

28. Rex rounds the number of ties sold during the sale to the nearest ten. He tells the cashier that 70 ties have been sold. What is the greatest number of ties that could have been sold?

29. Which town is 200 miles away from Sam's Super Store to the nearest hundred miles?

30. *Write a problem* that involves rounding. When writing it, pretend that Eva sells 52 belts and 49 wallets.

ACTIVITY

Using Tables

Dr. Martha Johnson, the principal at the Sojourner Truth School, needs to report to the school board on how students get to school. This table shows how many students take school buses to school.

STUDENT TRANSPORTATION

Grade	Students Taking Buses
3	143
4	98
5	151

WORKING TOGETHER

Other students walk to school: 37 in grade 3, 53 in grade 4, and 49 in grade 5.

1. Copy and complete this table to show how many students come to school by bus and by walking.

2. How do the labels help you complete the table?

3. In which grade do the most students come by bus? by walking?

STUDENT TRANSPORTATION

Grade	Number of Students	
	Bus	Walk

SHARING IDEAS

4. Compare your table to those of others. How are they the same? different?

5. What does your table tell you about how students get to school?

6. What are some other ways of getting to school? How could you show them on the table?

7. Why is a table a useful place to record data? What makes the data easy to read?

PRACTICE

Solve. Use the table for Problems 8–14.

8. In what order is the data in the **Day** column given?

9. Complete the column.

10. The same number of students brought their lunches on Monday as on Wednesday. Complete this column.

11. On which day did more students bring lunch than had the school lunch?

12. On which day did the most students buy lunch?

13. Each day the school prepares 120 lunches for the third grade. Is this enough? How do you know?

14. Do more third grade students usually bring lunch or do more eat the school's lunch? How do you know?

LUNCHES FOR THIRD GRADE

Day	School Lunch	Bring Lunch
Monday	100	80
Tuesday	93	75
Wednesday	80	■
■	115	69
■	78	102

Choose one activity. Ask students in your class questions to collect the needed information.

15. *Make a table* showing how the students in your class get to school. Compare your table to those of others. What do the tables tell you about how students get to school?

16. *Make a table* about something else you would like to know about the students in your class. Show your table to other students. Talk about what the table shows.

Mixed Review

Write the number or amount.

17. 4 hundreds 8 ones   **18.** 4 dimes, 3 pennies   **19.** $17 - 9 =$

ACTIVITY

Using Bar Graphs

The students in Una's class listed the continent from which one of their ancestors came. They recorded this data in a table.

They used these steps to show the data on a **bar graph**.

Step 1 Choose a scale.

Step 2 Draw and label the sides.

Step 3 Draw the bars on the graph.

Step 4 Write a title above the graph.

WHERE OUR ANCESTORS CAME FROM

Continent	Students
Africa	6
Asia	5
Europe	6
North America	7
South America	4

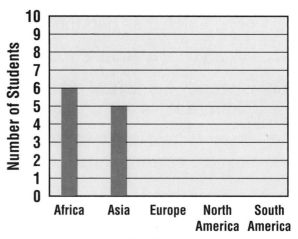

WORKING TOGETHER

1. Complete the bar graph.

2. Why were the numbers 0 to 10 used for the scale?

3. How tall did you make each bar? Why?

4. What is the tallest bar on the graph? What does this tell you?

5. What title did you write above the graph?

SHARING IDEAS

6. ***What if*** there were 14 students whose ancestors came from Asia? How would you change the scale?

7. From which continent did the fewest ancestors come? Is it easier to tell this from the table or the bar graph? Why?

8. Why is a bar graph a useful way to record data?

PRACTICE

Use the table and bar graph to answer Problems 9–12.

9. Una's class asked the rest of the students in the school where one of their ancestors came from. Copy and complete the bar graph.

10. There were 67 students whose ancestors came from Europe. Show this information on the graph. What do you have to do first?

11. No one's ancestors came from Australia or Antarctica. How would you show this?

12. Where did the most ancestors come from? Where did the least?

13. The students also voted for which continent they would like to visit. Nine said Africa, 6 said Asia, 9 said South America, 5 said Europe, and 3 said Australia. Make a table and then a bar graph. Compare them to those of others.

14. Choose a topic you can ask the students in your class about. Make a table and bar graph to show the results. Talk about your graph with the class.

WHERE OUR ANCESTORS CAME FROM

Continent	Number of Students (to the nearest ten)
Africa	40
Asia	50
North America	60
South America	10

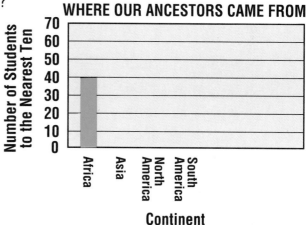

WHERE OUR ANCESTORS CAME FROM

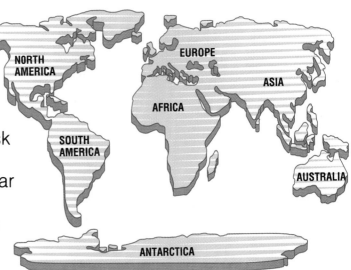

DECISION MAKING

Problem Solving: Choosing a Save-a-Tree Project.

SITUATION

The Ecology Club is planning a Save-a-Tree Project. The 20 members have three projects from which to choose.

PROBLEM

Which project should they choose?

DATA

Recycle Paper Project

- We will collect paper after school for recycling.
- Each member must stay after school for 1 hour, 1 day a week. There are 36 weeks in the school year.
- Each member must donate $1.00. The money will be used to buy art supplies to make posters.

Plant a Tree Project

- We will buy and care for a tree.
- A tree costs $50. A local nursery will donate the equipment needed to plant and care for it.
- Club members must donate $5.00 each or spend 5 hours helping to raise the money to buy the tree.
- Each member will be expected to work 1 hour every month of the year to help care for the tree.

Write Letters Project

- We will write letters to people about saving trees.
- Each member will spend about 2 hours writing the letters.
- Each member will spend about $2.50 for stamps, paper, and envelopes.

USING THE DATA

1. How much money will it cost each member to work on the:

   a. Recycle-Paper Project?
   b. Plant-a-Tree Project?
   c. Write-Letters Project?

2. How many hours each year will each member work on the:

   a. Recycle-Paper Project?
   b. Plant-a-Tree Project?
   c. Write-Letters Project?

MAKING DECISIONS

3. Which project would you choose if you want to spend the least amount of money? the greatest amount?

4. **What if** the members do not want to spend their own money? What can they do?

5. **What if** the members do not always have free time after school? Which project should they choose?

6. **What if** the members want to work on a long-term project, but can not work when school is closed for summer vacation? Which project should they choose?

7. **What if** the members want to work on a long-term project, but can not work after school each week? Which project should they chose?

8. **Write a list** of other things the members should think about when choosing a project.

9. Which project should the members choose? Why?

10. **Write a paragraph** about the type of project you would do and why.

Math and Social Studies

Thousands of years ago, there were no words for numbers. People showed "how many" in other ways.

They might tie a knot in a string for each sheep they had. Perhaps they lined up twigs to show the number of sunsets since the last rain.

You already know one way to show how many without numbers, the tally mark. You use tally marks when you gather data for a graph.

What if you saw these marks? There are 18 marks in each box. Which marks are easier to count?

Think: The marks in the second box are grouped in fives. You can skip-count by 5s.

So it is easier to count the grouped marks.

ACTIVITIES

1. Use tally marks to show how many boys and how many girls are in your class. Are there more boys or more girls?

2. Make up your own way of showing how many without numbers. You may want to use beads or paper clips. Use your method to show how many animals you pass on the way home from school.

Computer Graphing: Double-Bar Graph

Suki is interested in birds. She did research to find out the number of birds living in zoos in her state. She found the bird populations in 1985 and in 1990 for five zoos.

Suki uses a **double-bar graph** to show the number of birds in the zoos in 1985 and 1990. A double-bar graph compares related data. A computer makes it easy to draw a double-bar graph. All you have to do is enter the data.

AT THE COMPUTER

Run the computer graphing program called BIRDS. Look at the data shown in the table on the screen, then draw the graph.

1. What information is compared on this double-bar graph?

2. What does the first set of bars represent? What does the second set of bars represent?

3. Which two zoos had the same number of birds in 1985?

4. How is the data about Wild Woods different from the data about every other zoo?

5. What does the double-bar graph tell you about bird populations in the five zoos?

6. **What if** in 1985 there were 60 birds living in Green Park, 70 in Nature Land, and 90 in Ross Center? Change the data to show this and draw a new graph. Would your answer to Problem 4 change? Why or why not?

EXTRA PRACTICE

Regrouping Tens and Hundreds, page 55 ....

Use place-value models. Regroup tens to make more ones.

1. 2 hundreds 3 tens 4 ones = ■ hundreds ■ tens ■ ones

2. 5 hundreds 4 tens 0 ones = ■ hundreds ■ tens ■ ones

Regroup.

3. 16 ones   **4.** 30 ones   **5.** 19 tens   **6.** 41 tens

Numbers to Thousands, page 57 ....

Write the number or word name.

1. 8,000 + 300 + 20 + 4   **2.** 3 hundreds 2 tens 7 ones

3. 3,074   **4.** 4,207   **5.** 5,124   **6.** 3,333

Numbers to Ten Thousands, page 59 ....

Write the number.

1. 6 ten thousands 2 thousands 1 hundred 0 tens 4 ones

2. eighty thousand, two hundred twelve

3. twenty-two thousand, seven hundred five

Write the place and value of the digit 5 in the number.

4. 15,302   **5.** 51,000   **6.** 12,015   **7.** 4,588

Numbers to Hundred Thousands, page 61 ....

Write the number.

1. 2 hundred thousands 6 hundreds 5 tens 9 ones

2. three hundred nineteen thousand, seventy-seven

Write the place and value of the digit 1 in the number.

3. 21,284   **4.** 102,306   **5.** 62,186   **6.** 601,333

Problem Solving: Identifying Extra Information, page 63 ....

List the extra information. Then solve the problem.

1. The Recipe Club has $25.00 in the prize fund. David will contribute $5 this week and $6 next week. How much money will David contribute?

2. At one club meeting there were 7 new members, 4 regular members, and 8 children present. How many members were at the meeting?

3. The Art Club has 17 members who meet every other Monday. There are 9 women members. How many men are in the Art Club?

4. Ed gives Jo 4 recipes for bread and 3 recipes for salad. He also gives her a new pan. How many recipes does Ed give to Jo?

Counting, page 65 ....

1. Count by 2s. Write each missing number.

30   32   34   ■   38   ■   42   ■   ■   48   ■

2. Count by 3s. Write each missing number.

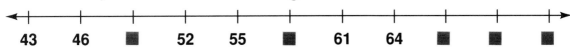

43   46   ■   52   55   ■   61   64   ■   ■   ■

3. Count by 5s. Write each missing number.

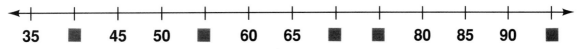

35   ■   45   50   ■   60   65   ■   ■   80   85   90   ■

Counting Money, page 67 ....

Solve.

1. Samantha wants to buy a muffin. She has 2 quarters, 2 dimes, and 1 nickel. How much money does Samantha have?

2. Amal is buying his lunch. He has 3 one-dollar bills, 4 dimes, and 4 pennies. How much money does Amal have?

EXTRA PRACTICE

Making Change, page 69

Write the number of each coin or bill needed to make the correct change. Count up to find the change.

	Cost	Given	$.01	$.05	$.10	$.25	$.50	$1.00	Total Change
1.	$3.25	$5.00	■	■	■	■	■	■	■
2.	$.63	$1.00	■	■	■	■	■	■	■

Comparing and Ordering Numbers, page 73

Compare. Use >, <, or =.

1. 16 ● 21   **2.** 110 ● 101   **3.** $1.43 ● $1.60   **4.** 1,202 ● 120

Order from least to greatest.

5. 252; 232; 460   **6.** $5.60; $.89; $3.25   **7.** 1,623; 4,196; 1,149

Order from greatest to least.

8. 341; 82; 1,463   **9.** $5.60; $5.06; $10.50   **10.** 4,263; 8,101; 3,478

Problem Solving Strategy: Using Number Sense, page 75

Use number sense to solve the problem.

1. Marci wants to buy a new radio. About how much money will she need?

    a. $.01   **b.** $1   **c.** $15

2. Al wants to buy a carton of eggs. About how much money will he need?

    a. $.10   **b.** $1   **c.** $30

Rounding Money, page 77

Round to the nearest dollar.

1. $1.45   **2.** $6.52

Round to the nearest ten dollars.

3. $63.40   **4.** $35.00

EXTRA PRACTICE

Rounding, page 79

Round to the nearest ten.

1. 27   **2.** 32

Round to the nearest hundred.

3. 810   **4.** 666

Using Tables, page 81

Copy the table. Use the table to answer Problems 1–4.

1. In what order is the data in the Day column given?

2. Complete this column.

3. The same number of students walked to school on Tuesday and Wednesday. Complete this column.

4. On which day did the most students walk to school?

TRANSPORTATION TO SCHOOL

Day	Walk to School	Bus to School
Monday	12	14
Tuesday	17	9
Wednesday	■	9
■	20	6
■	13	13

Using Bar Graphs, page 83

Use the bar graph to answer Problems 1–3.

1. There were 58 votes for news programs. Show this information on the graph. What do you have to do first?

2. No one voted for westerns. How would you show this on the graph?

3. Which type of show is the most popular? the least popular?

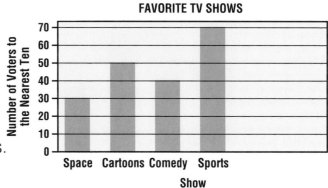

FAVORITE TV SHOWS

Number of Voters to the Nearest Ten

Space 30, Cartoons 50, Comedy 40, Sports 70

Show

PRACTICE PLUS

KEY SKILL: Numbers to Hundred Thousands (Use after page 61.)

Level A

Write the number.

1. three thousand, nine hundred twenty-one

2. twelve thousand, one hundred sixty-five

3. thirty thousand, two hundred seventy-three

Write the place and value of the digit 2 in the number.

4. 1,235   5. 14,892   6. 12,850   7. 65,125

Level B

Write the number.

8. seventy thousand, one hundred

9. six hundred thirty-nine thousand, twenty-five

10. two hundred five thousand, seven hundred forty

Write the place and value of the digit 9 in the number.

11. 89,137   12. 48,009   13. 34,892   14. 983,125

Level C

Write the place and value of the digit 5 in the number.

15. 35,207   16. 350,017   17. 517,389   18. 927,315

Write the number.

19. one hundred greater than 10,041

20. 100 less than 281,193

21. 1,000 greater than 309,508

22. one thousand less than 430,962

PRACTICE PLUS

KEY SKILL: Rounding (Use after page 79.)

Level A

Write the letter of the correct answer.

Round to the nearest ten.

1. 19   **a.** 20   **2.** 72   **a.** 80   **3.** 56   **a.** 50
       b. 10   **b.** 70   **b.** 60

Round to the nearest hundred.

4. 108   **a.** 110   **5.** 666   **a.** 600   **6.** 387   **a.** 400
        b. 100   **b.** 700   **b.** 300

7. Janice's grandmother lives 93 miles away. How many miles is this rounded to the nearest ten?

Level B

Round to the nearest ten.

8. 85   **9.** 52   **10.** 39   **11.** 41   **12.** 19

Round to the nearest hundred.

13. 665   **14.** 407   **15.** 333   **16.** 221   **17.** 450

18. Fred's Factory Outlet sold 375 TVs. How many TVs were sold to the nearest hundred?

Level C

19. Which numbers round to 40?
     45   39   44   50   41   30   35

20. Which numbers round to 800?
     750   888   799   849   723   812   700

21. Brittany's Baseball Store sold 565 baseball cards. About how many baseball cards were sold?

LANGUAGE AND MATHEMATICS

Complete the sentences. Use the words in the chart.

VOCABULARY
greater
expanded
regroup
less

1. You can ■ ten hundreds as one thousand.

2. The "arrow" > means ■ than.

CONCEPTS AND SKILLS

Write the number or word name.

3. seventy thousand, sixty-two   4. 634

Complete the pattern.   Compare. Use >, <, or =.

5. 5, 7, ■, 11, 13   6. 747 ■ 674   7. $.56 ■ $.65

Write the total amount.   Order from greatest to least:

8. 6 quarters, 4 nickels   9. 176; 761; 76

Round to the nearest hundred.   Round to the nearest $10.00.

10. 758   11. 906   12. $24.31   13. $87.17

Complete the table to answer Problem 14.

14. A store sold 26 pencils and 15 pens on Monday. It sold 32 pens and 39 pencils on Friday. On which day did the store sell more pens? more pencils?

STORE SALES

Day	Number Sold	
	Pen	Pencils
Monday	■	■
Friday	■	■

Complete the table. Write the number of each coin or bill needed to make the correct change.

	Cost	Amount Given	Count Up to Find the Change						Total Change
			$.01	$.05	$.10	$.25	$.50	$1.00	
15.	$1.67	$5.00	■	■	■	■	■	■	■
16.	$.37	$1.00	■	■	■	■	■	■	■

Critical Thinking

17. Ricco has 6 coins that total $.33. What coins does he have?

Mixed Applications

18. Amiko found 15 crabs in 3 days. She sold 7 of the crabs. How many crabs does she have left?

19. Talisha wants to buy a sweater. About how much money does she need?

    a. $2.00   **b.** $20.00   **c.** $2,000

20. Barbara is tenth in line. How many people are in front of her?

PERFORMANCE ASSESSMENT

Work with your group to solve the problem.

Suppose your town is redesigning the main road near your housing development. To show the town board that there is a lot of traffic into the development, you took a survey. Make a bar graph using the data.

MORNING TRAFFIC SURVEY

Day	Number of Cars
Sunday	115
Tuesday	338
Thursday	302
Saturday	546

1. *Think about:*
- how to round the numbers
- what steps are involved in making a bar graph

2. Write 3 sentences about the bar graph. Include the words "greater than" or "less than."

CUMULATIVE REVIEW

Choose the letter of the correct answer.

1. $15 - 6 = \blacksquare$
- **a.** 11
- **b.** 10
- **c.** 9
- **d.** not given

2. $6 + 2 = \underline{\blacksquare} + 6$
- **a.** 9
- **b.** 6
- **c.** 2
- **d.** not given

3. Round $44.50 to the nearest ten dollars.
- **a.** $40.00
- **b.** $50.00
- **c.** $60.00
- **d.** not given

4. Complete the pattern:
16, 20, 24, $\blacksquare$, 32.
- **a.** 26
- **b.** 28
- **c.** 30
- **d.** not given

5. $7 + 1 + 0 + 8 = \blacksquare$
- **a.** 17
- **b.** 16
- **c.** 8
- **d.** not given

6. $\underline{\blacksquare} - 7 = 4$
- **a.** 11
- **b.** 13
- **c.** 14
- **d.** not given

7. Ron has 9 shells. This is 7 more than Beth. How many shells does Beth have?
- **a.** 2
- **b.** 7
- **c.** 16
- **d.** not given

8. Choose the number for six hundred thousand.
- **a.** 600
- **b.** 6,000
- **c.** 60,000
- **d.** not given

9. $7 + 3 = 3 + \underline{\blacksquare}$
- **a.** 9
- **b.** 8
- **c.** 7
- **d.** not given

10. What is the amount of 2 quarters and 5 dimes?
- **a.** $.75
- **b.** $1.00
- **c.** $1.45
- **d.** not given

11. Choose the number for forty-four thousand, forty.
- **a.** 40,440
- **b.** 44,040
- **c.** 44,004
- **d.** not given

12. Compare: 794 ● 947
- **a.** >
- **b.** <
- **c.** =
- **d.** not given

13. Complete the pattern:
20, 23, 26, $\blacksquare$, 32
- **a.** 27
- **b.** 29
- **c.** 31
- **d.** not given

14. June caught 4 fish. Oscar caught 6 fish. How many fish did they catch in all?
- **a.** 2
- **b.** 8
- **c.** 24
- **d.** not given

ROMAN NUMERALS

Ancient Romans used letters called Roman numerals to name numbers. Roman numerals are still used today. You can see them on some clocks.

I	**V**	**X**
1	5	10

When letters are repeated, add.

III is 1 + 1 + 1, or 3.

When **I** is placed to the right of V or X, add 1.

VI is 5 + 1, or 6.

When **I** is placed to the left of V or X, subtract 1.

IV is 5 − 1, or 4.

What is **XI**?
Think: 10 + 1 is 11.

What is **IX**?
Think: 10 − 1 is 9.

Write the number.

1. VII   **2.** V   **3.** XX   **4.** XV   **5.** VI   **6.** XIV

Write the Roman numeral.

7. 2   **8.** 11   **9.** 17   **10.** 16   **11.** 19   **12.** 8

Write the time.

13.

14.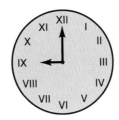

15.

INCA
Record Keeping

About 500 years ago, the Inca Empire stretched along the western coast of South America. The Inca produced many different things. Farmers raised crops and livestock. Miners dug metals and precious stones out of the earth. Craftspeople made cloth and other goods.

The Inca government kept records of how many people lived in different parts of the empire. The amounts of food and other goods the people produced were also recorded. Government officials recorded these numbers by a system involving tying knots in cords. A whole set of cords attached to one main cord was called a *quipu* (KEY-poo).

Cords of different colors on a *quipu* contained information about different people or items. For example, a *quipu* that showed the number of people living in one area might have had three cords of different colors to represent men, women, and children. Knots were tied in a cord in different positions to show hundreds, tens, and ones.

 For 1, the knot in the ones position was shaped like this.

 For 2 to 9, the knots had 2 to 9 turns. Here is the knot for 4.

 Knots like this were used for tens and hundreds.

Here is a *quipu* showing the numbers 28 and 154.

1. How is place value shown on a *quipu?*

2. What kind of information could you record using knots on a cord? Use this information to make a model or a drawing that looks like a *quipu*. Remember that each cord on a *quipu* can represent a different item.

Mental Math and Front-End Estimation

Red Canyon
Campground

A. There are 40 girls and 20 boys on the bus to the Red Canyon Campground. How many students are on the bus?

You can add mentally to find the sum.

Add: 20   *Think:* 2 tens + 4 tens = 6 tens
       + 40   20 + 40 = 60

There are 60 students on the bus.

1. How would you add mentally to find 7,000 + 9,000? What is the sum?

B. You can use mental math to help you estimate a sum.

Estimate: 53 + 67 + 29. Use the front digits.

53   *Think:* Add the tens.
67   5 tens + 6 tens + 2 tens = 13 tens
+ 29   50 + 60 + 20 = 130

The estimated sum of 53 + 67 + 29 is 130.

2. Why will the exact sum be greater than 130?

3. How would you use front digits to estimate 2,546 + 5,205 + 124? What is your estimate?

TRY OUT Add.

4. 40 + 50 + 60

5. 300 + 600 + 500

Estimate by using the front digits.

6. 350 + 478 + 713

7. 2,756 + 4,098 + 6,376

PRACTICE

Add. Use mental math.

8.	9.	10.	11.	12.
600 + 200	500 + 400	900 + 200	7,000 + 8,000	2,000 4,000 + 5,000

13. 80 + 50 = _■_ **14.** 400 + 700 = _■_ **15.** 800 + 900 = _■_

16. 4,000 + 8,000 = _■_ **17.** 200 + 300 + 400 = _■_

Estimate by using the front digits.

18.	19.	20.	21.	22.
69 + 44	217 + 274	65 509 + 117	2,052 598 + 1,500	6,189 3,001 + 5,404

23. 42 + 25 = _■_ **24.** 338 + 569 = _■_ **25.** 348 + 853 = _■_

26. 2,006 + 6,759 + 899 = _■_ **27.** 7,642 + 648 + 2,000 = _■_

Critical Thinking

28.   536
    102   Is the exact sum greater than or less
+ 221   than 900? How do you know?

Mixed Applications

29. The students traveled 40 kilometers after breakfast, 60 kilometers after lunch, and 20 kilometers after dinner. How far did they travel that day?

30. The first road sign shows 11 kilometers to the campground. The next road sign shows 2 kilometers. What is the distance between the two signs?

31. Karl counts 93 horses, 35 sheep, and 54 cows. Does he see more than 170 animals? How do you know?

32. It costs $3.30 to camp in Red Canyon. How can you pay using the least number of bills and coins?

EXTRA PRACTICE, page 130

Estimating Sums by Rounding

There are 382 girls, 267 boys, and 79 adults at the holiday show. About how many people see the show?

The word *about* means that an exact answer is not needed.

You can round to estimate the sum.
Estimate: 382 + 267 + 79

Step 1	Step 2
Round each number to the greatest place of the greatest number.	**Add the rounded numbers.**

$$
\begin{array}{rcr}
382 & \longrightarrow & 400 \\
267 & \longrightarrow & 300 \\
+\ \ 79 & \longrightarrow & +\ 100 \\
\end{array}
\qquad
\begin{array}{r}
400 \\
300 \\
+\ 100 \\
\hline
800 \\
\end{array}
$$

Think: Round to the nearest hundred.

About 800 people see the holiday show.

1. Why will the exact sum be less than 800?

2. Estimate by rounding: $31.67 + $24.03 + $23.08. Will the exact sum be greater than or less than your estimate? Why?

TRY OUT   Write the letter of the correct answer. Estimate by rounding.

3. 327 + 519   **a.** 800   **b.** 900   **c.** 1,000   **d.** 9,000

4. 2,345 + 4,790   **a.** 5,000   **b.** 6,000   **c.** 7,000   **d.** 70,000

5. 22 + 15 + 39   **a.** 50   **b.** 60   **c.** 80   **d.** 100

6. 998 + 4,602   **a.** 4,000   **b.** 6,000   **c.** 14,000   **d.** 60,000

PRACTICE

Estimate by rounding.

7. $512
+ 79

8. 4,125
+ 679

9. 6,900
+ 1,221

10. 3,980
2,099
+ 554

11. $676
262
+ 40

12. $1.85 + $1.69 =

13. $4.33 + $6.64 =

14. 246 + 590 + 79 =

15. 554 + 76 + 32 =

16. 235 + 51 + 560 =

17. 1,827 + 2,999 + 422 =

Estimate by rounding. Then write > or <.

18. 345 + 589 ● 800   **19.** 549 + 64 ● 700   **20.** 1,999 + 122 ● 2,200

Write the letter of the best estimate.

21. 432
217
+ 546
  a. less than 1,100
b. more than 1,100

22. 377
272
+ 94
  a. less than 800
b. more than 800

Mixed Applications

23. The students use 73 flags, 71 banners, and 81 caps in their show. Do they use over 200 items in the show?

24. Sheila buys a pair of red tights for $1.89. She pays $2.00. How can the cashier make change using the fewest number of coins?

MENTAL MATH

Find pairs of numbers with sums that are about 50, 100, or 150.

71   36   93
89   78   28
19   63

Adding 2-Digit Numbers: Regrouping Ones

A. Seth and Sara are selling nut bars to help pay for their class trip to the zoo. The first week they sell 58 bars. The next week they sell 24 bars. How many nut bars have they sold so far?

Seth estimates. 60 + 20 = 80
He uses place-value models to find the exact answer.

Add: 58 + 24

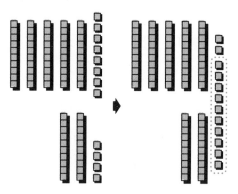 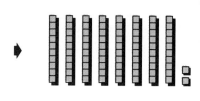

1. Tell how Seth combined the models to find the sum. Did he regroup? Why?

2. How many nut bars did Seth and Sara sell?

B. Sara knows a way to record how Seth adds. She can use this method to add without models.

	Step 1	**Step 2**
	Add the ones. Regroup if necessary.	Add the tens.
58 + 24	$\begin{array}{r} 1 \\ 5\,8 \\ +\,2\,4 \\ \hline 2 \end{array}$	$\begin{array}{r} 1 \\ 5\,8 \\ +\,2\,4 \\ \hline 8\,2 \end{array}$

Think: 12 ones = 1 ten 2 ones

SHARING IDEAS

3. Compare Sara's method to Seth's. How are they the same? How are they different?

4. How does estimating help you tell if an answer is reasonable?

5. How do you know when to regroup?

PRACTICE

Add. Use place-value models if needed.

6. 23 + 5	**7.** 51 + 9	**8.** 16 + 8	**9.** 48 + 8	**10.** 42 + 38	**11.** 24 + 29
12. 56 + 16	**13.** 78 + 19	**14.** 45 + 45	**15.** 18 + 77	**16.** 67 + 14	**17.** 76 + 15
18. 34 + 36	**19.** 12 + 19	**20.** 7 + 69	**21.** 59 + 14	**22.** 44 + 17	**23.** 33 + 48

24. 49 + 44 = ■   **25.** 32 + 58 = ■   **26.** 12 + 49 = ■

27. 57 + 6 = ■   **28.** 63 + 28 = ■   **29.** 27 + 35 = ■

Mixed Applications

30. There are 17 swans and 36 ducks swimming in the pond. How many birds are in the pond?

31. There are 32 baby deer and 38 grown deer eating grass. How many deer are there in all?

32. There are 30 people waiting to watch the seal show. Ed is fifth in line. How many people are behind him?

33. Sheryl has $8.00. How much money will she have left if she spends $7.00?

EXTRA PRACTICE, page 130

ACTIVITY

Adding 2-Digit Numbers: Regrouping Tens

A. At the school ball game Malcolm spends $.47 for a pennant and $.79 for a hat. How much does he spend at the game?

Malcolm estimates $.50 + $.80 = $1.30
Use models of coins to find the exact answer.
Then compare your method to the way Malcolm did it.

Add: $.47 + $.79

1. Tell how Malcolm combined the models to find the sum. Did he regroup? Why?

2. How much does he spend at the game?

B. You can record how Malcolm adds. You can use this method to add without models.

Step 1	Step 2	Step 3
Line up the decimal points. Add the cents. Regroup if necessary.	Add the dimes. Regroup if necessary.	Write the dollar sign and the decimal point in the answer.
$\begin{array}{r} {\scriptstyle 1} \\ \$\ .47 \\ +\ \ \ .79 \\ \hline 6 \end{array}$	$\begin{array}{r} {\scriptstyle 1} \\ \$\ .47 \\ +\ \ \ .79 \\ \hline 1\ 26 \end{array}$	$\begin{array}{r} {\scriptstyle 1} \\ \$\ .47 \\ +\ \ \ .79 \\ \hline \$1.26 \end{array}$
Think: 10 cents = 1 dime	*Think:* 10 dimes = 1 dollar	

3. Use place-value models to add 47 + 79.

SHARING IDEAS

4. Compare the two methods for adding money. How are they the same? How are they different?

5. Compare how you add money amounts to how you add whole numbers. What do you notice?

PRACTICE

Add. Use money or place-value models if needed.

6. $.46 + .74	**7.** 37 + 22	**8.** 86 + 17	**9.** 98 + 5	**10.** $.29 + .95
11. 8 + 88	**12.** 47 + 63	**13.** $.36 + .98	**14.** $.75 + .50	**15.** 48 + 82

16. 98 + 89 = ■ **17.** 72 + 39 = ■ **18.** $.69 + $.41 = ■

19. 9 + 99 = ■ **20.** 65 + 25 = ■ **21.** $.38 + $.83 = ■

Solve.

22. At the ball game Ellie spends $.65 for a can of grape juice and $.89 for a box of popcorn. How much does she spend in all?

23. The Yankee Doodles hit 47 home runs last year. They have hit 55 more home runs this year than last year. How many home runs have they hit this year?

Mixed Review

Compare. Write >, <, or =.

24. 6 + 2 ● 17 − 9

25. 10,000 ● 1,000 + 900 + 90

26. 15 − 7 ● 6

27. 0 + 9 ● 9 − 0

28. 10 + 6 ● 5 + 4 + 7

29. 4 ● 13 − 8

EXTRA PRACTICE, page 131

Column Addition

A. On an all-day hike some students count 18 crows, 9 robins, and 14 geese. How many birds do they count?

You can add to find the sum.

Add: 18 + 9 + 14

Step 1	Step 2	
Add the ones. Regroup if necessary.	Add the tens. Regroup if necessary.	Check by adding up.

$$\begin{array}{r} {\scriptstyle 2} \\ 1\,8 \\ 9 \\ +1\,4 \\ \hline 1 \end{array} \qquad \begin{array}{r} {\scriptstyle 2} \\ 1\,8 \\ 9 \\ +1\,4 \\ \hline 4\,1 \end{array} \qquad \begin{array}{r} 18 \\ 9 \\ +14 \\ \hline 41 \end{array}$$

They count 41 birds.

1. Why can you check an answer by adding up?

B. You can use what you know about addition facts to make adding easier.

You can use **doubles**.

$$3 + 3 = \ \begin{array}{r} 6 \\ +\ 5 \\ \hline 11 \end{array} \ \begin{array}{r} 32 \\ 55 \\ +\ 31 \\ \hline 118 \end{array}$$

You can look for a 10.

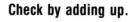

$$\begin{array}{r} {\scriptstyle 1} \\ \$\ .2\,8 \\ .6\,7 \\ +\ \ .1\,2 \\ \hline \$1.0\,7 \end{array} \qquad 8 + 2 = \begin{array}{r} 10 \\ +\ 7 \\ \hline 17 \end{array}$$

TRY OUT Add.

2. $.04 + $.32 + $.76 = ▪

3. 43 + 32 + 7 + 19 = ▪

4. 36 + 5 + 56 = ▪

5. $.14 + $.23 + $.06 = ▪

PRACTICE

Add.

6.	$.39	7.	27	8.	$.82	9.	32	10.	$.96
	.21		14		.90		78		.65
	+ .43		+ 12		+ .17		+ 18		+ .44

11. $.29 + $.92 + $.18 = ▦

12. 77 + 67 + 6 = ▦

13. 44 + 16 + 1 + 28 = ▦

14. 11 + 12 + 13 + 14 = ▦

15. 9 + 19 + 91 = ▦

16. $.99 + $.88 + $.77 ▦

17. 38 + 89 + 4 = ▦

18. 54 + 41 + 5 = ▦

Mixed Applications

Solve. Which method did you use?

ESTIMATION
MENTAL MATH
PAPER/PENCIL

19. Carrie buys wildlife books. The books cost $.75, $.95, $.98, and $.50. Will Carrie spend more or less than $4.00? How do you know?

20. Bob has 19 books about birds, 17 books about fish, and 23 books about plants. How many books does Bob have?

21. Sam hikes 17 kilometers. Kit hikes 9 kilometers. How many more kilometers does Sam hike than Kit?

22. Jena counts 50 red ants and 60 black ants. How many ants does she count in all?

ESTIMATION

You can use 2-digit front-end estimation to get a closer estimate.

4,721 + 217 → 4,700 + 200 = 4,900

Estimate using 2-digit front-end estimation.

1. 1,209 + 123 = ▦

2. 8,394 + 615 = ▦

3. 4,721 + 3,217 = ▦

4. 5,112 + 323 = ▦

PROBLEM SOLVING

Checking for a Reasonable Answer

The members of the third grade at Ridge School are visiting the airport. There are already 92 passengers on a jet plane. Another 62 passengers are waiting to get on the plane. How many passengers will be on the plane when it takes off?

Phyllis uses her calculator
to find the sum.

9 2 $+$ 6 2 $=$ $124.$

She estimates to see
if her sum is reasonable.

$$\begin{array}{r} 92 \rightarrow 90 \\ +62 \rightarrow 60 \\ \hline 150 \end{array}$$

Her sum is unreasonable
so she uses her
calculator again.

9 2 $+$ 6 2 $=$ $154.$

1. Is her sum reasonable? How do you know?

2. How many passengers will be on the plane?

3. Can you think of another way to check Phyllis's answer?

4. Why is it important to check that an answer is reasonable?

PRACTICE

Use estimation to decide which answer is reasonable. Write the letter of the correct answer.

5. There are 16 children and 38 adults on a tour. How many people are on the tour?
   a. 34   **b.** 54   **c.** 74

6. The fare between Houston and Atlanta is $119. What is the round-trip fare?
   a. $198   **b.** $238   **c.** $258

7. The students need 3 buses to go to the airport. One bus takes 42 students, another bus takes 45, and a third bus takes 39. How many students are going in all?
   a. 96   **b.** 106   **c.** 126

8. Baggage is being taken on two carts to be loaded on a plane. One cart has 34 suitcases on it. The other cart has 23 suitcases. How many suitcases will be loaded on the plane?
   a. 57   **b.** 67   **c.** 75

Strategies and Skills Review

9. A plane takes about 7 hours to fly from London to Boston, about 5 hours to fly from London to Cairo, and about 12 hours to fly from Boston to Cairo. How much longer does it take to fly from London to Boston than from London to Cairo?

10. On Wednesday 253 people checked their baggage, on Thursday 277 people checked their baggage, and on Friday 361 people checked their baggage. About how many people checked their baggage on these three days?

11. Tom sold 83 bottles of orange juice and 64 bottles of apple juice. How many bottles of juice did he sell?

12. *Write a problem* of your own. Solve the problem. Then ask others to solve your problem.

Using Number Concepts

On a sheet of paper, draw and color a triangle like the one at the right. Make the triangle larger.

Write the numbers 1, 2, 3, 4, 5, and 6 on another sheet of paper. Draw a circle around each number, then cut the numbers out. The number slips should fit inside the circles on your triangle.

1. Place one number slip on each circle. Can you place the numbers so that each side adds up to 9?

To start, look for sets of numbers that add up to 9. Make a list of the sets you find.

$$1 + 2 + 6 \qquad 1 + 3 + 5 \qquad 2 + 3 + 4$$

Now, look at your list. What numbers appear most often? There are 2 ones, 2 twos, and 2 threes. Try placing these numbers on the red circles. Then try to place the remaining numbers. Can you get each side to add up to 9?

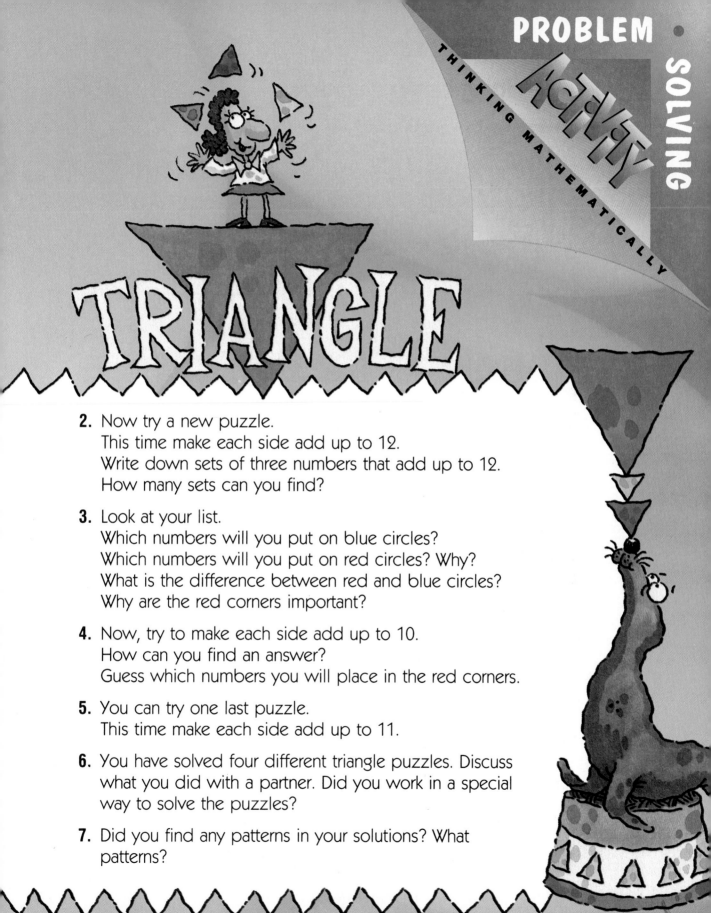

TRIANGLE

2. Now try a new puzzle.
This time make each side add up to 12.
Write down sets of three numbers that add up to 12.
How many sets can you find?

3. Look at your list.
Which numbers will you put on blue circles?
Which numbers will you put on red circles? Why?
What is the difference between red and blue circles?
Why are the red corners important?

4. Now, try to make each side add up to 10.
How can you find an answer?
Guess which numbers you will place in the red corners.

5. You can try one last puzzle.
This time make each side add up to 11.

6. You have solved four different triangle puzzles. Discuss what you did with a partner. Did you work in a special way to solve the puzzles?

7. Did you find any patterns in your solutions? What patterns?

ACTIVITY

Adding Larger Numbers

This table shows the number of cartons of juice sold last week at Pine School.

JUICE SOLD

Flavor	Number
Apple	618
Orange	595

WORKING TOGETHER

Estimate the sum. Then use your place-value models to find how many cartons of juice were sold in all.

1. How did you model each number?

2. In which order did you combine the models to find the sum?

3. Was it necessary to regroup the ones? the tens? the hundreds?

4. Record your results in a table like this.

Exercise	Did You Regroup?		
	Hundreds	Tens	Ones
618 + 595	■	■	■

Use your place-value models to find these sums. Record your results in the table.

5.   726
  +395

6.   635
  +297

7.   524
  +736

8.   586
  +643

9.   237
   585
  +402

SHARING IDEAS

10. How did you use what you know about adding 2-digit numbers to help you add larger numbers?

11. How do you know when to regroup?

12. How did you estimate the sums?

13. How many places can be in a sum when you add two 3-digit numbers? a 3-digit and a 4-digit number?

14. What mental math methods can you use to help you add larger numbers?

ON YOUR OWN

Solve. Use models if needed.

15. The school cooks baked muffins for the weekend food fair. They baked 278 muffins on Friday, 426 muffins on Saturday, and 568 muffins on Sunday. How many muffins did they bake?

16. The Pine School lunchroom served 327 hot lunches last week. It served 185 more cold lunches than hot lunches. How many cold lunches were served last week?

17. *Write a problem* using large numbers you find in newspapers and magazines. Ask others to solve it.

Adding 3-Digit Numbers: Regrouping Once

A. Students in the Green Thumb Garden Club want to know how many flowers they have planted.

FLOWERS PLANTED	
Tulips	191
Daisies	123

They estimate: 200 + 100 = 300. Then they use place-value models to find the exact answer.

Add: 191 + 123

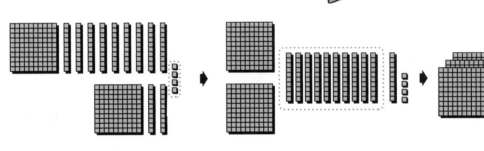

1. Tell how they combined the models to find the sum. Did they regroup? Why?

2. How many flowers have they planted?

B. Here is a way to record how the students add. You can use this method to add without models.

Step 1	Step 2	Step 3
Add the ones. Regroup if necessary.	Add the tens. Regroup if necessary.	Add the hundreds. Regroup if necessary.
191 + 123 ——— 4	¹ 191 + 123 ——— 1 4	¹ 191 + 123 ——— 3 1 4

Think: 11 tens = 1 hundred 1 ten

SHARING IDEAS

3. Compare the method in section A with the method shown in section B. What do you notice?

4. In which place is the regrouping necessary? Why? How is the regrouping recorded in the method shown in section B?

5. Why is 314 a reasonable answer?

PRACTICE

Add.

6.
$$\begin{array}{r} \$431 \\ +\ \ 234 \\ \hline \end{array}$$

7.
$$\begin{array}{r} 59 \\ +\ 625 \\ \hline \end{array}$$

8.
$$\begin{array}{r} \$645 \\ +\ \ 216 \\ \hline \end{array}$$

9.
$$\begin{array}{r} \$562 \\ +\ \ 282 \\ \hline \end{array}$$

10.
$$\begin{array}{r} 683 \\ +\ \ 91 \\ \hline \end{array}$$

11.
$$\begin{array}{r} 237 \\ 448 \\ +\ 309 \\ \hline \end{array}$$

12.
$$\begin{array}{r} 419 \\ 207 \\ +\ 135 \\ \hline \end{array}$$

13.
$$\begin{array}{r} \$395 \\ 192 \\ +\ \ 92 \\ \hline \end{array}$$

14.
$$\begin{array}{r} \$130 \\ 463 \\ 24 \\ +\ \ 252 \\ \hline \end{array}$$

15.
$$\begin{array}{r} 530 \\ 812 \\ 724 \\ +\ \ 23 \\ \hline \end{array}$$

16. $797 + 182 = $ ___

17. $\$337 + \$556 = $ ___

18. $\$987 + \$102 = $ ___

19. $426 + 29 + 438 = $ ___

Mixed Applications

20. Les counted 214 roses in the school garden. Nancy counted 148 lilies. How many flowers did they count?

21. *Write a problem* using this addition sentence: $321 + 345 + 433 = $ ___. Ask others to solve it.

Mixed Review

Compare. Use >, <, or =.

22. $400 + 50 + 25$ ● 500

23. $400 + 600$ ● $900 + 70$

24. $25 + 50 + 100$ ● $50 + 100 + 25$

Adding 3-Digit Numbers: Regrouping More Than Once

The Road Hog Bus Company uses 665 gallons of fuel during one week. The next week it uses 525 gallons of fuel. How much fuel does the company use during these two weeks?

Add: 665 + 525

Step 1	Step 2	Step 3
Add the ones. **Regroup if necessary.**	**Add the tens.** **Regroup if necessary.**	**Add the hundreds.** **Regroup if necessary.**
$\begin{array}{r} 1 \\ 6\,6\,5 \\ +\,5\,2\,5 \\ \hline 0 \end{array}$	$\begin{array}{r} 1 \\ 6\,6\,5 \\ +\,5\,2\,5 \\ \hline 9\,0 \end{array}$	$\begin{array}{r} 1 \\ 6\,6\,5 \\ +\,\;\,5\,2\,5 \\ \hline 1,1\,9\,0 \end{array}$
Think: 10 ones = 1 ten 0 ones		*Think:* 11 hundreds = 1 thousand 1 hundred

The Road Hog Bus Company uses 1,190 gallons of fuel during these two weeks.

1. Is the answer reasonable? How do you know?

2. How would you add $6.63 + $3.25 + $1.46? What is the sum?

T RY OUT   Write the letter of the correct answer.

3. 435 + 297   **a.** 622   **b.** 632   **c.** 732   **d.** 741

4. 548 + 73 + 12   **a.** 523   **b.** 533   **c.** 623   **d.** 633

5. 876 + 639 + 266   **a.** 1,632   **b.** 1,712   **c.** 1,732   **d.** 1,781

6. $4.56 + $.99   **a.** $4.45   **b.** $4.55   **c.** $5.55   **d.** $5.91

PRACTICE

Find the sum. Solve only for sums that are less than 1,000 or $10.00.

7.	628	**8.**	$6.71	**9.**	246	**10.**	$8.97	**11.**	609
	+ 492		+ .85		+ 347		+ 2.12		+ 390

12.	127	**13.**	892	**14.**	$1.29	**15.**	$2.57	**16.**	719
	282		203		1.29		4.98		118
	+ 95		+ 24		+ 7.37		+ 1.84		+ 154

17.	214	**18.**	486	**19.**	$5.39	**20.**	$3.99	**21.**	334
	32		78		.29		5.08		747
	+ 405		+ 41		+ 1.20		+ .14		+ 112

22. 296 + 127 + 89 + 7 = ▇   **23.** 333 + 333 + 333 = ▇

24. 40 + 675 + 125 + 60 = ▇   **25.** 766 + 333 + 1 = ▇

Mixed Applications

Solve. Which method did you use?

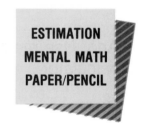

ESTIMATION
MENTAL MATH
PAPER/PENCIL

26. Mr. Wheeler drives the bus 165 miles on Monday, 94 miles on Tuesday, and 200 miles on Sunday. How many miles does he drive in one week?

27. The bus carries 165 students on Wednesday, 103 students on Thursday, and 152 students on Friday. About how many students ride the bus during the week?

28. The Road Hog Bus Company has 10 buses. If 3 of the buses are red, and the rest are green, how many buses are green?

29. Vinny rode the bus 20 times in March, 10 times in April, and 20 times in May. How many times did he ride the bus during these three months?

Choosing a Computation Method

The Ice Show has 27 skaters and 19 singers. How many people are in the show?

Add: 27 + 19

Lavar uses a calculator to find the sum.

$\boxed{2}\,\boxed{7}\,\boxed{+}\,\boxed{1}\,\boxed{9}\,\boxed{=}$ $\boxed{46}$

Anansa finds the sum mentally.
Think: 19 + 1 is 20
27 + 20 is 47
27 + 19 is 47 less 1, or 46

There are 46 people in the show.

1. Talk about how Anansa added mentally.

2. How can you use this method to add 642 and 198 mentally? What is the sum?

Add. Use mental math, paper and pencil, or a calculator.

3. 　　64
    　+ 28

4. 　　157
    　+ 265

5. 　　420
    　+ 390

6. 756 + 62 + 87 = ■　7. 5,000 + 6,000 = ■　8. 36 + 29 = ■

SHARING IDEAS

9. Which computation method did you use to find the answers for exercises 3 to 8? How did you decide?

10. When do you think it is easier to use mental math? paper and pencil? a calculator? Why?

PRACTICE

Add. Use mental math, calculator or paper and pencil.

11. $\begin{array}{r} 68 \\ +41 \\ \hline \end{array}$ **12.** $\begin{array}{r} 47 \\ +25 \\ \hline \end{array}$ **13.** $\begin{array}{r} 8 \\ +63 \\ \hline \end{array}$ **14.** $\begin{array}{r} 94 \\ +87 \\ \hline \end{array}$ **15.** $\begin{array}{r} \$.67 \\ +\ .46 \\ \hline \end{array}$

16. $\begin{array}{r} 495 \\ +186 \\ \hline \end{array}$ **17.** $\begin{array}{r} 812 \\ +103 \\ \hline \end{array}$ **18.** $\begin{array}{r} 245 \\ +578 \\ \hline \end{array}$ **19.** $\begin{array}{r} \$8.74 \\ +\ .66 \\ \hline \end{array}$ **20.** $\begin{array}{r} \$2.05 \\ +\ 3.98 \\ \hline \end{array}$

21. $45 + 48 = $ ___ ■   **22.** $326 + 526 = $ ___ ■   **23.** $750 + 25 = $ ___ ■

CRITICAL THINKING

24. This is how Pablo added $27 + 19$ mentally.
Add the tens.   Add on the ones.
$20 + 10 = 30$ $30 + 7 = 37$ $37 + 9 = 46$
Use this method to add 142 and 35.

**MENTAL MATH
CALCULATOR
PAPER/PENCIL**

Mixed Applications

Solve. Which method did you use?

25. Tickets to the Ice Show cost $5.50. Ian also spent $1.25 on a program and $.75 on popcorn. How much did he spend at the Ice Show?

26. Moe counts 19 skaters dressed in blue. Sara counts 9 skaters dressed in red. How many skaters do they count in all?

27. A group of students filled 2 buses going to the Ice Show. If there are 42 seats on each bus, about how many students went to the show?

28. If Mimi and Jan hike all the trails that begin at the Red Canyon Campground, how far will they walk? Use the information on page 518 in the Databank.

Mixed Review

Complete. Write $>$, $<$, or $=$.

29. $800 + 0 + 6$ ● 860

30. $792 + 380$ ● $1,172$

31. $10 + 20 + 30 + 40$ ● 100

32. $989 + 125$ ● $689 + 115$

PROBLEM SOLVING

UNDERSTAND
✓ PLAN
✓ TRY
CHECK
✓ EXTEND

Strategy: Drawing a Picture

Susan, Uri, David, and Ramona are in a race. Right now Susan is 6 meters ahead of Uri. David is 4 meters behind Susan. Uri is 9 meters behind Ramona. In what order are the runners from first to last?

You can draw a picture to help you solve the problem. Here is a way to show that Susan is 6 meters ahead of Uri.

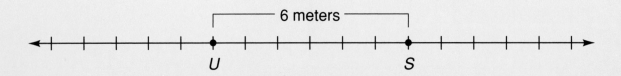

1. Copy the diagram. Draw a dot at the place that shows that David is 4 meters behind Susan. Write the letter *D* under the dot. Then draw a dot that shows Ramona's position. Write the letter *R* under the dot.

2. How far ahead of Uri is Ramona?

3. List the runners in order from first to last.

4. How far ahead of each other runner is the runner who is in first place?

5. **What if** Uri had been only 6 meters behind Ramona? How would this change the order of the runners?

6. How does drawing a picture help you solve problems like this?

PRACTICE

Draw a picture to help you solve the problem.

7. Eton, Marc, David, and Amet are skiing down a hill. David is first, and Eton is last. Amet is behind David. Marc is between Amet and Eton. In what order are they skiing down the hill?

8. Alice's birthday comes 1 day before Bob's. Donna's comes 3 days before Alice's. Carol's comes 2 days before Donna's. Whose birthday comes first?

9. The white car is 6 cars ahead of the red car. The blue car is 6 cars behind the red car. The green car is 5 cars ahead of the blue car. How many cars is the white car ahead of the green car?

10. Danny has planted some trees. The maple tree is to the right of his house. The willow tree is to the right of the maple tree and to the left of the apple tree. Which tree is farthest from the house?

Strategies and Skills Review

Solve. Use mental math, a calculator, or paper and pencil.

11. In a supermarket, the rice is to the left of the soups, and the soups are between the cereals and the rice. The cereals are between the soups and the bread. Which two items are in the middle?

12. The swimming pool has 6 lanes. The boys swim in lanes 2, 4, and 6. The girls swim in the other lanes. In which lanes do the girls swim?

13. In the morning 46 girls and 58 boys came to watch the race. There were also 77 adults. How many people came to watch the race?

14. *Write a problem* that can be solved with the help of a picture. Solve your problem. Then ask others to solve it.

ACTIVITY

Using Addition: Perimeter

Perimeter is the distance around an object.

You can use what you know about measuring to find the perimeter of objects around you.

WORKING TOGETHER

1. Estimate the distance around your math textbook.

2. Use pencils to measure the distance around the book. Compare your methods and measurements with those of others.

3. Place a piece of string around your math textbook. Then use a ruler to measure the length of the string to the nearest centimeter.

4. Record your measurement on a chart like this.

Object	Estimate	Perimeter

5. Can you think of a way to measure the perimeter of your textbook without using a piece of string? How?

6. Estimate and then measure the perimeter of other objects. Record your findings on the chart.

You can add the lengths of each side of an object to find the perimeter.

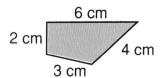

6 cm
2 cm
4 cm
3 cm

Think: 2 + 3 + 4 + 6 = 15
Perimeter = 15 centimeters

7. What is the perimeter of a triangle with the sides 3 meters, 4 meters, and 5 meters?

8. How many sides must you measure to find the perimeter of a rectangle? Why?

9. How many sides of a square must you measure to find its perimeter? Why?

10. Why is it better to use standard units than pencils when measuring perimeter?

PRACTICE

Estimate. Then measure to find the perimeter.

11.
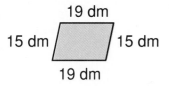

12.
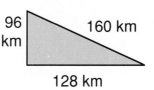

13.
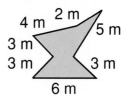

Find the perimeter.

14.
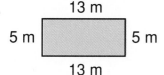
13 m
5 m   5 m
13 m

15.
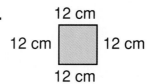
12 cm
12 cm   12 cm
12 cm

16.
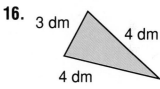
3 dm
4 dm
4 dm

17.

19 dm
15 dm   15 dm
19 dm

18.

96 km
160 km
128 km

19.

4 m   2 m
5 m
3 m
3 m   3 m
6 m

Solve.

20. The bus makes four stops on its trip around the perimeter of the zoo. If it is 2 kilometers between each stop, what is the perimeter of the zoo?

21. The fence around the monkey cage measures 8 meters by 4 meters by 8 meters by 4 meters. What is the perimeter of the cage?

DECISION MAKING

Problem Solving: Planning a Class Trip

SITUATION

Mr. Fish and his class want to take a day trip. Some students want to go to the zoo. Others want to go to the aquarium.

PROBLEM

Which trip should the class take?

DATA

TRIP TO ZOO	TRIP TO AQUARIUM
Admission: Students: $ .75 Adults: $ 1.50	Admission: Students: $ 1.50 Adults: $ 3.00
Transportation: School bus	Transportation: School bus
Travel time: 1 hour	Travel time: 30 minutes
Lunch: Outdoors at picnic grounds	Lunch: Indoors in cafeteria
Things to do: See bird show: "Bird Brains" Fee: $ 1.00	Things to do: See film: "The Great White Shark" Fee: $ .25

USING THE DATA

1. How much will it cost a student to visit the zoo?

2. How much will it cost a student to visit the aquarium and watch the film about sharks?

3. How much time will be spent traveling to and from the zoo? the aquarium?

4. If the class has 5 hours for the whole trip, how much time can students spend at the zoo? at the aquarium?

MAKING DECISIONS

5. What are some of the things the class should consider before deciding on which place to visit?

Which place should the class choose if it wants:

6. to study sharks?

7. to study how monkeys live in groups?

8. to have each student spend the least amount of money?

9. to spend more time at the place they are visiting?

10. **What if** the class is concerned with poor weather? Which place might students choose?

11. Which place would you choose? Why?

12. **Write a list** of places for a class trip. Then discuss the things you need to consider before choosing the trip.

CURRICULUM CONNECTION

Math and Geography

The Western Bike Club's next race is in Texas. The race route is marked in red on the map. It starts in Dallas at the Texas State Fair.

The riders race to Waco the first day. The Texas Ranger Hall of Fame is in Waco. Austin is the goal on the next day of the race. Austin is the capital of Texas.

The racers reach San Antonio the third day. Fort Alamo is in San Antonio. The race ends the fourth day in Lake Corpus Christi State Park.

How many miles is the race in all?

Think: Add. $82 + 94 + 74 + 100 = 350$. So the race is 350 miles in all.

Dallas
82 miles
Waco
94 miles
Austin
San Antonio
74 miles
100 miles
Lake Corpus Christi State Park

ACTIVITIES

1. Add the distance the racers ride on the first and second days. Add the distance they ride on the third and fourth days. Which distance is more miles?

2. Make up a race of your own. Draw a map that shows the route. Show the distance between each city. How long is the race?

Calculator: Palindromes

A **palindrome** is a word or a number that reads the same forward and backward.

These words are palindromes:

DAD   MOM   POP   NOON   SEES

These numbers are palindromes:

22   66   848   2,112   32,223

You can add to form palindromes.
Use your calculator and a sheet of paper.
Follow these steps to make a palindrome
from the number 43.

Write the number.	**43**
Reverse the digits.	**+34**
Add the two numbers.	**77** → a palindrome

Sometimes you have to reverse the digits and add a second time. Follow these steps to make a palindrome from the number 73.

Begin with the number.	**73**
Reverse it.	**+ 37**
Add.	**110** → not a palindrome yet
Reverse it.	**+011**
Add again.	**121** → a palindrome

USING THE CALCULATOR

Use your calculator to make a palindrome.

1. 24   **2.** 32   **3.** 51   **4.** 72

5. 16   **6.** 76   **7.** 20   **8.** 56

9. 53   **10.** 47   **11.** 14   **12.** 46

EXTRA PRACTICE

Mental Math and Front-End Estimation, page 101 ....

Add. Use mental math.

1. 300
   + 400

2. 200
   + 500

3. 800
   + 300

4. 6,000
   + 9,000

5. 1,000
   3,000
   + 4,000

6. 600 + 700 = ■

7. 2,000 + 3,000 + 7,000 = ■

Estimate by using the front digits.

8.   38
   + 24

9.   116
   + 363

10.   24
   419
   + 224

11. 3,073
   602
   + 2,189

12. 4,817
   2,385
   + 9,172

13. 307 + 225 = ■

14. 1,007 + 5,872 + 302 = ■

Estimating Sums by Rounding, page 103 ....

Estimate by rounding.

1. $300
   +   69

2. 650
   + 320

3. 5,017
   +   879

4. 3,072
   2,899
   +   374

5. $857
   226
   +   35

6. $1.62 + $1.38 = ■

7. 227 + 880 + 32 = ■

Adding 2-Digit Numbers: Regrouping Ones, page 105 ....

Add.

1. 23
   + 18

2. 38
   + 27

3. 43
   + 18

4. 17
   + 24

5. 65
   + 25

6. 37 + 54 = ■

7. 11 + 29 = ■

8. 42 + 48 = ■

9. 76 + 15 = ■

10. 28 + 27 = ■

11. 35 + 35 = ■

EXTRA PRACTICE

Adding 2-Digit Numbers: Regrouping Tens, page 107 ....

Add.

1. $.39 + .78	2. 46 + 63	3. 95 + 8	4. 98 + 8	5. 97 + 7
6. $.33 + .79	7. 9 + 99	8. 36 + 84	9. $.49 + .86	10. $.65 + .50

11. $.78 + $.63 = ▤   **12.** 58 + 45 = ▤   **13.** $.83 + $.48 = ▤

Column Addition, page 109 ....

Add.

1. $.27 .42 + .63	2. 16 17 + 35	3. $.71 .80 + .28	4. 61 38 + 27	5. $.88 .43 + .39

6. $.33 + $.82 + $.17 = ▤   **7.** 62 + 89 + 9 = ▤

8. 66 + 27 + 3 = ▤   **9.** 13 + 44 + 39 + 5 = ▤

Problem Solving: Checking for a Reasonable Answer, page 111 ....

Use estimation to decide which answer is reasonable.
Write the letter of the correct answer.

1. There are 22 women and 48 men on a ship. How many people are on the ship?
a. 50   **b.** 70   **c.** 80

2. Al saw 33 sailboats, 12 ferry boats, and 15 rowboats. How many boats did Al see?
a. 40   **b.** 60   **c.** 50

3. John loaded 83 boxes and Bill loaded 24 boxes. How many boxes were loaded in all?
a. 107   **b.** 284   **c.** 113

4. One bus holds 38 people, another holds 52 people, and a third holds 67 people. How many people do the buses hold?
a. 157   **b.** 143   **c.** 162

EXTRA PRACTICE

Adding 3-Digit Numbers: Regrouping Once, page 117 ....

Add.

1. $573
   + 134

2.   38
   + 403

3. $347
   + 214

4. $6.35
   + 2.71

5.   471
   + 87

6. $4.43 + $3.76 = ■

7. 975 + 112 + 1 = ■

8. $6.09 + $.39 + $1.01 = ■

9. 307 + 517 + 82 = ■

Adding 3-Digit Numbers: Regrouping More Than Once, page 119 ....

Find the sum. Solve only for sums that are less than 1,000 or $10.00.

1.   529
   + 518

2. $7.85
   + .66

3.   297
   + 475

4.   507
   + 618

5. $7.25
   + 2.80

6.   117
   373
   + 80

7.   572
   382
   + 278

8. $3.19
   3.19
   + 5.02

9. $1.63
   2.98
   + 2.87

10.   605
   152
   + 168

11. 375 + 109 + 87 + 5 = ■

12. 432 + 222 + 111 = ■

13. 30 + 542 + 107 + 50 = ■

14. 888 + 212 + 5 = ■

Mental Math: Adding Whole Numbers, page 121 ....

Find the sum. Use mental math.

1.   43
   + 67

2.   39
   + 26

3.   7
   + 47

4.   89
   + 11

5.   48
   + 23

6.   507
   + 83

7.   911
   + 75

8.   105
   + 475

9.   799
   + 18

10.   107
   + 289

11. 83 + 17 = ■

12. 50 + 21 = ■

13. 340 + 87 = ■

Problem Solving Strategy: Drawing a Picture, page 123 ....

Draw a picture to solve the problem.

1. Maria, Karen, Wayne, and Ernie are jogging down a hill. Wayne is first. Karen is last. Ernie is in front of Maria. In what order are they jogging down the hill?

2. Val, May, Jan, and Kay all have tryouts in the same week. Val's tryout comes 3 days after May's tryout. Jan's is 5 days before Val's. Kay's is 2 days before Jan's. Whose tryout comes first?

3. Four cyclists have completed the race. Kim is 3 kilometers ahead of Jon. Jon is 4 kilometers ahead of Lil. Bob is 6 kilometers ahead of Kim. In what order did the cyclists finish the race?

4. Chris plants some flowers. The roses are to the left of his house. The tulips are to the right of the daisies and to the left of the roses. The lilacs are to the left of the daisies. Which flowers are farthest from the house?

Using Addition: Perimeter, page 125...

Estimate. Then measure to find the perimeter.

1.

2.

3.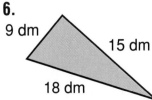

Find the perimeter.

4.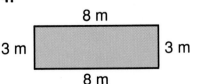

8 m
3 m   3 m
8 m

5.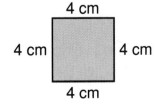

4 cm
4 cm   4 cm
4 cm

6. 9 dm
15 dm
18 dm

Practice PLUS

KEY SKILL: Column Addition (Use after page 109.)

Level A

Add.

1. 3	**2.** 12	**3.** 15	**4.** 6	**5.** 13	**6.** 8
4	4	11	21	3	61
+ 7	+ 1	+ 3	+ 12	+ 5	+ 31

7. Jo bought fruit to take on a hike. She spent $.14, $.87, and $.66. How much did she spend in all?

Level B

Add.

8. 62	**9.** $.75	**10.** 68	**11.** 41	**12.** $.73
78	.55	75	1	.69
+ 18	+ .23	+ 42	+ 67	+ .07

13. Jeb saw 25 elk, 18 deer, and 30 squirrels on the hike. How many animals did he see in all?

Level C

Add.

14. 43	**15.** $.74	**16.** 97	**17.** 8	**18.** $.59
39	.23	5	94	.43
5	.17	98	67	.79
+ 56	+ .97	+ 4	+ 78	+ .80

19. $.06 + $.49 + $.71 = ■

20. 45 + 62 + 9 = ■

21. Dee picked 87 blueberries. Eric picked 29 more berries than Dee. Ali picked 19 more berries than Eric. How many berries did Ali pick?

KEY SKILL: Adding 3-Digit Numbers (Use after page 119.)

Level A

Find the sum.

1.	2.	3.	4.	5.
43 + 289	777 + 29	409 + 390	321 + 203	$7.96 + 1.45

6. Hank drives 182 miles on Monday and 237 miles on Thursday. How many miles does he drive in all?

Level B

Find the sum.

7.	8.	9.	10.	11.
127 + 309	245 + 89	$5.45 .43 + .39	443 282 + 538	349 471 + 86

12. $2.99 + $3.00 + $1.93 = ■   13. 871 + 67 + 5 = ■

14. At the pet store Serge delivers 456 boxes of cat food and 349 boxes of dog food. How many boxes does he deliver?

Level C

Find the sum.

15.	16.	17.	18.	19.
697 816 + 524	788 47 + 289	$4.36 2.97 + 5.09	$5.76 .59 + 9.95	429 817 780 + 79

20. 287 + 421 + 7 + 9 = ■   21. 503 + 636 + 298 + 8 = ■

22. Sue is buying cards. She spends $5.67, $2.38, $1.76, and $.83. How much does she spend?

Chapter Review/Test

LANGUAGE AND MATHEMATICS

Complete the sentences. Use the words in the chart.

1. To show dollars and cents, you use a dollar sign and a ___ .

2. If you have a sum of ten or more in any place, you need to ___ .

CONCEPTS AND SKILLS

Estimate by using the front digits.

3.
$$\begin{array}{r} 26 \\ +15 \\ \hline \end{array}$$

4.
$$\begin{array}{r} 3,260 \\ +\ \ 519 \\ \hline \end{array}$$

5. $329 + 478 = $ ___

6. $4,329 + 3,891 + 555 = $ ___

Estimate by rounding.

7.
$$\begin{array}{r} \$431 \\ +\ \ 165 \\ \hline \end{array}$$

8.
$$\begin{array}{r} 5,129 \\ +\ \ 555 \\ \hline \end{array}$$

9. $\$2.75 + \$1.49 = $ ___

10. $1,727 + 351 + 7,388$ ___

Add.

11.
$$\begin{array}{r} 90 \\ +40 \\ \hline \end{array}$$

12.
$$\begin{array}{r} \$7.36 \\ +\ 3.58 \\ \hline \end{array}$$

13.
$$\begin{array}{r} 215 \\ 488 \\ +\ \ 52 \\ \hline \end{array}$$

14.
$$\begin{array}{r} \$1.28 \\ 9.53 \\ +\ 3.17 \\ \hline \end{array}$$

15.
$$\begin{array}{r} \$1.75 \\ +\ \ .53 \\ \hline \end{array}$$

16.
$$\begin{array}{r} \$2.08 \\ +\ 7.93 \\ \hline \end{array}$$

17. Find the perimeter.

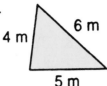

6 m

4 m

5 m

Critical Thinking

18. 408
         259
       + 182

Is the exact sum greater than or less than 700? How do you know?

Mixed Applications

19. In a bicycle race, Erik is 3 km ahead of Steve. Mike is 5 km behind Steve. Joey is 2 km ahead of Mike. How many km is Erik ahead of Joey?

20. There are 423 fish, 166 deer, and 760 birds in the zoo. How many animals are in the zoo?
a. 134   **b.** 349   **c.** 1,349

PERFORMANCE ASSESSMENT

Work with your group to solve the problem.

Suppose you are a rancher who wants to make 2 fenced-in areas in the shape of a rectangle. One area will be 120 feet long and 85 feet wide. The other will be 120 feet long and 65 feet wide. Draw a diagram of the 2 areas.

1. *Think about:*
   - what information to include in the diagram
   - how to draw the diagram

2. At the bottom of the diagram, find how much fencing you need for the 2 areas. Then write a paragraph explaining how you found the answer.

Choose the letter of the correct answer.

1. Estimate: $9.37 + $5.10
   a. $14.00   **c.** $16.00
   b. $15.50   **d.** $20.00

2. 4 + 8 = 8 + ■
   a. 0   **c.** 12
   b. 2   **d.** not given

3. $10.82 + $7.78 = ■
   a. $17.50   **c.** $88.70
   b. $18.60   **d.** not given

4. Round 7,482 to the nearest thousand.
   a. 8,000   **c.** 7,000
   b. 7,500   **d.** not given

5. Al is 8 meters from the line. Sue is 2 meters closer. How far is Sue from the line?
   a. 10 meters   **c.** 6 meters
   b. 8 meters   **d.** not given

6. Find the perimeter.

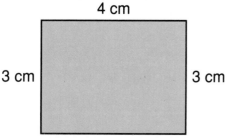

4 cm
3 cm   3 cm
4 cm

   a. 7 meters   **c.** 16 meters
   b. 11 meters   **d.** not given

7. Which number is greatest?
   a. 1,763   **c.** 7,136
   b. 1,736   **d.** 7,613

8. 388 + 67 + 639 = ■
   a. 1,689   **c.** 974
   b. 1,094   **d.** not given

9. Estimate: 4,332 + 198
   a. 3,000   **c.** 5,000
   b. 4,000   **d.** 6,000

10. Which unit is used to measure the length of a roof?
   a. centimeter   **c.** kilometer
   b. meter   **d.** not given

11. Compare: 8,947 ● 9,487
   a. >   **c.** =
   b. <   **d.** not given

12. A tree farm has 720 firs and 690 maples. Estimate how many trees there are in all.
   a. 1,100   **c.** 1,900
   b. 1,400   **d.** 2,000

13. Find the perimeter.

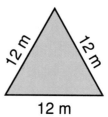

12 m   12 m
12 m

   a. 24 meters   **c.** 48 meters
   b. 36 meters   **d.** not given

14. Round $8.95 to the nearest ten dollars.
   a. $8.00   **c.** $10.00
   b. $9.00   **d.** not given

CLOCK ADDITION

The time shown on the face of the clock is eight o'clock. If you start at 8 and count ahead 6 hours, what time do you reach?

Think: $8 + 6 =$ ▪

The time is now two o'clock.

$8 + 6 = 2$

Use the face of the clock to add.

1. $10 + 3 =$ ▪

2. $11 + 4 =$ ▪

3. $5 + 6 =$ ▪

4. $8 + 7 =$ ▪

5. $4 + 9 =$ ▪

6. $12 + 5 =$ ▪

7. $6 + 7 =$ ▪

8. $8 + 8 =$ ▪

9. $3 + 7 =$ ▪

10. $12 +$ ▪ $= 12$

11. $9 +$ ▪ $= 4$

12. ▪ $+ 8 = 5$

13. $11 + 6 + 9 =$ ▪

14. $10 + 10 + 4 =$ ▪

15. $4 + 6 + 8 =$ ▪

16. $8 + 6 + 7 =$ ▪

17. $2 + 5 +$ ▪ $= 2$

18. $5 +$ ▪ $+ 9 = 5$

19. The time shown on the face of a clock is three o'clock. Count ahead 18 hours. What time is it now?

20. The time shown on the face of a clock is 8:00 A.M. Count ahead 12 hours. What time is it now?

21. The time shown on the face of a clock is seven o'clock. After counting ahead the time is three o'clock. What is the fewest number of hours that were counted ahead?

22. What is the greatest sum you can have adding on a clock face?

算盤

Fingers fly and beads click and clack. What makes these sounds? Someone is using a *suan pan* [swan-PAN], or Chinese abacus. *Suan pan* means counting board. Some people who are good at using the *suan pan* are faster with it than they are with a calculator!

THE CHINESE

Each dowel on the *suan pan* has two beads above the cross bar and five beads below it. An upper bead stands for 5. A lower bead stands for 1. This *suan pan* shows the number 8.

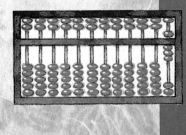

The *suan pan* uses place value. The dowel on the far right can be used as the ones place. The next dowel is the tens place, then hundreds, and so on. This *suan pan* shows the number 964.

1. What number does this *suan pan* show?

2. Draw a picture of a *suan pan* that shows the number 8,031.

3. What would you do to add 25 to the 964 on the *suan pan* above? Explain.

ASIA

China

Abacus

Mental Math and Front-End Estimation

A. There are 60 boys and 50 girls at the Junior Olympic Games. What is the difference between the number of boys and girls at the games?

You can subtract mentally to find the difference.

Subtract: 60   *Think:* 6 tens − 5 tens = 1 ten
          − 50   60 − 50 = 10

There are 10 more boys than girls at the games.

1. How would you subtract 8,000 − 6,000 mentally? What is the difference?

B. You can subtract mentally to estimate a difference. One way is front-end estimation.

Estimate: 843 − 126

Subtract the front digits.   843   *Think:* 8 − 1 = 7
Write zeros for the other digits. − 126   800 − 100 = 700
                                   700

2. Use the front digits to estimate: 7,283 − 460.

TRY **OUT**   Write the letter of the correct answer.

Subtract. Use mental math.

3. 800 − 500   **a.** 3   **b.** 30   **c.** 300   **d.** 1,300

4. 9,000 − 4,000   **a.** 5   **b.** 50   **c.** 500   **d.** 5,000

Estimate by using the front digits.

5. 4,323 − 1,199   **a.** 2,000   **b.** 3,000   **c.** 4,000   **d.** 5,000

6. 8,389 − 5,455   **a.** 3,000   **b.** 5,000   **c.** 8,000   **d.** 13,000

PRACTICE

Subtract. Use mental math.

7.	30 − 10	**8.**	80 − 20	**9.**	300 − 100	**10.**	700 − 400	**11.**	9,000 − 6,000

12.	900 − 600	**13.**	550 − 150	**14.**	8,100 − 4,100	**15.**	7,350 − 6,300	**16.**	1,910 − 1,900

17. 70 − 40 = ▪ **18.** 220 − 120 = ▪ **19.** 160 − 100 = ▪

Estimate by using the front digits.

20.	96 − 33	**21.**	833 − 444	**22.**	656 − 32	**23.**	3,122 − 1,009	**24.**	7,454 − 6,123

25.	222 − 111	**26.**	9,090 − 6,123	**27.**	9,499 − 7,252	**28.**	8,211 − 7,088	**29.**	8,481 − 321

30. 712 − 239 = ▪ **31.** 8,482 − 119 = ▪

Critical Thinking

32. Estimate 695 − 642 using front-end digits. How could you get an estimate that is closer to the exact answer?

Mixed Applications

33. Ira jogs 149 days a year. Sara jogs 238 days a year. About how many more days does Sara jog than Ira?

34. Hal sold about 150 tickets to the Junior Olympics. Meg sold about 200 tickets. About how many tickets did they sell?

35. Gwen does 45 sit-ups on Monday, 55 sit-ups on Tuesday, and 65 sit-ups on Friday. How many sit-ups does she do in one week?

36. *Write a problem* using this information: A ticket to the Junior Olympics costs $2.50. Ask others to solve your problem.

Estimating Differences by Rounding

A group of 429 runners started a long-distance race. There were 76 runners who did not finish the race. About how many runners completed the race?

The word *about* means that an exact answer is not needed. You can round to estimate the difference.

Estimate: 429 − 76

Step 1

Round each number to the greatest place of the greater number.

$$429 \longrightarrow 400$$
$$- 76 \longrightarrow 100$$

Step 2

Subtract the rounded numbers.

$$\begin{array}{r} 400 \\ - 100 \\ \hline 300 \end{array}$$

Think: Round to the nearest hundred.

About 300 runners completed the race.

1. How did you round these numbers?

2. Estimate by rounding: 341 − 224. Tell how you rounded the numbers.

TRY OUT Write the letter of the correct answer. Estimate by rounding.

3. 71 − 34   **a.** 40   **b.** 50   **c.** 60   **d.** 100

4. $.89 − $.29   **a.** $.50   **b.** $.60   **c.** $1.10   **d.** $1.20

5. 756 − 51   **a.** 200   **b.** 300   **c.** 600   **d.** 700

6. 4,889 − 1,111   **a.** 2,000   **b.** 3,000   **c.** 4,000   **d.** 5,000

PRACTICE

Estimate by rounding.

7. $\$.76$
   $- .09$

8. 91
   $- 66$

9. $\$4.56$
   $- 3.33$

10. 689
    $- 98$

11. $2,980$
    $- 1,099$

12. 534
    $- 108$

13. 635
    $- 287$

14. $\$946$
    $- 533$

15. $\$7.50$
    $- 3.09$

16. $5,555$
    $- 3,298$

17. $\$5.85 - \$4.13 = $ ▪

18. $\$8.99 - \$7.99 = $ ▪

Estimate by rounding. Then write > or <.

19. $236 - 23$ ● 200

20. $617 - 321$ ● 300

21. $575 - 187$ ● 500

22. $499 - 129$ ● 300

Critical Thinking

Write the letter of the best estimate.

23. 843
    $- 321$
    a. less than 500
    b. more than 500

24. $6,577$
    $- 4,977$
    a. less than 2,000
    b. more than 2,000

Mixed Applications

25. Otis buys a new hockey stick that costs $12.98. About how many dollars will the clerk give Otis if he pays with a $20.00 bill?

26. The Honkers Bike Club paid $180 for caps, $120 for shirts, and $200 for pants. How much did they spend in all?

MENTAL MATH

Estimate the differences. Then group the numbers with similar estimates.

1. $92 - 43 = $ ▪

2. $69 - 55 = $ ▪

3. $128 - 34 = $ ▪

4. $29 - 17 = $ ▪

5. $493 - 412 = $ ▪

6. $59 - 12 = $ ▪

Subtracting 2-Digit Numbers

A. Amy's class invites 54 parents to the school's track meet. There are 19 parents who cannot come. How many parents can come to the track meet?

Amy estimates $50 - 20 = 30$. She uses place-value models to find the exact answer.

Subtract: $54 - 19$

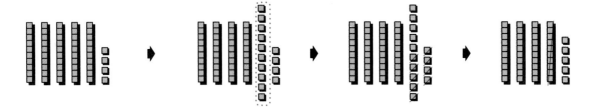

1. Tell how Amy uses the models to find the difference.

2. How many parents plan to come to the track meet?

B. Drew knows a way to subtract without models.

Step 1	Step 2	Step 3	Step 4
Subtract the ones. Not enough ones	Regroup.	Subtract the ones.	Subtract the tens.
$\begin{array}{r} 54 \\ -19 \\ \hline \end{array}$	$\begin{array}{r} {\scriptstyle 4\ 14} \\ \cancel{5}\ \cancel{4} \\ -1\ 9 \\ \hline \end{array}$	$\begin{array}{r} {\scriptstyle 4\ 14} \\ \cancel{5}\ \cancel{4} \\ -1\ 9 \\ \hline 5 \end{array}$	$\begin{array}{r} {\scriptstyle 4\ 14} \\ \cancel{5}\ \cancel{4} \\ -1\ 9 \\ \hline 3\ 5 \end{array}$
	Think: 5 tens 4 ones = 4 tens 14 ones		

You can check by adding: $35 + 19 = 54$.

SHARING IDEAS

3. How does Amy's method compare with Drew's?

4. How does estimating help you tell if an answer is reasonable?

5. How do you know when to regroup?

6. Why can you add to check your answer?

PRACTICE

Subtract. Use place-value models if needed.

7. 47 − 36	**8.** 78 − 24	**9.** 73 − 67	**10.** 95 − 47	**11.** 52 − 46	**12.** 91 − 65
13. 94 − 19	**14.** 46 − 38	**15.** 46 − 15	**16.** 83 − 46	**17.** 36 − 29	**18.** 32 − 17
19. 60 − 55	**20.** 52 − 15	**21.** 82 − 73	**22.** 69 − 18	**23.** 42 − 27	**24.** 85 − 32

25. $73 - 25 =$ ▆

26. $49 - 16 =$ ▆

27. $65 - 56 =$ ▆

28. $69 - 11 =$ ▆

29. $72 - 57 =$ ▆

30. $83 - 75 =$ ▆

Mixed Applications

31. There are 75 students in the track meet. If 36 are boys, how many girls are in the track meet?

32. A long-distance race takes about 3 hours to complete. What is the best metric unit to describe the distance?

33. There are 15 students in the long jump, 20 students in the high jump, and 10 students in the relay race. How many students are there in all?

34. *Write a problem* using the information found in the Databank on page 518. Ask others to solve your problem.

EXTRA **PRACTICE**, page 172

Activity — **M**ore Subtracting 2-Digit Numbers

A. Members of the swim club pay $.68 to rent a locker at the pool. Non-members pay $.75. How much less do members pay than non-members?

Estimate. $.80 − $.70 = $.10
Use models of coins to find the exact answer.
Then compare your method to the one below.

Subtract $.75 − $.68

1. Tell how you used models to find the difference. Did you regroup? Why?

2. How much less do members pay?

B. You can record how the models were used. You can use this method to subtract without using models.

Step 1	Step 2	Step 3	Step 4
Line up the decimal points. Subtract the cents. Not enough cents.	Regroup. Subtract the cents.	Subtract the dimes.	Write the dollar sign and the decimal point in the answer.

<table>
<tr><td>

$.75
− .68

</td><td>

  6 15
$ .7 5
− .6 8
⎯⎯⎯⎯
     7

</td><td>

  6 15
$ .7 5
− .6 8
⎯⎯⎯⎯
  0 7

</td><td>

  6 15
$ .7 5
− .6 8
⎯⎯⎯⎯
$ .0 7

</td></tr>
<tr><td></td><td>

Think:
7 dimes 5 cents =
6 dimes 15 cents

</td><td>

Think: For amounts less than $.10, a 0 is needed.

</td><td></td></tr>
</table>

3. Use place-value models to subtract 75 − 68.

SHARING IDEAS

4. Compare the two methods for subtracting money. How are they the same? How are they different?

5. Compare how you subtract money amounts to how you subtract whole numbers. What do you notice?

PRACTICE

Subtract. Use money or place-value models if needed.

6. 29	**7.** $.93	**8.** $.61	**9.** $.95	**10.** 70
− 4	− .65	− .02	− .84	− 18

11. $.96 − $.23 = ▪

12. 26 − 9 = ▪

13. 83 − 7 = ▪

14. $.75 − $.57 = ▪

15. 83 − 38 = ▪

16. 36 − 17 = ▪

Critical Thinking

17. How can you check an answer to a subtraction problem by subtracting, not adding?

Mixed Applications

18. There are 30 children at the swimming pool. If 6 of the children leave, how many children remain at the swimming pool?

19. The Sharks scored 14 points at their first water-polo match and 17 points at their second match. How many points did they score in all?

Mixed Review
Complete.

20. 8 + ▪ = 8

21. 5 quarters = $ ▪ . ▪ ▪

22. 348 + 229 = ▪

23. 7 − ▪ = 7

24. 730 = ▪ hundreds ▪ tens ▪ ones

EXTRA PRACTICE, page 173; **PRACTICE PLUS**, page 176

✓ UNDERSTAND
✓ PLAN
✓ TRY
✓ CHECK
✓ EXTEND

PROBLEM SOLVING

Strategy: Solving a Two-Step Problem

Mr. Grant's class is scheduled to play 15 volleyball games this season. They played 4 games in January and 5 games in February. How many more games are there left to play?

1. What information do you know?

2. What do you need to find out?

Sometimes it takes more than one step to solve a problem. When there is more than one step, it helps to make a **plan**.

3. What do you need to find out *before* you can decide how many more games are left to play?

Volleyball Game Schedule

January: 4th, 10th, 18th, 25th
February: 5th, 9th, 15th, 21st, 25th

Try your plan.

4. What do you need to do first?

What do you need to do next?

PLAN			
Step 1	4 + 5 = ■	
Step 2	15 − ■ = ■	

5. How many more games are there left to play?

6. Why is it important to make a plan when solving a two-step problem?

PRACTICE

Make a two-step plan. Then solve the problem.
Use mental math, a calculator, or paper and pencil.

7. On Friday, Saturday, and Sunday 98 people bought tickets for the game. On Saturday 38 people bought tickets. On Sunday 26 people bought tickets. How many people bought tickets on Friday?

8. Lucy bought a baseball bat for $13 and a baseball cap for $4. She gave the cashier a $20 bill. How much change did she receive?

9. Of the 21 students who came to practice, 12 played. The students who did not play joined the 62 students who came to watch. How many students watched?

10. George exercised 27 minutes one day and 18 minutes the next day. Ken exercised a total of 40 minutes in the two days. How much longer than Ken did George exercise?

Strategies and Skills Review

11. In the first 4 games of the season, a basketball player scored 27, 35, 18, and 26 points. He figured out that he had scored a total of 106 points. Is his answer reasonable? Why or why not?

12. There were 864 students at Monday's game and 977 students at Tuesday's game. The 99 senior citizens at the games did not have to pay. What was the total attendance for both games?

13. The Knock-Knock Hockey Team played 29 games this season. It won 14 games and lost 8. The rest of the games ended in a tie. How many games ended in a tie?

14. **_Write a problem_** with two steps. Solve it. Ask others to solve your problem. Compare your plans and answers.

SKIPPY THE CALCULATOR KANGAROO

Investigating Patterns

A. Skippy likes to jump. He jumps on a giant calculator.
Sometimes he jumps from one key to another.
Sometimes he jumps up and down on the same key.

1. Skippy jumps on these keys:

   [1] [+] [1] [=] [=] [=] [=] [=] [=].

   Try this on a calculator.
   What happens when Skippy keeps jumping on the
   [=] key?

2. Next, Skippy jumps on these keys:

   [5] [+] [5] [=] [=] [=] [=] [=] [=].

   Try it on your calculator. What happens?
   Skippy has found a way to skip-count by fives!

3. What do you think will happen when Skippy jumps on these keys?

⌨️ `2` `+` `2` `=` `=` `=` `=` `=` `=`

Try it out. Were you right?
Next, Skippy hits these keys:

⌨️ `1` `0` `0` `−` `1` `=` `=` `=` `=` `=` `=`

What happens when you try it?
How can Skippy count back by fives? by tens?

B. A calculator can help you make lists of numbers. Some lists of numbers have interesting patterns.

4. Look at this list:
2, 4, 6, 8, 10, 12, ▪
What do you know about this list?
What is the next number on this list?
How do you know?
Could 36 be a number on this list? Why or why not?
Could 55 be a number on this list? Why or why not?

5. What is the next number in this list?
How do you know?
1, 3, 6, 10, 15, 21, ▪

6. Some patterns go up and down. Can you find the next three numbers on this list? How do you know?
8, 11, 10, 13, 12, 15, 14, ▪, ▪, ▪

7. Look at the following lists. Try to discover the pattern. Write the missing numbers.
1, 10, 2, 11, 3, 12, ▪, ▪,
2, 2, 3, 3, ▪, 4, 5, 5, ▪, ▪, 7, ▪

8. Make up a pattern of your own. Ask a partner to find the next three numbers.

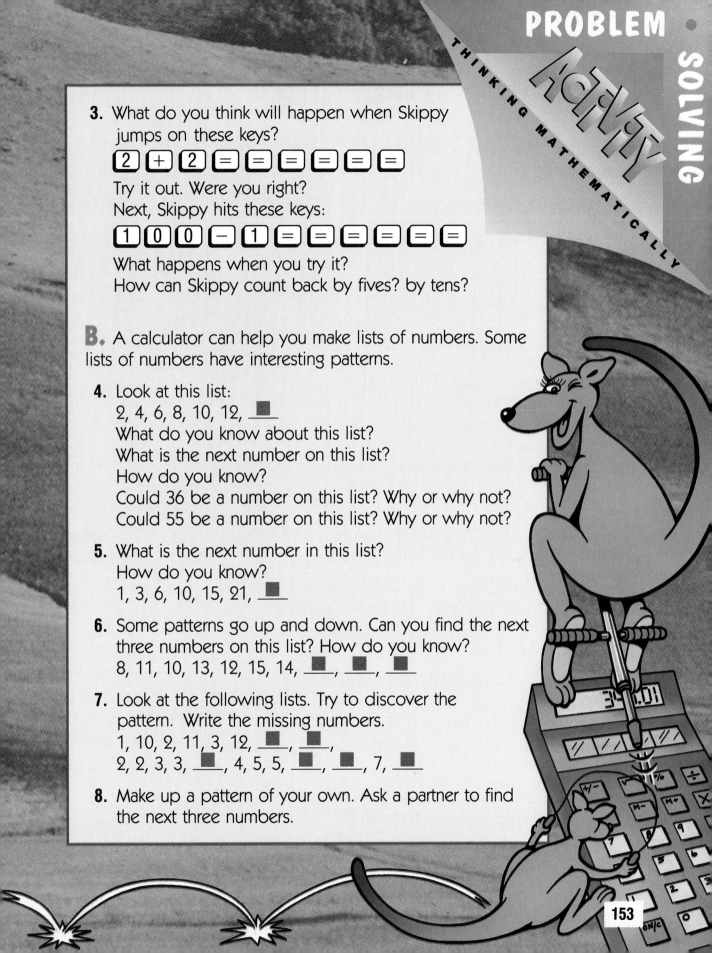

Activity

Subtracting Larger Numbers

This table shows the number of books in two city libraries.

NUMBER OF LIBRARY BOOKS

Library	Number of Books
Main Branch	784
Downtown Branch	295

WORKING TOGETHER

Estimate the difference. Then use your place-value models to find how many more books there are in the Main Branch Library than in the Downtown Branch Library.

1. How did you model 784?

2. In which order did you take away the models to find the difference?

3. What did you have to do before you took the 5 ones away? What did you have to do before you removed the 9 tens? Why?

4. How many more books are there in the Main Branch Library than in the Downtown Branch Library? Record your answer in a table like this.

Exercise	Did you regroup:	
784 − 295	hundreds as tens?	tens as ones?

Use your place-value models to find these differences. Record your results in the table.

5. 947 − 582	**6.** 835 − 829	**7.** 614 − 7	**8.** 490 − 92	**9.** 923 − 840

10. How did you use what you know about subtracting 2-digit numbers to help you subtract larger numbers?

11. How do you know when to regroup?

12. How did you estimate the differences?

13. How many places can there be in a difference when you subtract two 3-digit numbers? a 2-digit from a 3-digit number? a 1-digit from a 3-digit number? Show your work.

ON YOUR OWN

Solve. Use models if needed.

14. Lewis read a book with 355 pages. Photographs appear on 119 of the pages. How many pages do not have photographs?

15. The Main Branch Library loaned 122 books on Monday and 315 books on Friday. How many more books were borrowed on Friday than Monday?

16. **Write a problem** using subtraction. Use two 3-digit or larger numbers. Ask others to solve the problem.

ACTIVITY

Subtracting 3-Digit Numbers: Regrouping Once

A. The Jasper Library has 326 science books. Students borrow 173 of them. How many science books are still in the library?

Estimate. Use place-value models to find the exact answer.

Subtract: 326 − 173

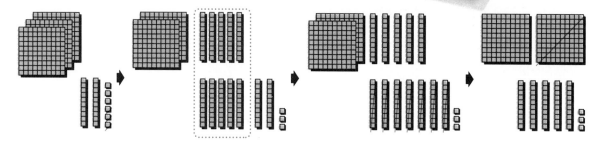

1. How did you use the models to find the difference? Did you regroup?

2. How many science books are still in the library?

B. Here is a way to subtract without models.

Step 1	Step 2	Step 3	Step 4
Subtract the ones. Regroup if necessary.	Subtract the tens. Not enough tens. Regroup.	Subtract the tens.	Subtract the hundreds.
3 2 6 − 1 7 3 ——— 3	2 12 3̶ 2̶ 6 − 1 7 3 ——— 3	2 12 3̶ 2̶ 6 − 1 7 3 ——— 5 3	2 12 3̶ 2̶ 6 − 1 7 3 ——— 1 5 3
	Think: 3 hundreds 2 tens = 2 hundreds 12 tens		

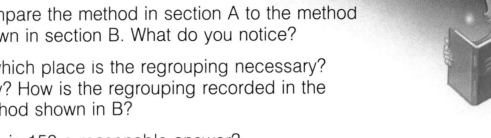

SHARING IDEAS

3. Compare the method in section A to the method shown in section B. What do you notice?

4. In which place is the regrouping necessary? Why? How is the regrouping recorded in the method shown in B?

5. Why is 153 a reasonable answer?

PRACTICE

Find the difference. Check by adding.

6. 958
− 522

7. 537
− 9

8. 986
− 107

9. 488
− 243

10. $4.81
− 2.43

11. 888
− 98

12. 847
− 792

13. 654
− 429

14. $9.67
− 1.38

15. $1.78
− .48

16. 349 − 261 = ■

17. $9.29 − $5.66 = ■

18. $8.47 − $.76 = ■

19. 834 − 29 = ■

Mixed Applications

20. Jasper School has 119 desks and 93 tables. How many more desks are there than tables?

21. Mr. Tee picks 27 boys and 27 girls to sing in the school choir. How many students will be in the choir?

Mixed Review
Find the answer. Which method did you use?

22. $7.50 + $7.50 = ■

23. 942 + 489 = ■

24. $30.00 − $9.00 = ■

25. 855 + 246 = ■

**MENTAL MATH
CALCULATOR
PAPER/PENCIL**

EXTRA PRACTICE, page 173

Subtracting 3-Digit Numbers: Regrouping Twice

The library shows a movie each week. There are enough seats for 320 people. At one show 189 seats are filled. How many seats are empty?

Subtract: 320 − 189

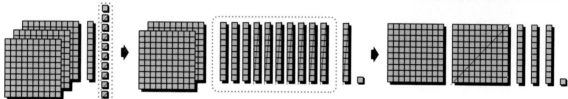

Step 1	Step 2	Step 3
Subtract the ones. Regroup if necessary.	Subtract the tens. Regroup if necessary.	Subtract the hundreds.

Step 1:
```
      1  10
   3  2  0
 - 1  8  9
 ─────────
         1
```

Think:
2 tens 0 ones = 1 ten 10 ones

Step 2:
```
         11
   2   1  10
   3   2   0
 - 1   8   9
 ──────────
       3   1
```

Think:
3 hundreds 1 ten = 2 hundreds 11 tens

Step 3:
```
         11
   2   1  10
   3   2   0
 - 1   8   9
 ──────────
   1   3   1
```

So 131 seats are empty.

1. How can you check the difference?

TRY OUT Write the letter of the correct answer.

2. 532 − 464   **a.** 68   **b.** 78   **c.** 168   **d.** 178

3. 313 − 76   **a.** 233   **b.** 237   **c.** 245   **d.** 263

4. 822 − 44   **a.** 768   **b.** 777   **c.** 778   **d.** 788

5. $4.65 − $2.98   **a.** $1.57   **b.** $1.67   **c.** $2.67   **d.** $2.77

PRACTICE

Subtract. Solve only for differences that are less than 500 or $5.00.

6. 941 − 144

7. 843 − 658

8. 932 − 894

9. 714 − 479

10. $7.65 − 3.76

11. 540 − 347

12. $3.48 − .69

13. 236 − 58

14. 313 − 238

15. $7.44 − 5.66

16. $6.47 − 2.59

17. 863 − 274

18. 656 − 150

19. 440 − 384

20. $3.56 − 1.97

21. 608 − 146 = ■____

22. $747 − $679 = ■____

23. 756 − 189 = ■____

24. $9.45 − $2.97 = ■____

25. 733 − 466 = ■____

26. 978 − 689 = ■____

Mixed Applications

Solve. Which method did you use?

> **ESTIMATION**
> **MENTAL MATH**
> **CALCULATOR**
> **PAPER/PENCIL**

27. The library rents sports movies from Movie Mania for $5.97 and from Video Vault for $7.50. How much does the library save when it rents from Movie Mania?

28. Best Plays Video has about 178 great plays in hockey, about 223 great plays in football, and about 194 great plays in basketball. About how many plays are on the video?

29. There were 353 people at the library movie the first week, 297 people the second week, 402 the third week, and 395 people the fourth week. How many people attended the movie in four weeks?

30. On his summer vacation Van read 8 books about the Olympic Games and 19 books about computer games. How many books about games did Van read over his summer vacation?

EXTRA PRACTICE, page 174

Subtracting Whole Numbers **159**

Subtracting Across Zeros

There are 403 tickets on sale for the Scooter School basketball game. The first day 247 tickets are sold. How many tickets are left?

Subtract: 403 − 247

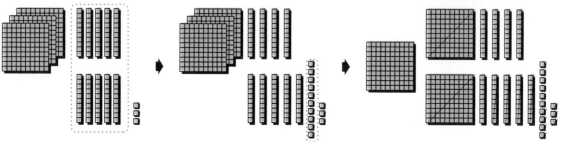

Step 1	Step 2	Step 3

Subtract the ones.
No tens.
Regroup the hundreds.

$$\begin{array}{cc} {\scriptstyle 3} & {\scriptstyle 10} \\ \cancel{4} & 0\ 3 \\ -2 & 4\ 7 \\ \hline \end{array}$$

Regroup the tens.

$$\begin{array}{ccc} & {\scriptstyle 9} & \\ {\scriptstyle 3} & {\scriptstyle \cancel{10}} & {\scriptstyle 13} \\ 4 & \cancel{0} & 3 \\ -2 & 4 & 7 \\ \hline \end{array}$$

Subtract the ones, tens, and hundreds.

$$\begin{array}{ccc} & {\scriptstyle 9} & \\ {\scriptstyle 3} & {\scriptstyle \cancel{10}} & {\scriptstyle 13} \\ 4 & \cancel{0} & 3 \\ -2 & 4 & 7 \\ \hline 1 & 5 & 6 \end{array}$$

Think:
4 hundreds 0 tens = 3 hundreds 10 tens

Think:
10 tens 3 ones = 9 tens 13 ones

So there are 156 tickets left.

TRY OUT   Write the letter of the correct answer.

1. 405 − 128 = ▪   **a.** 187   **b.** 323   **c.** 287   **d.** 277

2. 300 − 135 = ▪   **a.** 165   **b.** 65   **c.** 235   **d.** 175

3. $8.02 − $4.28 = ▪   **a.** $4.26   **b.** $2.74   **c.** $2.84   **d.** $3.74

4. 307 − 89 = ▪   **a.** 18   **b.** 118   **c.** 218   **d.** 208

PRACTICE

Subtract. Check by adding.

5.	802 − 53	**6.**	301 − 294	**7.**	501 − 9	**8.**	203 − 25	**9.**	$9.00 − 6.31
10.	200 − 5	**11.**	$4.07 − .98	**12.**	803 − 797	**13.**	$6.04 − 5.75	**14.**	300 − 144
15.	907 − 899	**16.**	$5.02 − 4.55	**17.**	600 − 467	**18.**	$7.05 − 6.69	**19.**	908 − 729

20. 906 − 98 = ▉   **21.** 400 − 391 = ▉   **22.** 807 − 9 = ▉

23. $4.00 − $2.17 = ▉   **24.** $7.00 − $.89 = ▉

Mixed Applications

Solve. You will need to use the Databank on page 518 for Problem 28.

25. Cheryl bought a ticket to the game for $3.50. She paid with a $5.00 bill. What was her change?

26. There are 403 box seats and 700 bleacher seats at the ballpark. How many more bleacher seats are there than box seats?

27. One side of a square fence around a playing field measures 8 meters. What is the perimeter of the fence?

28. Jen bought a cap, banner, and juice at the game. Did she spend more or less than $10.00?

Mixed Review

Find the answer. Which method did you use?

29. $4.50 + $5.50 = ▉   **30.** 165 + 86 = ▉

31. 903 − 603 = ▉   **32.** 853 − 317 = ▉

MENTAL MATH
CALCULATOR
PAPER/PENCIL

Choosing a Computation Method

The Milton School baseball team played 76 home games and 49 games in other towns. How many more games did they play at home than away?

Subtract: 76 − 49

Amy uses a calculator to find the difference.

 7 6 − 4 9 = ☐ 2 7

Glenn finds the difference mentally.

He adds 1 to both numbers.
76 + 1 = 77
49 + 1 = 50
77 − 50 = 27

1. Talk about how Glenn subtracted mentally

2. How can you use this method to subtract 68 from 173 mentally? What is the answer?

Subtract. Use mental math, a calculator, or paper and pencil.

3.
```
   461
 −  83
```

4.
```
  6,500
 − 3,200
```

5.
```
   394
 − 298
```

6. 864 − 278 = ■   7. 4,000 − 1,000 = ■   8. 84 − 29 = ■

SHARING IDEAS

9. Which computation methods did you use to find the answers for exercises 3 to 8? How did you decide?

10. When do you think it is easier to use mental math? a calculator? paper and pencil? Why?

PRACTICE

Subtract. Use mental math, calculator, or paper and pencil.

11. $.37
    − .19

12. 91
    − 36

13. 455
    − 26

14. 174
    − 57

15. 857
    −838

16. 994
    −416

17. $6.36
    − 4.37

18. $9.64
    − .39

19. 724
    −519

20. 952
    −464

21. 300
    −199

22. 736
    − 28

23. $2.72
    − 1.59

24. $9.62
    − 5.75

25. 914
    −699

26. 24 − 19 = ___■___

27. 273 − 39 = ___■___

28. 188 − 159 = ___■___

29. 40 − 28 = ___■___

30. 176 − 88 = ___■___

31. 993 − 894 = ___■___

32. 75 − 47 = ___■___

33. 487 − 38 = ___■___

34. 596 − 298 = ___■___

CRITICAL THINKING

35. Amy wants to subtract 43 − 29 mentally.

    Subtract the tens   Subtract the ones
    43 − 20 = 23   23 − 9 = 14

    Use this method to subtract 35 from 142.

Mixed Applications

Solve. Which method did you use?

MENTAL MATH
CALCULATOR
PAPER/PENCIL

36. The coach orders 118 baseballs and 89 bats. How many more baseballs than bats does the coach order?

37. The baseball team plays 172 games during the year. If it loses 106 games, how many games does it win?

38. Sal faced 30 batters in the first game he pitched, 40 batters in the second game, and 50 batters in the third game. How many batters did he face in the three games?

39. Tickets to the ball game cost $1.25. Dee also spends $2.89 for a cap and $1.29 for a cold drink. How much does Dee spend at the ball game?

PROBLEM SOLVING

Strategy: Using Estimation

A. The gymnastics coach wants everyone on the team to do at least 90 push-ups every three days. Jerry does 42 push-ups on Monday, 35 push-ups on Tuesday, and 31 push-ups on Wednesday. Does he need to do any more push-ups on Wednesday?

Jerry plans to use estimation to help him solve the problem. To make sure he has done enough push-ups, he decides to *underestimate*.

Jerry tries his plan. He rounds down the number of push-ups he has done each day and adds to find the total.

$42 \rightarrow 40$	40
$35 \rightarrow 30$	30
$31 \rightarrow 30$	+ 30
	100

1. Has Jerry done at least 90 push-ups? How can you tell?

2. *What if* the estimate is less than 90? Does this mean he must do more push-ups? Why or why not?

B. Jerry has saved $45 to spend on equipment. He wants to buy an exercise mat for $13.75 and a gym bag for $19.98.

Does he have enough money to buy these items? To make sure he has enough money, Jerry plans to *overestimate*

$\$13.75 \rightarrow \$20$	$20
$\$19.98 \rightarrow \$20$	+ 20
	$40

the cost of the items. So he rounds up each price.

3. Does he have enough money to buy the items? How can you tell?

4. *What if* the estimate is greater than $45? Does this mean he does not have enough money?

PRACTICE

Use estimation to solve. Did you overestimate or underestimate? Why?

5. The school record for the most points scored in a basketball season is 149 points. So far this season Rick has scored 89 points. Will he break the school record if he scores 73 more points?

6. If Jill's class collects 500 cans for recycling, they get to have a special party. The class collected 223 cans in March, 134 cans in April, and 241 cans in May. Have they collected enough cans to have their party?

7. The Funnybook Club wants to buy 2 new books for its library. One book costs $5.85 and the other book costs $5.95. Will $10 be enough money to buy the 2 books?

8. Jim's school hopes to sell 700 baseball programs this season. They have sold 321 programs so far. If they sell 433 more, will they meet their goal of selling 700 programs?

Strategies and Skills Review

9. Karen wants to buy a bag of peanuts and a can of juice. She has only $2 to spend. Peanuts cost $.95. A regular can of juice costs $.85. A large can costs $1.25. Which size can of juice can she buy?

10. Mel bought a baseball bat for $8.50. He paid for it with a $20 bill. What is the greatest number of dollar bills he could get in change?

11. *Write a problem* that can be solved by overestimating or underestimating. Solve your problem. Then ask others to solve it.

Subtracting Whole Numbers **165**

ACTIVITY

Median and Range

You can describe a group of numbers by finding their median and range.

WORKING TOGETHER

This table shows the number of books five students read over the last two months.

Step 1 Use cubes to build a tower for the number of books read by each student in the first month.

Step 2 Arrange the towers from least to greatest.

BOOKS READ

Student	Number of Books	
	1st Month	2nd Month
Joe	3	5
Jody	8	6
Gus	9	5
Sal	4	4
Meg	5	5

1. How many cubes are in the middle tower?

The number in the middle is the **median**.

2. How many more cubes are there in the tallest tower than in the shortest tower?

The difference between the greatest number and the least number is the **range**.

3. What number sentence can you write to show how you find the range?

4. Find the median and range for the number of books read in the second month.

5. Compare the medians and ranges of the two groups. What do you notice?

6. Pick five numbers from 1 to 9. Find the median and range of the five numbers. Do this several times. Then find the median and range for groups of seven numbers or nine numbers.

SHARING IDEAS

Compare your results with those of others.

7. Tell how you find the median and range of a group of numbers.

8. How does the median compare to the other numbers in a group if the range is small? if the range is large?

9. When is the median a good example of the numbers in a group?

ON YOUR OWN

10. Ask the age of five people in your class. Find the median and range of these ages. Compare your results with those of others.

11. Look in the sports section of a newspaper. Find your favorite team's scores for the last five games. Find the median and range of these scores. Is the median a good example of how much the team usually scores?

12. Look in newspapers and magazines for examples of when median and range are used. Talk about what they tell you about the information they describe.

DECISION MAKING

Problem Solving: Buying Sports Equipment

SITUATION

The members of the Lions School softball team need some new equipment. The team has $200 to spend on equipment.

PROBLEM

What equipment should the team buy?

DATA

EQUIPMENT NEEDED	NUMBER NEEDED	COST PER ITEM
Softball	10	$ 3
Bat	4	$ 6
Batter's helmet	3	$ 7
Team caps	10	$ 8
Team shirt	10	$ 10
Baseball mitt	5	$ 10
Equipment bag	3	$ 20
Catcher's mask	2	$ 25
Set of bases	1	$ 40

USING THE DATA

What is the total cost of the equipment?

1. 3 batter's helmets

2. 2 catcher's masks

3. 10 softballs

4. 3 team caps

5. 1 set of bases, 1 equipment bag

6. 1 softball, 1 baseball mitt, 1 batter's helmet

7. What equipment is the most expensive? the least expensive?

8. Does the team have enough money to buy all the equipment they need? How do you know?

MAKING DECISIONS

9. What equipment does the team need in order to play? Does the Lions School team have enough money?

10. **What if** the team must spend a total of $72 on a catcher's mask, a batter's helmet, and the set of bases? How much money will they have left? What other equipment can they buy?

11. What new equipment would you buy? Why?

12. **Write a list** of other methods of raising money to buy team equipment.

Math and Science

All animals do not move at the same speed. Animals that fly are the fastest animals. The fastest land animals move faster than the fastest water animals. The chart below shows the top speeds of six land animals in miles per hour. Notice that the animals are listed in order from the slowest to the fastest.

TOP SPEEDS OF SOME LAND ANIMALS

Animals	Speed (in miles per hour)	Animals	Speed (in miles per hour)
Snake	2	Giraffe	35
Chipmunk	10	Kangaroo	45
African Elephant	25	Cheetah	70

How much faster is a giraffe than a snake?

Think: Subtract. 35 − 2 = 33

A giraffe is 33 miles per hour faster than a snake.

ACTIVITIES

1. Here are the speeds of four more land animals: human being—20 miles per hour; greyhound—40 miles per hour; house cat—30 miles per hour; jackrabbit—45 miles per hour. Make a bar graph to compare the speeds of these animals with those in the chart.

2. Do you think a human being can run at top speed for a full hour? Why or why not? Talk about your answer with your class.

Computer Spreadsheet: Raffle Sales

Barton School students are selling raffle tickets. They want to raise money for the new hospital. The person with the winning ticket will get a new VCR. The students have set a goal. They are trying to sell 900 tickets.

The students use a **computer spreadsheet.** The spreadsheet keeps track of how many tickets they sell. The computer can calculate numbers in a spreadsheet quickly.

AT THE COMPUTER

Run the computer spreadsheet program called RAFFLE. Look at the data shown on the screen.

1. Describe how information is arranged in the spreadsheet.

2. The students in Mr. Diaz's class sold 127 tickets. Ms. Ellin's class sold 138 tickets, and Mr. Ford's class sold 145 tickets. Enter these numbers in the spreadsheet. Has the school reached its goal yet? If not, how many more tickets must be sold?

3. Choose the number of tickets sold by Ms. Gallo's and Ms. Hong's class. Use numbers between 75 and 125. Then check to see that 900 tickets have been sold? If not, enter different numbers until the goal is reached.

4. **What if** the students change the goal to 950 tickets? Change ticket sales for any three classes. Try to use numbers to make the total match the new goal exactly.

5. Describe how a spreadsheet can be helpful. What kinds of people might use spreadsheets in their jobs? Explain.

EXTRA PRACTICE

Mental Math and Front-End Estimation, page 143..........................

Subtract. Use mental math.

1.	**2.**	**3.**	**4.**	**5.**	**6.**
20 − 10	50 − 30	80 − 60	400 − 200	600 − 300	7,000 − 4,000

7. 90 − 40 = ■   **8.** 240 − 120 = ■   **9.** 1,400 − 600 = ■

Estimate by using the front digits.

10.	**11.**	**12.**	**13.**	**14.**
87 − 23	655 − 345	816 − 404	545 − 211	4,321 − 1,908

15. 817 − 324 = ■   **16.** 784 − 110 = ■   **17.** 5,003 − 2,981 = ■

Estimating Differences by Rounding, page 145.............................

Estimate by rounding.

1.	**2.**	**3.**	**4.**	**5.**
$.76 − .34	81 − 48	$3.89 − 1.23	532 − 107	7,007 − 3,009

6. $.65 − $.19 = ■ **7.** 467 − 187 = ■   **8.** 601 − 299 = ■

Estimate by rounding. Then write > or <.

9. 512 − 212 ● 200   **10.** 876 − 296 ● 700   **11.** 588 − 109 ● 600

Subtracting 2-Digit Numbers, page 147......................................

Subtract.

1.	**2.**	**3.**	**4.**	**5.**	**6.**
98 − 34	77 − 39	56 − 12	81 − 45	85 − 39	52 − 24

7. 86 − 34 = ■   **8.** 43 − 27 = ■   **9.** 76 − 58 = ■

10. 51 − 18 = ■   **11.** 87 − 8 = ■   **12.** 65 − 56 = ■

EXTRA PRACTICE

More Subtracting 2-Digit Numbers, page 149 ....

Subtract. Check by adding.

1. 63 − 26	**2.** 96 − 37	**3.** 72 − 13	**4.** 40 − 28	**5.** $.61 − .24	**6.** 53 − 34

7. $.65 − $.29 = ___   **8.** 25 − 8 = ___   **9.** 43 − 18 = ___

Problem Solving Strategy: Solving a Two-Step Problem, page 151 ......

Use a two-step plan to solve the problem.

1. On Saturday 40 people bought hot dogs. On Sunday 28 hot dogs were sold. If 96 hot dogs were sold on Friday, Saturday, and Sunday, how many were sold on Friday?

2. Mary exercises for 26 minutes one day and 15 minutes the next day. Sue exercises a total of 35 minutes in two days. How much longer does Mary exercise than Sue?

3. Frank and Nancy together sold 55 tennis programs on Saturday. Frank sold 22 of these programs. On Sunday Nancy sold 13 more programs. How many programs did Nancy sell on these two days?

4. Of the 19 members of the tennis team, 10 played in the tournament. The members who did not play joined the 54 students who came to watch. How many students watched the tournament?

Subtracting 3-Digit Numbers: Regrouping Once, page 157 ....

Find the difference. Check by adding.

1. 777 − 238	**2.** $6.72 − 3.25	**3.** 917 − 361	**4.** 586 − 192	**5.** 435 − 217
6. 510 − 8	**7.** $8.73 − 4.04	**8.** 652 − 24	**9.** $3.27 − .62	**10.** 668 − 29

11. 239 − 162 = ___   **12.** $8.16 − $3.08 = ___

Subtracting Whole Numbers **173**

EXTRA PRACTICE

Subtracting 3-Digit Numbers: Regrouping Twice, page 159...............

Subtract. Solve only for differences that are less than 500 or $5.00.

1. 451
− 273

2. 965
− 379

3. $5.25
− 2.78

4. 871
− 383

5. 382
− 194

6. 926
− 547

7. 384
− 195

8. $5.58
− 3.69

9. 654
− 75

10. 481
− 294

11. $7.23
− 2.47

12. 334
− 265

13. $3.17
− 1.28

14. $9.14
− .36

15. $6.52
− 4.76

16. $773 − $384 = ■

17. 658 − 79 = ■

18. $8.76 − $2.87 = ■

19. $5.15 − $.38 = ■

20. $6.12 − $4.23 = ■

21. 981 − 199 = ■

Subtracting Across Zeros, page 161...

Subtract. Check by adding.

1. 403
− 248

2. 800
− 267

3. 307
− 8

4. 501
− 75

5. $7.00
− 4.31

6. 501
− 319

7. 303
− 217

8. 700
− 203

9. 901
− 214

10. $8.07
− 5.48

11. 400
− 102

12. 608
− 19

13. $3.00
− 1.24

14. 804
− 458

15. $6.02
− 2.97

16. 805 − 78 = ■

17. 300 − 241 = ■

18. $5.00 − $3.25 = ■

19. $6.00 − $.78 = ■

Mental Math: Subtracting Whole Numbers, page 163.....................

Find the difference. Use mental math.

| 1. | 14
− 9 | 2. | 26
−17 | 3. | 44
− 23 | 4. | 445
− 36 | 5. | 232
− 30 |

| 6. | 326
− 127 | 7. | 973
− 50 | 8. | 612
−513 | 9. | 400
− 199 | 10. | 586
− 200 |

| 11. | 437
− 138 | 12. | 875
− 50 | 13. | 775
− 600 | 14. | 901
− 501 | 15. | 399
− 99 |

16. $36 - 18 = $ ■   **17.** $343 - 39 = $ ■   **18.** $954 - 845 = $ ■

19. $65 - 38 = $ ■   **20.** $147 - 29 = $ ■   **21.** $794 - 496 = $ ■

22. $75 - 50 = $ ■   **23.** $199 - 98 = $ ■   **24.** $900 - 499 = $ ■

Problem Solving Strategy: Using Estimation, page 165.....................

Use estimation to solve. Did you overestimate or underestimate? Why?

1. Jo wants to buy two gifts. If one gift costs $3.75 and the other gift costs $4.75, will $10 be enough to buy both gifts?

2. Jean hopes to sell 200 nut bars for her school. She has sold 91 nut bars so far. If she sells 72 more, will she reach her goal of selling 200 nut bars?

3. Bill and Liz need to collect 1,000 pounds of newspapers to earn $5.00. They collect 510 pounds on Saturday and 620 pounds on Sunday. Did they collect enough newspapers to earn $5.00?

4. The library wants to buy 3 new records. Each record costs $6.95. Will $20 be enough to buy the 3 records?

Practice *PLUS*

KEY SKILL: Subtracting 2-Digit Numbers (Use after page 149.)

Level A

Find the difference. Check by adding.

1. 49
    − 2

2. 66
    − 6

3. 54
    − 3

4. 69
    − 5

5. 48
    − 23

6. 41 − 20 = ■

7. 88 − 41 = ■

8. $.83 − $.62 = ■

9. The Tigers had 47 fans at the game. The Bulls had 33 fans. How many more fans did the Tigers have?

Level B

Find the difference. Check by adding.

10. 77
    − 8

11. 90
    − 4

12. $.81
    − .42

13. 56
    − 17

14. 97
    − 29

15. 51 − 5 = ■

16. $.75 − $.07 = ■

17. 60 − 7 = ■

18. Kristin had $.90. She spent $.78. How much money does she have left?

Level C

Find the difference. Check by adding.

19. 75
    − 8

20. 50
    − 9

21. $.32
    − .08

22. 35
    − 26

23. $.89
    − .59

24. 80 − 27 = ■

25. $.46 − $.27 = ■

26. 66 − 39 = ■

27. The Tigers played 58 games in April and 76 games in May. How many more games did they play in May?

KEY SKILL: Subtracting Across Zeros (Use after page 161.)

Level A

Find the difference. Check by adding.

1. 603 $- 6$	**2.** 803 $- 4$	**3.** 402 $- 7$	**4.** 302 $- 35$	**5.** 301 $- 82$

6. 406 $- 17$	**7.** 502 $- 276$	**8.** 603 $- 278$	**9.** 101 $- 34$	**10.** 304 $- 197$

11. There are 106 people on the field and 87 in the stands. How many more people are on the field?

Level B

Find the difference. Check by adding.

12. 700 $- 78$	**13.** 602 $- 207$	**14.** $8.00 $- .65$	**15.** 300 $- 129$	**16.** 607 $- 398$

17. 805 − 68 = ▪   **18.** 601 − 4 = ▪   **19.** $6.07 − $.89 = ▪

20. Emily buys nachos at the concert for $2.64. She pays with a $5.00 bill. What is her change?

Level C

Find the difference. Check by adding.

21. 607 − 98 = ▪   **22.** 502 − 3 = ▪   **23.** $9.04 − $3.69 = ▪

24. 108 $- 79$	**25.** 405 $- 87$	**26.** $5.07 $- 3.98$	**27.** $7.01 $- 4.55$	**28.** 803 $- 669$

29. Last year 758 people attended the State Fair. This year 906 people attended. How many more people attended this year than last year?

CHAPTER REVIEW/TEST

LANGUAGE AND MATHEMATICS

Complete the sentences. Use the words in the chart.

1. To subtract from a 2-digit number when there are not enough ones, you need to ▮.

2. The difference between the greatest number and the least number of a set of data is called the ▮.

3. You can ▮ to check a subtraction problem.

VOCABULARY

range
add
median
regroup

CONCEPTS AND SKILLS

Estimate by using the front digits.

4.	64 −35	5.	515 −329	6.	$6.75 − 3.46

Estimate by rounding.

7.	74 −48	8.	$.57 − .24	9.	6,459 −2,159

Subtract.

10.	50 −30	11.	61 − 9	12.	$.80 − .60	13.	765 −356

14.	674 − 88	15.	$7.00 − 5.31	16.	301 −264	17.	$5.06 − .97

Critical Thinking

18. Gene estimated the difference of 479 and 389. He said the estimate was less than 100. How did he know?

Mixed Applications

19. Ed wants to buy a book and a poster at the fair. The book costs $4.95 and the poster costs $5.50. Is $10 enough money to buy the two items?

20. Kathie bought two books. One cost $3.50 and the other cost $4.80. She gave the clerk a $10 bill. How much change did she receive?

PERFORMANCE ASSESSMENT

Work with your group to solve the problem.

Imagine that you are a newspaper reporter. You are given an assignment to write "The Story of 475 − 213." Write your first draft using rounded numbers and an estimated difference. Write your second draft using the actual numbers and the actual difference.

1. *Think about:*
   - how to round numbers
   - how to estimate in subtraction
   - how to subtract numbers

2. Explain how your story changed. Which numbers were more appropriate to use? Why?

CUMULATIVE REVIEW

Choose the letter of the correct answer.

1. $532 - 174 = $ ▪
   a. 468   **c.** 358
   b. 442   **d.** not given

2. $12 - 5 = $ ▪
   a. 7   **c.** 17
   b. 12   **d.** not given

3. Estimate: $6,209 - 2,093$
   a. 3,000   **c.** 4,500
   b. 4,000   **d.** 5,000

4. Al read 27 books this year and Dan read 19. If Cindi read 53, how many more did she read than Dan and Al?
   a. 7   **c.** 99
   b. 26   **d.** not given

5. Compare: 395 ● 539
   a. >   **c.** =
   b. <   **d.** not given

6. Choose the number for $40,000 + 300 + 70 + 6$.
   a. 43,760   **c.** 40,376
   b. 43,076   **d.** not given

7. Complete the pattern:
   12, ▪, 18, 21, 24
   a. 15   **c.** 13
   b. 14   **d.** not given

8. Estimate: $37.42 + $1.84
   a. $40.00   **c.** $36.00
   b. $39.00   **d.** $27.00

9. Estimate: $832 + 444$
   a. 1,000   **c.** 1,200
   b. 1,100   **d.** 1,400

10. $597 + 327 = $ ▪
   a. 814   **c.** 914
   b. 824   **d.** not given

11. $8 + 7 + 9 + 4 = $ ▪
   a. 31   **c.** 27
   b. 28   **d.** not given

12. $7.02 - $6.54 = $ ▪
   a. $.48   **c.** $1.58
   b. $1.52   **d.** not given

13. $742 + 952 + 31 = $ ▪
   a. 2,005   **c.** 1,625
   b. 1,725   **d.** not given

14. Which unit would you use to measure the distance from California to Florida?
   a. centimeter   **c.** kilometer
   b. meter   **d.** not given

MAGIC SQUARES

In a magic square, the sum of the numbers in each row, column, and diagonal is the same.

Add down.

1	8	3
6	4	2
5	0	7

■ ■ ■

Add across.

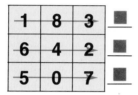

Add along the diagonals.

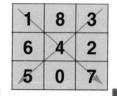

Complete.

The magic sum is ■.

Which of these is a magic square?
Find the magic sum.

1.

3	5	7
6	0	2
4	8	9

2.

8	4	3
0	5	10
7	6	2

3.

2	6	1
5	4	8
3	0	7

Copy and complete to make magic squares.

4.

6	7	2
1		9

5.

1		5
	4	0
3	2	

6.

6	7	
1		9
	3	4

IROQUOIS TURTLE CALENDAR

NEW YORK

In the Iroquois tradition, every living thing has a job. The job of the turtle is to mark the time. Its shell is used like a calendar.

The design on the turtle's shell has 13 parts, one for each moon, or month, in the Iroquois year. The 28 smaller parts around the outside of the shell mark each day in a moon cycle. The moon cycle is 28 days long. That's the time it takes for the moon to go from new moon to full moon and back to new moon again. Each section of the turtle's shell was marked to show the number of moons between important events.

Each Iroquois moon has its own special name:

NEW MOON	NAME	THE MOON OF—
First Moon	Nis-ko-wok-neh	the snow and blizzard
Second Moon	Ni-yo-not-ah	the winds
Third Moon	Oh-not-ah	the forming of the maple sugar
Fourth Moon	Ga-noh-gut	planting time
Fifth Moon	Wen-taa-kwo	the flowers
Sixth Moon	O-yeik-noh	strawberries
Seventh Moon	Ha-nyeah-na-ah	the gentle breeze
Eighth Moon	Stes-kies-neh	the hot weather
Ninth Moon	Ke-to-ok-neh	the harvest
Tenth Moon	Ke-oh-neh	the leaves
Eleventh Moon	Ka-suk-nyeh	the frost
Twelfth Moon	Jo-toh	the cold weather
Thirteenth Moon	Da-ya-we-goa-da-kwa	the snow shoes

1. How did the Iroquois name each moon?
2. Which Iroquois moon might include today's date?
3. During which Iroquois moon do you think your birthday falls? Explain.

Estimating Time

You can sing the song "Jingle Bells" in about one minute.

Your school lunch period lasts about one hour.

One day passes between lunch on Monday and lunch on Tuesday.

One week passes between this Saturday and next Saturday.

One month passes between January 1st and February 1st.

A year passes between your last birthday and your next birthday.

Units of Time
60 minutes (min) = 1 hour (h)
24 hours = 1 day (d)
7 days = 1 week (wk)
12 months (mo) = 1 year (y)
about 52 weeks = 1 year
365 days = 1 year
366 days = 1 leap year

Estimate the best unit of time for each activity. Choose *minutes, hours, days, weeks, months,* or *years.*

1. complete your homework

2. feed a pet

3. read a thick book

4. grow flowers in a garden

5. grow from a child to an adult

6. ride your bike to school

7. make a model

8. become a professional baseball player

9. learn to speak a foreign language

SHARING IDEAS

10. What are three activities that take about a minute to complete? an hour to complete?

11. What are three activities that take about a day to complete? a month to complete?

PRACTICE

What unit would you use to measure the time each activity takes? Write *minutes, hours, days, weeks, months,* or *years.*

12. run a kilometer

13. attend third grade

14. play a chess game

15. be a rock star

16. sprout a seed

17. watch a movie

Mixed Applications

18. Pablo's family drives 90 kilometers to Zippy's Apple Farm. What is the best unit to measure the time it takes them to reach the farm?

19. Jo buys a watch for $12.50. She gives the clerk a $20.00 bill. How much change will she receive?

CALCULATOR

Hint: Use the ⊟ button for repeating addition.

1. Use your calculator to find how many hours there are in a week.

2. Use the same method to find the number of minutes in a day.

Hour, Half Hour, and Quarter Hour

Ann is teaching her little sister how to tell time. She shows her how the hands of the clock show time passing.

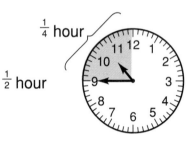

minute hand

hour hand

Ann begins at ten o'clock.

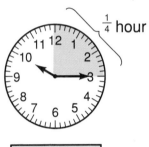

$\frac{1}{4}$ hour

$\frac{1}{4}$ hour

$\frac{1}{2}$ hour

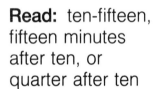

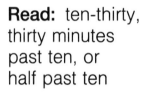

Read: ten-fifteen, fifteen minutes after ten, or quarter after ten

Write: 10:15

Read: ten-thirty, thirty minutes past ten, or half past ten

Write: 10:30

Read: ten forty-five, forty-five minutes past ten, or quarter to eleven

Write: 10:45

1. How far does the hour hand on the clock move in one hour?

2. How far does the minute hand move in one hour?

TRY OUT   Write the letter of the correct answer.

3.

a. 6:00   **c.** 4:30
b. 12:30   **d.** 1:30

4.

a. 12:00   **c.** 11:30
b. 12:30   **d.** 6:45

5.

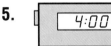

a. four o'clock
b. four forty-five
c. half past four
d. four-fifteen

PRACTICE

Write the time in words.

6. 　**7.** 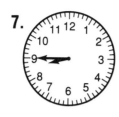　**8.** 4:15　**9.** 11:45

Write the time using numbers.

10. 　**11.** 　**12.** 　**13.**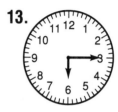

14. fifteen minutes after two

15. forty-five minutes past three

Mixed Applications

16. Rosa's dance class begins at quarter past three. Does her class begin closer to 3:00 or 4:00?

17. Karl gets to school at 7:30. Mary gets to school at 7:45. Which student arrives first?

18. Clara's Clock Shop is 20 meters long and 10 meters wide. What is the perimeter of the shop?

19. *Write a problem* using the information found on page 519 in the Databank. Give it to others to solve.

Mixed Review

Compare. Write >, <, or =.

20. 154 + 689 ● 800　**21.** 1 cm ● 1 dm　**22.** 4 quarters ● $1.00

Minutes

A. Erin entered the store.

Read: four twenty-three or
23 minutes after four

Write: 4:23

Erin left the store.

Read: four fifty-six or
four minutes to five

Write: 4:56

B. You use A.M. to show times
from 12 midnight to 12 noon.

8:30 A.M.

Use P.M. to show times from
12 noon to 12 midnight.

9:01 P.M.

TRY OUT Write the letter of the correct answer. Find the digital
clock with the same time.

1.

a.  `1:00`

b. 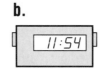 `11:54`

c. `12:05`

d. `11:00`

2.

a.  `5:20`

b.  `6:39`

c. 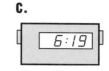 `6:19`

d.  `5:19`

PRACTICE

Write the time using numbers and A.M. or P.M. Then write the time in words.

3.

4.

5.

6.

7.

8.

9. What time will it be in 1 minute?

| 8:59 |

Mixed Applications

10. The Party Hut sells 3,000 hats a month. There are 1,552 hats. The clerk orders 2,000 more. Is this enough?

11. Marta and Sal leave to go to the party at 3 minutes after 12 noon. Write the time using numbers and A.M. or P.M.

LOGICAL REASONING

Happy Birthday

Put the story in order. Write 1, 2, 3, and 4.

Finding Elapsed Time

A. Andy gets on the school bus at 7:15 A.M.
The bus arrives at school at 7:35 A.M.
How much time does Andy's bus ride take?

Count by fives.

Begin at: 7:15

7:20

7:25

7:30

Stop at: 7:35

Think:

5 minutes

10 minutes

15 minutes

20 minutes

Andy's bus ride takes 20 minutes.

1. What are some other ways you could count the minutes?

B. It takes Maria 12 minutes to walk home from school. She leaves school at 2:25 P.M. At what time does Maria arrive home?

Count by fives.
Then count by ones.

Begin at: 2:25

2:30

2:35

2:36

Stop at: 2:37

Think:

5 minutes

10 minutes

11 minutes

12 minutes

Maria arrives home at 2:37 P.M.

2. Can you count the minutes another way? How?

TRY OUT Write the number.

What time will it be in 20 minutes?

3.    **4.** `11:05`   **5.**    **6.** `8:10`   **7.**

PRACTICE

How much time passes between:

8.  `9:10`

9:10 A.M. and
9:45 A.M.?

9. 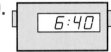 `6:40`

6:40 P.M. and
9:40 P.M.?

10.  `12:00`

12 noon and
9 P.M.?

What time will it be in:

11. `1:20`

15 minutes?

12. 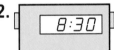 `8:30`

2 hours?

13.  `9:00`

60 minutes?

Critical Thinking

14. Karen's bus ride takes 20 minutes. She arrives at school at 7:50 A.M. At what time does Karen get on the bus? Tell how you solved the problem.

Mixed Applications

15. Sue wants to buy a book for $5.30. She has 5 one-dollar bills, 1 quarter, and 2 pennies. Does Sue have enough money?

16. **Write a problem** about the time you arrive at or leave school. Solve your problem. Then ask others to solve it.

PROBLEM SOLVING

Finding Needed Information

Joe Olmos and his family are having a picnic today, July 4, Independence Day. Joe's grandparents in Mexico want him to visit them for their Independence Day celebration in September. How many days must Joe wait from July 4 until he visits his grandparents?

1. What information does Joe know?

2. What does he need to find out?

Sometimes you do not have enough information to solve a problem.

3. What other information does Joe need before he can find the answer?

4. Can he find this needed information? Where?

Joe learns that Mexicans celebrate their country's independence from Spain on September 16.

Joe uses a calendar to count the number of days from July 4 to September 16.

5. How many days until Joe visits his grandparents?

6. On July 5, Joe's sister Rosa decided that on the next rainy day she will draw a picture of the picnic for her grandparents. How many days must she wait? What other information does she need to solve the problem? Can she find this information now?

7. Why is it important to list all the information needed to solve a problem? Can you always find this information?

PRACTICE

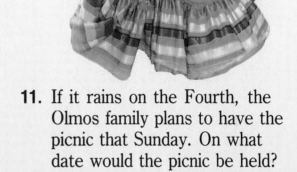

Solve. If there is not enough information,
write what is needed. Use mental math,
a calculator, or paper and pencil.

8. Joe has 2 rolls of film to take
family pictures at the picnic.
How many pictures can he take?

9. Mr. Olmos and Joe decide to
serve hot dogs and burritos at
5 P.M. At what time should
they start to cook them?

10. There are enough chairs to
seat 12 people. There will be 26
people at the picnic. How many
more chairs will be needed?

11. If it rains on the Fourth, the
Olmos family plans to have the
picnic that Sunday. On what
date would the picnic be held?

Strategies and Skills Review

12. There are 203 people in the
Fourth of July parade. Of
these, 86 are Scouts and
49 others play in the band.
The rest are schoolchildren.
How many schoolchildren are
marching in the parade?

13. They sing 3 songs at the
picnic, one right after another.
"De Colores" takes 5 minutes,
"America" takes 4 minutes,
and "Sloop John B" takes 9
minutes. Do the songs take
more than a half-hour?

14. Six girls and five boys are
dancing. Can they form a
circle so that no girl is next to
another girl? Can they make a
straight line so that no two
girls are next to each other?

15. Mrs. Olmos is reading a book
about the Mexican Revolution.
The book has 302 pages. So
far she has read 157 pages.
How many pages does she
have left to read?

16. How is Independence Day
celebrated in other countries?
What information do you need
to find? Where do you think
you can find it?

17. *Write a problem* that does not
have all the information needed
to solve it. Ask a student to
tell what other information is
needed and if it can be found.

Measure **for M**easure

Measurement

Try this experiment.
The results may surprise you.

You need:
- Two 8½ in. × 11 in. sheets of paper
- 2 pieces of cardboard
- Scissors
- Tape
- Macaroni

Make a pair of tubes from two sheets of paper.

Step 1
Roll the long sides of one sheet of paper into a tube. Tape the sides together where they meet.

Step 2
Roll the short sides of the other sheet of paper into a tube. Tape the sides together where they meet.

Step 3
Tape each tube to a piece of cardboard. They should look like this:

1. **What if** you filled the tubes with macaroni? Do you think both tubes hold the same amount? Why or why not? If not, which tube do you think holds more? Why?

2. Now check your guess. First, fill the tall tube with macaroni. Then, carefully empty the tall tube into the short tube. Is the short tube full? What does this mean?

3. Was your guess correct? What have you learned?

4. Make another pair of tubes. Use two sheets of paper that are the same size (but not the same size as the paper you used above). Guess which tube holds more. Did you guess correctly?

5. **What if** you make a pair of tubes and they both hold the same amount? What shape must the sheets of paper be? Check by experimenting.

Temperature

Temperature can be measured using a **Celsius thermometer.**

To read the temperature on a thermometer, look at the mark or number next to the top of the red column.

A bowl of hot soup is about 50°C.

A cold drink is about 5°C.

1. At what temperature does water freeze?

2. At what temperature does water boil?

3. What is room temperature?

4. Which is warmer, ⁻10°C or 10°C? How can you tell?

TRY OUT
Write the letter of the correct answer.
What is a reasonable temperature?

5. summer day   **a.** 5°C   **b.** 10°C   **c.** 26°C   **d.** 100°C

6. winter day   **a.** ⁻10°C   **b.** 25°C   **c.** 75°C   **d.** 100°C

7. spring day   **a.** 5°C   **b.** 17°C   **c.** 75°C   **d.** 100°C

8. normal body temperature   **a.** 0°C   **b.** 5°C   **c.** 10°C   **d.** 37°C

PRACTICE

Choose the most reasonable temperature.

9. hot bath   **a.** ⁻10°C   **b.** 5°C   **c.** 43°C   **d.** 99°C

10. ice cube   **a.** 0°C   **b.** 20°C   **c.** 25°C   **d.** 60°C

11. warm milk   **a.** 4°C   **b.** 38°C   **c.** 90°C   **d.** 110°C

12. tap water   **a.** ⁻7°C   **b.** 0°C   **c.** 20°C   **d.** 100°C

13. boiling an egg   **a.** ⁻2°C   **b.** 25°C   **c.** 50°C   **d.** 100°C

14. cool day   **a.** 10°C   **b.** 25°C   **c.** 75°C   **d.** 100°C

Write the temperature in degrees Celsius.

15. 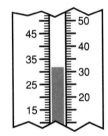   **16.** 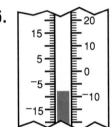   **17.**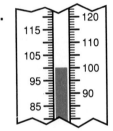

18. 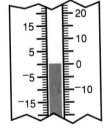   **19.** 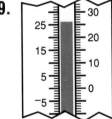   **20.**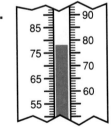

Solve.

21. Use a Celsius thermometer to find the air temperature of a sunny spot and a shady spot. Record your answers in a chart. Compare your findings with other students.

22. The thermometer outside Guy's window says that the air temperature is 23°C. Should he dress for warm weather or cold weather?

Measuring Capacity

The **capacity** of a container is the amount it can hold.

WORKING TOGETHER

Collect four different size cups.

CAPACITY TABLE

Kind of Cup	Number of Cups	
	Estimate	Actual
Teacup	■	■
Small paper cup	■	■
Large paper cup	■	■
Yogurt cup	■	■

1. About how many of each size cup will it take to fill a medium size juice bottle?

2. Compare the sizes and numbers of cups needed to fill the juice bottle. What do you notice?

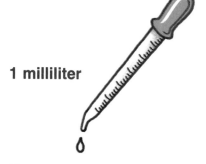

1 liter

The **liter (L)** is a metric unit for measuring large amounts of liquid.

1 milliliter

The **milliliter (mL)** is a metric unit for measuring smaller amounts of liquid.

SHARING IDEAS

3. What other kinds of containers have large capacities? small capacities? Which units would you use to measure their capacities?

4. What would happen if three people used containers of different sizes to measure the same capacity?

5. What would be a better way for three people to measure the same capacity?

PRACTICE

Write the letter of the better estimate.

6.

a. 150 milliliters
b. 150 liters

7.

a. 10 milliliters
b. 10 liters

8.

a. 1 milliliter
b. 1 liter

9.

a. 50 milliliters
b. 50 liters

10.

a. 15 milliliters
b. 15 liters

11.

a. 250 milliliters
b. 250 liters

Critical Thinking

12. Two containers have the same capacity. Must they have the same shape? Why or why not?

Solve.

13. Kay needs to make punch for a large group of people. Does the punch bowl hold about 5 milliliters or about 5 liters?

14. Spike fills his toy bear's toy cup with water. Does it hold about 10 milliliters or about 10 liters?

Mixed Review

Find the answer. Which method did you use?

| MENTAL MATH |
| CALCULATOR |
| PAPER/PENCIL |

15. $37 + 18 + 119 =$ ____

16. $98 - 60 =$ ____

17. $756 + 287 =$ ____

18. $7 + 8 + 2 + 3 =$ ____

19. $625 - 113 =$ ____

20. $880 - 240 =$ ____

ACTIVITY

Measuring Mass

Measuring **mass** is one way to tell how much of something there is. A large cat has more mass than a small cat.

WORKING TOGETHER

You can use **grams (g)** to measure the mass of lighter things.

1 gram

1. Choose several objects in your classroom and estimate the mass of each.

2. Place each object on one pan of a balance. Add grams to the other pan until the two pans are balanced.

3. Record your estimates and measurements in a chart.

Object	Estimate	Actual

The **kilogram (kg)** is a unit of mass used to measure heavier things. This math book has a mass of about 1 kilogram.

4. Estimate. Then use the balance scale to measure the actual mass of several objects in kilograms. Record your estimates and measurements.

1 kilogram

SHARING IDEAS

5. Name other objects that could be measured using grams.

6. Name other objects that could be measured using kilograms.

7. Why is it important that everyone use the same unit when measuring mass?

PRACTICE

Write the letter of the better estimate.

8.
a. 220 grams
b. 220 kilograms

9.
a. 250 grams
b. 250 kilograms

10.
a. 4 grams
b. 4 kilograms

11.
a. 9 grams
b. 9 kilograms

12.
a. 5 grams
b. 5 kilograms

13.
a. 4 grams
b. 4 kilograms

Critical Thinking

14. Does a larger object always have more mass than a smaller object? Give an example to explain your answer.

Mixed Applications

Solve. You may need to use the Databank on page 519.

15. A lion has a mass of about 160 kilograms. After he eats a meal his mass is about 195 kilograms. By how much does the lion's mass increase after he eats?

16. Is the total mass of an otter, a coyote, a seal, and a porcupine greater than or less than 70 kilograms?

17. Which animal has the greater mass, an alligator or a seal? How many kilograms greater is its mass?

18. *Write a problem* about comparing masses. Solve the problem. Then give it to another student to solve.

PROBLEM SOLVING

Strategy: Conducting an Experiment

Jason and Gail are planning a hopping race for their party. Each member of a team will have to hop about 5 times from the starting line to another line, turn around, then hop back. The first team to have all of its members complete the race will win. How far away from the starting line should they put the other line?

Sometimes the best way to solve a problem is to do an experiment.

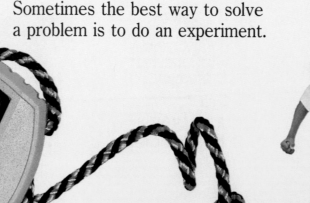

Plan your experiment.

You need to know how far someone goes when they hop 5 times. You can put a piece of tape on the floor to mark the starting line. Then hop 5 times and mark where you stopped. Use a tape measure to find how far you went.

Try your experiment.

Do the experiment. Hop 5 times. Then measure the distance.

1. How far did you hop?

2. Compare your measurement to those of others. Did you all go about the same distance? How might this affect where you put the other line?

3. Why should you do an experiment more than once?

PRACTICE

Do an experiment to solve.

4. You want to hang a banner across the top of the chalkboard for a class party. How long should the banner be?

5. Gail and Jason plan to have the hopping race at their party. How much time should they allow for the race?

6. At Jo's party everyone is going to have the outline of his or her body drawn on big pieces of paper that they can keep. How long should each piece be?

7. Thomas plans to serve juice at his party. How many small paper cups can he fill from a liter bottle?

Strategies and Skills Review

Solve. Use mental math, a calculator, or paper and pencil.

8. The Andersons had 18 people at the dinner party. Michelle helps wash the dishes. She washes 36 plates, 22 glasses, 18 knives and 36 forks. How many things does she wash?

9. Pete is planning a coin-toss game for his party. How far away from the throwing line should he place the cup that will catch coins tossed by guests?

10. Cass is setting up chairs for a game. She places them in a square with 4 chairs on each side. How many chairs does Cass use?

11. *Write a problem* that can be solved by doing an experiment. Solve your problem. Ask others to solve it. Compare your results.

Measuring Time, Capacity, and Mass **203**

DECISION MAKING

Problem Solving: Planning a Birthday Party

SITUATION

Jason and his mother are planning a birthday party for Jason. There will be 14 children at the party, including Jason. The party will last for 2 hours.

PROBLEM

What games and activities will Jason have at his party?

DATA

IDEAS FOR BIRTHDAY PARTY

ACTIVITY	HOW MANY MINUTES
Singing "Happy Birthday" and blowing out candles	5
Eating cake and ice cream	10
Magic Show	30
Opening presents	15
Cookie decorating	15
Giving out prizes and party favors	5
Playing musical chairs	15
Dancing	20
Playing video games	20
Watching cartoons	25
Scavenger hunt	20
Playing hide-and-seek	20
Playing tag	15
Singing Songs	15
Playing guessing games	15
Running relay races	10

USING THE DATA

What is the total time for each group of activities?

1. watching cartoons, magic show, playing video games, singing songs

2. decorating cookies, running relay races, magic show, playing musical chairs, dancing

3. scavenger hunt, playing musical chairs, dancing, playing hide-and-seek

4. opening presents, eating cake and ice cream, giving out prizes and party favors, singing "Happy Birthday" and blowing out candles

MAKING DECISIONS

5. What are some of the things that Jason and his mother should consider while planning a party?

6. Which activities are usually part of any birthday party?

7. Does the party last long enough to include all the activities that Jason and his mother have listed? Why or why not?

8. **What if** it rains the day of the party? Which activities should they not play indoors?

9. Which activities would you choose for Jason's birthday party? Why?

10. **Write a list** of things that you like to do at birthday parties. Then plan a 2-hour party. Talk about how you choose what to do.

Math and Social Studies

Sundials are the oldest known way of telling time. Sundials tell time by the movement of the sun. Every day the sun rises in the east and sets in the west. The shadow on the face of the sundial moves with the sun. As it moves, the shadow points to the hour markings on the sundial's face.

Candle clocks were also used to tell time. A candle was marked with 12 lines. It took one hour to burn from one line to the next.

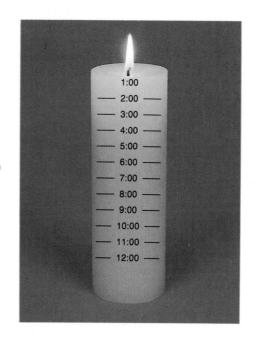

What if you lit a candle clock at 1:00 P.M.? If the candle burned to the third line, what time would it be?

Think: Add. 1 + 3 = 4
The candle burned for 3 hours.

The time would be 4:00 P.M.

ACTIVITIES

1. Use paper and pencil to make a sundial. Mark where the shadow is when school starts. Mark where the shadow is at lunch and at the end of school.

2. Discuss with your class why these old clocks might not have kept time very well.

Computer Graphing: Line Graph

Storm E. Weather gives the weather report on the TV news. Every day he uses a **line graph** to show the high temperatures for the past four days.

A line graph is used to show how data changes over time. A computer makes it easy to draw a line graph.

AT THE COMPUTER

Run the computer program called TEMPERATURE. Look at the data shown in the table on the screen, then draw the graph.

1. What information is given along the bottom of the graph? What information is given along the left of the graph?

2. What do the points along the line show?

3. Which two days had the same high temperature? Which day had the lowest temperature?

4. **What if** Storm predicts that the weather is getting warmer? Change the data to show a warming trend for the remaining three days of the week and draw a new graph.

5. **What if** Storm says temperatures will be dropping? Enter new temperatures for the last three days to show a cooling trend. Draw the new graph.

6. **What if** you heard the following weather forecast for another city? Sunday's high temperature was 20°C. Over the next two days, the temperature will fall sharply. For the rest of the week, it will rise steadily. Enter temperatures that fit the story. Draw a new graph.

EXTRA PRACTICE

Estimating Time, page 185.......................................

What unit would you use to measure the time each
activity takes? Write *minutes, hours, days, weeks,
months,* or *years.*

1. become a doctor

2. play a baseball
game

3. prepare for a play

4. wash your hair

5. winter vacation

6. grow your hair
long

Hour, Half Hour, and Quarter Hour, page 187.......................

Write the time in words.

1.
2.
3.
4.

Write the time using numbers.

5.
6.
7.
8.

9. fifteen minutes after three

10. thirty minutes after eight

Minutes, page 189.......................................

Write the time using numbers. Then write the
time in words.

1.
2.
3.

Finding Elapsed Time, page 191 . . . .

How much time passes between:

1.

8:30 A.M. and
8:55 A.M.?

2.

5:20 P.M. and
9:20 P.M.?

3.

7:00 P.M. and
9:00 P.M.?

4.

11:00 P.M. and
11:59 P.M.?

5.

3:05 P.M. and
4:10 P.M.?

6.

7:45 A.M. and
10:45 A.M.?

What time will it be in:

7.

3 hours?

8.

15 minutes?

9.

24 minutes?

Problem Solving: Finding Needed Information, page 193 . . . .

Tell what information is needed to solve the problem.

1. Mrs. Spencer is baking a pie. She wants to serve it at 6:00 P.M. What time should she put it in the oven?

2. The refreshments cost Sandy $7.85. How much change does Sandy receive?

3. Bonnie has a roll of film that takes 36 pictures. How many pictures are left in the roll?

4. Jim started cooking carrots at 6:15 P.M. When will they be cooked?

EXTRA PRACTICE

Temperature, page 197 ....

Choose the most reasonable temperature.

1. cold drink   **a.** 5°C   **b.** 20°C   **c.** 30°C   **d.** 40°C

2. hot shower   **a.** ⁻5°C   **b.** 10°C   **c.** 44°C   **d.** 100°C

3. boiling water   **a.** 30°C   **b.** 50°C   **c.** 70°C   **d.** 100°C

4. freezing water   **a.** ⁻10°C   **b.** 0°C   **c.** 5°C   **d.** 10°C

Write the temperature in degrees Celsius.

5.
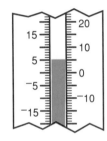

6.
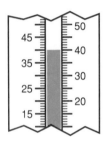

7.

Measuring Capacity, page 199 ....

Write the letter of the better estimate of capacity.

1.

a. 5 milliliters
b. 5 liters

2.
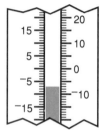
a. 10 milliliters
b. 10 liters

3.

a. 2 milliliters
b. 2 liters

4.

a. 30 milliliters
b. 30 liters

5.

a. 150 milliliters
b. 150 liters

6.

a. 5 milliliters
b. 5 liters

Measuring Mass, page 201

Write the letter of the better estimate of mass.

1.

    a. 14 grams
    b. 14 kilograms

2.

    a. 3 grams
    b. 3 kilograms

3.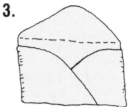

    a. 2 grams
    b. 2 kilograms

4.

    a. 150 grams
    b. 150 kilograms

5.

    a. 4 grams
    b. 4 kilograms

6.

    a. 5 grams
    b. 5 kilograms

Problem Solving Strategy: Conducting an Experiment, page 203

Do an experiment to solve.

1. You want to draw a mural that will cover part of your classroom wall. How long should the mural be?

2. Guy plans to hold a spelling bee. How much time should he allow for the spelling bee?

3. Jeb wants to make each person in his class a ribbon. How much ribbon will he need?

4. Amy is playing records so people can dance at her party. How many records will she need?

5. Jackie wants to wrap 4 small gifts. How many large sheets of wrapping paper will she need?

6. Sam wants to do his homework before dinner. How much time should he allow?

Practice PLUS

Level A

What time will it be in:

1.

30 minutes?

2.

15 minutes?

3. 4:15

10 minutes?

4. 1:05

45 minutes?

5. Wendy gets on the bus at 8:20. She gets to school at 8:40. How long is Wendy's bus ride?

Level B

What time will it be in:

6.

15 minutes?

7.

35 minutes?

8. 7:48

12 minutes?

9. 10:13

23 minutes?

10. Ed starts his breakfast at 7:15 A.M. He finishes it in 23 minutes. At what time does he finish?

Level C

11. How much time passes between 4:10 P.M. and 5:00 P.M.?

12. How much time passes between 9:13 A.M. and 9:36 A.M.?

13. It is 3:49 A.M. What time will it be in 3 hours?

14. It is 1:31 P.M. What time will it be in 60 minutes?

15. Gary finished his homework at 7:55 P.M. It took him 55 minutes. At what time did Gary start?

KEY SKILL: Measuring Mass (Use after page 201.)

Level A ....

Write the letter of the better estimate of mass.

1.
a. 2 grams
b. 2 kilograms

2.
a. 10 grams
b. 10 kilograms

3.
a. 1 gram
b. 1 kilogram

4. Arrange three objects in order of least to greatest mass.

Level B ....

Write the letter of the better estimate of mass.

5.
a. 2 grams
b. 2 kilograms

6.
a. 2 grams
b. 2 kilograms

7.
a. 5 grams
b. 5 kilograms

8. Name three objects that can be measured in grams.

Level C ....

Write the letter of the better estimate of mass.

9.
a. 2 grams
b. 2 kilograms

10.
a. 22 grams
b. 22 kilograms

11.
a. 4 grams
b. 4 kilograms

12. Name three objects that can be measured in kilograms.

CHAPTER REVIEW/TEST

LANGUAGE AND MATHEMATICS

Complete the sentences. Use the words in the chart.

1. The amount of liquid a container can hold is called its ___.

2. To show times from 12 noon to 12 midnight, use ___.

3. 52 weeks is about one ___ .

VOCABULARY

P.M.
capacity
A.M.
mass
year
month

CONCEPTS AND SKILLS

Write the time using numbers.

4.

5.

6.

7. eight minutes after one

8. forty-five minutes past six

What time will it be in:

9.

15 minutes?

10.

3 hours?

11.

25 minutes?

Choose the most reasonable temperature for each activity.

12. swimming **a.** ⁻10°C **b.** 15°C **c.** 30°C **d.** 90°C

13. ice skating **a.** ⁻3°C **b.** 20°C **c.** 50°C **d.** 80°C

Write the letter of the better estimate.

14.

15.

16.

17.

14. **a.** 1 milliliter
    b. 1 liter

15. **a.** 60 milliliters
    b. 60 liters

16. **a.** 5 grams
    b. 5 kilograms

17. **a.** 7 grams
    b. 7 kilograms

Critical Thinking

18. It takes Holly 30 minutes to get to the train station. If she has to catch a 10:00 A.M. train, by what time should she leave?

Mixed Applications

Solve. If there is not enough information, write what is needed.

19. There are 14 rows of seats in the theater. How many people can the theater seat?

Do an experiment to solve.

20. Ross plans to serve juice and pretzels during the intermission. How much time should he allow for the intermission?

PERFORMANCE ASSESSMENT

Work with your group to solve the problem.

Imagine that you are a producer of a television show. It is aired on Saturday from 9:00 to 10:00. You must plan 3 commercial breaks, each 3 minutes, 4 minutes, and 5 minutes long. Make a table of the show time and commercial times.

1. *Think about:*
    - what you must include in the table
    - what time each commercial starts and ends

2. Write a memo to your boss about the table.

CUMULATIVE REVIEW

Choose the letter of the correct answer.

1. Which unit would you use to measure the distance from New York to Texas?
   a. centimeter   c. kilometer
   b. meter   d. not given

2. Estimate: $7.25 + $8.43
   a. $14.00   c. $17.00
   b. $15.00   d. $18.00

3. What time will it be 22 minutes after 3:35?
   a. 4:07   c. 3:15
   b. 3:22   d. not given

4. $47.03 − $4.08 = ■
   a. $42.05   c. $44.05
   b. $43.95   d. not given

5. What time will it be 15 minutes before 7:30?
   a. 7:15   c. 8:20
   b. 7:45   d. not given

6. 8 + 4 = 4 + ■
   a. 7   c. 16
   b. 12   d. not given

7. Find the perimeter.

   6 cm

   4 cm [ ] 4 cm

   6 cm

   a. 10 meters   c. 24 meters
   b. 20 meters   d. not given

8. 429 − 185 = ■
   a. 364   c. 144
   b. 244   d. not given

9. 724 + 58 + 540 = ■
   a. 1,844   c. 1,212
   b. 1,322   d. not given

10. Which unit would you use to measure the mass of a pencil?
    a. gram   c. kilogram
    b. liter   d. not given

11. Estimate: 2,107 − 477
    a. 1,000   c. 2,500
    b. 2,000   d. 3,000

12. Which unit would you use to measure the amount of gas in a tank?
    a. gram   c. milliliter
    b. liter   d. not given

13. Compare: 521 + 776 ● 1,296
    a. >   c. =
    b. <   d. not given

14. What is the smallest 4-digit number using the digits 3, 4, 5, and 6?
    a. 3,564   c. 3,456
    b. 6,345   d. not given

TIME LINES

A time line shows important dates. This time line shows the years when different states joined the United States.

YEAR OF STATEHOOD

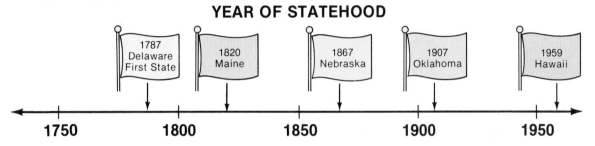

1. How is a time line like a number line?

2. How can you use a time line to help you see the order in which events happen?

3. In the time line above, how many years are between each mark?

4. Which state joined the Union first?

5. Did Nebraska or Oklahoma become a state first?

6. How many years after Nebraska did Hawaii become a state?

7. Wisconsin became a state in 1848. Between which two marks would you place the Wisconsin flag? Which mark would you place it closer to? Why?

Copy the time line on a piece of paper. Place and label a flag to show when the state entered the Union.

8. Ohio—1803   9. Washington—1889   10. Arizona—1912

11. Idaho—1890   12. Virginia—1788   13. West Virginia—1863

14. Make a time line that shows the important events in your own life or in the history of your town.

MASAI NUMBERS
USING HAND SIGNS

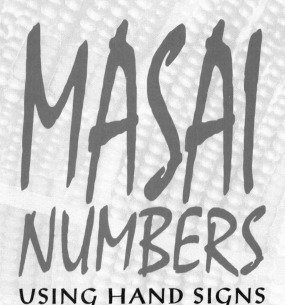

If you visit a market in Tanzania (TAN-zuh-NEE-uh), you might see people using hand signals as they buy and sell things. You might see a buyer and a seller discussing some beaded necklaces made by Masai (muh- SIGH) women who live in the area.

AFRICA

Kenya

Tanzania

The seller holds up four fingers of her right hand and moves them slightly to the right. The buyer says, "isiet." The seller is using her hand to tell the buyer the price, eight shillings. A shilling is a unit of money in Tanzania.

1 How many hands are used for making the Masai hand signals? What other things do you notice about each signal and the number it stands for?

2 What reason can you think of for holding up four fingers and moving them slightly to the right as a sign for "eight?"

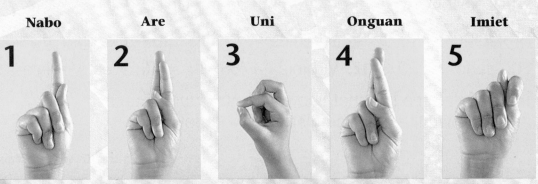

Nabo	Are	Uni	Onguan	Imiet
1	2	3	4	5

3 Why do you think the buyer said, "isiet," the Masai word for "eight" after seeing the seller's hand sign?

4 What are some hand signs you use or know? When are words used with the signs?

Ile
6

Naapishana
7

Isiet
8

Enderuj
9

ACTIVITY
The Meaning of Multiplication

Marta buys 3 packages of oranges. There are 4 oranges in each package. How many oranges does Marta buy?

WORKING TOGETHER

You can solve the problem by making a model.

Step 1 Model a package of oranges.

Think: There are 4 oranges.

Show a train of 4 cubes.

Step 2 Model 3 packages.

Think: Show 3 trains of 4 cubes.

1. Write an addition sentence to show what you have modeled.

2. How many cubes are there in all? How many oranges does Marta buy?

Compare the following **multiplication** sentence with your addition sentence and your model.

$$3 \quad \times \quad 4 \quad = \quad 12$$

| factor | times | factor | equals | product |

3. Which factor tells the number of addends? Which factor tells the number of groups?

4. Which factor names the addend? Which factor tells how many in each group?

5. What does the sum or product tell you?

Use cubes to model and solve these problems.
Then write an addition sentence to show what you
have modeled.

6. $4 \times 2 = $

7. $2 + 3 + 5 = $

8. $1 + 3 + 5 = $

9. $5 \times 3 = $

10. Can you write a multiplication sentence for each problem? Why or why not?

SHARING IDEAS

11. When can an addition sentence be written as a multiplication sentence?

12. When can you multiply to find how many in all?

ON YOUR OWN

13. *Write a problem* in which you can find how many in all by multiplying. Ask others to model the problem and then write the multiplication sentence.

Informal Algebra: Multiplication Properties

James buys 2 bags of apples. Each bag holds 3 apples. Erin buys 3 bags of apples. Each bag holds 2 apples. Did James and Erin buy the same number of apples?

WORKING TOGETHER

1. Place two-color counters on a sheet of paper. Group the counters to show how many apples are in each bag that James buys. Circle each group. Now do the same for the apples Erin buys.

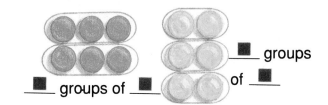

___ groups of ___

___ groups of ___

2. Write a multiplication sentence for each model.

3. What do you notice about the products? Did James and Erin buy the same number of apples?

Number of Groups	×	Number in each Group	=	Product
■	×	■	=	■

4. Use your counters to model the following pairs of multiplication sentences:

   $6 \times 2 =$ ___ and $2 \times 6 =$ ___

   $9 \times 3 =$ ___ and $3 \times 9 =$ ___

   $5 \times 4 =$ ___ and $4 \times 5 =$ ___

5. How do the products compare in each pair of sentences?

6. Use counters to model the following sentences:

   $3 \times 1 =$ ___ $1 \times 9 =$ ___ $1 \times 7 =$ ___ $4 \times 1 =$ ___

7. What factor is common to all these sentences?

8. Compare the product to both factors in each sentence. What pattern do you see?

This picture shows 3 rows with 0 objects in each row.

9. Complete the multiplication sentence: $3 \times 0 =$ ___

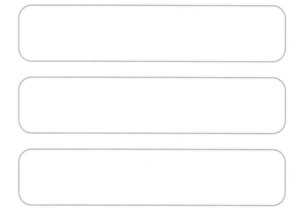

10. Draw pictures for these multiplication sentences.

$7 \times 0 =$ ___ $5 \times 0 =$ ___

$9 \times 0 =$ ___ $4 \times 0 =$ ___

11. What factor is common to all sentences?

12. Compare the product to both factors in each sentence. What pattern do you see?

SHARING IDEAS

13. What happens to the product of two factors if you change the order of the factors?

14. What is the product of two factors if one factor is one?

15. What is the product if one factor is zero?

PRACTICE

Find the product. Use pictures and what you have learned about multiplication properties.

16.	**17.**	**18.**	**19.**	**20.**	**21.**
2	1	3	2	5	0
$\times 1$	$\times 2$	$\times 2$	$\times 3$	$\times 0$	$\times 5$

22. $3 \times 6 =$ ___   **23.** $1 \times 5 =$ ___   **24.** $8 \times 0 =$ ___

Solve.

25. Tex has 3 bags with 4 pears in each bag. Vera has 4 bags with 3 pears in each bag. How many pears does each person have?

26. Rita has 3 bags of flour. Each bag weighs 1 pound. How many pounds of flour does Rita have?

2 and 5 as Factors

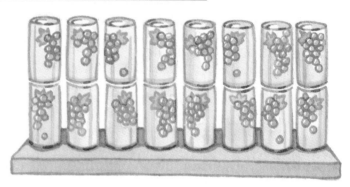

A. Leo stacks cans of grape juice in groups of 2. He puts 8 pairs of cans on a shelf. How many cans does Leo put on the shelf?

You can skip-count by 2s to find the product.

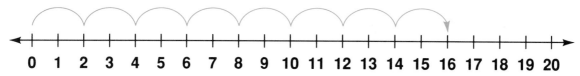

Number of Skips	Times	Size of Skips	Equals	Product
8	×	2	=	16

Leo puts 16 cans of juice on the shelf.

1. Use skip-counting to find the product of 7 × 2.

2. What is 4 × 2? 6 × 2?

3. You know that 8 × 2 = 16. What is 2 × 8? How do you know?

B. You can use a calculator to skip-count by 5s.

4. Enter 5 + 5 = on the calculator. What does the calculator show? How many skips of 5 have you made? Complete the number sentence.

___ × 5 = ___

5. Press the = sign again. What does the calculator show? How many skips of 5 have you made in all? Write a multiplication sentence.

6. Keep pressing = to skip count by 5. Look at what the calculator shows each time that you press =. Then write a multiplication sentence. Stop when the calculator shows 45.

TRY OUT Find the product. Use a number line or a calculator.

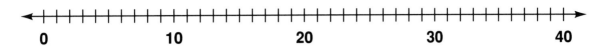

0   10   20   30   40

7. $9 \times 2 =$ ___ **■**

8. $6 \times 5 =$ ___ **■**

9. $8 \times 2 =$ ___ **■**

10. $8 \times 5 =$ ___ **■**

PRACTICE

Multiply.

11.	**12.**	**13.**	**14.**	**15.**	**16.**	**17.**
2 $\times 5$	5 $\times 3$	5 $\times 1$	2 $\times 3$	5 $\times 7$	2 $\times 6$	5 $\times 4$

18.	**19.**	**20.**	**21.**	**22.**	**23.**	**24.**
5 $\times 2$	1 $\times 2$	0 $\times 5$	7 $\times 2$	0 $\times 2$	2 $\times 4$	4 $\times 5$

25. $2 \times 2 =$ ___ **■**   **26.** $5 \times 5 =$ ___ **■**   **27.** $9 \times 5 =$ ___ **■**

Use a calculator to complete the multiplication table.

28. Rule: Multiply by 2.

0	1	2	3	4	5	6	7	8	9
■	■	■	■	■	■	■	■	■	■

29. Rule: Multiply by 5.

0	1	2	3	4	5	6	7	8	9
■	■	■	■	■	■	■	■	■	■

30. What patterns do you see?

31. What patterns do you see?

Mixed Applications

32. Ty stacks 8 cartons of cereal. There are 5 boxes in each carton. How many boxes does Ty stack in all?

33. Sal spends $1.25 for bread and $3.75 for turkey. He gives the clerk a $10.00 bill. What is his change?

EXTRA PRACTICE, page 250

3 and 4 as Factors

A. Leah places cups of lemonade in rows on her table. She puts 3 cups in each row. How many cups are in 4 rows?

You can count by 3s to find the number of cups in 4 rows.

Think: Count four 3s: **3, 6, 9, 12**

$$4 \times 3 = 12$$

There are 12 cups in 4 rows.

1. How many cups would there be in 7 rows? What is 7×3?

B. To find multiplication facts with 4 as a factor, you can use multiplication facts with 2 as a factor.

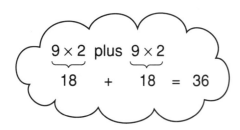

$$9 \times 2 \text{ plus } 9 \times 2$$
$$18 \quad + \quad 18 \quad = \quad 36$$

9 × 4 = 36

9×4 9×2 plus 9×2

TRY OUT   Find the product.

2. $2 \times 3 =$ ▪

3. $6 \times 3 =$ ▪

4. $3 \times 9 =$ ▪

5. $5 \times 4 =$ ▪

6. $8 \times 4 =$ ▪

7. $4 \times 7 =$ ▪

PRACTICE

Multiply.

8. 3
   × 1

9. 4
   × 2

10. 3
    × 3

11. 4
    × 3

12. 3
    × 5

13. 4
    × 4

14. 4
    × 9

15. 7
    × 3

16. 6
    × 4

17. 4
    × 1

18. 5
    × 4

19. 2
    × 5

20. 0
    × 4

21. 3
    × 9

22. 8 × 3 = ___

23. 5 × 7 = ___

24. 2 × 3 = ___

25. 6 × 3 = ___

26. 0 × 3 = ___

27. 3 × 7 = ___

28. 7 × 4 = ___

29. 4 × 8 = ___

30. 4 × 3 = ___

Complete the multiplication table.
Use the rule to complete.

31. Rule: Multiply by 3.

0	1	2	3	4	5	6	7	8	9
■	■	■	■	■	■	■	■	■	■

32. Rule: Multiply by 4.

0	1	2	3	4	5	6	7	8	9
■	■	■	■	■	■	■	■	■	■

33. What pattern do you see?

34. What pattern do you see?

Mixed Applications

35. Dee is planning a picnic for 4 people. Each person will need a cup, plate, spoon, and fork. How many items will she need?

36. A grocer totaled the number of watermelons he sold in three days: 27, 32, and 51. How many watermelons did he sell in all?

37. Roy picks 32 apples. Fay picks 16 fewer apples than Roy. How many apples does Fay pick?

38. The picnic starts at 1:30 P.M. It lasts 3 hours. At what time does the picnic end?

PROBLEM SOLVING

Strategy: Finding a Pattern

A. Ken needs to buy 20 small cans of juice for the class field trip. He sees that Stan's Supermarket sells packs of 4 cans for $2.00, 8 cans for $4.00, and 12 cans for $6.00. How much will the 20 cans cost?

Ken plans to make a table to help him find a pattern to solve the problem.

He knows that for every pack of 4 he buys, the cost goes up $2.00.

1. What can he do to find how many cans he has each time he buys another pack?

2. What can he do to find the total cost each time he buys another pack?

3. Complete the table. How much will 20 cans cost?

Cans	4	8	12		
Cost	$2	$4	$6		

B. Stan announced that there would be five special sales. The last three will be at 9:00 P.M., 7:00 P.M., and 5:00 P.M. If this pattern continues, when will the first sale be?

Sometimes you do not need a table to find a pattern.

4. How much time passes between each sale?

5. What can you do to find when the next sale will be?

6. Continue the pattern. When will the first sale be?

7. How does finding a pattern help you solve problems like these?

PRACTICE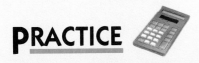

Find a pattern to solve. Use a table if needed.
Use mental math, a calculator, or paper and pencil.

8. Peanuts are sold 3 bags for $2.00, 6 bags for $4.00, and 9 bags for $6.00. Paula buys 15 bags of peanuts for the class. How much does she pay?

9. Stan gives away 2 free samples for every $5.00 spent, 4 samples for every $10.00, and 6 for every $15.00. Emile got 16 free samples. How much did he spend?

10. Stan sells 12 boxes of crackers the first day, 15 boxes the second day and 18 boxes the third day. If the pattern continues, how many boxes will he sell the sixth day?

11. Aisha stacks 6 rows of cans in a pattern. There are 18 cans in the bottom row, 15 cans in the next row, and 12 cans in the row above. How many cans will be in the last row?

Strategies and Skills Review

12. Martin orders 25 loaves of white bread, 15 loaves of rye bread, and 10 loaves of seven-grain bread. How many more loaves of white bread does he order than rye bread?

13. Mabel sells 3 kinds of Swiss cheese at the deli counter. She sells 5 more kinds of cheddar cheese than Swiss cheese. How many kinds of cheddar cheese does she sell?

14. There is an airplane ride outside the store. A 5-minute ride costs 10¢. A 10-minute ride costs 20¢. A 15-minute ride costs 30¢. How much would a 25-minute ride cost?

15. ***Write a problem*** that can be solved by finding a pattern. Solve your problem. Ask others to solve it.

EXTRA PRACTICE, page 251

SUBTRACTION CONTRAPTION

Using Number Concepts

First, make a set of 9 playing cards, one for each of the numbers 1 to 9. Use blank cards or cut sheets of paper into pieces the same size.

Next, on another sheet of paper, draw a board like the one at the right. The spaces should be about the same size as your cards.

1. Pick any 5 cards. Which numbers did you pick?
   Now place your cards in the spaces.
   Then solve the subtraction problem.
   What is the difference?

Now try to fill the spaces so that you get the GREATEST possible difference. Use any 5 cards you want.

2. What is the greatest 3-digit number you can make? Put those cards in the top row.

3. What is the least 2-digit number you can make with the remaining cards? Put that number in the bottom row. This will give you the greatest possible difference. How do you know?

4. Now try to find the LEAST possible difference. What number will you put in the top row? Why? What number will you put in the bottom? Why? What is the difference?

5. Try to find the difference closest to 200. What numbers will you use? Why? Is there another way?

6. Suppose the cards were face-down and you picked these numbers:

1   4   5   7   8

How will you place these numbers on your board to get the greatest possible difference? —the least possible difference?

7. Now turn all your playing cards face-down. Pick 5 cards. Use only the numbers you have chosen. Find the greatest possible difference. Find the least possible difference. Find the difference closest to 200.

8. Discuss how you solved Problems 6 and 7 with a partner. Did you both work the same way?

9. Make up your own questions using the subtraction board. Try them out with a partner.

6 and 7 as Factors

A. Each truck has 6 tires. There are 4 trucks. How many tires are there in all?

Since one of the factors is 4, you can use a multiplication fact that you know to solve the problem.

$$4 \times 6 = 24$$

There are 24 tires in all.

B. To find new multiplication facts with 6 as a factor, you can use multiplication facts with 3 as a factor.

6 × 3 plus 6 × 3
18 + 18 = 36

6 × 6 = 36

7 × 3 plus 7 × 3
21 + 21 = 42

7 × 6 = 42

8 × 3 plus 8 × 3
24 + 24 = 48

8 × 6 = 48

1. What is the product of 9 × 6?

C. To find new multiplication facts with 7 as a factor, you can add on.

6 × 7 plus 7 more
42 + 7 = 49

7 × 7 = 49

7 × 7 plus 7 more
49 + 7 = 56

8 × 7 = 56

8 × 7 plus 7 more
56 + 7 = 63

9 × 7 = 63

TRY OUT Find the product.

2. 4 × 7 = ___

3. 6 × 8 = ___

4. 6 × 9 = ___

5. 7 × 8 = ___

6. 5 × 6 = ___

7. 7 × 9 = ___

PRACTICE

Multiply.

8. $\begin{array}{r} 6 \\ \times\,2 \\ \hline \end{array}$	**9.** $\begin{array}{r} 7 \\ \times\,4 \\ \hline \end{array}$	**10.** $\begin{array}{r} 6 \\ \times\,5 \\ \hline \end{array}$	**11.** $\begin{array}{r} 7 \\ \times\,5 \\ \hline \end{array}$	**12.** $\begin{array}{r} 6 \\ \times\,6 \\ \hline \end{array}$	**13.** $\begin{array}{r} 7 \\ \times\,8 \\ \hline \end{array}$	**14.** $\begin{array}{r} 6 \\ \times\,9 \\ \hline \end{array}$
15. $\begin{array}{r} 6 \\ \times\,0 \\ \hline \end{array}$	**16.** $\begin{array}{r} 3 \\ \times\,7 \\ \hline \end{array}$	**17.** $\begin{array}{r} 6 \\ \times\,8 \\ \hline \end{array}$	**18.** $\begin{array}{r} 7 \\ \times\,7 \\ \hline \end{array}$	**19.** $\begin{array}{r} 6 \\ \times\,7 \\ \hline \end{array}$	**20.** $\begin{array}{r} 7 \\ \times\,9 \\ \hline \end{array}$	**21.** $\begin{array}{r} 5 \\ \times\,7 \\ \hline \end{array}$

22. $1 \times 6 = \underline{\blacksquare}$

23. $2 \times 7 = \underline{\blacksquare}$

24. $3 \times 6 = \underline{\blacksquare}$

25. $6 \times 7 = \underline{\blacksquare}$

26. $1 \times 7 = \underline{\blacksquare}$

27. $7 \times 6 = \underline{\blacksquare}$

28. $7 \times 2 = \underline{\blacksquare}$

29. $6 \times 4 = \underline{\blacksquare}$

30. $0 \times 7 = \underline{\blacksquare}$

Complete the multiplication table.
Use the rule to complete.

31. Rule: Multiply by 6.

0	1	2	3	4	5	6	7	8	9
■	■	■	■	■	■	■	■	■	■

32. Rule: Multiply by 7.

0	1	2	3	4	5	6	7	8	9
■	■	■	■	■	■	■	■	■	■

Mixed Applications

Solve. Which method did you use?

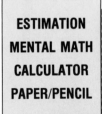

ESTIMATION
MENTAL MATH
CALCULATOR
PAPER/PENCIL

33. Vito drives a delivery truck 4 days a week. He makes 7 deliveries each day. How many deliveries does he make in one week?

34. Ira's business earns $6,734 in one month. He spends $3,758 on supplies and help. How much money does Ira have left?

35. Don spends $6.75 for gasoline and $2.75 for oil. He has $10.00. Does he have enough money?

36. Fred made 8 deliveries. Jan made 5 deliveries. How many more deliveries did Fred make than Jan?

EXTRA **PRACTICE,** page 251

8 and 9 as Factors

Rose knows most of the multiplication facts that have 8 or 9 as factors.

Here are the new multiplication facts she needs to know.

8 × 8 =

9 × 8 = ___

8 × 9 = ___

9 × 9 = ___

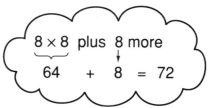

Here is how she found 8 × 8 and 9 × 8.

8 × 4 plus 8 × 4
32 + 32 = 64

8 × 8 = 64

8 × 8 plus 8 more
64 + 8 = 72

9 × 8 = 72

1. What is the product of 8 × 9? Why?

2. Find the product of 9 × 9. How did you find the product?

TRY **OUT**   Find the product.

3. 6 × 9 = ___

4. 8 × 7 = ___

5. 9 × 5 = ___

6. 7 × 9 = ___

7. 8 × 4 = ___

8. 5 × 8 = ___

PRACTICE

Multiply.

9. 8   **10.** 9   **11.** 8   **12.** 9   **13.** 8   **14.** 9   **15.** 8
    ×2   ×4   ×5   ×5   ×0   ×8   ×1

16. 9   **17.** 7   **18.** 9   **19.** 3   **20.** 8   **21.** 6   **22.** 8
    ×2   ×9   ×3   ×8   ×7   ×9   ×8

23. $4 \times 8 = $ ▦

24. $7 \times 9 = $ ▦

25. $1 \times 9 = $ ▦

26. $9 \times 9 = $ ▦

27. $8 \times 6 = $ ▦

28. $0 \times 9 = $ ▦

29. $9 \times 8 = $ ▦

30. $8 \times 5 = $ ▦

31. $8 \times 7 = $ ▦

32. $9 \times 6 = $ ▦

33. $8 \times 8 = $ ▦

34. $9 \times 3 = $ ▦

Complete the multiplication table.
Use the rule to complete.

35. Rule: Multiply by 8.

0	1	2	3	4	5	6	7	8	9
▦	▦	▦	▦	▦	▦	▦	▦	▦	▦

36. Rule: Multiply by 9.

0	1	2	3	4	5	6	7	8	9
▦	▦	▦	▦	▦	▦	▦	▦	▦	▦

Mixed Applications

Solve. Which method did you use?

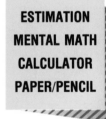

**ESTIMATION
MENTAL MATH
CALCULATOR
PAPER/PENCIL**

37. Rose has 4 hamsters. She takes 9 photographs of each hamster. How many photographs does she take of her hamsters?

38. The doctor sees 186 dogs and 405 cats in one week. How many more cats than dogs does she see?

39. The pet store sold 122 white hamsters and 115 brown hamsters last year. Did the store sell over 300 hamsters last year?

EXTRA **PRACTICE,** page 252

Patterns on a Multiplication Table

You can use patterns that you see on a multiplication table to help you remember multiplication facts.

×	0	1	2	3	4	5	6	7	8	9
0	0	0	0	0	0	0	0	0	0	0
1	0	1	2	3	4	5	6	7	8	9
2	0	2	4	6	8	10	12	14	16	18
3	0	3	6	9	12	15	18	21	24	27
4	0	4	8	12	16	20	24	28	32	36
5	0	5	10	15	20	25	30	35	40	45
6	0	6	12	18	24	30	36	42	48	54
7	0	7	14	21	28	35	42	49	56	63
8	0	8	16	24	32	40	48	56	■	■
9	0	9	18	27	36	45	54	63	■	■

1. Look under the 5s column and across the 5s row. Look at the ones digit. What pattern do you see?

2. What pattern do you see under the 2s column and across the 2s row?

3. What pattern do you see under the 9s column and across the 9s row?

4. Under which columns and across which rows are all the numbers even?

5. Look for other patterns. Talk about them.

TRY OUT Find the product.

6. $3 \times 3 =$ ■

7. $5 \times 9 =$ ■

8. $8 \times 9 =$ ■

9. $6 \times 7 =$ ■

10. $7 \times 7 =$ ■

11. $9 \times 3 =$ ■

PRACTICE

Multiply.

12. $\begin{array}{r} 3 \\ \times 7 \\ \hline \end{array}$ **13.** $\begin{array}{r} 4 \\ \times 7 \\ \hline \end{array}$ **14.** $\begin{array}{r} 9 \\ \times 2 \\ \hline \end{array}$ **15.** $\begin{array}{r} 2 \\ \times 7 \\ \hline \end{array}$ **16.** $\begin{array}{r} 4 \\ \times 8 \\ \hline \end{array}$ **17.** $\begin{array}{r} 8 \\ \times 3 \\ \hline \end{array}$ **18.** $\begin{array}{r} 5 \\ \times 6 \\ \hline \end{array}$

19. $\begin{array}{r} 8 \\ \times 9 \\ \hline \end{array}$ **20.** $\begin{array}{r} 9 \\ \times 9 \\ \hline \end{array}$ **21.** $\begin{array}{r} 7 \\ \times 6 \\ \hline \end{array}$ **22.** $\begin{array}{r} 6 \\ \times 6 \\ \hline \end{array}$ **23.** $\begin{array}{r} 9 \\ \times 7 \\ \hline \end{array}$ **24.** $\begin{array}{r} 8 \\ \times 7 \\ \hline \end{array}$ **25.** $\begin{array}{r} 9 \\ \times 5 \\ \hline \end{array}$

26. $2 \times 6 = $ ■   **27.** $3 \times 6 = $ ■   **28.** $8 \times 4 = $ ■

29. $7 \times 4 = $ ■   **30.** $4 \times 4 = $ ■   **31.** $4 \times 5 = $ ■

32. $6 \times 9 = $ ■   **33.** $9 \times 7 = $ ■   **34.** $9 \times 8 = $ ■

35. $7 \times 5 = $ ■   **36.** $4 \times 9 = $ ■   **37.** $8 \times 8 = $ ■

Mixed Applications

38. Mike practices his guitar for 2 hours a day. How many hours does he practice in 6 days?

39. Agnes needs $4.75 for new guitar strings. She has $1.89. How much more money does she need?

40. Gus has 8 tapes of his favorite songs. Each tape has 9 songs on it. How many songs does Gus have in all?

41. *Write a problem* using the information found on page 519 in the Databank. Solve the problem. Then give it to another student to solve.

Mixed Review

Find the answer. Which method did you use?

42. $3 \times 3 = $ ■   **43.** $500 - 217 = $ ■

44. $704 - 369 = $ ■   **45.** $145 + 689 = $ ■

46. $9 \times 8 = $ ■   **47.** $\$7.00 - \$6.20 = $ ■

```
MENTAL MATH
CALCULATOR
PAPER/PENCIL
```

EXTRA PRACTICE, page 252; PRACTICE *PLUS*, page 254

Three Factors

Sam has boxes of canned apple juice. Each box has 4 cans of juice. Sam puts the cans from 2 boxes of juice on each of 3 different shelves. How many cans of juice in all did Sam put on the shelves?

1. Write the multiplication sentence to show the total number of cans of juice.

Number of Boxes	Number of Cans in Each Box	Number of Shelves	Total Number of Cans
■ ×	■ ×	■ =	■

Sam put 24 cans of juice on the shelves.

You use ( ) to show which factors you multiply first.

2. Rewrite the multiplication sentence using ( ).

3. What is $(4 \times 2) \times 3 =$ ___■___ ? $2 \times (4 \times 3) =$ ___■___ ?

4. What is $(3 \times 2) \times 4 =$ ___■___ ? $2 \times (3 \times 4) =$ ___■___ ?

SHARING IDEAS

5. What do you notice about the factors in Exercises 3 and 4?

6. What happens to the product when you change the ways the factors are grouped?

7. Use other numbers to write your own multiplication sentences. Give them to other students to solve.

PRACTICE

Multiply.

8. $6 \times (3 \times 1) =$ ___

9. $(2 \times 4) \times 7 =$ ___

10. $8 \times (3 \times 3) =$ ___

11. $(2 \times 3) \times 1 =$ ___

12. $5 \times (3 \times 2) =$ ___

13. $(6 \times 1) \times 7 =$ ___

14. $8 \times 0 \times 7 =$ ___

15. $2 \times 2 \times 8 =$ ___

16. $3 \times 3 \times 9 =$ ___

17. $3 \times 2 \times 6 =$ ___

18. $0 \times 9 \times 6 =$ ___

19. $8 \times 1 \times 6 =$ ___

20. $2 \times 3 \times 8 =$ ___

21. $4 \times 9 \times 1 =$ ___

22. $3 \times 3 \times 5 =$ ___

23. $7 \times 1 \times 9 =$ ___

24. $4 \times 2 \times 6 =$ ___

25. $2 \times 2 \times 9 =$ ___

Find the missing number.

26. ___ $\times 5 \times 5 = 25$

27. $9 \times$ ___ $\times 5 = 0$

28. ___ $\times 8 \times 1 = 8$

29. $2 \times$ ___ $\times 9 = 0$

30. $6 \times 4 \times$ ___ $= 24$

31. $6 \times 7 \times$ ___ $= 0$

Mixed Applications

32. José unpacks 2 boxes of strawberries. There are 4 jars in each box. If there are 9 strawberries in each jar, how many strawberries are there in all?

33. Alina's class collected 150 empty cans and 175 empty bottles. How many cans and bottles did they collect?

MENTAL MATH

Ben found the product $2 \times 9 \times 2$ mentally. What did Ben do?

$$2 \times 2 \times 9 =$$
$$4 \times 9 = 36$$

Multiply mentally.

1. $3 \times 8 \times 2 =$ ___

2. $2 \times 7 \times 4 =$ ___

3. $3 \times 7 \times 3 =$ ___

4. $4 \times 7 \times 2 =$ ___

5. $3 \times 9 \times 2 =$ ___

6. $2 \times 8 \times 4 =$ ___

PROBLEM SOLVING

✓UNDERSTAND
✓PLAN
✓TRY
CHECK
✓EXTEND

Strategy: Choosing the Operation

The students in Mrs. Chen's class are planning a picnic. They have formed 3 teams. Each team has 5 students on it. How many students are working on teams?

You can use the five-step process to solve this problem.

UNDERSTAND What do I know?	I know that there are 3 teams. There are 5 students on each team.
What do I need to find out?	I need to find out how many students are working on teams.
PLAN What can I do?	Since each team has the same number of students, I can multiply the number of students on each team by the number of teams.
TRY Let me try my plan.	Number of students on each team ↓ **3 × 5 = 15** ↑ Number of teams So 15 students are working on teams.
CHECK Have I answered the question?	Yes. There are 15 students working on teams.
Does my answer make sense?	Yes. I get the same answer if I add. 5 + 5 + 5 = 15
EXTEND What have I learned?	I can use multiplication to solve problems that combine groups of the same size. I can check my answer by adding.

PRACTICE

**Decide which operation to use. Then solve the problem.
Use mental math, a calculator, or paper and pencil.**

1. There are 5 picnic tables. Each table seats 8 people. How many people can sit at the tables?

2. Mrs. Chen made 4 apple pies and 8 cherry pies for the picnic. How many pies did she make in all?

3. At the picnic 8 students played volleyball and 14 students played dodgeball. How many more students played dodgeball than volleyball?

4. There were 8 teams in the relay race. Each team had 4 runners. How many runners took part in the relay race?

Strategies and Skills Review

5. Raoul drove 20 minutes to get to the picnic. Could he have driven 15 miles? 150 miles? 500 miles?

6. Carrie collected 7 pine cones. Jerry collected 5 times as many leaves. How many leaves did he have?

7. In the ball-throwing contest, Althea threw the ball 78 feet, 64 feet, and 71 feet. The scorekeeper said that this is a total distance of 213 feet. Is this distance reasonable? Why?

8. Clem and Dawn are walking on their hands. Clem takes 23 steps before falling over. Dawn takes 37 steps. How many more steps does Dawn take than Clem before falling over?

9. Claude lives 1 mile from the picnic. He wants to walk to the picnic grounds. Can he get there in 3 minutes? Why or why not?

10. **Write a problem** that can be solved by addition, subtraction, or multiplication. Solve your problem. Ask others to solve your problem.

ACTIVITY Area

You can use counters to explore area.

WORKING TOGETHER

1. Use the two-color counters. Estimate the number of counters it takes to cover a 3-inch by 5-inch index card. Then count to find the exact number.

2. Estimate the number of square counters it takes to cover the same index card. Then count to find the exact number.

3. What do you notice about how the different shapes cover the area?

The **area** of an object is the number of square units it takes to cover the surface of the object.

4. Draw large figures like these on plain paper. Use your squares to find the area of each figure.

5. Use your squares to make a rectangle that has 3 rows with 4 squares in each row. What is the area?

SHARING IDEAS

6. Why are square units better to use to measure an area than curved units?

7. Why are figures with square corners easier to measure than figures with curves?

8. When you measured the figures with square corners, did everyone always agree about the area? Why or why not?

ON YOUR OWN

9. Estimate the number of squares needed to cover the areas of small objects around you. Then use the squares to find the areas of the objects. Make a table. Compare your areas with those of other students.

Object	Estimate	Area
book		

10. *Write a problem* about people who need to measure area. Solve the problem. Then give it to another student to solve.

ACTIVITY

Finding Area

The **square centimeter** can be used as a unit for measuring area.

square centimeter

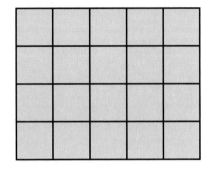

1. What is the length of each side of a square centimeter?

Count to find the area of each figure in square centimeters.

2.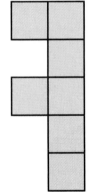

3.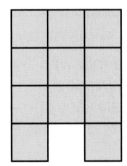

4.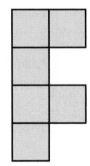

SHARING IDEAS

5. Why is it better to use square centimeters rather than the squares you cut yourself to measure an area?

6. Are square centimeters more useful measuring large areas or small areas? Why?

7. What metric unit of measure would be useful in measuring larger areas?

PRACTICE

Find the area in square centimeters.

8.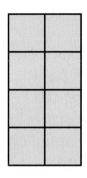

9.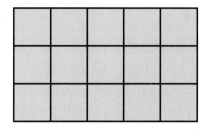

10.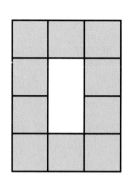

Critical Thinking

11. In Exercises 8 and 9, how can you find the area without counting all the squares?

Find the area. Tell how you did it.

12.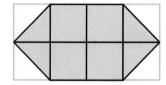

13.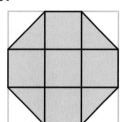

14.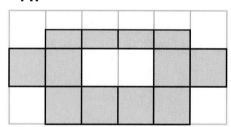

CHALLENGE

Estimate the area. Tell how you estimated. The first one is done for you.

1.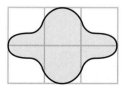

2.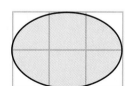

3.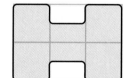

The area is about 3 square centimeters.

DECISION MAKING

Problem Solving: Planning a Picnic

SITUATION

The students in Paula's class are planning a picnic. They plan to serve hot dogs, hamburgers, and other picnic foods. There will be 24 students and 6 adults at the picnic. They know that 18 students want hot dogs. The rest of the students and all of the adults want hamburgers.

PROBLEM

How many packages of hot dogs, rolls, hamburger patties, and buns should the students buy?

DATA

Packages of Hot-Dog Rolls

6 Rolls $.90
12 Rolls $1.50

PACKAGES OF HAMBURGER PATTIES

8 PATTIES $4.00

Packages of Hot Dogs

8 Hot Dogs $2.50

PACKAGES OF HAMBURGER BUNS
8 BUNS $1.00
12 BUNS $1.65

USING THE DATA

How many of each food item do they need?

1. hot dogs

2. hamburgers

How many packages of each food item do they need to buy?

3. hot dogs

4. hamburgers

5. hot-dog rolls in packages of six

6. hot-dog rolls in packages of 12

7. hamburger buns in packages of 8

8. hamburger buns in packages of 12

Find the cost of each.

9. 2 packages of 12 hot-dog rolls

10. 3 packages of 6 hot-dog rolls

11. 2 packages of 8 hamburger buns

12. 1 package of 12 hamburger buns

MAKING DECISIONS

13. What other things do the students need to think about when planning a picnic?

14. What size packages of hot-dog rolls would you buy for the picnic? Tell how you made your choice.

15. *What if* you know some people will want more than one hot dog or hamburger? How would this change how many packages of each item you would buy?

16. How many packages of hot dogs, rolls, hamburger patties and buns should the students buy?

17. *Write a list* of what you would buy for a picnic if you had $20 to spend.

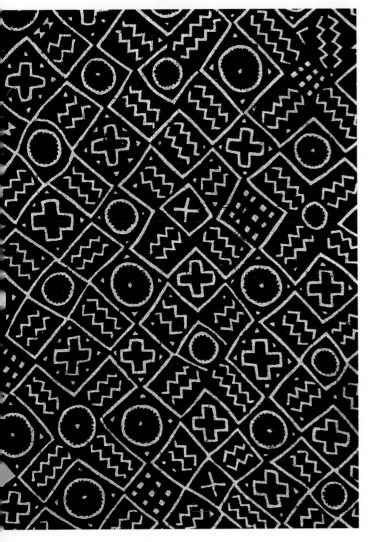

Math and Art

The Ashanti people of Ghana, Africa, have made cloth since long ago. Each piece of cloth has a pattern that is one of a kind.

The artists weave the cloth. Then they carve many designs into hard shells. Each shell is dipped into dye and stamped onto the fabric. The artists stamp the designs onto the fabric in patterns that they choose. The picture shows how the artists mix and repeat designs to create different patterns.

What if an artist stamped one design in 8 rows? The design will fit 7 times in each row. How many times will the design be repeated?

Think: Multiply. 8 × 7 = 56

The design is repeated 56 times.

ACTIVITIES

1. Use graph paper and colored markers. Create a pattern for a piece of cloth. Choose the color and design you want to put in each square. Display your design.

2. Find pictures of other cloth with repeating patterns. Compare the cloth you find with the Ashanti cloth. Talk with your class about how they are the same and how they are different.

Computer: Exploring Area of Rectangles

You can use Logo commands to build shapes with different areas.

AT THE COMPUTER

This program will have the computer draw square units. Enter the following program.

```
TO UNIT
REPEAT 4 [FD 10 RT 90] FD 10
END
```

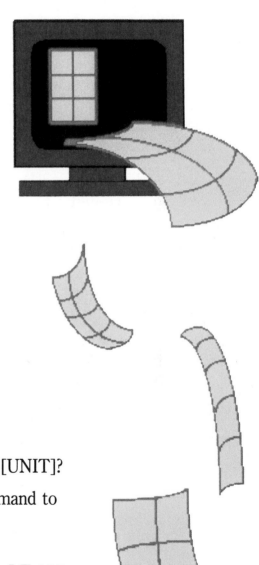

1. Type UNIT. Then press RETURN. Repeat the command a few more times. What happens?

Clear the screen. Then enter these commands.

```
REPEAT 4 [UNIT]
RT 90 FD 20 RT 90
REPEAT 4 [UNIT]
LT 180
REPEAT 4 [UNIT]
```

2. What happens after you enter REPEAT 4 [UNIT]?

3. How would you change the REPEAT command to build a column with 3 square units?

4. Tell what happens after you enter:
   a. RT 90   b. FD 20   c. LT 180

5. Clear the screen. Then build a square with an area of 9 square units. What did you enter?

6. Ask a partner to draw a figure with an area greater than 12 square units but smaller than 20 square units. Take turns drawing several different shapes.

EXTRA PRACTICE

Multiplication Properties, page 223

Find the product.

1. 3 ×1	**2.** 1 ×3	**3.** 4 ×2	**4.** 2 ×4	**5.** 0 ×6	**6.** 6 ×0
7. 5 ×2	**8.** 0 ×3	**9.** 6 ×1	**10.** 2 ×6	**11.** 1 ×0	**12.** 3 ×4

13. $1 \times 7 = $ ___ **14.** $2 \times 3 = $ ___ **15.** $6 \times 2 = $ ___ **16.** $7 \times 0 = $ ___

2 and 5 as Factors, page 225

Multiply.

1. 2 ×4	**2.** 0 ×5	**3.** 4 ×2	**4.** 5 ×4	**5.** 2 ×5	**6.** 1 ×2
7. 2 ×0	**8.** 5 ×8	**9.** 2 ×8	**10.** 6 ×2	**11.** 1 ×5	**12.** 9 ×2

13. $6 \times 5 = $ ___ **14.** $2 \times 3 = $ ___ **15.** $5 \times 3 = $ ___ **16.** $7 \times 2 = $ ___

3 and 4 as Factors, page 227

Multiply.

1. 0 ×3	**2.** 4 ×3	**3.** 3 ×7	**4.** 5 ×4	**5.** 1 ×3	**6.** 4 ×7
7. 2 ×3	**8.** 4 ×6	**9.** 3 ×9	**10.** 1 ×4	**11.** 6 ×4	**12.** 3 ×6

13. $0 \times 4 = $ ___ **14.** $8 \times 3 = $ ___ **15.** $2 \times 4 = $ ___ **16.** $9 \times 4 = $ ___

EXTRA PRACTICE

Problem Solving Strategy: Finding a Pattern, page 229 ....

Look for a pattern. Then solve the problem.

1. Ava wants to buy 15 packets of seeds for her garden. The Garden Shop sells 3 packets of seeds for $4.00, 6 packets of seeds for $8.00, and 9 packets of seeds for $12.00. How much will 15 packets of seeds cost?

2. There are 5 library classes a day at the Village Elementary School. The last three classes are at 11:30 A.M., 11:00 A.M., and 10:30 A.M. If this pattern continues, when is the first library class?

3. A radio station broadcasts 5 minutes of news at 12:00 noon, 2 P.M., and 4 P.M. If this pattern continues, at what time will the next news broadcast take place?

4. Don wants to buy 18 cans of cat food. The Pet Store sells 3 cans of cat food for $1.50, 6 cans for $3.00, and 12 cans for $6.00. How much will 18 cans of cat food cost?

6 and 7 as Factors, page 233 ....

Multiply.

1. 2×7
2. 4×6
3. 0×6
4. 7×5
5. 6×3
6. 1×7

7. 6×5
8. 7×3
9. 6×1
10. 9×7
11. 6×6
12. 7×8

13. $0 \times 7 = \blacksquare$
14. $6 \times 7 = \blacksquare$
15. $7 \times 7 = \blacksquare$
16. $2 \times 6 = \blacksquare$

17. $7 \times 4 = \blacksquare$
18. $8 \times 6 = \blacksquare$
19. $8 \times 4 = \blacksquare$
20. $9 \times 6 = \blacksquare$

Use the rule to complete the table.

21. Rule: Multiply by 6.

0	1	2	3	4
$\blacksquare$	$\blacksquare$	$\blacksquare$	$\blacksquare$	$\blacksquare$

22. Rule: Multiply by 7.

5	6	7	8	9
$\blacksquare$	$\blacksquare$	$\blacksquare$	$\blacksquare$	$\blacksquare$

EXTRA PRACTICE

8 and 9 as Factors, page 235 ....

Multiply.

| **1.** 8 $\times 8$ | **2.** 3 $\times 9$ | **3.** 9 $\times 8$ | **4.** 9 $\times 4$ | **5.** 8 $\times 6$ | **6.** 0 $\times 9$ |

7. $8 \times 7 =$ ___ **8.** $6 \times 9 =$ ___ **9.** $4 \times 8 =$ ___ **10.** $9 \times 7 =$ ___

Patterns on a Multiplication Table, page 237 ....

Multiply.

| **1.** 6 $\times 4$ | **2.** 3 $\times 7$ | **3.** 5 $\times 5$ | **4.** 9 $\times 8$ | **5.** 4 $\times 7$ | **6.** 1 $\times 6$ |

| **7.** 3 $\times 4$ | **8.** 6 $\times 0$ | **9.** 8 $\times 5$ | **10.** 7 $\times 7$ | **11.** 9 $\times 3$ | **12.** 5 $\times 4$ |

13. $6 \times 2 =$ ___ **14.** $3 \times 9 =$ ___ **15.** $8 \times 8 =$ ___ **16.** $2 \times 7 =$ ___

17. $9 \times 9 =$ ___ **18.** $0 \times 2 =$ ___ **19.** $7 \times 4 =$ ___ **20.** $1 \times 3 =$ ___

Three Factors, page 239 ....

Multiply.

1. $4 \times (2 \times 3) =$ ___ **2.** $(3 \times 2) \times 6 =$ ___ **3.** $7 \times (2 \times 4) =$ ___

4. $(1 \times 7) \times 2 =$ ___ **5.** $6 \times (2 \times 1) =$ ___ **6.** $(5 \times 2) \times 7 =$ ___

7. $3 \times 0 \times 5 =$ ___ **8.** $2 \times 2 \times 6 =$ ___ **9.** $1 \times 9 \times 0 =$ ___

10. $4 \times 2 \times 4 =$ ___ **11.** $5 \times 2 \times 3 =$ ___ **12.** $4 \times 1 \times 6 =$ ___

Find the missing numbers.

13. ___ $\times 4 \times 4 = 16$ **14.** $8 \times$ ___ $\times 6 = 0$ **15.** ___ $\times 7 \times 1 = 7$

16. $3 \times$ ___ $\times 6 = 0$ **17.** $3 \times 7 \times$ ___ $= 21$ **18.** $4 \times 8 \times$ ___ $= 0$

Problem Solving Strategy: Choosing the Operation, page 241 ....

Decide which operation to use. Then solve the problem.

1. After the picnic 7 students went to play on the monkey bars and 10 played on the merry-go-round. How many more students played on the merry-go-round than on the monkey bars?

2. There are 6 pounds of chicken for dinner. Each pound has 9 pieces of chicken. How many pieces of chicken will there be for dinner?

3. Ms. Palmer's class brought lemonade to the picnic. Eight students drank regular lemonade. Nine students drank pink lemonade. How many children drank lemonade at the picnic?

4. There were 6 teams in the sack race. Each team had 2 players. How many players took part in the sack race?

Finding Area, page 245 ....

Find the area in square centimeters.

1.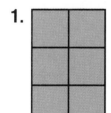

2.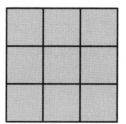

3.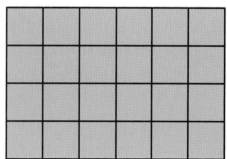

4.

5.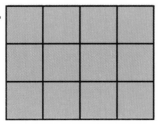

6.

Practice PLUS

KEY SKILL: Multiplication Facts (Use after page 237.)

Level A ....
Multiply.

1. 3	**2.** 1	**3.** 2	**4.** 5	**5.** 6	**6.** 8
$\times 0$	$\times 7$	$\times 4$	$\times 3$	$\times 3$	$\times 2$

7. $1 \times 4 = $ ▆   **8.** $3 \times 2 = $ ▆   **9.** $5 \times 0 = $ ▆   **10.** $6 \times 4 = $ ▆

11. Sandy practices the piano 3 hours a day. How many hours does she practice in 3 days?

Level B ....
Multiply.

12. 4	**13.** 8	**14.** 7	**15.** 5	**16.** 2	**17.** 9
$\times 4$	$\times 3$	$\times 6$	$\times 4$	$\times 6$	$\times 3$

18. $6 \times 0 = $ ▆   **19.** $9 \times 5 = $ ▆   **20.** $6 \times 6 = $ ▆   **21.** $5 \times 7 = $ ▆

22. Dan has 9 records of popular songs. Each record has 6 songs on it. How many songs does Dan have all together?

Level C ....
Multiply.

23. 6	**24.** 8	**25.** 7	**26.** 4	**27.** 8	**28.** 5
$\times 8$	$\times 8$	$\times 6$	$\times 7$	$\times 3$	$\times 7$

29. $7 \times 8 = $ ▆   **30.** $9 \times 9 = $ ▆   **31.** $4 \times 3 = $ ▆   **32.** $7 \times 9 = $ ▆

33. There are 8 records in a box. Each record sells for $9. How much does a box of records cost?

PRACTICE PLUS

KEY SKILL: **Three Factors** (Use after page 239.)

Level A ....

Multiply.

1. $4 \times (2 \times 1) = $ ■   **2.** $(2 \times 2) \times 3 = $ ■   **3.** $4 \times (1 \times 3) = $ ■

4. $(2 \times 3) \times 5 = $ ■   **5.** $2 \times (6 \times 1) = $ ■   **6.** $(3 \times 3) \times 2 = $ ■

7. $0 \times 6 \times 5 = $ ■   **8.** $3 \times 1 \times 4 = $ ■   **9.** $5 \times 1 \times 3 = $ ■

10. Julio packs 3 boxes of pickles. Each box has 2 jars of pickles. If there are 4 pickles in each jar, how many pickles are there in all?

Level B ....

Multiply.

11. $6 \times (4 \times 2) = $ ■   **12.** $(3 \times 3) \times 6 = $ ■   **13.** $(2 \times 3) \times 6 = $ ■

14. $9 \times (2 \times 4) = $ ■   **15.** $5 \times 0 \times 9 = $ ■   **16.** $2 \times 4 \times 4 = $ ■

17. $1 \times 7 \times 6 = $ ■   **18.** $9 \times 1 \times 9 = $ ■   **19.** $4 \times 2 \times 8 = $ ■

20. Colin puts the cans from 4 boxes of juice on each of 2 different shelves. Each box has 4 cans of juice. How many cans of juice does he put on the shelves?

Level C ....

Multiply.

21. $9 \times (4 \times 1) = $ ■   **22.** $2 \times 4 \times 9 = $ ■   **23.** $2 \times 4 \times 7 = $ ■

24. $8 \times (3 \times 1) = $ ■   **25.** $4 \times 2 \times 1 = $ ■   **26.** $2 \times 3 \times 4 = $ ■

Find the missing number.

27. ■ $\times 5 \times 6 = 30$ **28.** $7 \times 3 \times$ ■ $= 21$ **29.** $6 \times$ ■ $\times 8 = 0$

30. Hank unpacks 2 boxes of olives. There are 4 cans of olives in a box. If there are 9 olives in one can, how many olives are there all together?

CHAPTER REVIEW/TEST

LANGUAGE AND MATHEMATICS

Complete the sentences. Use the words in the chart.

1. The number of square units it takes to cover the surface of an object is the ___.

2. The answer to a multiplication problem is called the ___.

3. The number 9 in the multiplication sentence $9 \times 2 = 18$ is called a ___.

VOCABULARY
product
factor
area
perimeter

CONCEPTS AND SKILLS

Multiply.

4.	5.	6.	7.	8.	9.
4 $\times 3$	3 $\times 7$	7 $\times 5$	1 $\times 6$	6 $\times 6$	2 $\times 5$

10.	11.	12.	13.	14.	15.
0 $\times 8$	5 $\times 9$	8 $\times 7$	4 $\times 4$	9 $\times 8$	8 $\times 2$

16. $(2 \times 3) \times 4 = $ ___

17. $9 \times (1 \times 7) = $ ___

Find the missing number.

18. $9 \times $ ___ $ = 0$

19. ___ $\times 5 = 5$

20. $9 \times 6 = $ ___ $\times 9$

Find the area in square centimeters.

21.
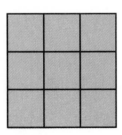

22.
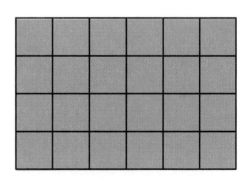

Critical Thinking

Write *always*, *sometimes*, or *never*.

23. The product of a number multiplied by 1 is ▬ the number.

Mixed Applications

24. There are 6 books in 1 box, 12 books in 2 boxes, and 18 books in 3 boxes. How many books are in 5 boxes?

25. Each team has 9 swimmers at the meet. There are 5 teams. How many swimmers are at the meet?

PERFORMANCE ASSESSMENT

Work with your group to solve this problem.

Suppose you are cleaning out your closet. You find:

Number of Items	Number on Cube	Multiplication Sentence
0 elephants 1 sweater 2 radios 3 gerbils 4 games 5 sneakers		

Choose one of the items and toss a number cube. Record the number tossed. Write a multiplication sentence using the number tossed and the number of items as factors. Take turns until you have completed the table.

1. *Think about:*
- how to find the product of the two factors
- how to write each multiplication sentence

2. Choose one of the multiplication sentences in the table. Write a word problem for it.

Cumulative Review

Choose the letter of the correct answer.

1. $8 \times 5 =$ ■
   a. 4
   b. 40
   c. 400
   d. not given

2. $487 + 579 + 82 =$ ■
   a. 938
   b. 1,138
   c. 1,148
   d. not given

3. $5 \times 1 =$ ■
   a. 1
   b. 5
   c. 6
   d. not given

4. Which is the best estimate to measure the capacity of a bottle of milk?
   a. 1 milliliter
   b. 1 liter
   c. 1 gram
   d. not given

5. Estimate: $3,478 - 399$
   a. 3,000
   b. 2,000
   c. 4,000
   d. 4,100

6. Choose the temperature at which you could go skiing.
   a. ⁻5°C
   b. 25°C
   c. 100°C
   d. not given

7. How many apples are in 5 bags if each bag has 6 apples?
   a. 17
   b. 34
   c. 78
   d. not given

8. $\$7.65 - \$2.74 =$ ■
   a. $5.91
   b. $5.11
   c. $4.91
   d. not given

9. $0 \times 4 =$ ■
   a. 0
   b. 1
   c. 4
   d. not given

10. $3,304 - 1,228 =$ ■
    a. 2,184
    b. 2,176
    c. 2,026
    d. not given

11. Find the perimeter of a figure with sides: 8 cm, 9 cm, 8 cm, and 9 cm.
    a. 17 cm
    b. 34 cm
    c. 72 cm
    d. not given

12. $7 \times 6 =$ ■
    a. 36
    b. 42
    c. 49
    d. not given

13. Which is the best estimate to measure the weight of a bean?
    a. 3 liters
    b. 3 kilograms
    c. 3 grams
    d. not given

14. What time will it be 18 minutes after 7:39?
    a. 8:07
    b. 7:57
    c. 7:41
    d. not given

ANOTHER MODEL OF MULTIPLICATION

Prairie Village has ten roads. Four roads run east and west. Six roads run north and south.

1. In how many places do the roads cross?

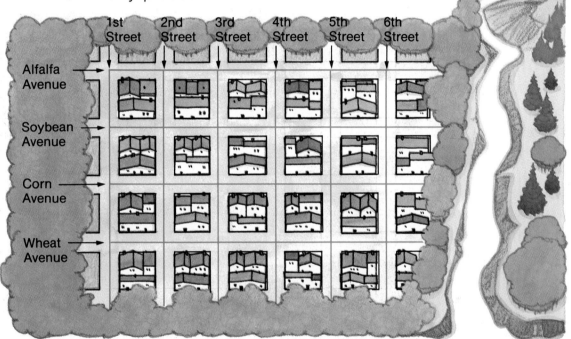

2. You can draw a line model to show the number of times the streets cross. Write two multiplication sentences.

3. Draw a line model to show 7 × 5. How many times do the lines cross?

4. Draw a line model to show 8 × 7. How many times do the lines cross?

5. Draw a line model to show 6 × 9. How many times do the lines cross?

6. Draw line models of your own. Trade your models with others and have them write two multiplication sentences for each.

A Japanese Folktale and Equality

The Japanese folktale *The Two Foolish Cats* tells of two hungry cats who find a large rice cake and a small rice cake. The cats cannot decide which one of them should get the large cake. They argue and argue.

Finally, the cats ask the wise old monkey of the mountain to settle their argument once and for all. The monkey puts the rice cakes on a balance scale. Of course, the large cake is heavier, so the monkey nibbles at both cakes, pretending to make them equal. The monkey keeps taking big bites. After every bite, one cake is still larger than the other. He keeps biting until he has eaten both cakes. The argument is settled—both cakes are equally gone!

1 What important lesson do you think the cats learned?

2 How might the two cats have shared the rice cakes?

3 Discuss sharing with your class. Tell about a time when you and some friends divided things to make equal shares.

Russia

China   JAPAN

ACTIVITY

The Meaning of Division

Alicia put 12 dog biscuits in bags. She put 4 biscuits in each bag. How many bags did she use?

WORKING TOGETHER

You can solve the problem by making a model.

Step 1 Model the number of biscuits in all.

Think: There are 12 biscuits, so show 12 counters.

Step 2 Model the number of biscuits in each bag.

Think: Take away as many groups of 4 as you can.

1. How many groups of 4 did you take away from 12? How many bags did Alicia use?

Compare the following **division sentence** to your model:

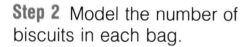

$$12 \div 4 = 3$$

dividend divided by divisor equals quotient

$$\text{3} \leftarrow \text{quotient}$$
$$\text{or } 4\overline{)12} \leftarrow \text{dividend}$$
$$\uparrow$$
$$\textbf{divisor}$$

2. Which number tells you the total number of biscuits?

3. Which number tells you the number in each group?

4. Which number tells you the number of equal groups?

5. ***What if*** Alicia had 12 biscuits and 3 bags? If each bag held the same number of biscuits, how many biscuits would be in each bag?

6. Complete the tables. Model using counters.

Number in All		Number in Each Group		Number of Equal Groups
12	÷	4	=	■
12	÷	3	=	■
18	÷	3	=	■
24	÷	4	=	■

Number in All		Number of Equal Groups		Number in Each Group
12	÷	3	=	■
12	÷	4	=	■
18	÷	9	=	■
24	÷	8	=	■

7. Try to separate the numbers in all into other equal groups. Record your results in the tables. Try this with other numbers.

SHARING IDEAS

8. Look at the tables. What pattern do you see?

9. What can you find if you know the number in all and the number in each group?

10. What can you find if you know the number in all and the number of groups?

ON YOUR OWN

Solve. Use counters if needed.

11. Jon puts 15 cat's toys in boxes. He puts 5 toys in each box. How many boxes does he use?

12. Lulu puts 30 water bowls in 5 boxes. She puts the same number of bowls in each box. How many bowls are in each box?

13. *Write a problem* that can be solved using division. Solve the problem. Then ask others to solve it.

ACTIVITY

Informal Algebra: Relating Multiplication and Division

WORKING TOGETHER

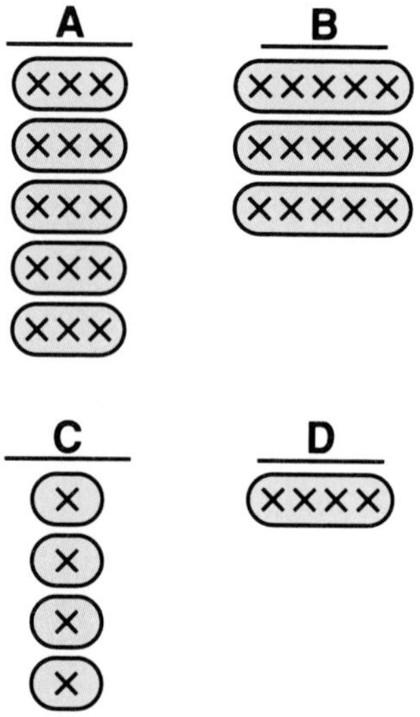

You can use pictures and number sentences to learn about division and multiplication.

Answer the questions for each picture shown.

A
(xxx)
(xxx)
(xxx)
(xxx)
(xxx)

B
(xxxxx)
(xxxxx)
(xxxxx)

1. How many counters are there in all? How many equal groups of counters are there? How many are in each group?

C
(x)
(x)
(x)
(x)

D
(xxxx)

2. Write a division sentence and a multiplication sentence for each picture. Record your sentences in tables like these.

Number in All		Number of Groups		Number in Each Group
	÷		=	

Number of Groups		Number in Each Group		Number in All
	×		=	

3. Compare the number sentences. What do you notice?

4. Draw a picture for each pair of number sentences. Find the missing numbers. What patterns do you see?

$16 \div 2 =$ ___ and ___ $\times 2 = 16$

$16 \div 8 =$ ___ and ___ $\times 8 = 16$

5. Draw a picture and write a multiplication sentence for each division sentence.

$5 \div 5 =$ ___ $5 \div 1 =$ ___ $7 \div 7 =$ ___ $7 \div 1 =$ ___

$6 \div 6 =$ ___ $6 \div 1 =$ ___ $8 \div 8 =$ ___ $8 \div 1 =$ ___

6. Compare the dividends, divisors, and quotients. What patterns do you see?

This picture shows 0 counters separated into 5 groups.

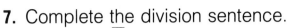

7. Complete the division sentence.
$0 \div 5 =$ _____

8. Draw pictures for these division sentences.

$0 \div 2 =$ _____ $0 \div 3 =$ _____ $0 \div 7 =$ _____ $0 \div 8 =$ _____

9. Compare the quotients to the dividends and divisors. What patterns do you see?

10. Can you draw a picture for the sentence $5 \div 0 =$ _____ ? Why or why not? Think: $0 \times$ _____ $= 5$

SHARING IDEAS

11. How are division and multiplication related?

12. What happens when you divide the dividend in a division sentence by the quotient?

13. What happens when you divide a number by itself? by one?

PRACTICE

Find the quotient. Use pictures and what you have learned about the properties of division.

14. $20 \div 5 =$ _____   **15.** $20 \div 4 =$ _____   **16.** $9 \div 1 =$ _____

17. $9 \div 9 =$ _____   **18.** $0 \div 9 =$ _____   **19.** $0 \div 4 =$ _____

20. $16 \div 4 =$ _____   **21.** $25 \div 5 =$ _____   **22.** $3 \div 3 =$ _____

23. $4\overline{)4}$ **24.** $1\overline{)9}$ **25.** $5\overline{)5}$ **26.** $2\overline{)10}$ **27.** $6\overline{)6}$

Solve.

28. Sol has 5 fish. He puts 1 fish in each bowl. How many bowls does he need?

29. Ida has 6 fish. She puts the same number in 3 tanks. How many fish are in each tank?

Dividing by 2 and 5

A. Ed has 10 kittens in all. He wants to put 2 kittens in each of a number of boxes. How many boxes does Ed need?

Divide 10 by 2.

Ed starts at 10 and skip-counts backward by 2s until he gets to zero. He counts 5 skips.

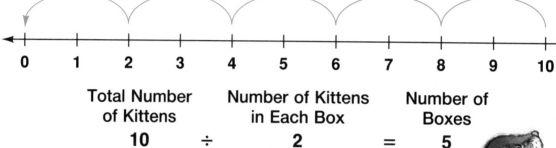

Total Number of Kittens		Number of Kittens in Each Box		Number of Boxes
10	$\div$	2	=	5

Ed needs 5 boxes for his kittens.

1. Tell how you would use the number line to find how many 2s are in 6. What is the quotient?

2. What is $8 \div 2$? How big is each skip on the number line? How many skips do you make?

3. How many 2s are in 4? How big is each skip on the number line? How many skips do you make?

B. Use the number line below to skip-count backward by 5s.

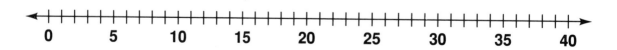

4. How many 5s are in 10?

5. Divide 40 by 5.

TRY OUT Find the quotients.

6. $2\overline{)12}$ **a.** 14   **b.** 10   **c.** 6   **d.** 4

7. $15 \div 5 =$    **a.** 20   **b.** 15   **c.** 10   **d.** 3

8. How many 2s in 18?   **a.** 2   **b.** 9   **c.** 16   **d.** 20

9. Divide 8 by 4.   **a.** 2   **b.** 4   **c.** 8   **d.** 12

PRACTICE

Divide.

10. $2\overline{)4}$ **11.** $5\overline{)25}$ **12.** $2\overline{)2}$ **13.** $5\overline{)10}$ **14.** $2\overline{)16}$

15. $2\overline{)10}$ **16.** $5\overline{)45}$ **17.** $2\overline{)14}$ **18.** $5\overline{)20}$ **19.** $2\overline{)0}$

20. $2 \div 1 =$ ■   **21.** $35 \div 5 =$ ■   **22.** $5 \div 1 =$ ■

23. $0 \div 5 =$ ■   **24.** $12 \div 2 =$ ■   **25.** $15 \div 3 =$ ■

26. $25 \div 5 =$ ■   **27.** $18 \div 2 =$ ■   **28.** $30 \div 5 =$ ■

29. How many 5s are in 5?   **30.** How many 2s are in 6?

31. Divide 14 by 2.   **32.** Divide 45 by 5.

Complete the table. Use the rule to complete.

33. Rule: Divide by 2.

0	2	4	6	8	10	12	14	16	18
■	■	■	■	■	■	■	■	■	■

34. Rule: Divide by 5.

0	5	10	15	20	25	30	35	40	45
■	■	■	■	■	■	■	■	■	■

Solve.

35. Juan has 5 fighting fish. He puts them in 5 tanks. How many fish are in each tank?

36. Tia has 10 fish tanks. She puts 1 tank in each carton. How many cartons does she use?

Dividing by 3 and 4

A. Jerry takes care of 12 horses. He ties the same number of horses to each of 4 hitching posts. How many horses does Jerry tie to each post?

How many 4s are in 12?

Think: $\underline{\blacksquare} \times 4 = 12$
$ 3 \times 4 = 12$

$12 \div 4 = 3$ or $4\overline{)12}$ with quotient 3

Jerry ties 3 horses to each post.

1. What related division sentence can you write?

2. **What if** Jerry ties 24 horses to 4 hitching posts? If each post has the same number of horses, how many horses does he tie to each post? What division sentence did you use?

TRY OUT Find the quotient.

3. $4\overline{)20}$ 4. $4\overline{)16}$ 5. $3\overline{)18}$ 6. $4\overline{)36}$ 7. $3\overline{)21}$

8. $6 \div 3 = \underline{\blacksquare}$ 9. $28 \div 4 = \underline{\blacksquare}$ 10. $24 \div 3 = \underline{\blacksquare}$

PRACTICE

Divide.

11. $3\overline{)3}$ **12.** $4\overline{)8}$ **13.** $3\overline{)9}$ **14.** $1\overline{)4}$ **15.** $3\overline{)27}$

16. $4\overline{)16}$ **17.** $3\overline{)12}$ **18.** $4\overline{)20}$ **19.** $3\overline{)15}$ **20.** $4\overline{)28}$

21. $3 \div 1$ ▪ **22.** $12 \div 4 =$ ▪ **23.** $18 \div 3 =$ ▪

24. $24 \div 4 =$ ▪ **25.** $0 \div 3 =$ ▪ **26.** $24 \div 3 =$ ▪

27. $0 \div 4 =$ ▪ **28.** $27 \div 3 =$ ▪ **29.** $15 \div 3 =$ ▪

30. Divide 4 by 4. **31.** Divide 12 by 3.

32. How many 3s are in 24? **33.** How many 4s are in 32?

Complete the table. Use the rule to complete.

34. Rule: Divide by 3.

0	3	6	9	12	15	18	21	24	27
▪	▪	▪	▪	▪	▪	▪	▪	▪	▪

35. Rule: Divide by 4.

0	4	8	12	16	20	24	28	32	36
▪	▪	▪	▪	▪	▪	▪	▪	▪	▪

Mixed Applications

Solve. Which method did you use?

> **ESTIMATION**
> **MENTAL MATH**
> **CALCULATOR**
> **PAPER/PENCIL**

36. Fred's horse weighs 938 pounds. His sister's pony weighs 321 pounds. About how much more does the horse weigh than the pony?

37. A riding stable has 12 horses. There are 3 people who care for an equal number of horses. How many horses does each person care for?

38. Ed feeds 56 horses. Jan feeds 47 horses. How many horses do they feed in all?

39. Extra saddle blankets are stored in 4 drawers. There are 4 blankets in each drawer. How many blankets are there in all?

PROBLEM SOLVING

Strategy: Solving a Multistep Problem

The pet store has 3 cages with 4 puppies in each cage. There are 3 fewer kittens than puppies. How many animals are there in all?

1. What information do you know?

2. What do you need to find out?

Some problems take several steps to solve. When there is more than one step, you should first make a plan.

3. What do you need to find out *before* you can decide how many animals there are?

Try your plan.

4. What can you do first?

5. What can you do next?

6. What can you do last?

7. How many animals are there in all?

8. How does a plan help you solve multistep problems?

PLAN		
Step 1	$3 \times 4 =$	12
Step 2	$12 - 3 =$	9
Step 3	$12 + 9 =$	■

PRACTICE

Make a plan. Then solve the problem. Use mental math, a calculator, or paper and pencil.

9. One carton of pet food contains 4 rows with 6 cans in each row. The other carton contains 3 rows with 8 cans in each row. How many cans are there in the two cartons?

10. Ray has 3 reptile cards and 5 elephant cards. He has 4 times as many bird cards as the total number of reptile and elephant cards. How many animal cards does he have?

11. Margie walks dogs on weekends. She charges $2 for each dog she walks. Last weekend she earned $8. This weekend she walked 3 dogs on Saturday and 5 dogs on Sunday. How much did she earn on the two weekends?

12. The pet store keeps its starfish in 3 bowls. One bowl has 4 starfish. The second bowl has 3 times as many starfish as the first bowl. The third bowl has 6 fewer than the second bowl. How many starfish does the store have?

Strategies and Skills Review

13. Kelly changes the water in her fish tank 4 times a month and cleans it twice a month. It takes her 5 minutes to change the water and 9 minutes to clean the tank. How many minutes does she spend each month taking care of her tank?

14. The pet store sells two sizes of leashes. The regular size is 3 feet long. The large size is twice as long. The regular size costs $3.95, and the large size costs $5.60. How much more does the large size cost than the regular size?

15. Gary left his home at 7:25 A.M. to walk his dog. What other information do you need in order to find how long it took Gary to walk his dog?

16. ***Write a problem*** that takes several steps to solve. Ask others to solve it. Talk about whether there is more than one way to solve the problem.

EXTRA PRACTICE, page 291

NIM-ATICS

Visual Reasoning

Follow these rules to play NIM. Arrange 12 coins or counters as shown:

- 5 in the top row
- 4 in the middle row
- 3 in the bottom row

Two players take turns. A player may remove any number of coins as long as the coins are from the same row. The winner is the player who takes the last coin.

Rita and Sam play NIM. Rita goes first. She removes 2 coins from the top row.	
Next, Sam removes all 3 coins from the bottom row.	
Then, Rita removes 2 coins from the middle row.	
Sam removes 2 coins from the top row.	

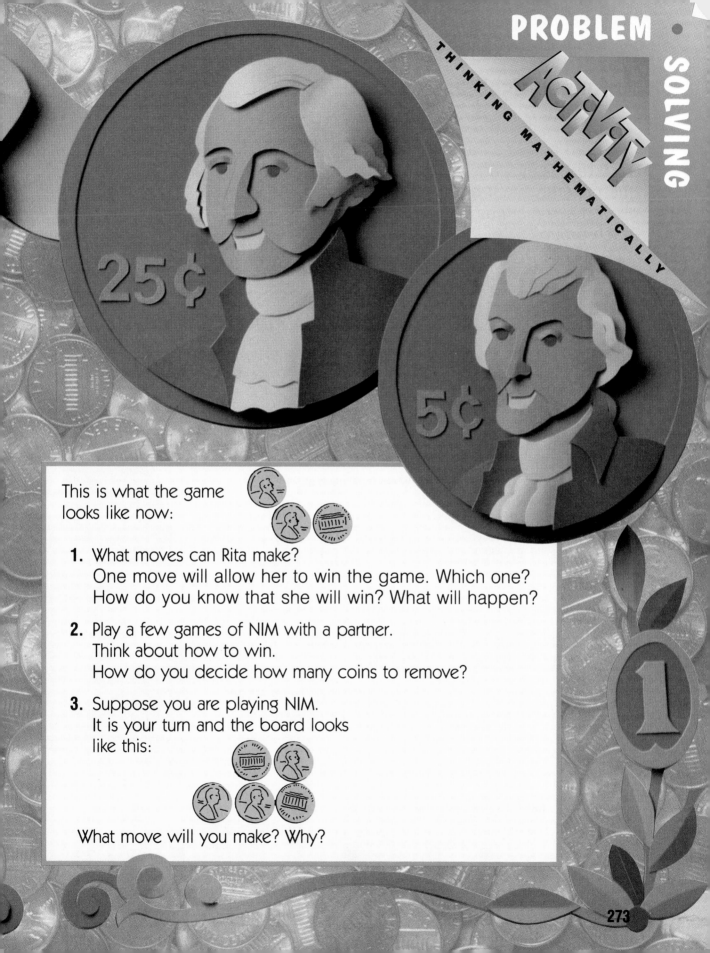

This is what the game looks like now:

1. What moves can Rita make?
   One move will allow her to win the game. Which one?
   How do you know that she will win? What will happen?

2. Play a few games of NIM with a partner.
   Think about how to win.
   How do you decide how many coins to remove?

3. Suppose you are playing NIM.
   It is your turn and the board looks
   like this:

   What move will you make? Why?

273

Informal Algebra: Fact Families

A. Stan and Lee have 36 animal pictures. They want to separate the pictures into 4 equal groups. How many pictures will be in each group?

Stan says he can divide to find the answer. He thinks:

$36 \div 4 =$ ▦

Lee says she can multiply to find the answer. She thinks:

▦ $\times 4 = 36$

1. Write the division sentence.

2. Write the multiplication sentence.

3. How many pictures are in each group?

B. Number sentences that use the same numbers are related. They belong to the same fact family.

4. *What if* Stan and Lee want to put 40 animal pictures into 5 equal groups? How many pictures will be in each group? Write the fact family.

C. Some fact families are smaller than others.

5. Write the fact family for 4, 4, and 16. Write the fact family for 3, 3, and 9.

6. How are these fact families different from other fact families you have written? Why?

TRY OUT Complete the fact families.

7. $30 \div$ ▦ $= 6$
　　▦ $\times 6 = 30$
　　$30 \div 6 =$ ▦
　　▦ $\times 5 = 30$

8. $4 \times$ ▦ $= 36$
　　$36 \div 4 =$ ▦
　　$9 \times$ ▦ $= 36$
　　$36 \div 9 =$ ▦

9. $72 \div$ ▦ $= 9$
　　▦ $\times 9 = 72$
　　▦ $\times 8 = 72$
　　▦ $\div 9 = 8$

PRACTICE

Find the missing number.

10. $4 \times \underline{\blacksquare} = 16$ **11.** $18 \div \underline{\blacksquare} = 9$ **12.** $45 \div \underline{\blacksquare} = 9$

13. $49 \div 7 = \underline{\blacksquare}$ **14.** $\underline{\blacksquare} \div 5 = 4$ **15.** $3 \times \underline{\blacksquare} = 21$

16. $24 \div 3 = \underline{\blacksquare}$ **17.** $15 \div \underline{\blacksquare} = 3$ **18.** $8 \times \underline{\blacksquare} = 32$

19. $18 \div \underline{\blacksquare} = 3$ **20.** $\underline{\blacksquare} \times 7 = 35$ **21.** $10 \div 5 = \underline{\blacksquare}$

Complete the fact family.

22. 3, 7, 21

$\underline{\blacksquare} \times 3 = 21$
$\underline{\blacksquare} \times 7 = 21$
$21 \div \underline{\blacksquare} = 3$
$21 \div \underline{\blacksquare} = 7$

23. 2, 8, 16

$2 \times \underline{\blacksquare} = 16$
$8 \times \underline{\blacksquare} = 16$
$16 \div 8 = \underline{\blacksquare}$
$16 \div 2 = \underline{\blacksquare}$

24. 5, 7, 35

$5 \times \underline{\blacksquare} = 35$
$7 \times \underline{\blacksquare} = 35$
$35 \div \underline{\blacksquare} = 7$
$35 \div \underline{\blacksquare} = 5$

25. 6, 7, 42

$\underline{\blacksquare} \times 7 = 42$
$\underline{\blacksquare} \times 6 = 42$
$42 \div 7 = \underline{\blacksquare}$
$42 \div 6 = \underline{\blacksquare}$

26. 3, 3, 9

$\underline{\blacksquare} \times 3 = 9$
$\underline{\blacksquare} \div \underline{\blacksquare} = \underline{\blacksquare}$

27. $\underline{\blacksquare}, \underline{\blacksquare}, \underline{\blacksquare}$

$8 \times \underline{\blacksquare} = 64$
$\underline{\blacksquare} \div \underline{\blacksquare} = 8$

Mixed Applications

Solve. You may need to use the Databank on page 520.

28. Kim makes 9 animal puppets. She makes an equal number of birds, cats, and dogs. How many of each puppet does she make?

29. Ali wants to buy a T-shirt, a large poster, and a key ring at the Gift Shop. Can she buy these things for $20.00?

Mixed Review

Compare. Write $>$, $<$, or $=$.

30. $4 + 6 \bullet 15 - 4$ **31.** $100 \text{ cm} \bullet 1 \text{ m}$ **32.** $9 \text{ kg} \bullet 9 \text{ g}$

33. $\$7.50 \bullet \$0.75$ **34.** $2{,}005 \bullet 2{,}050$ **35.** $3 \times 4 \bullet 2 \times 6$

Dividing by 6 and 7

Holly has 12 pet birds and 6 cages. She puts an equal number of birds into each cage. How many birds does Holly put into each cage?

How many 6s are in 12?

Think: $\underline{\blacksquare} \times 6 = 12$
$2 \times 6 = 12$

$$12 \div 6 = 2 \quad \text{or} \quad 6\overline{)12}^{\,2}$$

Holly puts 2 birds in each cage.

1. Write the related division sentence.

2. Complete the fact family for 2, 6, and 12.

3. ***What if*** Holly has 14 birds and wants to put 2 birds in each of a number of cages? How many cages does she need? Write the fact family.

TRY OUT Write the letter of the correct answer.

4. $6\overline{)54}$ **a.** 4   **b.** 5   **c.** 9   **d.** 60

5. $7\overline{)56}$ **a.** 5   **b.** 6   **c.** 7   **d.** 8

6. $24 \div 6 = \underline{\blacksquare}$ **a.** 3   **b.** 4   **c.** 18   **d.** 30

7. $35 \div 7 = \underline{\blacksquare}$ **a.** 5   **b.** 6   **c.** 28   **d.** 42

PRACTICE

Divide.

8. $6\overline{)18}$ **9.** $7\overline{)28}$ **10.** $6\overline{)24}$ **11.** $7\overline{)14}$ **12.** $6\overline{)12}$

13. $7\overline{)21}$ **14.** $6\overline{)6}$ **15.** $7\overline{)49}$ **16.** $6\overline{)30}$ **17.** $7\overline{)35}$

18. $7 \div 7 = \blacksquare$ **19.** $0 \div 6 = \blacksquare$ **20.** $36 \div 6 = \blacksquare$

21. $12 \div 6 = \blacksquare$ **22.** $42 \div 7 = \blacksquare$ **23.** $48 \div 6 = \blacksquare$

24. Divide 6 by 6.   **25.** Divide 54 by 6.

26. How many 7s are in 56?   **27.** How many 7s are in 63?

Complete the table. Use the rule to complete.

28. Rule: Divide by 6.

0	6	12	18	24	30	36	42	48	54
■	■	■	■	■	■	■	■	■	■

29. Rule: Divide by 7.

0	7	14	21	28	35	42	49	56	63
■	■	■	■	■	■	■	■	■	■

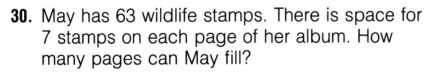

Solve.

30. May has 63 wildlife stamps. There is space for 7 stamps on each page of her album. How many pages can May fill?

31. *Write a problem* using division. Solve your problem. Then ask others to solve it.

Mixed Review

Find the answer. Which method did you use?

32. $400 + 10 + 7 = \blacksquare$ **33.** $318 - 289 = \blacksquare$

34. $9 \times 8 = \blacksquare$ **35.** $107 - 69 = \blacksquare$

36. $650 + 550 = \blacksquare$ **37.** $4 \times 7 \times 2 = \blacksquare$

Dividing by 8 and 9

A. There are 56 monkeys living in a forest. An equal number of monkeys sit in 8 different trees. How many monkeys sit in each tree?

Think: What is 56 divided by 8?

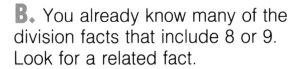

$$56 \div 8 = \underline{\blacksquare} \quad \text{or} \quad 8\overline{)56}$$

There are 7 monkeys sitting in each tree.

1. Write the division sentence.

2. Write the related division sentence.

3. Complete the fact family for 7, 8, and 56.

B. You already know many of the division facts that include 8 or 9. Look for a related fact.

4. ***What if*** there are 63 monkeys sitting in a number of trees? If 9 monkeys sit in each tree, how many trees have monkeys in them?

5. What is 54 divided by 9?

TRY OUT   Write the letter of the correct answer.

6. $8\overline{)24}$ **a.** 3   **b.** 8   **c.** 16   **d.** 32

7. $9\overline{)45}$ **a.** 4   **b.** 5   **c.** 36   **d.** 54

8. $64 \div 8 = \underline{\blacksquare}$ **a.** 72   **b.** 64   **c.** 56   **d.** 8

9. $81 \div 9 = \underline{\blacksquare}$ **a.** 90   **b.** 81   **c.** 9   **d.** 8

PRACTICE

Divide.

10. $8\overline{)16}$ **11.** $9\overline{)27}$ **12.** $8\overline{)8}$ **13.** $9\overline{)18}$ **14.** $8\overline{)24}$

15. $1\overline{)9}$ **16.** $8\overline{)32}$ **17.** $9\overline{)36}$ **18.** $8\overline{)56}$ **19.** $9\overline{)45}$

20. $48 \div 8$ ▪   **21.** $0 \div 9 =$ ▪   **22.** $64 \div 8 =$ ▪

23. $72 \div 9 =$ ▪   **24.** $8 \div 1 =$ ▪   **25.** $54 \div 6 =$ ▪

26. $0 \div 8 =$ ▪   **27.** $36 \div 9 =$ ▪   **28.** $56 \div 8 =$ ▪

29. What is 54 divided by 9?   **30.** What is 40 divided by 8?

31. Divide 9 by 9.   **32.** Divide 72 by 8.

Complete the table. Use the rule to complete.

33. Rule: Divide by 8.

0	8	16	24	32	40	48	56	64	72
▪	▪	▪	▪	▪	▪	▪	▪	▪	▪

34. Rule: Divide by 9.

0	9	18	27	36	45	54	63	72	81
▪	▪	▪	▪	▪	▪	▪	▪	▪	▪

Mixed Applications

35. Two hens have a total of 18 chicks. Both hens have the same number of chicks. How many chicks do each of the hens have?

36. Bev helps feed 9 baby seals at the zoo. She feeds each seal 5 fish. How many fish in all does she give to the baby seals?

Mixed Review

Find the answer. Which method did you use?

37. $325 - 125 =$ ▪   **38.** $5 \times$ ▪ $= 40$

39. $469 + 279 =$ ▪   **40.** ▪ $\times 6 = 36$

41. $42 \div$ ▪ $= 7$ **42.** $\$6.00 + \$6.00 =$ ▪

> MENTAL MATH
> CALCULATOR
> PAPER/PENCIL

Another Look at Division Facts

A. There are 56 legs in all. Each spider has 8 legs. How many spiders are there?

You divide to find the quotient.
56 ÷ 8 = ___

Think: Look for the missing factor.

    8 × ___ = 56

    8 × 7 = 56

So there are 7 spiders.

Solve. Look for the missing factor.

(■ × 9 = 45)   (■ × 6 = 54)   (■ × 7 = 35)

1. 45 ÷ 9 = ___   **2.** 54 ÷ 6 = ___   **3.** 35 ÷ 7 = ___

B. Use fact families to find the quotient.

4. 36 ÷ 9 = ___   **5.** 24 ÷ 8 = ___   **6.** 63 ÷ 7 = ___
    4 × 9 = 36   3 × 8 = 24   7 × 9 = 63
    9 × 4 = 36   8 × 3 = 24   9 × 7 = 63

7. 36 ÷ 4 = ___   **8.** 24 ÷ 3 = ___   **9.** 63 ÷ 9 = ___

TRY OUT   Choose the letter of the correct answer.

10. 6)42   **a.** 48   **b.** 36   **c.** 7   **d.** 6

11. 7)49   **a.** 56   **b.** 42   **c.** 9   **d.** 7

12. 27 ÷ 3 = ___   **a.** 3   **b.** 9   **c.** 24   **d.** 30

13. 63 ÷ 9 = ___   **a.** 6   **b.** 9   **c.** 7   **d.** 72

PRACTICE

Divide.

14. $3\overline{)9}$ **15.** $5\overline{)25}$ **16.** $7\overline{)14}$ **17.** $9\overline{)36}$ **18.** $2\overline{)12}$

19. $4\overline{)16}$ **20.** $6\overline{)24}$ **21.** $8\overline{)40}$ **22.** $7\overline{)56}$ **23.** $3\overline{)27}$

24. $1\overline{)4}$ **25.** $8\overline{)64}$ **26.** $8\overline{)48}$ **27.** $9\overline{)63}$ **28.** $7\overline{)7}$

29. $14 \div \blacksquare = 7$ **30.** $\blacksquare \div 7 = 3$ **31.** $36 \div \blacksquare = 6$

32. $\blacksquare \div 4 = 7$ **33.** $0 \div 5 = \blacksquare$ **34.** $\blacksquare \div 7 = 8$

35. $49 \div \blacksquare = 7$ **36.** $\blacksquare \div 9 = 9$ **37.** $45 \div 5 = \blacksquare$

38. $54 \div 6 = \blacksquare$ **39.** $10 \div 5 = \blacksquare$ **40.** $0 \div 1 = \blacksquare$

41. How many 4s are in 16? **42.** How many 7s are in 56?

43. How many 5s are in 45? **44.** How many 8s are in 24?

45. Divide 35 by 5. **46.** Divide 20 by 5.

47. Divide 32 by 8. **48.** Divide 42 by 6.

Mixed Applications

49. Joe has a total of 25 gerbils. There are 5 cages with an equal number of gerbils in each cage. How many gerbils are in each cage?

50. *Write a problem* using the information on page 520 in the Databank. Solve the problem. Then ask others to solve it.

CHALLENGE

You can use facts to name a number in different ways.

Example: $4 = 3 + 1 = 6 - 2 = 2 \times 2 = 8 \div 2$

Write four facts to rename the number. Compare your answer to those of others.

1. 7 **2.** 8 **3.** 9 **4.** 6

PROBLEM SOLVING

Strategy: Choosing the Operation

A. The pet store has 12 canaries. Sarah wants to put 4 canaries in each cage. How many cages does she need?

Sarah knows that she is separating the canaries into groups of the same size.

1. What can she do to find the number of cages she needs?

$$12 \div 4 = \underline{\blacksquare}$$

2. How many cages does she need?

B. Sarah feeds the parakeets. There are 9 cages with 7 parakeets in each cage. How many parakeets does she feed?

Sarah plans to combine 9 groups of parakeets. Each group has 7 parakeets.

3. What can Sarah do to find the total number of parakeets?

$$9 \times 7 = \underline{\blacksquare}$$

4. How many parakeets does she feed?

5. Which operation can you use when you separate a larger group into smaller groups of the same size?

6. Which operation can you use when you combine groups of the same size?

PRACTICE

Decide which operation to use to solve the problem. Use mental math, a calculator, or paper and pencil.

7. Jack has 21 carrots. He gives 3 carrots to each rabbit. How many rabbits does Jack feed?

8. There are 18 guppies and 6 goldfish in the fish tank. How many more guppies are there than goldfish?

9. Dog vitamins are sold in packages of 8. Cheri buys 4 packages. How many vitamin tablets does she buy?

10. Some dog food comes in 5-pound bags. How many 5-pound bags do you need to buy if you need 20 pounds of dog food?

11. Michael's dog ate 6 treats on Saturday and 12 treats on Sunday. How many treats did Michael's dog eat over the two days?

12. The pet store has 126 cans of cat food on its shelves. Eileen bought 28 cans. How many cans of cat food are left on the shelves?

Strategies and Skills Review

13. Larry scored a total of 35 points in 3 basketball games. He scored 12 in the first game and 9 in the second game. How many points did he score in the third game?

14. The basketball team practices 3 times every week. At the end of 9 weeks, how many times have they practiced?

15. Forty people play in a basketball tournament. There are 5 players on each team. How many teams played in the tournament?

16. ***Write a problem*** that can be solved by addition, subtraction, multiplication, or division. Solve your problem. Ask others to solve it.

ACTIVITY
Using Pictographs

Craig asked students in his school to vote for their favorite kinds of movies.

He uses these steps to show the data in a pictograph.

Step 1 List each kind of movie.

Step 2 Choose a picture to represent the number of votes.

Step 3 Draw pictures for each movie. Let ⊛ = 5 votes.

Step 4 Write the title above the graph.

Step 5 Write the number of votes each picture represents below the graph.

FAVORITE KINDS OF MOVIES

Kind of Movie	Number of Votes
Adventure	25
Animal	35
Comedy	40
Monster	15
Space	20

Kind of Movie	Number of Votes
Adventure	⊛ ⊛ ⊛ ⊛ ⊛
Animal	⊛ ⊛ ⊛ ⊛ ⊛ ⊛ ⊛
Comedy	⊛ ⊛ ⊛ ⊛ ⊛ ⊛ ⊛ ⊛
Monster	
Space	
Each ⊛ = 5 votes	

WORKING TOGETHER

1. Copy and complete the pictograph.

2. How do you find the number of pictures for each kind of movie?

3. What title did you write above the graph?

SHARING IDEAS

4. Why do pictographs use one picture to show many items?

5. Why is a pictograph a useful way to record data?

PRACTICE

Use this pictograph.

6. How many votes is each picture worth?

7. Which hobby is the most popular? the least popular?

8. How many more people like sewing than drawing?

9. How many people said that they liked drawing the best? sewing the best?

10. List the hobbies from the least favorite to most favorite.

11. *Write a problem* using the information in the pictograph. Solve the problem. Then ask others to solve it.

12. Use a table to make a pictograph. Ask students in your school about their favorite indoor games. Compare your pictographs with those of others.

FAVORITE KINDS OF HOBBIES

Kind of Hobby	Number of Votes
Making Models	𝍐 𝍐 𝍐 𝍐 𝍐 𝍐 𝍐
Collecting Coins	𝍐 𝍐
Drawing	𝍐 𝍐 𝍐 𝍐
Writing Stories	𝍐 𝍐 𝍐
Sewing	𝍐 𝍐 𝍐 𝍐 𝍐
Each 𝍐 = 4 votes	

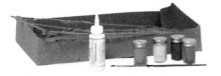

DECISION MAKING

COOPERATIVE LEARNING

Problem Solving: Setting Up an Aquarium

SITUATION

The students at Johnson School want to set up a class aquarium. They have a 20-gallon tank, air filter, and water heater.

PROBLEM

Which types of fish should they buy for their aquarium? How many of each should they buy?

DATA

Type of Fish	Care		How They Should Be Grouped	Adult Size	Comments
	Food	Aquarium Water Temperature			
Angelfish	All-Purpose Fish Food	75° to 86°F	1 or more	5 inches	Best kept in larger tanks
Black molly	All-Purpose Fish Food Vegetable Food	75° to 86°F	pair	2 inches	See food
Goldfish	Goldfish Food	65° to 75°F	1 or more	4 inches	Best not mixed with other fish
Guppy	All-Purpose Fish Food Vegetable Food	75°F	pair	2 inches	Special guppy food is available

Guide: Keep no more than 1 inch of fish for each gallon of water.

USING THE DATA

1. How many inches of fish will their tank hold?

How many adult-size fish will fit in the tank?

2. angelfish   **3.** goldfish   **4.** guppies   **5.** black mollies

Will the combination fit in the tank?

6. 2 black mollies
2 angelfish
6 guppies

7. 1 goldfish
4 guppies
2 angelfish

8. 4 guppies
2 angelfish

MAKING DECISIONS

9. What things should the students think about when deciding which fish to put in their tank?

10. *What if* they want to buy just one kind of food? Which fish should they put in their tank?

11. *What if* they would like as many fish as possible? Which types of fish should they choose? Why?

12. *What if* the fourth-grade students want to give the third graders 3 goldfish? How would the third-graders set up their aquarium now?

13. What types of fish would the third-graders choose to put in the tank? How many of each would you choose? Give reasons for your decisions.

14. *Write a list* of things you would think about before setting up an aquarium in your home.

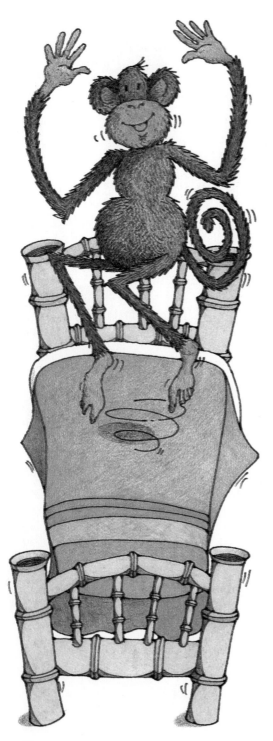

Math and Literature

Like "Three Blind Mice," many nursery rhymes use numbers. Here is another rhyme that uses numbers:

Five little monkeys jumping on the bed; one fell down and broke his head. Called the doctor and the doctor said, "No more monkeys jumping on the bed!"

Four little monkeys jumping on the bed; one fell down and broke his head. . . .

What if you want to explain the number pattern in the poem?

Think: The poem begins with 5 monkeys. Then there are 4 monkeys. If the pattern goes on, 1 less monkey will be in each verse of the poem.

ACTIVITIES

1. Think of other number rhymes you know, such as "One, Two, Buckle My Shoe." Talk about the patterns you find in them with your class.

2. Write some words that rhyme with the numbers from one to ten. For *one*, you might choose *fun*, *run*, or *sun*. Then write your own number rhyme.

Calculator: The Meaning of Division

You have 56 monster cards that you want to share among 8 friends. How many cards will you give to each?

You can divide to solve the problem. Find out how many 8s are in 56.

Recall that you can think of division by a number as *taking away* groups of that number.

First make a guess. How many groups of 8 are in 56? Then use your calculator. Use its constant feature to do repeated subtractions of 8.

Keep track of how many times you subtract.

$$\boxed{5}\ \boxed{6}\ \boxed{-}\ \boxed{8}\ \boxed{=}\ \boxed{=}\ \boxed{=}\ \boxed{=}\ \boxed{=}\ \boxed{=}\ \boxed{=}$$

You can subtract 8 from 56 seven times.

Count   1 2 3 4 5 6 7

So $56 \div 8 = 7$.

You will give each friend 7 cards.

USING THE CALCULATOR

Use repeated subtraction to find the quotient.

1. $72 \div 9 = $ ___
2. $63 \div 9 = $ ___
3. $81 \div 9 = $ ___
4. $54 \div 6 = $ ___
5. $70 \div 5 = $ ___
6. $90 \div 6 = $ ___
7. $84 \div 7 = $ ___
8. $78 \div 3 = $ ___
9. $65 \div 5 = $ ___
10. $64 \div 4 = $ ___
11. $51 \div 3 = $ ___
12. $48 \div 4 = $ ___
13. $99 \div 9 = $ ___
14. $85 \div 5 = $ ___

EXTRA PRACTICE

Relating Multiplication and Division, page 265 ....

Find the quotient.

1. $3\overline{)3}$ **2.** $1\overline{)8}$ **3.** $1\overline{)9}$ **4.** $8\overline{)8}$ **5.** $6\overline{)0}$

6. $10 \div 2 = \blacksquare$ **7.** $18 \div 1 = \blacksquare$ **8.** $8 \div 8 = \blacksquare$ **9.** $15 \div 3 = \blacksquare$

10. $0 \div 7 = \blacksquare$ **11.** $18 \div 9 = \blacksquare$ **12.** $20 \div 4 = \blacksquare$ **13.** $7 \div 7 = \blacksquare$

14. $6 \div 6 = \blacksquare$ **15.** $16 \div 4 = \blacksquare$ **16.** $12 \div 6 = \blacksquare$ **17.** $12 \div 2 = \blacksquare$

18. $9 \div 3 = \blacksquare$ **19.** $25 \div 5 = \blacksquare$ **20.** $14 \div 2 = \blacksquare$ **21.** $14 \div 7 = \blacksquare$

Dividing by 2 and 5, page 267 ....

Divide.

1. $2\overline{)6}$ **2.** $5\overline{)20}$ **3.** $2\overline{)12}$ **4.** $5\overline{)5}$ **5.** $2\overline{)18}$

6. $2\overline{)16}$ **7.** $5\overline{)15}$ **8.** $2\overline{)8}$ **9.** $5\overline{)10}$ **10.** $2\overline{)2}$

11. $5 \div 1 = \blacksquare$ **12.** $40 \div 5 = \blacksquare$ **13.** $0 \div 2 = \blacksquare$ **14.** $2 \div 1 = \blacksquare$

15. $20 \div 5 = \blacksquare$ **16.** $14 \div 2 = \blacksquare$ **17.** $35 \div 5 = \blacksquare$ **18.** $8 \div 2 = \blacksquare$

19. How many 2s are in 16?   **20.** Divide 45 by 5.

Dividing by 3 and 4, page 269 ....

Divide.

1. $4\overline{)12}$ **2.** $3\overline{)6}$ **3.** $4\overline{)16}$ **4.** $3\overline{)15}$ **5.** $4\overline{)20}$

6. $3\overline{)27}$ **7.** $4\overline{)28}$ **8.** $3\overline{)18}$ **9.** $3\overline{)24}$ **10.** $3\overline{)21}$

11. $21 \div 3 = \blacksquare$ **12.** $16 \div 4 = \blacksquare$ **13.** $20 \div 4 = \blacksquare$ **14.** $32 \div 4 = \blacksquare$

15. $24 \div 4 = \blacksquare$ **16.** $18 \div 3 = \blacksquare$ **17.** $24 \div 3 = \blacksquare$ **18.** $15 \div 3 = \blacksquare$

19. Divide 36 by 4.   **20.** Divide 30 by 3.

21. How many 3s are in 6?   **22.** How many 4s are in 20?

Problem Solving Strategy: Solving a Multistep Problem, page 271 ......

Make a plan. Then solve the problem.

1. José is unpacking 2 cartons of hair products. The carton of shampoo is packed in 8 rows with 5 bottles in each row. The hair spray is packed in 6 rows with 4 bottles in each row. How many hair products are there in the 2 cartons?

2. Bill has 4 red rocks and 6 blue rocks. He has 5 times as many green rocks as the total number of red and blue rocks. How many rocks does he have?

3. Sam collects model airplanes. He has 4 biplanes and 2 cargo planes. He has three times as many jets as the total number of biplanes and cargo planes. How many airplanes does Sam have all together?

4. Lee washes cars on weekends. She earns $3 for each car she washes. Last weekend she earned $24. This Saturday she washed 3 cars, and on Sunday she washed 4 cars. How much more did she earn last weekend than this weekend?

Fact Families, page 275 ....

Find the missing number.

1. $3 \times \blacksquare = 9$

2. $16 \div 4 = \blacksquare$

3. $24 \div 6 = \blacksquare$

4. $6 \times \blacksquare = 30$

5. $\blacksquare \div 4 = 7$

6. $5 \times \blacksquare = 15$

7. $\blacksquare \times 7 = 49$

8. $20 \div 5 = \blacksquare$

9. $6 \times \blacksquare = 36$

10. $32 \div 8 = \blacksquare$

11. $\blacksquare \div 5 = 7$

12. $7 \times \blacksquare \quad 21$

Complete the fact family.

13. 3, 8, 24
$\blacksquare \times 3 = 24$
$\blacksquare \times 8 = 24$
$24 \div \blacksquare = 3$
$24 \div \blacksquare = 8$

14. 2, 7, 14
$2 \times \blacksquare = 14$
$7 \times \blacksquare = 14$
$14 \div 2 = \blacksquare$
$14 \div 7 = \blacksquare$

15. 5, 8, 40
$5 \times \blacksquare = 40$
$8 \times \blacksquare = 40$
$40 \div \blacksquare = 5$
$40 \div \blacksquare = 8$

16. 5, 5, 25
$\blacksquare \times 5 = 25$
$\blacksquare \div \blacksquare = \blacksquare$

EXTRA PRACTICE

Dividing by 6 and 7, page 277

Divide.

1. $6\overline{)12}$ 2. $7\overline{)14}$ 3. $6\overline{)30}$ 4. $7\overline{)21}$ 5. $6\overline{)42}$

6. $7\overline{)28}$ 7. $6\overline{)36}$ 8. $7\overline{)35}$ 9. $6\overline{)24}$ 10. $7\overline{)63}$

11. $6 \div 6 =$ ___   12. $49 \div 7 =$ ___   13. $48 \div 6 =$ ___   14. $0 \div 6 =$ ___

15. $42 \div 7 =$ ___   16. $30 \div 6 =$ ___   17. $56 \div 7 =$ ___   18. $54 \div 6 =$ ___

19. Divide 7 by 7.   20. How many 7s are in 21?

Dividing by 8 and 9, page 279

Divide.

1. $8\overline{)24}$ 2. $9\overline{)9}$ 3. $8\overline{)16}$ 4. $9\overline{)27}$ 5. $8\overline{)64}$

6. $9\overline{)36}$ 7. $8\overline{)48}$ 8. $8\overline{)40}$ 9. $9\overline{)54}$ 10. $8\overline{)32}$

11. $9 \div 1 =$ ___   12. $81 \div 9 =$ ___   13. $48 \div 8 =$ ___   14. $18 \div 9 =$ ___

15. $8 \div 8 =$ ___   16. $72 \div 9 =$ ___   17. $56 \div 8 =$ ___   18. $63 \div 9 =$ ___

19. What is 45 divided by 9?   20. Divide 64 by 8.

Another Look at Division Facts, page 281

Divide.

1. $4\overline{)28}$ 2. $5\overline{)45}$ 3. $1\overline{)8}$ 4. $7\overline{)49}$ 5. $8\overline{)24}$

6. $6\overline{)6}$ 7. $4\overline{)32}$ 8. $9\overline{)54}$ 9. $2\overline{)18}$ 10. $5\overline{)30}$

11. $18 \div 9 =$ ___   12. $42 \div 7 =$ ___   13. $72 \div 8 =$ ___   14. $7 \div 7 =$ ___

15. $0 \div 3 =$ ___   16. $20 \div 5 =$ ___   17. $40 \div 5 =$ ___   18. $64 \div 8 =$ ___

19. How many 8s are in 56?   20. How many 4s are in 36?

21. Divide 40 by 5.   22. Divide 49 by 7.

EXTRA PRACTICE

Problem Solving Strategy: Choosing the Operation, page 283 ....

Decide which operation to use. Then solve the problem.

1. Birdseed comes in 2-pound bags. How many 2-pound bags do you buy if you need 8 pounds of birdseed?

2. There are 17 parrots and 4 hummingbirds waiting to be sold. How many more parrots are waiting to be sold than hummingbirds?

3. Lisa feeds the fish in the pet shop. There are 6 tanks with 9 fish in each. How many fish does she feed?

4. The pet store sold 12 turtles on Friday and 3 more on Saturday. How many turtles did the pet store sell?

5. The pet store has 21 boxes of dog treats. They sell 3 boxes of treats. How many boxes of dog treats remain?

6. Bart has 24 apples. He gives each of his horses 6 apples. How many horses does Bart feed?

Using Pictographs, page 285 ....

Use this pictograph to answer Problems 1–5.

1. How many votes is each book worth?

2. Which book is the most popular? the least popular?

3. How many more people said they liked adventure books than animal books?

4. How many people said they liked nature books the best? sports the best?

5. List the books from the least favorite to the most favorite.

FAVORITE KINDS OF BOOKS

Kind of Book	Number of Votes
Sports	⚊⚊⚊⚊⚊⚊
Adventure	⚊⚊⚊⚊⚊
Animal	⚊⚊
Nature	⚊
Fiction	⚊⚊⚊⚊
Each ⚊ = 6 votes	

PRACTICE *PLUS*

KEY SKILL: Division Facts (Use after page 277.)

Level A ....
Divide.

1. $6\overline{)12}$ **2.** $7\overline{)14}$ **3.** $6\overline{)24}$ **4.** $7\overline{)28}$ **5.** $6\overline{)18}$

6. $21 \div 7 = \blacksquare$ **7.** $36 \div 6 = \blacksquare$ **8.** $35 \div 7 = \blacksquare$

9. $42 \div 7 = \blacksquare$ **10.** $12 \div 6 = \blacksquare$ **11.** $20 \div 4 = \blacksquare$

12. Zack has 42 photos of wild animals. There is space for 7 photos on each page of his album. How many pages can Zack fill?

Level B ....
Divide.

13. $5\overline{)45}$ **14.** $6\overline{)0}$ **15.** $4\overline{)32}$ **16.** $6\overline{)30}$ **17.** $7\overline{)56}$

18. $54 \div 6 = \blacksquare$ **19.** $40 \div 5 = \blacksquare$ **20.** $42 \div 6 = \blacksquare$

21. $36 \div 4 = \blacksquare$ **22.** $48 \div 6 = \blacksquare$ **23.** $0 \div 7 = \blacksquare$

24. Kim has 54 hamsters and 6 cages. She puts an equal number of hamsters into each cage. How many hamsters does Kim put into each cage?

Level C ....
Divide.

25. $7\overline{)63}$ **26.** $6\overline{)54}$ **27.** $7\overline{)49}$ **28.** $6\overline{)48}$ **29.** $7\overline{)56}$

30. Divide 36 by 6.   **31.** Divide 35 by 7.

32. How many 7s are in 42?   **33.** How many 6s are in 30?

34. Margie has 63 cat toys and 7 bags. She puts an equal number of toys into each bag. How many toys does she put into each bag?

KEY SKILL: Another Look at Division Facts (Use after page 281.)

Level A

Divide.

1. $4\overline{)8}$　　　**2.** $3\overline{)3}$　　　**3.** $2\overline{)10}$　　　**4.** $1\overline{)5}$　　　**5.** $3\overline{)12}$

6. $5\overline{)15}$　　　**7.** $2\overline{)14}$　　　**8.** $3\overline{)6}$　　　**9.** $6\overline{)12}$　　　**10.** $1\overline{)2}$

11. $16 \div 8 =$ ▪　　　**12.** $0 \div 3 =$ ▪　　　**13.** $6 \div 6 =$ ▪

14. $9 \div 3 =$ ▪　　　**15.** $15 \div 3 =$ ▪　　　**16.** $18 \div 2 =$ ▪

17. A pet store has a total of 16 dogs for sale. There are 2 dogs in each cage. How many cages are there?

Level B

Divide.

18. $6\overline{)24}$　　　**19.** $3\overline{)21}$　　　**20.** $5\overline{)35}$　　　**21.** $5\overline{)10}$　　　**22.** $4\overline{)16}$

23. $4\overline{)20}$　　　**24.** $9\overline{)18}$　　　**25.** $7\overline{)28}$　　　**26.** $6\overline{)48}$　　　**27.** $4\overline{)36}$

28. $54 \div 9 =$ ▪　　　**29.** $49 \div 7 =$ ▪　　　**30.** $42 \div 6 =$ ▪

31. There are 64 legs in all. Each ladybug has 8 legs. How many ladybugs are there?

Level C

Divide.

32. $9\overline{)81}$　　　**33.** $7\overline{)63}$　　　**34.** $6\overline{)54}$　　　**35.** $8\overline{)72}$　　　**36.** $8\overline{)16}$

37. $5\overline{)40}$　　　**38.** $8\overline{)56}$　　　**39.** $5\overline{)25}$　　　**40.** $9\overline{)27}$　　　**41.** $8\overline{)64}$

42. $63 \div 9 =$ ▪　　　**43.** $21 \div 7 =$ ▪　　　**44.** $42 \div 7 =$ ▪

45. Al cleans 72 cages a day. He cleans 9 cages an hour. How many hours does he work in a day?

CHAPTER REVIEW/TEST

LANGUAGE AND MATHEMATICS

Complete the sentences. Use the words in the chart.

1. The ■ tells you the total number being divided.

2. A number divided by itself is equal to ■.

3. Zero divided by another number is equal to ■.

VOCABULARY
divisor
zero
one
dividend

CONCEPTS AND SKILLS

Divide.

4. $2\overline{)14}$　　　**5.** $3\overline{)15}$　　　**6.** $4\overline{)16}$　　　**7.** $5\overline{)45}$

8. $6\overline{)30}$　　　**9.** $7\overline{)56}$　　　**10.** $9\overline{)72}$　　　**11.** $9\overline{)36}$

12. $6 \div 6 =$ ■ 　　　　　　**13.** $32 \div 8 =$ ■

14. $63 \div 7 =$ ■ 　　　　　　**15.** $40 \div 5 =$ ■

Use the pictograph for questions 16 to 19.

16. What food is the most popular?

17. How many people liked apples the best?

18. How many more people liked pizza than burgers?

19. How many ⚘ would show 30 votes?

FAVORITE FOODS

Food	Votes
Pizza	⚘ ⚘ ⚘ ⚘ ⚘ ⚘
Nuts	⚘
Soup	⚘ ⚘
Burgers	⚘ ⚘ ⚘ ⚘
Apples	⚘ ⚘ ⚘
Each ⚘ = 6 votes	

Find the missing number.

20. $10 \div 5 =$ ■ 　　　**21.** $54 \div$ ■ $= 9$ 　　　**22.** $12 \div 4 =$ ■

　　$10 \div$ ■ $= 5$ 　　　　　$54 \div$ ■ $= 6$ 　　　　　$12 \div$ ■ $= 4$

　　$5 \times$ ■ $= 10$ 　　　　　■ $\times 9 = 54$ 　　　　　$4 \times$ ■ $= 12$

　　$2 \times$ ■ $= 10$ 　　　　　■ $\times 6 = 54$ 　　　　　$3 \times$ ■ $= 12$

Critical Thinking

Write true or false. Tell how you decided.

23. You can find the quotient to 0 ÷ 1,237 without dividing.

Mixed Applications

24. Jo has $7.90. Her mother gives her $2.50 more. Then she spends $3.00. How much money does she have left?

25. Ken picks 8 bags of apples each day for 4 days. Which operation can you use to find how many he picked in all? Find the number.

PERFORMANCE ASSESSMENT

Work with your group to solve this problem.

Imagine you are a scout leader planning a camping trip. There are 24 girls, 48 boys, and 24 adults. The smaller cabins hold 6 people and the larger ones hold 8. The boys and girls must be in separate cabins. There must be at least 1 adult in every cabin. How many small and large cabins will you reserve?

1. ***Think about:***
   - using different methods to solve the problem
   - there may be more than 1 correct answer

2. Compare your answer with others. Write a paragraph telling how you solved the problem.

CUMULATIVE REVIEW

Choose the letter of the correct answer.

1. $9\overline{)81}$
- **a.** 5
- **b.** 6
- **c.** 9
- **d.** not given

2. What time will it be 18 minutes after 6:00?
- **a.** 5:22
- **b.** 6:00
- **c.** 6:18
- **d.** not given

3. $8 \times 8 =$ ___
- **a.** 0
- **b.** 16
- **c.** 46
- **d.** not given

4. $21 \div 7 =$ ___
- **a.** 3
- **b.** 14
- **c.** 28
- **d.** not given

5. $4 + 4 =$ ___ $\times 4$
- **a.** 0
- **b.** 2
- **c.** 8
- **d.** not given

6. Estimate: $8,711 - 3,099$
- **a.** 4,000
- **b.** 6,000
- **c.** 7,000
- **d.** 12,000

7. Which is the best estimate for the mass of a small shell?
- **a.** 15 kilograms
- **b.** 15 grams
- **c.** 15 liters
- **d.** not given

8. $6 \times$ ___ $= 0$
- **a.** 0
- **b.** 1
- **c.** 6
- **d.** not given

9. Which multiplication sentence goes with $24 \div 6 = 4$?
- **a.** $8 \times 3 = 24$
- **b.** $12 \times 2 = 24$
- **c.** $6 \times 4 = 24$
- **d.** not given

10. $565 - 485 =$ ___
- **a.** 20
- **b.** 80
- **c.** 180
- **d.** not given

11. Which is the best estimate for the capacity of a spoon?
- **a.** 5 milliliters
- **b.** 5 liters
- **c.** 5 grams
- **d.** not given

12. $8\overline{)56}$
- **a.** 5
- **b.** 6
- **c.** 8
- **d.** not given

13. $3 \times 7 =$ ___
- **a.** 4
- **b.** 10
- **c.** 21
- **d.** not given

14. Which multiplication sentence goes with $18 \div 2 = 9$?
- **a.** $9 \times 2 = 18$
- **b.** $6 \times 3 = 18$
- **c.** $18 \times 1 = 18$
- **d.** not given

EVEN AND ODD NUMBERS

Even numbers end in 0, 2, 4, 6, or 8.
Odd numbers end in 1, 3, 5, 7, or 9.

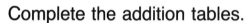

+	1	3	5
3			
5			
7			

+	2	4	6
4			
6			
8			

Complete the addition tables.

1. Is the sum of two even numbers even or odd?

2. Is the sum of two odd numbers even or odd?

3. Is the sum of an even number and an odd number even or odd? Make your own table to find out.

Use the addition tables and what you know about addition and subtraction to answer these questions.

4. Is the difference of two even numbers even or odd?

5. Is the difference of two odd numbers even or odd?

6. Is the difference of an even number and an odd number even or odd?

Find the products of even and odd numbers. Answer questions 7–10. Then complete the table to show your results.

7. If you multiply an even number by an even number, is the product even or odd?

8. If you multiply an odd number by an odd number, is the product even or odd?

9. If you multiply an even number by an odd number, is the product even or odd?

10. If you multiply an odd number by an even number, is the product even or odd?

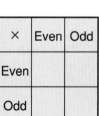

×	Even	Odd
Even		
Odd		

SPANISH PIECES

Hundreds of years ago in Spain, a silver coin worth 8 *reals* [ray-AHLS] was known as a "Spanish dollar." Spanish traders traveled to other parts of the world, bringing their 8-*real* coins with them. Soon, people began to call the coins "pieces of eight."

MATH *CONNECTION*: Statistics

FRACTIONS

EUROPE

Spain

# of EIGHT

But sometimes people needed smaller amounts
of money. The silver was soft enough to cut,
so they would cut an 8-*real* coin
into smaller parts known as *bits*.
A popular size was $\frac{1}{4}$ of the coin,
which was called *two bits*.

1 How many *reals*
is a Spanish
half-dollar worth?

2. In the United
States, what coin
is worth one-
fourth of a dollar?

3 If you had a silver
dollar, what would
you do to get a
smaller amount
of money?

The Meaning of Fractions

Mr. Grover wants to separate his garden into 4 equal parts. What can each part look like?

You can fold paper to make a model of Mr. Grover's garden.

WORKING TOGETHER

Step 1 Fold a piece of paper into 4 equal parts.

Step 2 Use scissors to cut along the folds. Place each part on top of the other to see if they are equal.

1. Compare your equal parts to those of others. How are they the same? How are they different?

Fractions name equal parts of a whole. Each equal part you made is **one-fourth** of the whole square.

2. Fold a piece of paper into 8 equal parts. Is there more than one way to do this? How?

3. What do you think each of the equal parts is named?

4. Try folding squares to show other fractions. Compare your fractions to those of others.

You can use counters to explore parts of sets.

Put out 5 counters and one cube.

1 of the 6 objects is a cube. **One-sixth** of the objects is a cube.

5. What fraction of the objects are counters?

6. Pick other amounts of cubes and counters. Tell what fraction of the set are cubes and what fraction are counters. Compare your results to those of others.

SHARING IDEAS

7. How is finding part of a whole like finding part of a set? How is it different?

8. What do you need to know to name a fraction?

ON YOUR OWN

Tell which of these figures show thirds. Tell why or why not.

9. 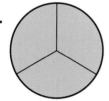 **10.** 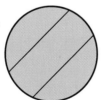 **11.** 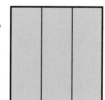 **12.**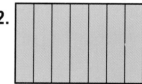

Solve. Use paper or counters.

13. Eight friends have a square garden plot to share equally. What fraction names the part each friend gets?

14. Mr. Grover has 5 tools he uses in his garden. Two of the tools are hoes. What fraction of the tools are hoes?

15. *Write a list* of things at home that are separated into fractions. Compare your list to those of others.

ACTIVITY

Parts of a Whole

Eva cuts the carrot cake she baked into 6 equal pieces. She decorates 5 of the pieces for her friends. Each friend gets a different decoration. What fraction of the cake did she decorate?

WORKING TOGETHER

You can use fraction strips to model the problem.

Step 1 Find the models that show a strip cut into 6 equal pieces. Place them with the labeled side down.

Step 2 Turn over pieces to show how many pieces Eva decorated.

Step 3 Complete to write the fraction.

number of pieces decorated → ■ ← numerator

total number of pieces → ■ ← denominator

1. How would you write this fraction in words?

2. What fraction of the cake did Eva keep?

3. What fraction of the cake did Eva bake?

4. What fraction of the cake has candles on it?

5. Work with a partner. One student writes a fraction. The other uses fraction strips to make a model of that fraction. Take turns. Record each fraction and draw a picture of its model.

Compare your fractions and models.

6. What does the numerator tell you? the denominator?

7. As you divide a whole into more and more parts, what happens to the size of the parts?

PRACTICE

Write the fraction for each part that is shaded.

8.

9.

10.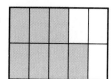

11.

Write the fraction.

12. two-thirds   **13.** three-fifths   **14.** four-sixths   **15.** three-tenths

Critical Thinking

Which of these pictures show fourths? Tell why or why not.

16.

17.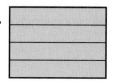

18.

19.

Mixed Application

Solve. Use fraction strips if needed.

20. Pat makes a cake with 5 layers. The top layer is banana nut. What fraction of the cake is banana nut?

21. Gary bakes 3 cakes. He puts 8 cherries on the top of each cake. How many cherries does Gary use?

ACTiViTy
Parts of a Set

Wally chose 8 flowers.
He has 3 red roses and
5 yellow daisies. What fraction
of the flowers are roses?

WORKING TOGETHER

You can use counters to make
a model of the problem.

Step 1 Put out 8 counters with
the yellow side up.

Step 2 Turn over counters to
show how many flowers are
red roses.

Step 3 Complete to write
the fraction.

number of red roses → ■ ← numerator
total number of flowers → ■ ← denominator

1. How would you write this fraction
   in words?

2. What fraction of the flowers are yellow?

3. **What if** all of the flowers have buds? What fraction
   of the flowers have buds?

4. What fraction of the flowers are tulips?

5. Select a handful of counters and toss them on a
   table. Write a fraction to name the part that is red.
   Write another fraction to name the part that is
   yellow. Record each fraction and draw a picture of
   its model.

Compare your fractions and models.

6. What does the numerator tell you?

7. What does the denominator tell you?

8. Look at the set of flowers in the problem. Do all of the parts of a set have to be exactly the same? Why or why not?

PRACTICE

Write the fraction for the parts that are red.

9.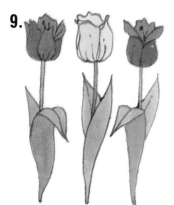

10.

11.

12. Five of the twelve shovels are red.

13. None of the seven rakes is red.

14. Four of the ten flowerpots are red.

15. All of the ten roses are red.

Mixed Applications

16. Ali planted 12 tulips. Ten of them came up. What fraction of Ali's tulips came up?

17. Lena picked 9 pink roses and 6 red roses. How many roses did she pick?

18. One of Aaron's 10 rosebushes has yellow flowers. What fraction of the rosebushes have yellow flowers?

19. Max planted 7 rows of bushes. He put 8 bushes in each row. How many bushes did he plant?

ACTIVITY Finding Parts of a Set

Peter bought 12 pizzas for the Green Thumb Club party. One-half of them had peppers. How many of the pizzas had peppers?

WORKING TOGETHER

1. Use counters to make a model of the pizzas. How many counters do you need? Why?

2. How many equal groups should you make?

3. How many counters are in 1 of the 2 equal groups? What is $\frac{1}{2}$ of 12? How many of the pizzas had peppers?

4. Record your results in a table like this.

5. Now use counters to find these parts and fill in the table.

   a. $\frac{1}{3}$ of 12   **b.** $\frac{1}{4}$ of 12   **c.** $\frac{1}{6}$ of 12

Part	Total Number in the Set	Number of Groups	Number in Each Group
$\frac{1}{2}$ of 12		2	■

SHARING IDEAS

6. Look at the table. How can you use division to find a part of a set when the numerator of the fraction is 1?

7. Write the division sentence for the numbers in your table.

8. Can you show $\frac{1}{5}$ of 12? Why or why not?

308 Lesson 8–4

PRACTICE

Find the part.

9. $\frac{1}{2}$ of 10

10. $\frac{1}{3}$ of 9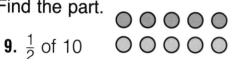

11. $\frac{1}{4}$ of 16   **12.** $\frac{1}{8}$ of 24   **13.** $\frac{1}{5}$ of 15   **14.** $\frac{1}{3}$ of 21

Critical Thinking

15. The club members spent $9.00 for their party snacks. This is one-fourth of the money they collected. How much money did they collect? Use counters to model the fractions.

Mixed Applications

Solve. Which method did you use?

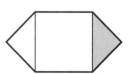

ESTIMATION
MENTAL MATH
CALCULATOR
PAPER/PENCIL

16. Hal has 21 balloons. He gives an equal number of balloons to 7 people. How many balloons does he give to each person?

17. Di buys 18 hats, 21 cups, and 11 candles for the party. About how many items does she buy?

18. There are 133 children at the movies. If 58 of them are boys, how many girls are at the movies?

19. Kit cuts the cake into 8 equal parts so that 8 people get an equal share. What fraction is each slice of cake?

ESTIMATION

Is the shaded part close to the fraction?

1. $\frac{1}{2}$    **2.** $\frac{1}{4}$ **3.** $\frac{2}{3}$ **4.** $\frac{1}{2}$

If your answer is no, draw a picture to show the correct part.

EXTRA PRACTICE, page 330

PROBLEM SOLVING

Strategy: Working Backward

Frank used straws, ice-cream sticks, and pipe cleaners to build a model house of the future. He used twice as many pipe cleaners as straws and 5 more sticks than pipe cleaners. He used 35 ice-cream sticks. How many straws did he use?

Frank plans to work backward to solve the problem. He starts with what he knows at the end and works back to the beginning.

He knows that he used 35 ice-cream sticks and that he used 5 more sticks than pipe cleaners.

1. What can he do to find the number of pipe cleaners he used? $35 - 5 = $ _____

2. How many pipe cleaners did he use?

Frank also knows that he used twice as many pipe cleaners as straws.

3. What can he do to find the number of straws he used? $30 \div 2 = $ _____

4. How many straws did he use?

5. How can you check your answer?

PRACTICE

Work backward to solve the problem. Use mental math, a calculator, or paper and pencil.

6. June cuts a piece of wood into 3 pieces of the same length. After she cuts off 2 feet from one of the pieces, she is left with a piece that is 5 feet long. What is the length of the piece of wood she started with?

7. Elaine bought some material to build a doll house. She paid $15.33 for wood, $2.47 for nails, and $3.20 for wood cement. She received $4 in change. How much did she give the clerk?

8. Tom uses nails, screws, and pegs to build a model house. He uses twice as many screws as pegs and 3 fewer nails than screws. He uses 15 nails. How many pegs does he use?

9. Steve gives 10 model buildings to David. This is twice as many as he gives to Sue. He keeps the last 4 models. How many models did Steve start with?

Strategies and Skills Review

10. A three-story mansion has 2 more windows on the second floor than on the first floor and twice as many windows on the second floor as on the third floor. There are 9 windows on the third floor. How many windows are there on the first floor?

11. There are 5 classrooms next to each other on one side of the school building. Grade 5 is to the left of Grade 4 and to the right of Grade 1. Grade 4 is between Grades 2 and 3. Grade 3 is between Grades 4 and 5. List the rooms in order from left to right.

12. Carlo lives on the 6th floor of his apartment building. Maria lives 2 floors above Carlo and Ben lives 3 floors below Maria. On which floor does Ben live?

13. **_Write a problem_** which can be solved by working backward. Solve your problem. Ask others to solve it.

EXTRA **PRACTICE**, page 331

MR. AND MRS. FIZZ'S QUIZZES

Visual Reasoning

A. Mr. Fizz is sewing a quilt.
It will have four large squares.
Two squares will be blue.
Two squares will be red.

How many different designs can Mr. Fizz make?
Here is one design:

Designs are the same if they can be matched by turning.
The three designs below all come from turning the first design.
They are all the same.

1. There is one other different design. What is it?

Mr. Fizz decides to make a larger quilt.
It will have six squares.
Three squares will be red.
Three squares will be blue.

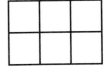

2. How many different designs can he make?
Show each design on graph paper.
Use crayons or colored markers.

B. Mrs. Fizz draws this shape. She wants to divide it into two equal pieces. Equal pieces have the same size *and* the same shape.

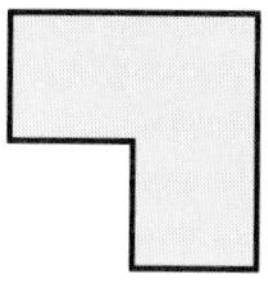

First, she tries dividing the shape like this:
But the two pieces are not equal.

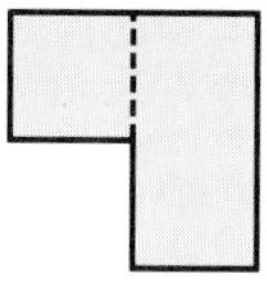

Next, she tries dividing it like this. Are the two shapes equal?

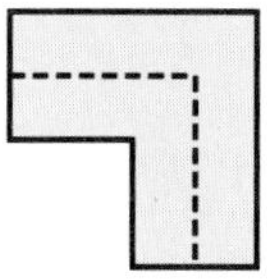

Finally, she finds the right line:

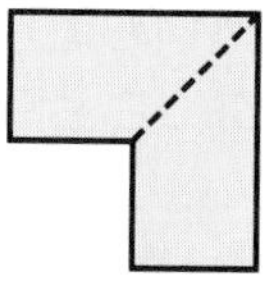

3. Can you see a way for Mrs. Fizz to divide this shape into three equal pieces? Draw a picture.

Mrs. Fizz draws another shape:

4. Copy the shape on a sheet of paper. Can you divide the shape into two equal pieces? three equal pieces? six equal pieces?

Equivalent Fractions

Different fractions can name the same amount.
Such fractions are called **equivalent fractions**.

WORKING TOGETHER

1. Find a fraction strip for $\frac{1}{2}$. Look for other fraction strips that show the same amount. When you find a match, write the fraction in a table.

2. Use fraction strips to find equivalent fractions for $\frac{1}{4}$ and $\frac{3}{4}$. Write the fractions in your table.

EQUIVALENT FRACTIONS
$\frac{1}{2}, \frac{2}{4}$

3. Use fraction strips to find equivalent fractions for $\frac{1}{3}$ and $\frac{2}{3}$. Write the fractions in your table.

4. Use your fraction strips to model other fractions and their equivalent fractions. Write the fractions in the table.

SHARING IDEAS

5. Look at the numerators and the denominators in each set of equivalent fractions. What patterns do you see?

6. Use the pattern you found to predict what equivalent fraction you could show for $\frac{1}{6}$. Use fraction strips to check.

7. Use the pattern to write two equivalent fractions for each.

   a. $\frac{1}{5}$ **b.** $\frac{1}{7}$ **c.** $\frac{1}{9}$

Solve. Use fraction strips.

8. Alec and Beth have bags of soil the same size. Alec used $\frac{1}{3}$ of his soil. Beth needs to use the same amount. How many sixths should she use?

9. Carlos poured $\frac{1}{2}$ of a can of water on his bean plants. He used the same amount on his tomato plants. How many fourths of a can did he use on his tomato plants?

10. **Write a list** of examples of equivalent fractions you see in school and at home. Compare your list with those of others. (*Hint:* Think of things that people measure.)

ACTIVITY

Finding Equivalent Fractions

Myra and Ned are filling window boxes in their flower shop. Myra planted red flowers in $\frac{1}{3}$ of her window box. Ned planted red flowers in $\frac{2}{6}$ of his window box. Did they use the same amount of space for red flowers?

Myra drew a picture to find out. $\frac{1}{3}$ and $\frac{2}{6}$ are **equivalent fractions**.

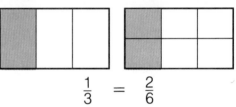

$$\frac{1}{3} = \frac{2}{6}$$

1. You can use pictures to show other equivalent fractions. Show $\frac{2}{3}$ and $\frac{4}{6}$. Are they equivalent fractions?

2. Copy and shade the diagrams to find their equivalent fractions.

a.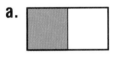

$$\frac{1}{2} = \frac{\blacksquare}{4}$$

b.

$$\frac{1}{2} = \frac{\blacksquare}{8}$$

c.

$$\frac{8}{10} = \frac{\blacksquare}{5}$$

SHARING IDEAS

3. Look at your diagrams and pairs of fractions. How do you know that you have shown equivalent fractions?

4. Look for patterns in this list of equivalent fractions. What is the next fraction in the pattern? Tell how you found the answer.

$$\frac{8}{16} = \frac{4}{8} = \frac{2}{4} = \frac{\blacksquare}{\blacksquare}$$

PRACTICE

Name the equivalent fraction.

5.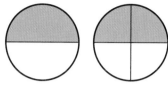

$$\frac{1}{2} = \frac{\blacksquare}{\blacksquare}$$

6.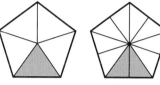

$$\frac{1}{5} = \frac{\blacksquare}{\blacksquare}$$

7.

$$\frac{2}{3} = \frac{\blacksquare}{\blacksquare}$$

8.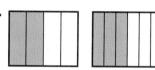

$$\frac{2}{4} = \frac{\blacksquare}{\blacksquare}$$

9.

$$\frac{3}{6} = \frac{\blacksquare}{\blacksquare}$$

10.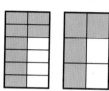

$$\frac{8}{12} = \frac{\blacksquare}{\blacksquare}$$

Mixed Applications

11. One-fourth of Su's garden has beans. Two-eighths has corn. Do the corn and the beans take up the same amount of space in the garden?

12. Van picked 24 ears of corn. He gave away $\frac{1}{4}$ of them. How many ears of corn did Van give away?

13. Ellen used 2 bags of soil for each window box. She filled 8 boxes. How many bags of soil did she use?

14. **Write a problem** using this information: Zack worked in his garden for $\frac{1}{2}$ hour; Rod worked for $\frac{2}{4}$ hour. Give your problem to others to solve.

Mixed Review

Solve. Which method did you use?

MENTAL MATH
CALCULATOR
PAPER/PENCIL

15. $7.02 - $4.58 = \underline{\blacksquare}$ **16.** $810 - 200 = \underline{\blacksquare}$

17. $9 \times 8 = \underline{\blacksquare}$ **18.** $697 + 986 = \underline{\blacksquare}$ **19.** $56 \div 8 = \underline{\blacksquare}$

EXTRA PRACTICE, page 331; **PRACTICE PLUS**, page 335

PROBLEM SOLVING

Strategy: Guess, Test, and Revise

The Van Hovens are planting 48 tulip bulbs for the Dutch Tulip Festival. They will plant bulbs in 10 rows. Some rows will have 6 bulbs each. The rest will have 4 bulbs each. How many rows should they plant with 6 bulbs? How many with 4 bulbs?

To solve the problem John Van Hoven plans to use the Guess, Test, and Revise strategy.

John first guesses that he should plant 5 rows with 6 bulbs each and 5 rows with 4 bulbs each. Then he tests his guess.

Guess

5 rows of 6 and
5 rows of 4

1. Is his guess correct? Why or why not?

2. Why should John lower his guess?

Test

$5 \times 6 = \quad 30$
$5 \times 4 = +20$
Total $= \quad 50$

John lowers his guess. He tries 4 rows with 6 bulbs each and 6 rows with 4 bulbs each.

Revised Guess

4 rows of 6 and
6 rows of 4

3. Is his guess correct? Why or why not?

Test

$4 \times 6 = $ ■
$6 \times 4 = $ ■
Total $= $ ■

4. ***What if*** they wanted to plant some rows with 3 bulbs each and the rest with 9 bulbs each? How many rows of each would they plant?

5. How did you make your guess? Did you have to revise it? Why or why not?

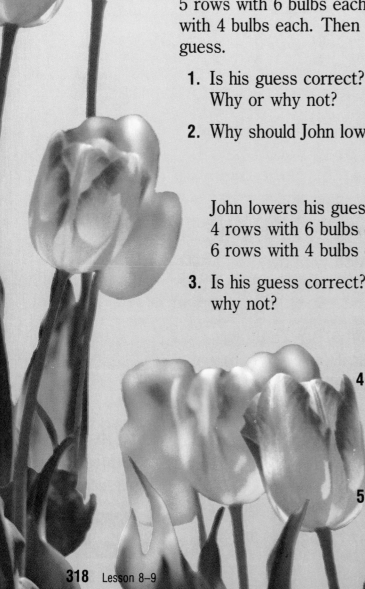

PRACTICE

Use the Guess, Test, and Revise strategy to solve the problem.
Use mental math, a calculator, or paper and pencil.

6. John bought some potting soil. He received 55 cents in change, all in nickels and dimes. There were 8 coins. How many coins were nickels and how many were dimes?

7. Amy Brinker needs 85 pounds of fertilizer. She buys 12 bags. Some are 5-pound bags. The rest are 10-pound bags. How many bags of each kind does she buy?

8. A pot filled with bulbs for the Holland town square weighs 25 pounds. The pot weighs 7 pounds more than all the bulbs. How much do the bulbs weigh?

9. Meg Van Hoven puts 66 tulips in 7 boxes. Some boxes have 6 red tulips, and the rest have 12 yellow tulips. How many boxes of each kind of tulip does she have?

Strategies and Skills Review

10. Mr. Jacobs planted tulip bulbs 5 inches apart in a row. The distance between the first and the last bulb in the row is 20 inches. How many bulbs did he plant in the row?

11. The perimeter of Amy's rectangular garden is 26 yards. The longer sides are 3 yards longer than the shorter sides. What is the length of a shorter side? of a longer side?

12. The picture on a bag of bulbs shows 8 tulips, each with 5 petals, and 10 tulips, each with 4 petals. How many tulips does the bag show?

13. *Write a problem* that can be solved using the Guess, Test, and Revise strategy. Solve the problem. Ask others to solve your problem.

ACTIVITY Comparing Fractions

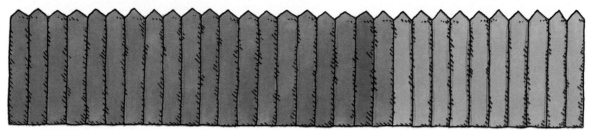

Lucia painted $\frac{1}{3}$ of the garden fence. Jan painted $\frac{2}{3}$ of the fence. Who painted more?

WORKING TOGETHER

Step 1 You can use fraction strips to compare fractions. Work with a partner. Model the fraction $\frac{1}{3}$. Have your partner model the fraction $\frac{2}{3}$.

Step 2 Compare your fraction model with your partner's fraction model.

1. Whose fraction is greater?

2. Who painted more of the fence?

3. Use >, <, or = to compare the two fractions. Write the sentences in a table.

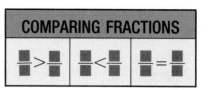

4. Work with your partner to model and compare these fractions. Complete the table.

    a. $\frac{3}{4}$ and $\frac{1}{4}$ **b.** $\frac{4}{6}$ and $\frac{5}{6}$ **c.** $\frac{7}{8}$ and $\frac{6}{8}$ **d.** $\frac{1}{2}$ and $\frac{1}{3}$ **e.** $\frac{6}{8}$ and $\frac{9}{12}$

SHARING IDEAS

5. When the denominators of two fractions are the same, which fraction is greater?

6. When the numerators of two fractions are the same, which fraction is greater?

PRACTICE

Compare. Write >, <, or =.

7.

$\frac{1}{4}$ ● $\frac{1}{3}$

8.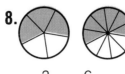

$\frac{3}{5}$ ● $\frac{6}{10}$

9.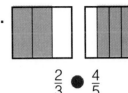

$\frac{2}{3}$ ● $\frac{4}{5}$

10.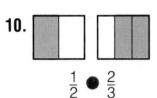

$\frac{1}{2}$ ● $\frac{2}{3}$

11.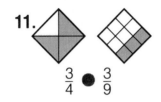

$\frac{3}{4}$ ● $\frac{3}{9}$

12.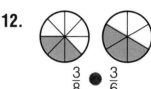

$\frac{3}{8}$ ● $\frac{3}{6}$

Use the number line to help with Exercises 13–16.

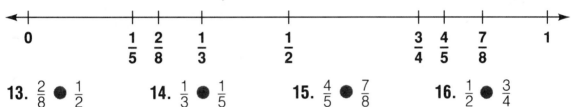

13. $\frac{2}{8}$ ● $\frac{1}{2}$ **14.** $\frac{1}{3}$ ● $\frac{1}{5}$ **15.** $\frac{4}{5}$ ● $\frac{7}{8}$ **16.** $\frac{1}{2}$ ● $\frac{3}{4}$

Mixed Applications

Solve. You may need to use the Databank on page 520.

17. Carl worked in the garden for $\frac{1}{2}$ hour. Nat worked for $\frac{3}{4}$ hour. Who worked more?

18. How high does a tomato plant grow in one week? in two weeks?

19. Lucia's bean seeds grew to $\frac{1}{2}$ inch in 2 weeks. How does this compare to the seeds the Garden Club planted?

20. *Write a problem* which compares information found in the Databank. Solve your problem. Then ask others to solve it.

Mixed Review

MENTAL MATH
CALCULATOR
PAPER/PENCIL

Find the answer. Which method did you use?

21. $7 \times 9 = $ ▬   **22.** $802 - 17 = $ ▬   **23.** $90 + 60 = $ ▬

Adding and Subtracting Fractions

Amy weeded $\frac{1}{4}$ of her garden in the morning. After lunch she weeded another $\frac{1}{4}$. Did she finish weeding the whole garden?

WORKING TOGETHER

You can use fraction strips to explore adding and subtracting fractions.

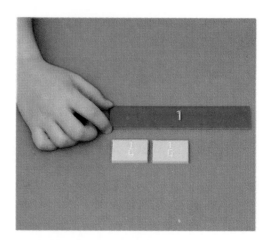

Step 1 Show $\frac{1}{4}$ with fraction strips. Then show another $\frac{1}{4}$ next to it.

Step 2 Compare them to a whole strip.

1. How many fourths are there in all? How do they compare to one whole?

2. Write the sentence to show how you added the two fractions.

3. Did Amy finish weeding her garden? How do you know?

Use fraction strips to show each of these sums.

4. $\frac{1}{6} + \frac{1}{6} = \blacksquare$ 5. $\frac{1}{4} + \frac{2}{4} = \blacksquare$ 6. $\frac{1}{8} + \frac{7}{8} = \blacksquare$

Step 3 Put together fraction strips to show $\frac{2}{4}$. Take away one of the strips.

7. How many fourths are left? Write sentences to show how you subtracted the fractions.

Use fraction strips to show these differences.

8. $\frac{2}{6} - \frac{1}{6} = \blacksquare$ 9. $\frac{3}{4} - \frac{1}{4} = \blacksquare$ 10. $\frac{6}{8} - \frac{4}{8} = \blacksquare$

SHARING IDEAS

11. Look at your addition sentences. What pattern do you see in the denominators? in the numerators?

12. Look at your subtraction sentences. What pattern do you see in the denominators? in the numerators?

ON YOUR OWN

Find the sum. Use the pattern or fraction strips.

13. $\frac{2}{4} + \frac{1}{4} = \frac{\blacksquare}{\blacksquare}$ **14.** $\frac{1}{6} + \frac{3}{6} = \frac{\blacksquare}{\blacksquare}$ **15.** $\frac{5}{8} + \frac{1}{8} = \frac{\blacksquare}{\blacksquare}$

Find the difference. Use the pattern or fraction strips.

16. $\frac{3}{4} - \frac{2}{4} = \frac{\blacksquare}{\blacksquare}$ **17.** $\frac{3}{6} - \frac{1}{6} = \frac{\blacksquare}{\blacksquare}$ **18.** $\frac{2}{8} - \frac{1}{8} = \frac{\blacksquare}{\blacksquare}$

Complete the table.

19. Rule: Add $\frac{1}{6}$.

$\frac{1}{6}$	$\frac{2}{6}$	$\frac{3}{6}$	$\frac{4}{6}$	$\frac{5}{6}$
$\frac{\blacksquare}{\blacksquare}$	$\frac{\blacksquare}{\blacksquare}$	$\frac{\blacksquare}{\blacksquare}$	$\frac{\blacksquare}{\blacksquare}$	$\frac{\blacksquare}{\blacksquare}$

20. Rule: Subtract $\frac{1}{8}$.

$\frac{5}{8}$	$\frac{4}{8}$	$\frac{3}{8}$	$\frac{2}{8}$	$\frac{1}{8}$
$\frac{\blacksquare}{\blacksquare}$	$\frac{\blacksquare}{\blacksquare}$	$\frac{\blacksquare}{\blacksquare}$	$\frac{\blacksquare}{\blacksquare}$	$\frac{\blacksquare}{\blacksquare}$

Solve. Use fraction strips or mental math. Tell whether you added or subtracted.

21. Ray had $\frac{7}{8}$ of a pizza. He and some friends ate $\frac{4}{8}$ of the pizza. How much of the pizza was left?

22. Nell jogged for $\frac{3}{4}$ hour on Saturday and $\frac{1}{4}$ hour on Sunday. How long did she jog on the weekend?

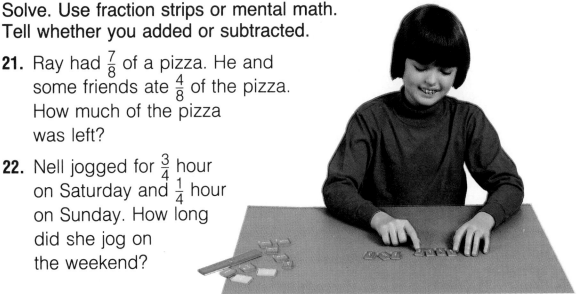

Activity

Using Pictographs

The members of Lisa's class are collecting containers for recycling. They have collected the containers shown in the table. They used these steps to show the data in a **pictograph**.

Step 1 List each item.

Step 2 Choose a picture.

Step 3 Draw pictures for each item. Let ⏝ = 10 containers.

Step 4 Write a title above the graph.

Step 5 Write what the picture means below the graph.

CONTAINERS COLLECTED

Type of Container	Number Collected
Aluminum	70
Large plastic	35
Small plastic	65
Large glass	50
Small glass	25

Container	Number Collected
Aluminum	⏝⏝⏝⏝⏝⏝⏝
Large plastic	⏝⏝⏝⏝
Small plastic	⏝⏝⏝⏝⏝⏝⏝
Large glass	
Small glass	

Each ⏝ = 10 containers

WORKING TOGETHER

1. What does one half of the picture, ⏝, mean?

2. Why are there 3 whole pictures and 1 half picture for the large plastic containers?

3. Complete the pictograph. Which container was collected the most? What does this tell you?

SHARING IDEAS

4. How does your pictograph compare to those of others?

5. What if you had used ⏝ to mean 5 containers? How would your graph be different?

6. How did you choose a picture to use in a pictograph?

PRACTICE

Use the table and pictograph to answer questions 7–10.

PAPER PRODUCTS COLLECTED

Type of Product	Amount Collected
Newspapers	65 kilograms
Magazines	55 kilograms
Paper bags	40 kilograms
Catalogs	85 kilograms

7. The members of Lisa's class collected paper products to recycle. Copy and complete the pictograph.

8. The students collected the greatest mass of which type of paper product? the least mass of which type?

PAPER PRODUCTS COLLECTED

Product	Amount Collected
Newspapers	🗞🗞🗞🗞🗞🗞🗞
Magazines	🗞🗞🗞🗞🗞🗞
Paper bags	
Catalogs	

Each  = 10 kilograms

9. The students helped to make a park in the former landfill. Use the table to make a pictograph to show the types of plants that were used. Compare your graph to those of others.

PLANTS IN NEW TOWN PARK

Type of Plant	Number Used
Rosebush	80
Daisies	75
Maple tree	45
Oak tree	35
Pine tree	30

10. **Make a tally** list of the cartons, bottles, and other containers your family uses in one month. Make a pictograph to show the results.

EXTRA PRACTICE, page 333

DECISION MAKING

Problem Solving: Planning a Garden

SITUATION

The Armstrongs want to plan a garden for their backyard. They can plant beans, cucumbers, peas, and eggplant. The garden is 3 feet long and 2 feet wide.

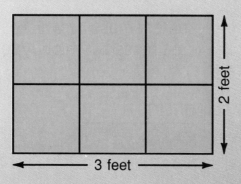

2 feet

3 feet

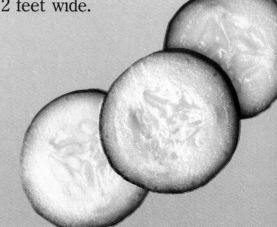

PROBLEM

What should they plant in their garden?

DATA

← 1 foot →	← 1 foot →	← 1 foot →	← 1 foot →

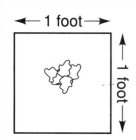

1 square foot

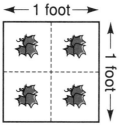

1 square foot

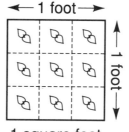

1 square foot

1 square foot

Eggplants	Cucumbers	Beans	Peas
• grow from seedlings	• grow from seeds	• grow from seeds	• grow from seeds
• 12 weeks to harvest	• 9 weeks to harvest	• 9 weeks to harvest	• 10 weeks to harvest

USING THE DATA

1. Which plants need the most space in the garden? the least space?

2. Which plants take the most time to grow to harvest? the least time?

3. How many pea plants can fit in 1 square foot of the garden?

4. How many bean plants can fit in one-third of the garden?

5. One eggplant will take up what fraction of the garden?

6. How many cucumber plants can fit in one-half of the garden?

MAKING DECISIONS

7. What should you think about when planning a garden? Make a list.

8. Is it a good idea to grow only one crop in a small garden? Why or why not? Which crop would you choose? Why?

9. **What if** the Armstrongs decide to plant all four crops in their garden? How could they divide the space?

10. What vegetables would you plant in the garden? Why?

11. **Write a list** of the vegetables you would plant in your garden. Then discuss the things you need to consider before planting your garden.

Math and Music

Do you know the five groups of instruments that make up most music groups?

Guitars and violins are **stringed** instruments. Saxophones and flutes are **woodwinds.** Drums are **percussion** instruments. Tubas and trumpets are **brass** instruments. Pianos and organs are **keyboard** instruments.

What if a band has 2 guitar players, 1 flute player, 1 piano player, and 1 drummer? What fraction of the band plays a percussion instrument?

Think: There are 5 players in the band. One of the 5 plays drums.

So $\frac{1}{5}$ of the band plays a percussion instrument.

ACTIVITIES

1. How many members play in your favorite musical group? What fraction of the instruments in the group are stringed, wind, keyboard, and percussion?

2. Make up your own musical group and draw a picture of it. How many players are in your group? What instruments do they play? Give your group a name and make some music of your own!

Computer: Patterns

The pattern below is formed by using the same shape in different positions.

1 2 3 4

The part of the pattern that repeats is called the rule.

1. What is the rule for this pattern?

2. What is the number of the shape that comes next in the pattern?

You can use a computer to explore patterns.

AT THE COMPUTER

Run the computer program called PATTERN3. Work with a partner.

3. Have the computer make a pattern. Choose the number of the shape that will complete the pattern.

4. What is the rule for this pattern? Describe the pattern to your partner.

5. Complete several more patterns and give their rules.

6. Now make your own patterns. Think of a rule for a pattern that uses the shapes on the screen. Enter the rule. Your partner completes the pattern and gives the rule. Take turns.

7. Make a pattern in which every third shape is the same. Have your partner complete the pattern and give the rule.

8. Why is a computer helpful in exploring patterns?

EXTRA PRACTICE

Parts of a Whole, page 305

Write the fraction for the part that is red.

1.
2.
3.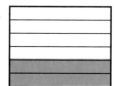
4.

Write the fraction.

5. one-third

6. three-tenths

7. four-sixths

8. two-fifths

9. six-eighths

10. three-fourths

Parts of a Set, page 307

Write the fraction for the parts that are red.

1.
2.
3.

Write the fraction.

4. Six of the 7 wagons are red.

5. Four of the 9 roses are yellow.

6. Three of the 8 trees are aspen.

7. None of the 6 roses are yellow.

8. All of the 10 lilacs are purple.

9. One of the 10 lilacs have buds.

Finding Parts of a Set, page 309

Find the part.

1. $\frac{1}{2}$ of 12

2. $\frac{1}{4}$ of 8

3. $\frac{1}{3}$ of 18

4. $\frac{1}{5}$ of 20

5. $\frac{1}{8}$ of 32

6. $\frac{1}{2}$ of 14

7. $\frac{1}{3}$ of 21

8. $\frac{1}{5}$ of 40

9. $\frac{1}{6}$ of 36

10. $\frac{1}{10}$ of 30

11. $\frac{1}{4}$ of 20

12. $\frac{1}{8}$ of 16

EXTRA PRACTICE

Problem Solving Strategy: Working Backward, page 311.....................

Work backward to solve the problem.

1. Sam buys items to make banana bread. He pays $2 for nuts. He pays twice as much for flour as he does for nuts. He pays $1 less for the bananas than for the nuts. He gets $3 change. How much does he give the cashier?

2. Charla wants to build a model of the Eiffel Tower. She uses twice as many screws as sticks of wood and 16 fewer nails than screws. She uses 34 nails. How many sticks of wood will she use?

3. Wanda has 36 Cincinnati Reds baseball cards. She found 4 more cards under her book. She now has 5 times the number of cards she wants to trade. How many cards does she want to trade?

4. Andy cuts a piece of fabric into 4 pieces of the same length. After he cuts off 3 feet from one of the pieces, he is left with a piece that is 2 feet long. What is the length of the piece of fabric he started with?

Finding Equivalent Fractions, page 317.....................................

Write the equivalent fraction.

1.

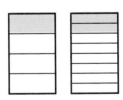

$\frac{1}{4} = \frac{\blacksquare}{\blacksquare}$

2.

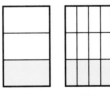

$\frac{1}{3} = \frac{\blacksquare}{\blacksquare}$

3.

$\frac{3}{6} = \frac{\blacksquare}{\blacksquare}$

4.

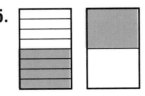

$\frac{1}{2} = \frac{\blacksquare}{\blacksquare}$

5.

$\frac{4}{8} = \frac{\blacksquare}{\blacksquare}$

6.

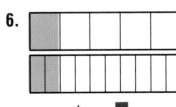

$\frac{1}{5} = \frac{\blacksquare}{\blacksquare}$

EXTRA PRACTICE

Guess, test, and revise to solve the problem.

1. April went to the flower shop to buy some daisies. She received 85¢ in change, all nickels and dimes. She received 10 coins in all. How many were nickels and how many were dimes?

2. Todd needs 65 pounds of potting soil. He buys 8 bags. Some are 5-pound bags and the rest are 10-pound bags. How many bags of each does he buy?

3. Peg has 51 tomato plants. She will plant them in 9 rows. Some rows will have 3 plants in each. The rest of the rows will each have 6 plants. How many rows should she plant with 3 plants in each row? How many with 6 plants in each row?

4. Jimmy, Gary, and Bill make 11 posters for the school election. Each boy makes a different number of posters. Each boy makes fewer than 6 posters. How many posters does each boy make?

5. Jessica has 10 coins in her wallet. They add up to $.57. What are they?

6. Quentin has 5 coins in his pocket. They add up to $.26. What are they?

7. Mrs. Jenkins has 2 girls. The sum of their ages is 18. The product of their ages is 72. How old is each girl?

8. A book is open to two facing pages. The sum of the page numbers is 45. Neither number is above 25. What are the page numbers?

Comparing Fractions, page 321 ....

Compare. Write >, <, or =.

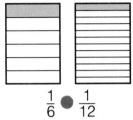 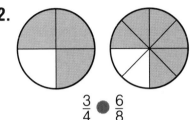 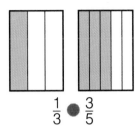

1. $\frac{1}{6} \bullet \frac{1}{12}$ **2.** $\frac{3}{4} \bullet \frac{6}{8}$ **3.** $\frac{1}{3} \bullet \frac{3}{5}$

Use the number line to help with Exercises 4–11.

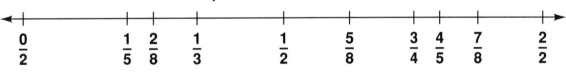

$\frac{0}{2}$ $\frac{1}{5}$ $\frac{2}{8}$ $\frac{1}{3}$ $\frac{1}{2}$ $\frac{5}{8}$ $\frac{3}{4}$ $\frac{4}{5}$ $\frac{7}{8}$ $\frac{2}{2}$

4. $\frac{2}{8} \bullet \frac{7}{8}$ **5.** $\frac{1}{3} \bullet \frac{1}{2}$ **6.** $\frac{4}{5} \bullet \frac{3}{4}$ **7.** $\frac{1}{3} \bullet \frac{1}{5}$

8. $\frac{1}{5} \bullet \frac{3}{4}$ **9.** $\frac{1}{3} \bullet \frac{7}{8}$ **10.** $\frac{3}{4} \bullet \frac{1}{2}$ **11.** $\frac{1}{2} \bullet \frac{2}{2}$

Using Pictographs, page 325 ....

Use the table and pictograph to answer Questions 1–5.

1. The members of Larry's class sold calendars to raise money for the new library. Copy and complete the pictograph.

2. How many calendars is each ☐ worth?

3. What does one half of the picture ☐ mean?

4. Which type of calendar sold the most? the least?

5. How many pictures are needed to show that 80 calendars were sold?

CALENDARS SOLD

Type of Calendar	Amount Sold
Nature	30
Kittens	75
Cartoons	25
Horses	40

CALENDARS SOLD

Type of Calendar	Amount Sold
Nature	☐☐☐
Kittens	☐☐☐☐☐☐☐◗
Cartoons	
Horses	
Each ☐ = 10 calendars	

Practice PLUS

KEY SKILL: Parts of a Set (Use after page 307.)

Level A ....

Write the fraction for the part that is red.

1. ○○
2. ○○○○
3. ○○○
4. ○○○ ○○
5. ○○○ ○○○
6. ○○○○ ○○○○

7. Pat bought 3 pairs of gloves. One of the 3 pairs is red. Write the fraction for the part that is red.

Level B ....

Write the fraction for the part that is red.

8. ○○ ○○
9. ○○○ ○○○
10. ○○○ ○○

11. Four of the 9 rakes are red.

12. Three of the 9 roses are red.

13. Eight of the 10 pairs of gloves are red.

14. James bought 7 rakes at the garden shop. Two of the 7 rakes are damaged. Write the fraction for the part that is damaged.

Level C ....

Write the fraction.

15. Two of the 9 roses are red.

16. Six of the 7 cars are red.

17. One of the 8 rocks is blue.

18. All 4 of the roses are red.

19. Janet has 12 roses. None of the roses are pink. Write the fraction for the part that is pink.

KEY SKILL: Finding Equivalent Fractions (Use after page 317.)

Level A

Name the equivalent fraction.

1.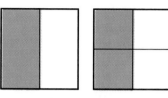

$\frac{1}{2} = \frac{\blacksquare}{\blacksquare}$

2.

$\frac{3}{5} = \frac{\blacksquare}{\blacksquare}$

3.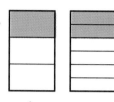

$\frac{1}{3} = \frac{\blacksquare}{\blacksquare}$

4. One-half of Ling's garden has corn. Two-sixths has lettuce. Do the corn and the lettuce take up the same amount of space?

Level B

Name the equivalent fraction.

5.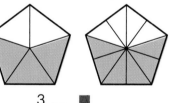

$\frac{3}{5} = \frac{\blacksquare}{\blacksquare}$

6.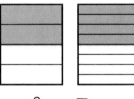

$\frac{2}{4} = \frac{\blacksquare}{\blacksquare}$

7.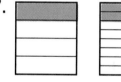

$\frac{1}{4} = \frac{\blacksquare}{\blacksquare}$

8. Three-sixths of Jason's garden has lilacs. One-half of the garden has roses. Do the lilacs and the roses take up the same amount of space?

Level C

Find the missing number.

9. $\frac{2}{3} = \frac{\blacksquare}{6}$

10. $\frac{1}{2} = \frac{\blacksquare}{10}$

11. $\frac{6}{8} = \frac{\blacksquare}{4}$

12. Jill plants roses in $\frac{8}{12}$ of her garden. Ed plants roses in $\frac{2}{3}$ of his garden. Do they use the same fractional part of their gardens?

CHAPTER REVIEW/TEST

LANGUAGE AND MATHEMATICS

Complete the sentences. Use the words in the chart.

1. In the fraction $\frac{2}{3}$, the 2 is the ___.

2. Four equal parts are ___.

3. In the fraction $\frac{3}{4}$, the 4 is the ___.

> **VOCABULARY**
> fourths
> denominator
> numerator
> thirds

CONCEPTS AND SKILLS

Write the fraction for the part that is shaded.

4.
5.
6.
7.

Write the fraction.   Find the part.

8. two-fifths

9. six-eighths

10. $\frac{1}{4}$ of 24

11. $\frac{1}{3}$ of 27

Name the equivalent fraction.

12.

$$\frac{1}{4} = \frac{\blacksquare}{\blacksquare}$$

13.

$$\frac{1}{2} = \frac{\blacksquare}{\blacksquare}$$

14.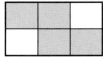

$$\frac{3}{5} = \frac{\blacksquare}{\blacksquare}$$

Compare. Use $>$, $<$, or $=$.

15. $\frac{5}{7}$ ● $\frac{3}{7}$

16. $\frac{1}{3}$ ● $\frac{1}{4}$

17. $\frac{1}{2}$ ● $\frac{4}{8}$

Use the pictograph to answer problems 18 to 20.

18. What does one half of the picture, ⚹, mean?

19. Which month had the most rainy days?

20. How many ⚹ would show 14?

Month	Number of Rainy Days
April	⚹ ⚹ ⚹
May	⚹ ⚹ ⚹ ⚹
June	⚹ ⚹ ⚹ ⚹ ⚹ ⚹
Each ⚹ = 2 rainy days	

Critical Thinking

Which of these pictures show thirds? Tell why or why not.

21.

22.

23.

Mixed Applications

24. Grove Farm has 4 times more apple trees than pear trees and 4 fewer plum trees than apple trees. If Grove Farm has 12 plum trees, how many pear trees does it have?

25. Peter received 65 cents in change, all in nickels and dimes. There were 8 coins. How many coins were nickels and how many were dimes?

PERFORMANCE ASSESSMENT

Work with your group to solve the problem.

There are 12 cars in a parking lot. $\frac{1}{4}$ of the cars are red, $\frac{1}{6}$ are blue, $\frac{1}{2}$ are white, and $\frac{1}{12}$ are green. Draw a picture that shows the numbers of cars of each color in the parking lot. Label the picture using the fractions.

1. **Think about:**
   - how to find the number of cars of each color
   - how to label the picture

2. Write 3 sentences about the fractions using your picture. Use "greater than" and "less than."

CUMULATIVE REVIEW

Choose the letter of the correct answer.

1. $\frac{1}{5}$ of 45
   a. 9   c. 7
   b. 8   d. not given

2. $54 \div 6 = \underline{\blacksquare}$
   a. 9   c. 7
   b. 8   d. not given

3. What time will it be 29 minutes after 3:40?
   a. 3:59   c. 4:19
   b. 3:61   d. not given

4. Compare: $\frac{3}{6} \bullet \frac{1}{2}$
   a. >   c. =
   b. <   d. not given

5. $4\overline{)16}$
   a. 5   c. 12
   b. 6   d. not given

6. Which is the best estimate to measure the mass of a dog?
   a. 10 kilograms   c. 10 grams
   b. 10 liters   d. not given

7. Compare: $\frac{1}{9} \bullet \frac{4}{9}$
   a. >   c. =
   b. <   d. not given

8. Which is the same as 7 + 7 + 7 + 7?
   a. 5 × 7   c. 7
   b. 4 × 7   d. not given

9. $\frac{1}{8}$ of 32
   a. 3   c. 5
   b. 4   d. not given

10. Which is the same as 3 + 3 + 3 + 3?
    a. 4 × 3   c. 12 × 1
    b. 6 × 2   d. not given

11. $9 \times 8 = \underline{\blacksquare}$
    a. 63   c. 72
    b. 64   d. not given

12. Compare: $\frac{1}{4} \bullet \frac{1}{5}$
    a. >   c. =
    b. <   d. not given

13. $86 - 24 = \underline{\blacksquare}$
    a. 63   c. 62
    b. 26   d. not given

14. $10 \times 0 = \underline{\blacksquare}$
    a. 10   c. 0
    b. 1   d. not given

VENN DIAGRAMS

You can use **Venn diagrams** to show how sets of items are related. This Venn diagram shows which musical instruments five students play.

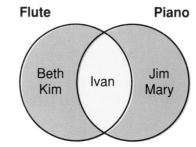

Flute **Piano**

Beth, Kim, and Ivan play the flute.
Jim, Mary, and Ivan play the piano.

1. Which student plays both the flute and the piano?

2. How does the diagram show this?

This Venn diagram shows students in Mr. Bach's class who joined musical groups.

3. How many students joined the chorus? List their names.

4. How many students joined the band? List their names.

5. How many students joined the orchestra? List their names.

6. Which student joined all three musical groups?

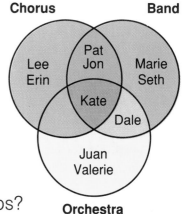

Chorus **Band**

Orchestra

7. Draw a Venn diagram to show which musical instruments these students play:

  a. Sam and Bruce play the drums.
  b. Sharon and Wayne play the trumpet.
  c. David and Maureen play the clarinet.
  d. Dick plays the clarinet and the drums.
  e. Jane plays the clarinet and the trumpet.
  f. Leon plays all three instruments.

People all over the world have used parts of their bodies as units of measure. Ancient Romans used the width of their thumbs to measure. They called this width the *uncia* [UHN-chee-uh]. The word inch comes from *uncia*. Twelve *unciae* [UHN-chee-ay] made one *pes* [pess], which was about as long as a man's foot.

A Roman *passus* [PASS-us] was two steps, or about 5 feet. In English, we say "pace." One thousand paces equaled one Roman mile.

Ancient Egyptians used the width of a person's finger as a measurement. They called it a *digit*. Four *digits* made a *palm*.

The Egyptians called the length from a person's elbow to finger tip a *cubit*. A *cubit* was equal to 6 *palms* or 24 *digits*.

1. Why do you think people used parts of the body to measure things? How would it be difficult measuring this way?

2. Which of the ancient measurements would you use to measure the length of a pencil? Which might be best for finding the length of your classroom?

ANCIENT
MEASUREMENT

ACTIVITY

Whole Numbers and Mixed Numbers

There are pictures of animals on 1 whole bulletin board and $\frac{3}{4}$ of another bulletin board.

You can write this amount as a **mixed number.**
Write: $1\frac{3}{4}$ **Read:** one and three-fourths

WORKING TOGETHER

1. How many fourths are there? What fraction can you write?

2. ***What if*** the last part of the bulletin board was filled? What fraction could you write? What whole number could you write?

3. Write a whole number or a mixed number.

a.

b.

4. Draw pictures to show the following numbers.

   a. $1\frac{7}{8}$ **b.** $3\frac{2}{5}$ **c.** $\frac{10}{5}$ **d.** $2\frac{2}{3}$ **e.** $\frac{8}{8}$

SHARING IDEAS

5. What two parts does a mixed number have?

6. How can you tell if a fraction is greater than 1?

7. How can you tell if a fraction is another name for a whole number?

PRACTICE

Write the whole number or the mixed number to tell
what part is shaded.

8.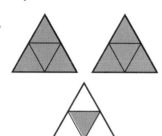

9.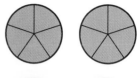

10.

11.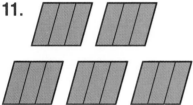

12.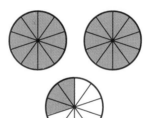

13.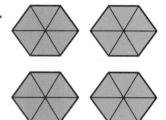

Write the mixed number.

14. seven and one-half

15. nine and four-fifths

16. three and seven-eighths

17. eight and six-tenths

Mixed Applications

Solve. Use models if necessary.

18. Lisa gave the elephants 3 whole bags of peanuts
and $\frac{1}{2}$ of another bag. Write the mixed number.

19. Ben used seven-eighths of a can of paint to
make a zoo sign. Write the fraction.

20. Hal has 49 photos of dogs and 38 photos of
cats. How many photos does he have in all?

21. Bev buys 4 rolls of film. There are 10
pictures on each roll. How many pictures
can Bev take?

EXTRA PRACTICE, page 368; **PRACTICE PLUS,** page 372

Comparing Mixed Numbers

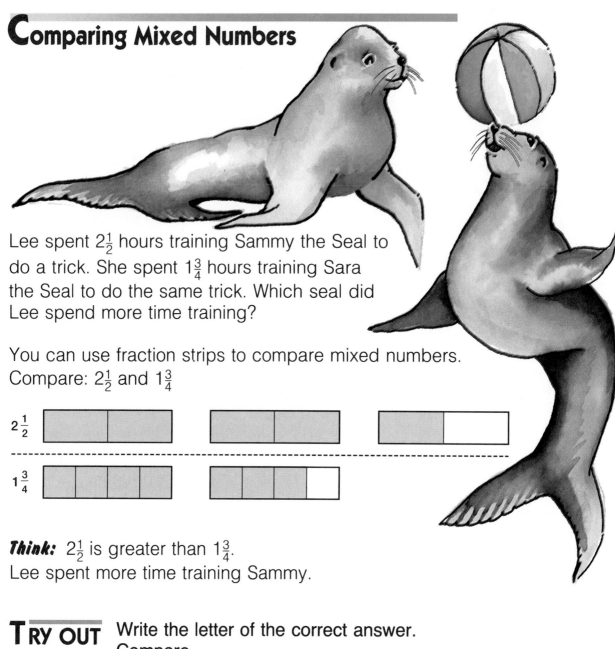

Lee spent $2\frac{1}{2}$ hours training Sammy the Seal to do a trick. She spent $1\frac{3}{4}$ hours training Sara the Seal to do the same trick. Which seal did Lee spend more time training?

You can use fraction strips to compare mixed numbers. Compare: $2\frac{1}{2}$ and $1\frac{3}{4}$

Think: $2\frac{1}{2}$ is greater than $1\frac{3}{4}$.
Lee spent more time training Sammy.

TRY OUT Write the letter of the correct answer.
Compare.

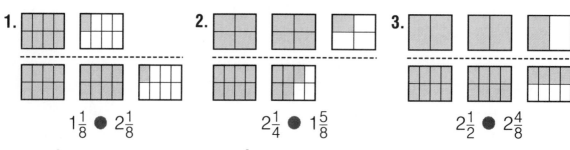

1. $1\frac{1}{8} \bullet 2\frac{1}{8}$

a. >   b. <   c. =

2. $2\frac{1}{4} \bullet 1\frac{5}{8}$

a. >   b. <   c. =

3. $2\frac{1}{2} \bullet 2\frac{4}{8}$

a. >   b. <   c. =

PRACTICE

Compare. Write $>$, $<$, or $=$.

4.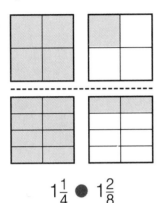

$1\frac{1}{4}$ ● $1\frac{2}{8}$

5.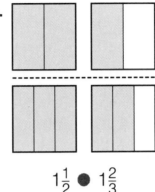

$1\frac{1}{2}$ ● $1\frac{2}{3}$

6.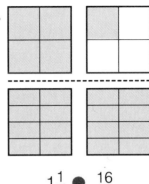

$1\frac{1}{4}$ ● $\frac{16}{8}$

7. $1\frac{1}{4}$ ● $2\frac{3}{4}$

8. 1 ● $2\frac{1}{3}$

9. 3 ● $\frac{2}{3}$

Critical Thinking

You are comparing two mixed numbers. Write *true* or *false.* If you write *false,* give an example to show why the statement is false.

10. The mixed number that has the greater fraction is always the greater number.

11. The mixed number that has the greater whole number is always the greater number.

12. If both mixed numbers have the same fraction, then the numbers are always equal.

Mixed Applications

13. Sammy the Seal swam for $1\frac{1}{4}$ hours. Sara the Seal swam for $\frac{3}{4}$ hour. Which seal spent more time swimming?

14. Lee had 6 fish to feed the seals. Sammy ate $\frac{1}{3}$ of the fish. How many fish did Sammy eat?

Mixed Numbers and Decimals **345**

ACTIVITY

Measuring Length

An **inch (in.)** is a customary unit of length. To measure to the nearest inch:

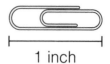

1 inch

Step 1 Line up the end of the object with the 0 mark of the ruler.

Step 2 Look at the right end of the object. Find the closest inch mark.

1. Find the length of the lizard to the nearest inch.

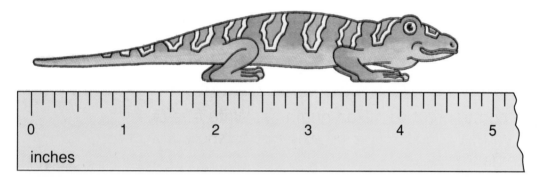

You can also measure length to the nearest **half inch ($\frac{1}{2}$ in.).**

2. What is the length of the lizard to the nearest half inch?

3. Work with a partner. Measure each other's arm length and hand span to the nearest inch. Then measure again to the nearest half inch.

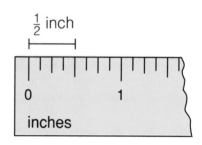

$\frac{1}{2}$ inch

SHARING IDEAS

4. Compare your two groups of measurements. When were they the same? Why?

5. Why would you want to measure something using a smaller unit? Make a list.

PRACTICE

Measure to the nearest inch.

6.

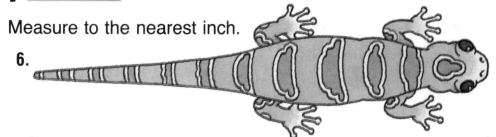

7.

Measure to the nearest half inch.

8.

9.

10. Which animal in Exercises 6–9 is the longest?
Which is the shortest?

Draw a line for each length.

11. 7 inches   **12.** 4 inches   **13.** $3\frac{1}{2}$ inches   **14.** $5\frac{1}{2}$ inches

Critical Thinking

15. ***What if*** you have a piece of paper that is 4 inches
long? How could you mark the inches on the piece
of paper without using a ruler?

Mixed Applications

16. Teri spent $1.50 for toys and
$2.75 for a book. How much
money did she spend in all?

17. Dan's lizard is $6\frac{1}{2}$ inches
long. Cal's is 5 inches long.
Whose lizard is longer?

ACTIVITY

Estimating Length: Customary Units

Foot (ft), yard (yd), and **mile (mi)**
are other customary units of length.

1 foot

A foot is about the length of your arm from elbow to fingertip.

A yard is about the width of
your classroom door.

← 1 yard →

A mile is about how far a person can walk in 30 minutes.

WORKING TOGETHER

1. Choose a unit of length.

2. Estimate and then measure
   each real object to the
   nearest unit you chose.

> 12 inches (in.) = 1 foot (ft)
> 3 feet = 1 yard (yd)
> 36 inches = 1 yard
> 1,760 yards = 1 mile (mi)
> 5,280 feet = 1 mile

a.

b.

c.

d.

e.
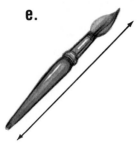

f.

g.

h.

3. For which things did you choose inches? feet? yards? Why?

4. For which units of measure were your estimates closest? Why do you think that happened?

Practice

Write the letter of the best estimate.

5. length of a football field
   a. 100 inches
   b. 100 yards
   c. 100 miles

6. length of a bicycle
   a. 5 inches
   b. 5 feet
   c. 5 yards

7. distance between two state capitals
   a. 100 feet
   b. 100 yards
   c. 100 miles

8. length of a paintbrush
   a. 9 inches
   b. 9 feet
   c. 9 yards

9. width of your bed
   a. 3 inches
   b. 3 feet
   c. 3 miles

Mixed Applications

Solve. You may need to use the Databank on page 521.

10. Which bird has the greater average length, the fish crow or the American crow?

11. *Write a problem* about comparing the length of birds. Ask others to solve it.

Mixed Review

Find the answer. Which method did you use?

MENTAL MATH
CALCULATOR
PAPER/PENCIL

12. $7 \times 5 = $ ___

13. $762 + 188 = $ ___

14. $4 + 9 + 6 = $ ___

15. $670 - 418 = $ ___

16. $30 \div 6 = $ ___

17. $250 - 30 = $ ___

ACTIVITY

Perimeter and Area

Dan and his grandfather are making a pen for their pet rabbit. To put wire fence around the pen, they must find the pen's perimeter. To build the pen floor they must find the pen's area.

Think: **Perimeter** is the distance around an object. **Area** is the number of square units it takes to cover the surface of something.

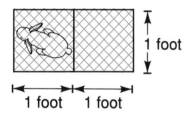

1 foot

1 foot   1 foot

WORKING TOGETHER

1. What is the perimeter of the pen?

2. How much wire is needed to fence in the pen's perimeter?

3. What is the area of the pen floor?

4. How much wood is needed to make the pen floor?

5. Estimate and then measure the perimeter and area of objects in your classroom. Make a table.

6. Use inch graph paper to draw different shapes that have an area of 8 square inches. Find the perimeter of each shape. What do you notice?

SHARING IDEAS

7. Why can you multiply to find the perimeter of a square?

8. Two rectangles have the same area. Must they have the same perimeter? Give two examples to support your answer.

PRACTICE

Find the perimeter and the area.
Each equals 1 square inch.

9.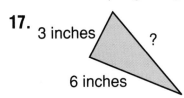

10.

11.

12.

13.

14.

15.

16.

Critical Thinking

Find the missing length.

17.
3 inches
6 inches
?

Perimeter: 16 inches

18. 3 yards   3 yards
4 yards   4 yards
?

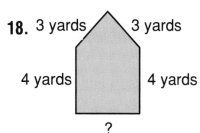

Perimeter: 18 yards

Solve.

19. The walls around the seal pool measure 12 yards, 15 yards, 12 yards, and 15 yards. What is the perimeter of the pool?

20. The area of the lamb's pen is 21 square yards. The area of the goat's pen is 28 square yards. Which pen has the greater area?

Mixed Review

Find the answer. Which method did you use?

**MENTAL MATH
CALCULATOR
PAPER/PENCIL**

21. $2 + 7 + 8 =$ ___

22. $400 - 168 =$ ___

23. $42 \div 7 =$ ___

24. $347 + 86 =$ ___

25. $6 \times 9 =$ ___

26. $\$1.98 + \$.75 =$ ___

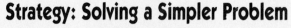
✓ UNDERSTAND
✓ PLAN
✓ TRY
CHECK
✓ EXTEND

Strategy: Solving a Simpler Problem

Jesse ate 530 calories for breakfast, 760 calories for lunch, and 1,150 calories for dinner. How many calories did he eat in all?

Oat Bran

Jesse cannot decide what he can do to solve the problem, so he plans to solve a simpler problem by using smaller numbers.

Jesse thinks: "If I had eaten 30 calories for breakfast, 40 calories for lunch, and 50 calories for dinner, I could add to solve the problem."

$$30 + 40 + 50 = 120$$

1. What can he do to solve the original problem?

$$530 + 760 + 1{,}150 = \underline{\blacksquare}$$

2. How many calories did he eat in all?

3. **What if** Jesse wants to know how many more calories he ate for dinner than for breakfast? Write a simpler problem by using smaller numbers. Then solve the original problem.

4. How can solving a simpler problem help you solve more difficult problems?

PRACTICE

Solve. Do a simpler problem first if you need to.
Use mental math, a calculator, or paper and pencil.

5. Hugh wants to eat 2,150 calories per day. He has eaten 1,275 calories for breakfast and lunch. How many calories does he need to eat for dinner?

6. Mrs. Hernandez ordered 305 apples for the school cafeteria. When the order came in, 76 apples were spoiled. How many apples can she serve?

7. The Organic Farm shipped 355 pounds of plums to one market, 590 pounds of plums to a second market, and 415 pounds of plums to a third market. How many pounds of plums were shipped in all?

8. One month a health-food store sold $134.37 worth of bran. The next month the store sold $162.14 worth. How much more money did the store collect in the second month?

Strategies and Skills Review

Solve. You may need to use the Databank on page 521.

9. Sally gave 7 carrot sticks to Maurice and divided the rest equally between Valerie and Margaret. Margaret then had 12 carrot sticks. How many carrot sticks did Sally have at first?

10. Mrs. Solo displays apples in a 6-row pattern. There are 3 apples in the first row, 6 apples in the second row, and 9 apples in the third row. How many apples do you think are in the next three rows?

11. The Sears started dinner at 6:15 P.M. What other information do you need in order to find out at what time they finished dinner?

12. Abby uses 1 cup of berries and 3 bananas to make fruit salad. How many bananas should she use to make twice as much fruit salad?

13. Heather has $5 to spend at the Plum Health Food Bar. Does she have enough money to buy a health salad and carrot juice?

14. **Write a problem.** Solve the problem. Ask others to solve your problem by first writing a simpler problem.

Mixed Numbers and Decimals **353**

CREATURE FEATURE

Visual Reasoning

A. Pretend you are a scientist looking at strange new creatures. These are all snords:

A B 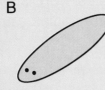 C

What features do the snords all have in common?

These creatures are not snords:

D E 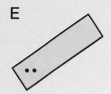 F

Compare the creatures in each group. What makes the creatures different?

Compare A and B with D and E. Look at the bodies. What is the difference?

The snords' bodies are curved. Now you know that snords have curved bodies.

Compare C with F. Both creatures have curved bodies. But F is not a snord. How can this be?

F does not have two eyes. Now you know that all snords have two eyes.

1. Which of the creatures below are snords? How do you know?

A   B   C   D   E   F

2. Draw four new snords on a sheet of paper.

B. Now make believe you have discovered another creature. These are crispids:

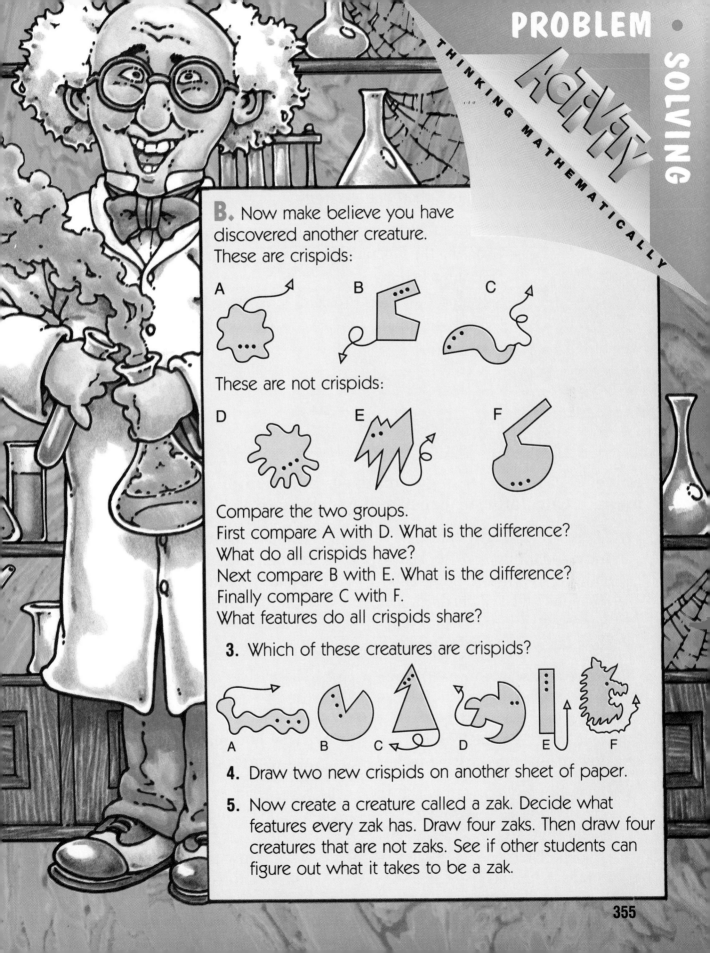

A   B   C

These are not crispids:

D   E   F

Compare the two groups.
First compare A with D. What is the difference?
What do all crispids have?
Next compare B with E. What is the difference?
Finally compare C with F.
What features do all crispids share?

3. Which of these creatures are crispids?

A   B   C   D   E   F

4. Draw two new crispids on another sheet of paper.

5. Now create a creature called a zak. Decide what features every zak has. Draw four zaks. Then draw four creatures that are not zaks. See if other students can figure out what it takes to be a zak.

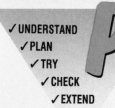

✓UNDERSTAND
✓PLAN
✓TRY
✓CHECK
✓EXTEND

PROBLEM SOLVING

Strategies Review

Use these problem-solving strategies to solve the problems. Remember that some problems can be solved using more than one strategy.

- Using Number Sense
- Choosing the Operation
- Drawing a Picture
- Solving a Two-Step Problem
- Using Estimation

- Conducting an Experiment
- Finding a Pattern
- Solving a Multistep Problem
- Working Backward
- Guess, Test, and Revise

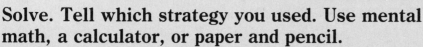

Solve. Tell which strategy you used. Use mental math, a calculator, or paper and pencil.

1. There are 240 seats in the zoo's auditorium. At the last showing of a movie on giraffes, 86 adults and 112 children were seated in the auditorium. How many seats were empty?

2. The zoo has 6 cages with 3 monkeys in each cage. There are also 15 monkeys who live in an open space. How many monkeys live in cages?

3. Mr. Watts wants to band trees in the zoo's rain forest. He cuts a long plastic strip into 8 pieces of the same length. How many cuts must he make?

4. The cashier at the zoo gives Kim $.75 in nickels, dimes, and quarters. If Kim receives 7 coins, how many nickels, dimes, and quarters does she have?

5. Drew has $50.00 with which to buy two nature books. The books cost $16.95 and $29.98. Does he have enough money to buy the books?

6. Kitty read 24 books about wildlife during her summer vacation. She read 3 books a week. How many weeks did it take her to read all the books?

7. Marie wants to buy a souvenir that costs $3.12 at the zoo's shop. She has $2.98. How much money does she need to borrow from her friend?

8. Erin wants to buy a zoo pennant at the gift shop. How much money does she need? $3? $30? $300?

9. The lion house has 3 jaguars and 4 cages with 2 lions in each cage. The rest of the animals are cougars. If there are 15 animals in the lion house, how many are cougars?

10. Donna gave twice as many animal cards to Millie as to Ellie. She gave David 6 fewer cards than she gave Millie. If David got 4 cards, how many cards did Donna start with?

11. The bears' cage has a climbing tower made up of 6 rows of rocks that are in a pattern. There are 2 rocks on the top, 5 rocks in the next row, and 8 rocks in the third row. How many rocks do you think are in the bottom three rows?

12. JoJo, the elephant, eats 8,000 pounds of hay in one month. JoJo has already eaten 6,275 pounds of hay this month. If the zoo buys another 2,100 pounds, will there be enough hay to feed JoJo for the rest of the month?

ACTIVITY **D**ecimals: Tenths and Hundredths

Four of the ten parking spaces are filled. You can name the part of the parking area that is filled in many ways.

WORKING TOGETHER

Step 1 Make a model of 1 whole parking area. Draw a 10-cm by 10-cm square on graph paper. Draw lines to show each parking space.

Step 2 Shade the square to show the parking spaces that are filled.

1. What fraction of the whole parking area is each parking space?
2. What fraction of the whole area is filled?

You can also name this part of the parking area as the **decimal** four tenths, or 0.4.

3. What fraction of the parking spaces are empty? What decimal can you write?

Ones		Tenths
0	.	4

↑_____decimal point

4. ***What if*** 25 out of 100 parking spaces were filled? Draw a picture on graph paper to show this. What fraction of the whole area would be filled?

You can name this part as the decimal 25 hundredths, or 0.25.

Ones		Tenths	Hundredths
0	.	2	5

5. *What if* 9 out of 100 parking spaces were filled? Draw a picture to show this. What fraction of the whole area would be filled? What decimal could you write?

Ones		Tenths	Hundredths
0	.	0	9

6. Write a fraction and a decimal. Draw a diagram.

   a. three tenths   **b.** ninety hundredths   **c.** seven hundredths

SHARING IDEAS

7. How are fractions and decimals the same? How are they different?

8. Look at the pictures you have drawn. How many hundredths are there in one tenth?

9. What does the 0 after the decimal point mean in the decimal 0.09?

10. What other decimal can you write for ninety hundredths?

ON YOUR OWN

Draw a diagram. Then write a fraction and a decimal.

11. seven tenths   **12.** forty-five hundredths   **13.** three hundredths

14. *Write a list* of the ways you have seen decimals used.

Tenths and Hundredths

A. The members of the Science Club are running a book sale. Each time they sell a book, they shade in a square on a chart. What part of the chart have they shaded?

You can name this part as a fraction or as a decimal.

$\frac{45}{100}$ or 0.45

They have shaded 0.45 of the chart.

Ones		Tenths	Hundredths
0	.	4	5

Read: forty-five hundredths

1. Complete: 45 hundredths = ▆ tenths ▆ hundredths

2. **What if** they had only shaded 8 squares on the chart? Write the fraction and decimal to name this part.

B. By the end of the sale, they had shaded one chart completely. They had also shaded $\frac{7}{10}$ of another chart.

You can name the shaded parts as a mixed number or as a decimal.

$1\frac{7}{10}$ or 1.7

Ones		Tenths
1	.	7

Read: one and seven tenths

3. **What if** they had only shaded $\frac{4}{100}$ of the second chart? Write the mixed number and decimal.

SHARING IDEAS

4. How does the place-value chart help you to read a decimal?

5. How is regrouping hundredths to tenths like regrouping one to tens?

6. How do you know if a decimal is close to 0, $\frac{1}{2}$, or 1?

PRACTICE

Write the decimal.

7.

8.

9.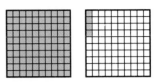

10. $\frac{8}{10}$ **11.** $\frac{72}{100}$ **12.** $\frac{2}{10}$ **13.** $\frac{6}{100}$ **14.** $\frac{53}{100}$

15. $3\frac{3}{10}$ **16.** $4\frac{6}{10}$ **17.** $7\frac{1}{100}$ **18.** $6\frac{38}{100}$ **19.** $2\frac{5}{100}$

20. five-tenths   **21.** eleven-hundredths   **22.** seventy-five hundredths

Use the number line. Write a decimal for each point.

23. A   **24.** B   **25.** C   **26.** D

Mixed Applications

27. Jan shades seventy-two of one hundred squares in her chart. What part of the chart is shaded?

28. Mr. Carr buys a book for $5.75. He gives the clerk a ten-dollar bill. How much change will Mr. Carr receive?

29. Marta has 12 bags of birdseed. She gives one-third of them to Su. How many bags of seed does she give to Su?

CALCULATOR

You can use a calculator to help you write a fraction or decimal.

$\frac{1}{2}$ = ☐1☐ ÷ ☐2☐ = ☐ 0.5 ☐

1. $\frac{1}{4}$ **2.** $\frac{3}{4}$ **3.** $\frac{1}{5}$ **4.** $\frac{2}{5}$ **5.** $\frac{3}{5}$

EXTRA PRACTICE, page 371; **PRACTICE PLUS**, page 373

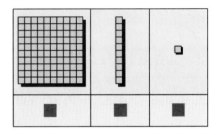

Adding and Subtracting Decimals

Marc is making models of the animals he saw at the zoo. He uses 0.75 kg of clay to make a bear. He uses 0.38 kg to make a rabbit. How much clay does he use?

You can use place-value models to add 0.75 and 0.38.

WORKING TOGETHER

Step 1 Show each decimal. Use a flat to show ones, a long to show tenths, and a unit to show hundredths. Arrange them on a chart like this.

Step 2 Combine the models. Regroup when necessary. Record how many of each type of model you used for each decimal. Then record the total.

Ones		Tenths	Hundredths
	.	■	■
	.	■	■
■	.	■	■

1. In which order did you combine the models to find the sum?

2. Was it necessary to regroup the hundredths? the tenths?

3. How much clay does he use?

What if Marc had used 0.15 kg less clay to make the bear? How much clay would he have used all together?

Step 3 Take away 0.15 from your total. Regroup when necessary.

4. In what order did you take away the models to find the difference?

5. Was it necessary to regroup the tenths? the ones?

6. How much would he have used?

Use models to add or subtract.

7. 0.25
      + 0.33

8. 0.74
      − 0.42

9. 1.56
      + 0.67

10. 2.74
       − 1.86

11. 1.42
       − 0.78

12. 0.84 + 0.93 = ___ **13.** 0.45 − 0.09 = ___ **14.** 1.03 − 0.45 = ___

SHARING IDEAS

Look at the number sentences you have written in
Exercises 7–14. Compare them with those of others.

15. When do you need to regroup when you add
decimals? subtract decimals?

16. How can you use what you know about adding and
subtracting whole numbers and money amounts to
help you add and subtract decimals?

ON YOUR OWN

Solve. Use models if needed.

17. Marc walked 1.75 kilometers
on the Nature Trail. Then he
walked 0.25 kilometer
through the animal park.
How many kilometers did he
walk all together?

18. Sal had 2.33 liters of paint.
He used 0.66 liter to paint a
picture of a deer. How much
paint does he have left?

DECISION MAKING

Problem Solving: Buying a Cage

SITUATION

Ben owns a rabbit. He has $50 to spend on a cage and other items to care for the rabbit.

PROBLEM

Should he build a cage from a kit or buy a cage from the pet store?

DATA

HAL'S HOBBY HUT

It's easy to put together the Bunny Palace! Complete kit—only $12.50!

- Made of strong wood and wire!
- Large enough for two bushy bunnies!
- 6 feet long and 2 feet wide with an area of 12 square feet!
- Any adult and child can build the Bunny Palace in about one hour!

Pete's Pet Shop Spring Sale

Buy the Rabbit House for only $18!

- Built of strong stainless steel wire!
- Perfect for your favorite rabbit!
- 3 feet long and 3 feet wide!
- A cozy 9 square feet!
- Ready to use in just 5 minutes!

USING THE DATA

1. Which cage has the larger area? How much larger is its area?

2. Which cage costs more? How much more does it cost?

3. How much money will Ben have left if he buys the Bunny Palace? the Rabbit House?

4. About how much longer does it take to build the Bunny Palace than it does to set up the Rabbit House?

= 1 square foot

CAGE AREA

MAKING DECISIONS

5. *Write a list* of the things that Ben should consider before choosing which cage to buy.

6. Why might Ben choose to buy the Bunny Palace? the Rabbit House?

7. Which cage should Ben buy if he wants to have money left to spend on other items for his rabbit?

8. *What if* Ben wants to get another rabbit? Which cage should be buy? Why?

9. *What if* this drawing shows the area in which Ben plans to keep his rabbit. Which cage should he buy? Why?

10. Which rabbit cage would you choose to buy? Why?

Math and Social Studies

The numbers we use today were introduced to Europe by Arab mathematicians. They had learned them from Indian mathematicians.

Before the invention of the decimal system, arithmetic with Roman numerals was hard. Most shopkeepers used wooden or metal counters.

For the first time, the decimal system made it easy to do arithmetic with only pencil and paper!

What if a shopkeeper compares 1 kilogram of flour and 0.5 kilogram of oats? Which has the greater mass?

Think: Any number to the right of the decimal point is less than 1.

So 1 kilogram of flour has a greater mass than 0.5 kilograms of oats.

ACTIVITY

1. Be a decimal detective. Make a chart showing the places where decimals are used. Look in the grocery store, a tool box, the bank, and a gas station. Share your findings with others.

Computer: Perimeter

You can use Logo commands to explore the perimeter of rectangles and squares.

In the picture, A is the length of the rectangle and B is the width of the rectangle.

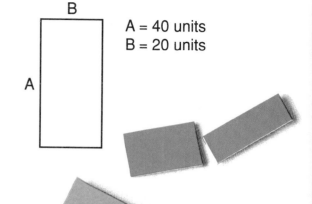

B

A

A = 40 units
B = 20 units

AT THE COMPUTER

Enter the following program.

```
TO RECT :A :B
REPEAT 2 [FD :A RT 90 FD :B RT 90]
PR SE [PERIMETER =] :A + :B + :A + :B
END
```

1. Enter RECT 40 20. What does the computer draw? Which side of the shape is drawn first?

2. What is the perimeter of the rectangle?

Remember to clear the screen before drawing a new figure.

3. Enter RECT 20 40. How are the two rectangles different? How are they the same?

4. Draw a rectangle with a perimeter of 80. Then draw a different rectangle with the same perimeter. What did you enter?

5. Draw a square with a perimeter of 100. What did you enter?

6. Work with a partner. Challenge each other to draw rectangles with different perimeters.

Extra Practice

Whole Numbers and Mixed Numbers, page 343 . . . .

Write the whole number or mixed number for the part
that is shaded.

1. 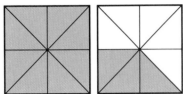   **2.** 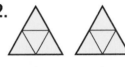   **3.**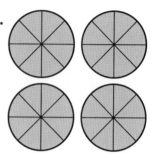

Write the mixed number.

4. eight and one-third   **5.** six and five-ninths

6. two and four-fifths   **7.** nine and seven-tenths

8. one and one-third   **9.** seven and six-sevenths

Comparing Mixed Numbers, page 345 . . . .

Compare. Write $>$, $<$, or $=$.

1. 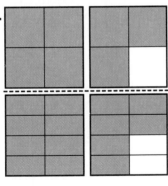   **2.** 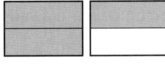   **3.**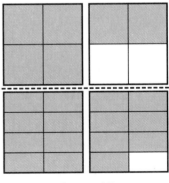

$1\frac{3}{4} \bullet 1\frac{6}{8}$ $1\frac{1}{2} \bullet 1\frac{1}{3}$ $1\frac{2}{4} \bullet \frac{15}{8}$

4. $1\frac{1}{2} \bullet 2\frac{1}{3}$ **5.** $2 \bullet 1\frac{3}{4}$ **6.** $4 \bullet \frac{2}{4}$ **7.** $2\frac{3}{5} \bullet \frac{5}{7}$

8. $1\frac{3}{4} \bullet 2$ **9.** $3 \bullet \frac{1}{3}$ **10.** $2\frac{1}{5} \bullet 5$ **11.** $\frac{3}{7} \bullet 1\frac{1}{2}$

Measuring Length, page 347...

Measure to the nearest inch.

1.

2.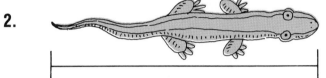

3.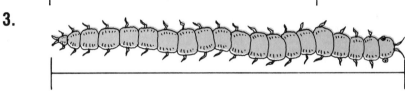

Measure to the nearest half inch.

4. 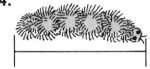   **5.**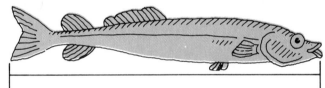

Draw a line for each length.

6. 4 inches   **7.** 3 inches   **8.** $2\frac{1}{2}$ inches   **9.** $6\frac{1}{2}$ inches

Estimating Length: Customary Units, page 349.....................................

Write the letter of the best estimate.

1. the length of a skirt   **a.** 15 inches   **b.** 15 feet   **c.** 15 miles

2. the distance between
two cities   **a.** 20 feet   **b.** 20 yards   **c.** 20 miles

3. the width of your feet   **a.** 3 inches   **b.** 3 feet   **c.** 3 miles

4. the length of a brush   **a.** 8 miles   **b.** 8 feet   **c.** 8 inches

5. the width of a table   **a.** 3 inches   **b.** 3 feet   **c.** 3 miles

6. the height of a ladder   **a.** 6 inches   **b.** 6 feet   **c.** 6 miles

EXTRA PRACTICE

Perimeter and Area, page 351...

Find the perimeter and the area. Each □ equals
1 square inch.

1.

2.

3.

4.

5.

6.

7.

8.

Problem Solving Strategy: Solving a Simpler Problem, page 353........

Solve the problem. Solve a simpler problem first
if you need to.

1. Rachel needs to eat 913 calories for lunch. She has
   eaten 678 calories so far. How many more calories
   does she need to eat?

2. Patrick buys 906 bags of mulch for use on his farm.
   The delivery service forgot to deliver 369 bags. How
   many bags of mulch did Patrick receive?

3. A watchmaker shipped 868 watches to Japan,
   928 to the United States, and 984 to England.
   How many watches did he ship in all?

4. Anne buys $8.47 worth of tickets for her school
   play. For the next play she buys $9.12 worth of
   tickets. How much more money did she spend
   for the second play?

Problem Solving: Strategies Review, page 357 ....

Solve. Tell which strategy you used.

1. Thomas Jefferson was born in 1743. It took him about $2\frac{1}{2}$ weeks to write the Declaration of Independence. He died on July 4, 1826. How many years did Jefferson live?

2. There are 8 rows of flags in a pattern. There are 4 flags in the first row, 6 flags in the second row, 8 flags in the third row, and 10 flags in the fourth row. How many flags are there in each of the last 4 rows?

3. The O'Neill Uniform Company made 320 uniforms for this year's parade. They sold 180 uniforms to boys and 110 to girls. How many uniforms did they have left to sell?

4. Cal has saved $15 to spend. He wants to buy a book for $9.98 and a Burger Platter for $3.15. Does he have enough money to buy the book and lunch?

Tenths and Hundredths, page 361 ....

Write the decimal.

1.

2.

3.

4. $\frac{6}{10}$

5. $\frac{74}{100}$

6. $\frac{3}{10}$

7. $\frac{8}{10}$

8. $\frac{57}{100}$

9. $4\frac{7}{10}$

10. $3\frac{8}{10}$

11. $8\frac{3}{100}$

12. $7\frac{36}{100}$

13. $1\frac{3}{100}$

Use the number line. Write a decimal for each point.

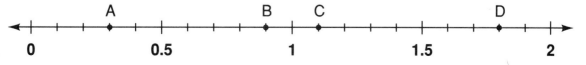

14. A

15. B

16. C

17. D

Practice PLUS

KEY SKILL: Whole Numbers and Mixed Numbers
(Use after page 343.)

Level A ....

Write the whole number or the mixed number for the part that is shaded.

1. 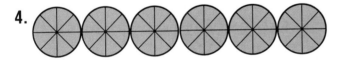   2.

3. Bo gave the birds 4 whole bags of seeds and $\frac{1}{2}$ of another bag. Write the mixed number.

Level B ....

Write the whole number or mixed number for the part that is shaded.

4.   5.

Write the whole number or the mixed number.

6. four and seven-tenths   7. seven and two-thirds

8. Janice fed the squirrels 8 bags of peanuts and $\frac{3}{4}$ of another bag.

Level C ....

Write the whole number or the mixed number.

9. thirteen and four-fifths   10. seven-thirds

11. three-thirds   12. ten and one-seventh

13. ten-fifths   14. eight-fourths

15. Jon has 3 full bags of oats and 5 eighths of another bag.

PRACTICE PLUS

KEY SKILL: Tenths and Hundredths (Use after page 361.)

Level A

Write the decimal.

1. 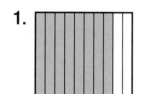   2. 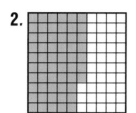   3. 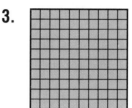   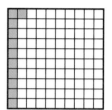

4. $\frac{9}{10}$ 5. $\frac{25}{100}$ 6. $\frac{4}{10}$ 7. $\frac{31}{100}$ 8. $\frac{1}{10}$

9. $\frac{67}{100}$ 10. $\frac{5}{10}$ 11. $\frac{37}{100}$ 12. $\frac{6}{10}$ 13. $\frac{43}{100}$

Level B

Write the decimal.

14. $\frac{8}{10}$ 15. $3\frac{2}{10}$ 16. $\frac{4}{100}$ 17. $8\frac{54}{100}$ 18. $\frac{7}{100}$

Write a decimal for the point on the number line.

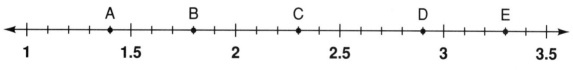

19. A   20. B   21. C   22. D   23. E

Level C

Write the decimal.

24. $\frac{2}{10}$ 25. $3\frac{3}{100}$ 26. $7\frac{9}{10}$ 27. $5\frac{1}{100}$ 28. $8\frac{5}{100}$

Write a decimal for the point on the number line.

29. A   30. B   31. C   32. D   33. E

Mixed Numbers and Decimals   **373**

CHAPTER REVIEW / TEST

LANGUAGE AND MATHEMATICS

Complete the sentences. Use the words in the chart.

1. The width of a door is about 1 ___.

2. $3\frac{3}{4}$ is called a ___ number.

3. ___ is the number of square units it takes to cover the surface of something.

VOCABULARY

mixed
perimeter
area
yard
foot

CONCEPTS AND SKILLS

Write the number or word name.

4. three and one-fourth

5. nine and three-eighths

6. $5\frac{2}{9}$

7. $2\frac{1}{2}$

Compare. Use >, <, or =.

8. $2\frac{1}{3}$ ● $2\frac{2}{3}$

9. 3 ● $3\frac{1}{2}$

10. $1\frac{1}{2}$ ● $\frac{1}{2}$

Write the letter of the best estimate.

11. the length of a parking lot   **a.** 1 inch   **b.** 100 feet   **c.** 10 miles

12. the length of a toothbrush   **a.** 6 inches   **b.** 6 feet   **c.** 6 yards

13. the width of a car   **a.** 3 inches   **b.** 3 feet   **c.** 3 miles

14. Draw a line 5 inches long.

15. Draw a line $2\frac{1}{2}$ inches long.

Write the decimal.

16.

17.

18. $\frac{3}{10}$

19. $\frac{8}{100}$

20. $1\frac{16}{100}$

Write the word name.

21. 2.2

22. 1.02

Critical Thinking

23. Bo says she can multiply to find the perimeter of a square that measures 3 meters on a side. Tell how she would do this.

Mixed Applications

24. A square field measures 50 feet on each side. What is the perimeter of the field?

25. Justin ships 376 pounds of apples, 485 pounds of pears, and 976 pounds of cherries. How many pounds of fruit does he ship?

PERFORMANCE ASSESSMENT

Work with your group to solve this problem.

Suppose you are president of a club. You just had a dinner dance and you have 3 kinds of pie left over. There are $1\frac{1}{2}$ apple pies, $1\frac{3}{8}$ blueberry pies, and $1\frac{1}{4}$ cherry pies left over. Make a poster of the leftover pies. Find what kind of pie had the most left over and what kind of pie had the least.

1. *Think about:*
   - what model you will use for the pies

2. Write 3 sentences about the mixed numbers using your poster. Use "greater than" and "less than."

CUMULATIVE REVIEW

Choose the letter of the correct answer.

1. $\frac{1}{3}$ of 21
   - **a.** 6
   - **b.** 7
   - **c.** 10
   - **d.** not given

2. Choose the mixed number for five and six-sevenths.
   - **a.** $5\frac{6}{7}$
   - **b.** $6\frac{5}{7}$
   - **c.** $6\frac{6}{7}$
   - **d.** $7\frac{5}{6}$

3. Choose the decimal for $\frac{37}{100}$.
   - **a.** 0.037
   - **b.** 0.37
   - **c.** 3.700
   - **d.** 37.00

4. $72 \div 9 = \underline{\blacksquare}$
   - **a.** 81
   - **b.** 63
   - **c.** 9
   - **d.** 8

5. Compare: $5\frac{3}{4} \bullet 5\frac{1}{4}$
   - **a.** >
   - **b.** <
   - **c.** =
   - **d.** not given

6. Compare: $\frac{5}{8} \bullet \frac{6}{8}$
   - **a.** >
   - **b.** <
   - **c.** =
   - **d.** not given

7. $7 \times 7 = \underline{\blacksquare}$
   - **a.** 0
   - **b.** 14
   - **c.** 49
   - **d.** not given

8. Compare: $1\frac{2}{3} \bullet 2\frac{2}{3}$
   - **a.** >
   - **b.** <
   - **c.** =
   - **d.** not given

9. $\underline{\blacksquare} \times 20 = 0$
   - **a.** 50
   - **b.** 20
   - **c.** 0
   - **d.** not given

10. $151 + 324 + 6 = \underline{\blacksquare}$
    - **a.** 481
    - **b.** 471
    - **c.** 461
    - **d.** not given

11. $8\overline{)48}$
    - **a.** 4
    - **b.** 6
    - **c.** 8
    - **d.** not given

12. $\frac{1}{7}$ of 42
    - **a.** 6
    - **b.** 7
    - **c.** 8
    - **d.** not given

13. Compare: $3\frac{9}{10} \bullet 4\frac{1}{10}$
    - **a.** >
    - **b.** <
    - **c.** =
    - **d.** not given

14. Which multiplication sentence goes with $20 \div 5 = 4$?
    - **a.** $4 \times 5 = 20$
    - **b.** $10 \times 2 = 20$
    - **c.** $20 \times 1 = 20$
    - **d.** not given

ENRICHMENT FOR ALL

FINDING THE COVERED AREA

Jill's family plans to add a
rectangular patio to their home.
Each square in the drawing
represents a square meter.
Some of the patio is covered
by the roof of the house.

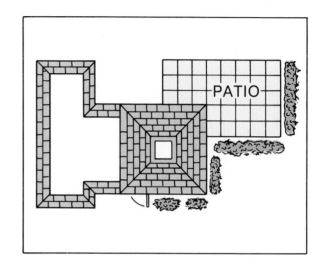

1. What is the total area of the
   patio in square meters?

2. How much of the patio is
   covered by the roof of
   the house?

3. Tell how you found the area of the patio.

Find the total area of each rectangular patio in square
meters. Tell how much of each patio is covered by the
roof of the house.

4.

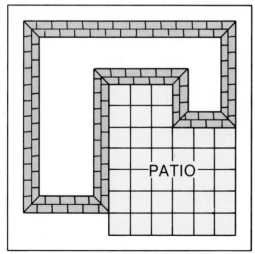

5.

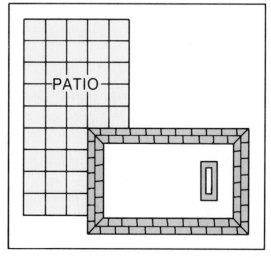

6. Use graph paper to make your own plans for a covered patio.
   Trade your plans with others and have them find the area.

THE INDIAN GAME
PACHISI

Grown-ups and children all over the world enjoy playing games. One very popular game played in India is called *pachisi* [pah-CHEE-zee]. *Pachisi* has been played for hundreds of years and is considered India's national game. In the 1500s, the Emperor Akbar the Great made *pachisi* the royal game. The game was first played in the royal courtyard.

Huge stone and marble squares formed the game board. People served as counters. One garden where life-size *pachisi* was played still exists today. It is at the palace of Agra in India.

ASIA

India

Pachisi comes from a Hindu word that means "twenty-five." In the game, 25 is the highest score possible in one turn. Players take turns rolling six brightly colored cowrie shells. For every shell that lands mouth up, a counter can be moved one space. If no shells land mouth up, the counter can be moved 25 spaces.

1 When a game of *pachisi* begins, do all the players have the same chance of winning? Why or why not?

2 What games are similar to *pachisi*? How are they the same? How are they different?

Measuring Capacity: Customary Units

The **capacity** of a container is the amount it can hold.

WORKING TOGETHER

The **cup (c)**, **pint (pt)**, **quart (qt)**, and **gallon (gal)** are units you can use to measure amounts of liquids.

1. Collect containers of different sizes. Estimate and measure the capacities of the containers. Use a cup container and a pint container. Make a table.

Container	Cups		Pints	
	Estimate	Measure	Estimate	Measure
Soup bowl	▦	▦	▦	▦
Juice jar	▦	▦	▦	▦
Milk carton	▦	▦	▦	▦
Large pot	▦	▦	▦	▦

2. Compare the numbers of cups and pints needed to fill each container. What do you notice?

SHARING IDEAS

3. What other containers have small capacities? large capacities? Which unit would you use to measure their capacities?

4. Two containers have different shapes. Must they have different capacities? Why or why not?

5. Look at containers at home and in stores. Make a list of the types of containers and the ways their capacities are labeled. Share your list with other students.

PRACTICE

Choose the better estimate.

6.

a. 1 cup
b. 1 quart

7.

a. 1 cup
b. 1 gallon

8.

a. 1 pint
b. 1 gallon

9.

a. 1 pint
b. 1 quart

10.

a. 1 cup
b. 1 quart

11.

a. 30 quarts
b. 30 gallons

Mixed Applications

12. Ron fills a large pail with water to hold some fish. Does he put in only 5 cups of water or 5 gallons of water?

13. Sue saves 132 egg cartons. She gives 25 of them to Ann. How many egg cartons does Sue have now?

14. Kay has a filled jar of lemonade. Does the jar hold 10 cups or 10 quarts of lemonade?

15. Mike buys a pail for $2.85 and a shovel for $1.29. How much money does he spend?

LOGICAL REASONING

You have two empty jars. The first jar holds 2 pints, and the second jar holds 5 pints. How can you use these two jars to get 3 pints of water from the faucet?

Measuring Weight: Customary Units

Measuring **weight** tells you how heavy something is.

WORKING TOGETHER

You can use **ounces (oz)** to measure
the weight of lighter things.

1. Estimate the weights of several
   objects in your classroom.

2. Place each object on one pan of a
   balance scale. Add 1-ounce
   weights to the other pan until the
   two pans are balanced.

3. Record your estimates and
   measurements in a chart.

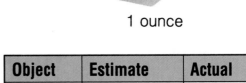

1 ounce

Object	Estimate	Actual

The **pound (lb)** is a unit of weight used
to measure heavier things.

4. Estimate. Then use the balance
   scale to measure the weight of
   several objects in pounds. Record
   your estimates and measurements
   in a chart like the one above.

1 pound

SHARING IDEAS

5. Name other objects that could be measured using
   ounces.

6. Name other objects that could be measured using
   pounds.

7. Why is it important that everyone use the same
   unit when measuring weight?

PRACTICE

Choose the better estimate.

8.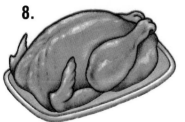
  a. 12 ounces
  b. 12 pounds

9.
  a. 1 ounce
  b. 1 pound

10.
  a. 15 ounces
  b. 15 pounds

11.
  a. 1 ounce
  b. 1 pound

12.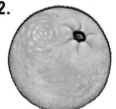
  a. 6 ounces
  b. 6 pounds

13.
  a. 1 ounce
  b. 1 pound

Critical Thinking

14. Meg wants to weigh her cat. The cat will not stay on the scale. What can Meg do to find the cat's weight?

Mixed Applications

15. Pat's father bought a 7-pound chicken and a 15-pound turkey. How much more did the turkey weigh?

16. A 16-ounce box of pasta makes 8 servings. How much does each serving weigh?

Mixed Review

> MENTAL MATH
> CALCULATOR
> PAPER/PENCIL

Find the answer. Which method did you use?

17. $148 - 30 = $ ▆

18. $283 + 529 = $ ▆

19. $64 \div 8 = $ ▆

20. $6 + 7 + 4 = $ ▆

21. $626 - 375 = $ ▆

Temperature

You can use a **Fahrenheit** thermometer to measure temperature.

To read the temperature on a thermometer, look at the mark or number next to the top of the red column.

A hot cup of cocoa is about 120°F.

A glass of cold water is about 40°F.

°F

Water boils

Hot cocoa

98.6 °F
Normal body
temperature

Room
temperature

Cold water
Water freezes

Each line shows
2 degrees Fahrenheit.

1. At what temperature does water boil?

2. At what temperature does water freeze?

3. What is normal body temperature?

4. Which is colder, 5°F or ⁻5°F? How can you tell?

TRY OUT Write the letter of the correct answer.
Which is the most reasonable temperature?

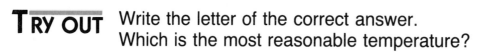

5. winter day   **a.** 18°F   **b.** 55°F   **c.** 72°F   **d.** 95°F

6. summer day   **a.** 25°F   **b.** 48°F   **c.** 85°F   **d.** 140°F

7. fall day   **a.** ⁻12°F   **b.** 58°F   **c.** 75°F   **d.** 100°F

8. room temperature   **a.** 20°F   **b.** 30°F   **c.** 48°F   **d.** 68°F

PRACTICE

Write the letter of the most reasonable temperature.

9. hot soup   **a.** 20°F   **b.** 35°F   **c.** 115°F   **d.** 200°F

10. cold juice   **a.** ⁻4°F   **b.** 25°F   **c.** 32°F   **d.** 38°F

11. bath water   **a.** 0°F   **b.** 35°F   **c.** 60°F   **d.** 95°F

12. warm day   **a.** 92°F   **b.** 72°F   **c.** 98°F   **d.** 105°F

Write the temperature in degrees Fahrenheit.

13. 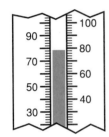   **14.** 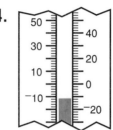   **15.**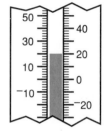

16. 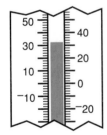   **17.** 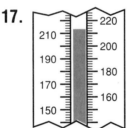   **18.**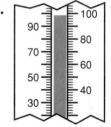

Mixed Applications

Solve. You may need to use the Databank on page 521.

19. In Boston, how much warmer is the normal temperature in September than in December?

20. How much colder is the normal December temperature in Chicago than in Houston?

21. The temperature at 12 noon in Keane was 54°F. It was 3° higher by 3:00 P.M. What was the temperature in Keane at 3:00 P.M.?

22. *Write a problem* about comparing normal monthly temperatures. Ask others to solve your problem.

✓ UNDERSTAND
✓ PLAN
✓ TRY
CHECK
✓ EXTEND

PROBLEM SOLVING

Strategy: Using Number Sense

Activity	Time
Weed the garden	about ½ hour
Do homework	about 1½ hours
Ride bicycles	about 1 hour
Have a snack	about ¼ hour
Visit grandparents	about 2 hours
Help Uncle Vinh with English lesson	about 1 hour

Trang and Connie get out of school at 2:00 P.M. every Wednesday. They must be home by 4:00 P.M. to help with dinner. They make a list of things they want to do after school and how long they think each thing takes. Do they have enough time to weed the garden and ride their bikes?

Trang and Connie use number sense to solve the problem.

They know they have 2 hours of free time after school.

It takes them about $\frac{1}{2}$ hour to weed the garden and 1 hour to ride their bikes.

$1\frac{1}{2}$ is less than 2.

They do have enough time.

1. Do they have enough time to weed the garden and visit their grandparents? Why or why not?

2. How did Trang and Connie use what they know about fractions and mixed numbers to help them solve the problem?

PRACTICE

Use number sense to solve. Tell how you made your choice.

3. Connie can watch television for 1 hour before dinner. Does she have enough time to watch two $\frac{1}{2}$-hour programs?

4. Trang has a very narrow table that is $2\frac{1}{2}$ feet long. Can she put a 2-foot long platter and a $\frac{3}{4}$-foot long bowl on this table?

5. Mrs. Huynh needs $1\frac{1}{2}$ pounds of shrimp for dinner. She has $\frac{1}{4}$ pound of shrimp. Mr. Huynh brings home 1 more pound of shrimp from his boat. Does she have enough shrimp?

6. Vinh is filling a large pitcher that can hold 2 quarts of juice. Can he mix 1 quart of apple juice with $\frac{3}{4}$ quart of grape juice in the pitcher?

Strategies and Skills Review

Solve. Use mental math, a calculator, or paper and pencil.

7. Connie places the soup spoon to the left of the salad fork on the left side of the plate. The dinner fork is next to the plate and just to the right of the salad fork. Which is farthest from the plate?

8. Trang has 13 more oatmeal cookies than raisin cookies. She has twice as many bran cookies as oatmeal cookies. She has 15 raisin cookies. How many bran cookies are there?

9. To make 1 tray of spring rolls, Vinh needs $3\frac{1}{4}$ cups of vegetables. He has 4 cups of vegetables. Can he make 2 trays of spring rolls? Why or why not?

10. *Write a problem* that can be solved using number sense. Solve your problem. Ask others to solve it.

ROLL, ROLL, ROLL YOUR CUBE

Experimenting and Predicting

A. Take a number cube with the numbers 1, 2, 3, 4, 5, and 6 on its faces. How many times do you think you will have to roll the cube to get a 3?

Roll the cube. Did you get a 3? If you did, it took you only one roll. If you didn't, roll again. Keep rolling the cube until you get a 3. How many rolls did it take?

1. Draw a chart like the one below. Put the number of rolls it took you in the box for Experiment #1

Experiment #	1	2	3	4	5	6	7	8	9	10
Number of rolls it took to roll a 3										

2. Now try the experiment nine more times.
   Record your results each time.
   What number appears most often in your chart?

3. Compare charts with other students.
   About how many rolls did it take to roll a 3?

4. How many rolls do you think it would take you to roll a 4? Why?
   Now try it.

B. How many rolls do you think it will take you to roll an odd number? What are the odd numbers on your cube?

5. Copy the chart below. Try the experiment ten times. Record your results on your chart.

Experiment #	1	2	3	4	5	6	7	8	9	10
Number of rolls it took to roll an odd number										

Look at the results of your two charts. Discuss what you learned.

6. How many rolls do you think it will take to roll a number greater than 4? Do you think the number of rolls will be more or less than the number of rolls for getting an odd number? What makes you think so? Try one more set of experiments to see if you are right.

Experiment #	1	2	3	4	5	6	7	8	9	10
Number of rolls it took to roll a number greater than 4										

PROBLEM SOLVING

Strategy: Making an Organized List

Alma, Betty, Chaka, and Dorothy are cousins. One day they met at a health food store. Each cousin hugged each of the other cousins. How many hugs were given?

Alma plans to make an organized list to solve the problem.

First Alma lists all the cousins she hugged.

Hugs
Alma↔Betty
Alma↔Chaka
Alma↔Dorothy

1. How many hugs did Alma list?

Then she lists the cousins Betty hugged. Alma is careful not to list the hug Betty gave her because she has already counted it.

2. How many hugs did Alma list for Betty?

Betty↔Chaka
Betty↔Dorothy

3. Which hug has not been listed?

4. How many hugs were given in all?

5. **What if** they had also met Alma's friend Emily? How many hugs would they have given then?

6. How does making an organized list help solve problems like this?

PRACTICE

Make an organized list to solve the problem.

7. A snack bar serves ham, tuna, cheese, or egg sandwiches. It serves milk or juice to drink. Joyce wants to buy a sandwich and a drink for lunch. How many different lunches can she choose? What are they?

8. David, Eleanor, Frank, and Kate are doing a nutrition project. They plan to form teams of 2 students each. How many different teams can they form? What are they?

9. There are 4 kinds of granola bars at the health-food store: lemon, grape, orange, and apple. Joe is choosing 3 flavors. How many different choices does he have? What are they?

10. Jane wants to take 2 books on nutrition out of the library. She chooses from 3 books by the authors Atlas, Boles, and Carlson. In how many different ways can Jane choose the 2 books? What are they?

Strategies and Skills Review

Solve. Use mental math, a calculator, or paper and pencil.

11. A small can of peas costs $.59, and a large can costs $.76. A small can of soup costs $.83, and a large can costs $1.28. Sharon buys a can of peas and a can of soup. What are all possible amounts she could have spent?

12. Dorothy's lunch has more calories than Alma's lunch, but fewer calories than Chaka's lunch. Alma's lunch has more calories than Betty's lunch. Whose lunch has the most calories?

13. Carlos wants to buy a chicken for $3.92, a head of lettuce for $.70, and potatoes for $.85. Is $5.00 enough to cover the cost of these items?

14. **Write a problem** that can be solved with the help of an organized list. Solve the problem. Ask others to solve your problem.

EXTRA **PRACTICE**, page 404   Measuring Capacity and Weight/Probability   **391**

ActiVity Probability

Probability is the chance that something will happen. If you toss a 2-color counter, there are 2 possible outcomes: It will come up red or it will come up yellow. What is the probability that the counter will come up red when you toss it?

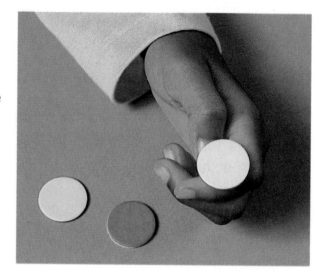

WORKING TOGETHER

You can explore the probability that the counter will come up red.

Step 1 Toss the counter. Did it come up red or yellow? Record the outcome in a table like this. Use a tally mark.

Red	|||
Yellow	|||||	

Step 2 Toss the counter until you have made 20 tosses. Record each outcome. Find the total of each.

 1. Did the counter come up more often red, more often yellow, or about the same?

 2. Do you think the outcome will be red or yellow if you toss again? Why?

 3. **What if** you tossed the counter 40 times? About how many times do you think it would come up red? Why do you think so?

Step 3 Toss the counter 40 times. Record each outcome.

 4. How close was your prediction?

Now use a spinner to explore probability.

5. What are the possible outcomes of spinning the pointer on this spinner?

6. Are all possible outcomes equally likely? Why or why not?

7. Pick one of the colors. Predict how many times you will spin your color in 40 times.

8. Spin 40 times and record the outcomes. How close was your prediction?

SHARING IDEAS

Which statements do you agree with? Which do you disagree with? Why?

9. The chance of the counter coming up red or yellow is equally likely.

10. The chance of the counter coming up red is 1 chance out of 2.

11. If you toss the counter and it comes up red, then it will come up yellow on the next toss.

ON YOUR OWN

12. Use a spinner like this one. Pick a number. Predict how many times you will spin your number in 30 spins. Test your prediction.

13. Make up your own probability experiment. Describe your experiment to other students and share the results.

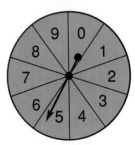

ACTIVITY

Finding Probability

From which jar would you pick if you wanted a better chance of picking a red cube?

1. How many cubes are in the first jar? How many cubes in the first jar are red? The chance of picking a red cube is ■ out of ■

2. How many cubes are in the second jar? How many cubes in the second jar are red? The chance of picking a red cube is ■ out of ■.

3. What is the probability of picking:

   a. a blue cube from the first jar? from the second jar?

   b. a yellow cube from the first jar? from the second jar?

   c. a green cube from the first jar? from the second jar?

4. From which jar do you have an equally likely chance of picking any color cube?

5. From which jar do you have a more likely chance of picking a red cube?

6. Put cubes of the same number and color as shown above in two jars. Pick a cube from each jar without looking. Put them back in the jars and pick again. Do this 20 times. Record the number of times you picked each color from each jar.

7. How can you tell when the outcomes of a probability experiment are equally likely?

8. Why do you use two numbers to describe a probability?

9. Did your outcomes agree with the probabilities? Compare your results with those of others.

PRACTICE

Find the probability of picking the color.

10. red

11. green

12. yellow

Find the probability of spinning:

13. red.

14. blue.

15. Which color are you more likely to spin?

Mixed Applications

16. There are 10 buttons in a bag. One button is black. If you pick a button without looking, what is the probability that it will be black?

17. There are 1 yellow, 4 blue, 3 white, and 2 red buttons in a bag. If you pick 1 button without looking, which color are you most likely to pick? least likely to pick?

18. There are 7 marbles in a bag. Three of them are purple. What fraction of the marbles are purple?

19. There are 12 marbles in a bag. There are the same number of each of 4 colors. How many marbles of each color are there?

ACTIVITY
Probability and Statistics

Graphing the results of a probability experiment can help you make predictions.

WORKING TOGETHER

Step 1 Without anyone else looking, have someone in your group put either 2 blue and 1 red cube or 1 blue and 2 red cubes in a jar.

Step 2 Have everyone else in your group take turns picking a cube from the jar. Record the outcomes on a bar graph.

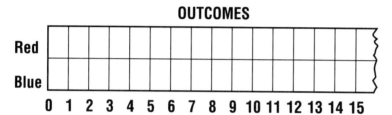

OUTCOMES

Red

Blue

0 1 2 3 4 5 6 7 8 9 10 11 12 13 14 15

Step 3 Put the cube back and shake the jar. Pick again and record the results. Do this 20 times.

1. Look at your graph. How often was a red cube picked? How often was a blue cube picked?

2. How many red cubes do you think are in the jar? how many blue cubes? Why?

3. Count how many red and blue cubes are in the jar. Was your prediction correct?

4. What is the probability of picking red? blue?

SHARING IDEAS

5. Tell how you predicted which cubes were in the jar. Compare your methods to those of others.

6. Did your results agree with the probabilities?

PRACTICE

Alex put 6 cubes in a bag. Some were blue and some were red. There were 2 cubes of one color, and 4 cubes of the other color. Sara took 20 turns picking cubes. She graphed her results.

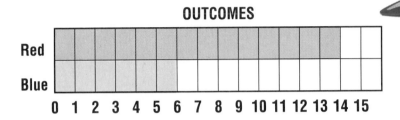

OUTCOMES

Use Sara's graph to answer Problems 7–9.

7. Which color did she pick most often? least often?

8. Predict how many cubes of each color are in the bag.

9. If your prediction is correct, what would be the probability of picking red? of picking blue?

10. Put 8 different-colored crayons in a box. Shake the box. Make predictions about what crayons you will pick in 20 turns. Then take 20 turns and graph your results.

11. Ask students in another class to vote for their favorite sandwich. Make a bar graph of the data.

12. **What if** you were in charge of the school cafeteria? How would you use your data to plan the lunch menu?

Mixed Review

Find the answer. Which method did you use?

13. $850 - 310 =$ ▇

14. $176 + 582 =$ ▇

15. $48 + 75 =$ ▇

16. $240 + 110 =$ ▇

17. $286 - 88 =$ ▇

> **MENTAL MATH**
> **CALCULATOR**
> **PAPER/PENCIL**

DECISION MAKING

Problem Solving: Planning a Healthy Breakfast

SITUATION

The Mills family is planning a healthy breakfast for Grandmother on her birthday. They know that a healthy breakfast should contain fruit or fruit juice, cereal or bread, and milk.

PROBLEM

What should they prepare for their grandmother's breakfast?

DATA

"Choose a Healthy Breakfast"

Item	Serving Size	Calories	Grams of Fat
Fruit and Fruit Juices			
Banana	1 medium	110	0
Orange	1 small	65	0
Orange juice	6 ounces	80	0
Cereals and Breads			
Cereals			
Grits	$\frac{1}{2}$ cup	300	0
Oatmeal	$\frac{1}{2}$ cup	221	4
Bran flakes	1 ounce	70	1
Breads			
Corn bread	1 piece	256	16
Whole-wheat bread	1 piece	60	3
White bread	1 piece	70	4
Milk Products			
Low-fat milk	1 cup	120	5
Yogurt (plain)	1 cup	140	4
Yogurt with fruit	1 cup	280	6

YOUR FAMILY MAGAZINE

USING THE DATA

1. Which fruit has the most calories? the least?

2. Which cereal has the most grams of fat? the least?

3. Which dairy product has the most grams of fat? the least?

4. Which breads have less than 100 calories?

How many calories are in the breakfast? how many grams of fat?

5. "Sunshine Special"
   1 cup of plain yogurt
   1 small orange
   1 slice of whole-wheat bread

6. "Yum-Yum Delight"
   1 piece of corn bread
   1 yogurt with fruit
   6-ounce glass of orange juice

7. "Stick to Your Ribs"
   $\frac{1}{2}$ cup of oatmeal
   6-ounce glass of orange juice
   1 cup of low-fat milk

8. "Munch & Crunch"
   1 ounce of bran flakes
   1 medium banana
   1 cup of low-fat milk

MAKING DECISIONS

9. What should you think about when planning a healthy breakfast? Make a list.

10. *What if* Grandmother is on a low-fat diet? Which foods would be best to choose?

11. What would you choose to fix for breakfast? Why?

12. *Write a list* of other things that you like to have as a healthy breakfast. Talk about your list with others.

Math and Science

You may not believe it, but an African elephant weighs about 250 pounds when it is born. At its adult weight, it can weigh over 12,000 pounds!

Look at the table below to find the birth weights and adult weights of four different animals.

Animal	Approximate Birth Weight (in pounds)	Approximate Adult Weight (in pounds)
Bear	2	900
Deer	4	200
Gorilla	5	350
Seal	10	195

What if someone asked you, "Are animals that are the heaviest at birth always the heaviest as adults?"

Use the table to answer the question.

Think: Of the animals in the table, the seal is the heaviest at birth. As an adult, the seal weighs the least of all the animals in the table.

So animals that are the heaviest at birth are not always the heaviest as adults.

ACTIVITIES

1. Find the birth weight and adult weight of your three favorite animals. Draw a picture. Show how different each animal looked as a baby and as an adult. List the birth and adult weight for each animal.

Computer Simulations: Coin Toss

Predict how many times a penny would land heads up, if you tossed it 50 times. You can use a computer to re-create or simulate the coin toss experiment. All you have to do is enter the total number of tosses you want. The computer will calculate the number of heads and tails.

AT THE COMPUTER

Run the computer probability program called COINTOSS.

1. Enter 50 for the number of tosses you want. How many heads did you get? How many tails did you get? How do the outcomes compare with your prediction?

2. Repeat the simulation in Problem 1 nine more times. What do you notice about the outcomes?

3. Run a new simulation with 500 tosses. Predict the number of heads. Repeat the simulation several times. How do the outcomes compare with your predictions? How do they compare to the total in Problem 2?

4. Predict outcomes for even greater numbers of coin tosses. Run the simulation several times. How do the outcomes compare with your predictions?

5. Heads have come up five times. Can you be sure that the next toss will come up tails?

6. Why is it helpful to use a computer to do probability experiments?

EXTRA PRACTICE

Measuring Capacity: Customary Units, page 381 ....

Choose the better estimate.

1.

    a. 1 cup
    b. 1 quart

2.

    a. 32 cups
    b. 32 gallons

3.

    a. 1 quart
    b. 1 gallon

4.

    a. 1 cup
    b. 1 quart

5.

    a. 9,000 quarts
    b. 9,000 gallons

6.

    a. 1 pint
    b. 1 gallon

Measuring Weight: Customary Units, page 383 ....

Choose the better estimate.

1.

    a. 8 ounces
    b. 8 pounds

2.

    a. 3 ounces
    b. 3 pounds

3.

    a. 100 ounces
    b. 100 pounds

4.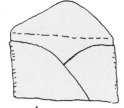

    a. 1 ounce
    b. 1 pound

5.

    a. 14 ounces
    b. 14 pounds

6.

    a. 90 ounces
    b. 90 pounds

EXTRA PRACTICE

Temperature, page 385 ....

Write the letter of the most reasonable temperature.

1. iced tea   **a.** ⁻5°F   **b.** 10°F   **c.** 40°F   **d.** 75°F

2. summer day   **a.** 20°F   **b.** 50°F   **c.** 65°F   **d.** 80°F

3. hot cocoa   **a.** 35°F   **b.** 110°F   **c.** 70°F   **d.** 50°F

4. winter day   **a.** 32°F   **b.** 80°F   **c.** 90°F   **d.** 100°F

5. room temperature   **a.** ⁻5°F   **b.** 20°F   **c.** 30°F   **d.** 68°F

6. ice cubes   **a.** 30°F   **b.** 60°F   **c.** 70°F   **d.** 95°F

Write the temperature in degrees Fahrenheit.

7.    **8.**    **9.**

Problem Solving Strategy: Using Number Sense, page 387 ....

Use number sense to solve. Tell how you made
your choice.

1. Lou practices his guitar for $\frac{1}{4}$ of an hour in the morning and $\frac{1}{4}$ of an hour after dinner. Does he practice for more than 1 hour?

2. Kate's black cat weighs $10\frac{1}{2}$ pounds. Her white cat weighs $9\frac{3}{4}$ pounds. Does her white cat weigh more than her black cat?

3. Ben has a 5-gallon bucket. He wants to pour $3\frac{3}{4}$ gallons of water into the bucket. Is the 5-gallon bucket large enough to hold the water?

4. Abraham is $4\frac{1}{2}$ feet tall. Rebecca is $3\frac{1}{2}$ feet tall. Is Abraham taller than Rebecca?

EXTRA PRACTICE

Problem Solving Strategy: Making an Organized List, page 391..........

Make an organized list to solve the problem.

1. Tony has a half dollar. He needs dimes and nickels for the fruit juice machine. Tony asks the cashier for change. How many different combinations of coins could the cashier give him for the half dollar?

2. Mel has 3 cardboard shapes: a square, a circle, and a triangle. She has 2 colors of paint: yellow and blue. How many different color shapes can she make?

3. Aaron is making the salad for dinner. He has 3 kinds of lettuce: Bibb, iceberg, and red leaf. He has 3 kinds of dressing: oil and vinegar, French, and Italian. How many different salads can he make?

4. Joan is packing for a hiking trip. She is taking a pair of brown shorts and a pair of navy blue shorts. She is also taking 4 T-shirts: white, orange, yellow, and blue. How many different outfits can she wear?

5. Miguel wants to give his mother flowers. He has enough money to buy her three kinds. The florist has tulips, roses, mums, and carnations. How many different choices does Miguel have?

6. Sara, Betty, Jim, and William are in charge of organizing a May Fair for the children at a nearby hospital. They want to form teams of two to share the work. How many different teams can they form?

7. The "All Natural Frugurt" shop sells raspberry, banana, blueberry, and peach "frugurt." Arnie wants to order a combination of 2 flavors. How many choices does he have?

8. Vicki is working on 2 book reports. She can choose to read a biography, a folktale, a book on nature or history. How many different ways can Vicki choose the 2 books?

Finding Probability, page 395 ....

Find the probability of picking the color:

1. red

2. green

3. blue

Find the probability of spinning:

4. blue

5. red

6. yellow

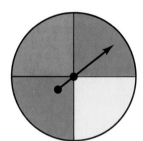

Probability and Statistics, page 397 ....

Phyllis put 8 crayons in a box. Two crayons were yellow and 6 were purple. Bruce took 20 turns picking crayons from the box. He graphed his results.

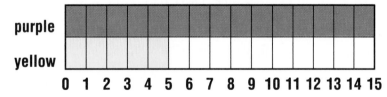

1. Which color did he pick most often? least often?

2. What is the probability of picking a purple crayon? a yellow crayon?

3. Put 10 different colored cubes in a bag. Shake the bag. Make predictions about what cubes you will pick in 20 turns. Then take 20 turns and graph your results.

Practice PLUS

KEY SKILL: Customary Weight (Use after page 383.)

Level A ....

Choose the better estimate.

1.
a. 12 ounces
b. 12 pounds

2.
a. 15 ounces
b. 15 pounds

3.
a. 5 ounces
b. 5 pounds

4. Duncan bought a 3-pound squash and a 12-pound pumpkin. How much more did the pumpkin weigh?

Level B ....

Choose the better estimate.

5.
a. 5 ounces
b. 5 pounds

6.
a. 12 ounces
b. 12 pounds

7.
a. 1 ounce
b. 1 pound

8. Don weighs 55 pounds. Bob weighs 72 pounds. How much more does Bob weigh?

Level C ....

Choose the better estimate.

9.
a. 12 ounces
b. 12 pounds

10.
a. 1 ounce
b. 1 pound

11.
a. 2 ounces
b. 2 pounds

12. Paul's hog weighs 102 pounds. Nancy's hog weighs 89 pounds. How much heavier is Paul's hog?

KEY SKILL: Probability (Use after page 395.)

Level A ....

1. Which color is most likely to
be chosen? least likely?

Give the probability of picking the color.

2. blue   **3.** green   **4.** orange

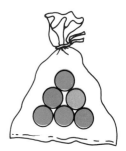

5. There are 8 cubes in a box. One cube is purple.
What is the probability of picking a purple cube?

Level B ....

6. Which color is the spinner
most likely to land on?

Give the probability of spinning:

7. red.   **8.** yellow.

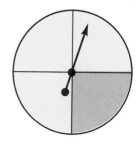

9. There are 3 blue, 5 yellow, 2 white, and 1 pink
cube in a box. If you pick one cube, which
color are you most likely to pick? least likely?

Level C ....

10. Which color is the most likely
to be chosen? least likely?

Give the probability of picking the color.

11. blue   **12.** green   **13.** orange

14. There are 2 blue rocks and 4 red rocks in a box.
What is the probability of picking a red rock?

CHAPTER REVIEW/TEST

LANGUAGE AND MATHEMATICS

Complete the sentences. Use the words in
the chart.

VOCABULARY
weight
capacity
Fahrenheit
probability
temperature

1. The amount a container can hold is its ___.

2. ___ tells how heavy an object is.

3. ___ is the chance that something will happen.

CONCEPTS AND SKILLS

Choose the better estimate
for the capacity.

4.

a. 2 cups
b. 2 quarts

5.

a. 1 pint
b. 1 gallon

Choose the better estimate for
the weight.

6.

a. 1,200 ounces
b. 1,200 pounds

7.

a. 6 ounces
b. 6 pounds

Write the temperature in degrees Fahrenheit.

8.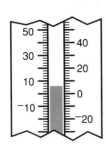

9.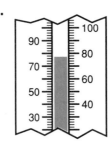

10.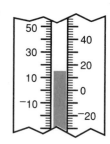

Choose the most reasonable temperature.

11. temperature of cold milk   **a.** ⁻10°F   **b.** 40°F   **c.** 100°F

12. temperature on a warm day   **a.** 0°F   **b.** 250°F   **c.** 80°F

Use the spinner at the right for questions 13 to 17.

13. What is the probability of spinning A?

14. What is the probability of spinning B?

15. What is the probability of spinning C?

16. If you were to spin the spinner 20 times, about how many times would it stop on A?

17. About how many times would it stop on B?

Critical Thinking

18. A small pot holds 3 cups of water and a large pot holds 7 cups of water. How would you use these two containers to get 4 cups of water?

Mixed Applications

19. Ira needs $1\frac{1}{2}$ cups of juice. He mixes $\frac{1}{4}$ cup of grape juice with 1 cup of apple juice. Did he mix enough?

20. There are 3 kinds of toppings: onion, cheese, and meatball. Sam is choosing 2 kinds. How many choices does he have? What are they?

PERFORMANCE ASSESSMENT

Work together with your group to solve the problem.

Choose a "mystery" container and put it in a bag. Describe the container on the outside of the bag. Use terms such as capacity, weight, and temperature.

1. *Think about:*
   - how you can clearly describe your container.

2. Write a paragraph about your description.

CUMULATIVE REVIEW

Choose the letter of the correct answer.

1. Which unit would you use to measure a small glass of water?
- **a.** cup
- **b.** quart
- **c.** gallon
- **d.** not given

2. $8 \times 5 =$ ___
- **a.** 20
- **b.** 30
- **c.** 40
- **d.** not given

3. $\frac{1}{3}$ of 9
- **a.** 2
- **b.** 4
- **c.** 5
- **d.** not given

4. A bag holds 3 red and 4 blue buttons. What are the chances of pulling a red?
- **a.** 1 out of 3
- **b.** 3 out of 4
- **c.** 3 out of 7
- **d.** not given

5. Choose the decimal for $\frac{3}{10}$.
- **a.** 0.03
- **b.** 0.3
- **c.** 3.0
- **d.** not given

6. Compare: $\frac{5}{8}$ ● $\frac{3}{8}$
- **a.** >
- **b.** <
- **c.** =
- **d.** not given

7. $45 + 36 =$ ___
- **a.** 21
- **b.** 32
- **c.** 81
- **d.** not given

8. Find the perimeter of a figure with sides 4 ft, 4 ft and 4 ft.
- **a.** 8 ft
- **b.** 12 ft
- **c.** 16 ft
- **d.** not given

9. Compare: $3\frac{1}{8}$ ● $2\frac{7}{8}$
- **a.** >
- **b.** <
- **c.** =
- **d.** not given

10. Complete the pattern: 2, 4, ___, 8, 10
- **a.** 3
- **b.** 4
- **c.** 6
- **d.** not given

11.
$$\begin{array}{r} 182 \\ -97 \\ \hline \end{array}$$
- **a.** 56
- **b.** 65
- **c.** 72
- **d.** not given

12. $9 \times 8 =$ ___
- **a.** 52
- **b.** 72
- **c.** 84
- **d.** not given

13. $54 \div 9 =$ ___
- **a.** 6
- **b.** 7
- **c.** 9
- **d.** not given

14. Compare: 0.8 ● 0.08
- **a.** >
- **b.** <
- **c.** =
- **d.** not given

TREE DIAGRAMS

John has 2 sweaters and 3 pairs of pants. You can use a tree diagram to help you find the number of different outfits John can wear.

1. How many different outfits can John wear with his green sweater?

2. How many different outfits can John wear with his red sweater?

3. How many different outfits can he wear in all?

4. How does a tree diagram help you to organize data to solve problems?

Draw a tree diagram to help you solve the problem.

5. Amy is making lunch for her class. She has 3 kinds of bread and 3 kinds of meat. How many different sandwiches can she make?

6. Burt is buying a new bicycle. He has a choice of 3 models and 4 colors. How many different bicycles does Burt have to choose from?

The circle is a shape that has special meaning to many people around the world. In the Lakota tradition, the circle is an especially important concept.

Gary Fields is a Native American musician and dancer. Some of his ancestors were Lakota. He says this about the circle:

"One of the things that seems to be fairly universal (among Indians) is the understanding of the importance of the circle. . . . The Indian people, a long time ago, if they would go out on the prairies, they could look around and see the horizon make a circle. The sun makes a circle as it goes through its path in the day. . . . We'd see that the seasons would go in circles. . . ."

Gary Fields describes a Round dance, a dance performed by men, women, and children in a circle:

"Round Dance is done in a circle. When we dance in an arena, we dance in a circle. When a Round Dance is done, we talk about the circle of friendship. . . ."

LAKOTA ROUND DANCE

1 The circle is a powerful shape in Lakota tradition. What other things found in nature are shaped like circles?

2 What is a "circle of friendship?" Why is a Round Dance a good way to show a circle of friendship?

3 Think of another shape. What things found in nature have this shape?

MONTANA NORTH DAKOTA MINNE-SOTA

SOUTH DAKOTA

ACTIVITY Geometry Around Us

Rima built a model castle to use in a play with puppets.

WORKING TOGETHER

1. Which figures in the castle have curved surfaces? Which have flat surfaces?

2. Which figures have corners? How many corners do they have?

3. Look for things that are shaped like the figures in the castle. Sort the things. Tell why you put the things in each group.

Come and See!
The Brave Prince

Les used flat figures to make an ad for the school play.

4. Which figures have curved sides? straight sides?

5. In which figures are some sides the same length?

6. Which figures have corners? How many corners do they have?

7. Look for things and parts of things that are shaped like the figures in the ad. Sort the things. Make a list for each group. Trace around the smaller things. Talk about why you put the things in each group.

8. Which figures do you see most often in the real world? Why?

9. Tell about how different shapes are used for different things. Why are certain shapes more useful than other shapes? Give examples.

10. How is geometry used in the world around us?

ON YOUR OWN

11. Look in magazines for pictures of things with the shapes you know. Sort the pictures and paste them in groups on pieces of paper.

12. *Write a list* of things in school, on the playground, on the way home from school, and at home that are shapes you know. Share your list and help make a class list.

ACTiViTY Lines, Line Segments, Rays, and Angles

You can fold paper to explore geometry.

WORKING TOGETHER

1. Fold a sheet of paper in any way. Open it and look at the fold.

You have made a **line segment**. It is straight and has two **endpoints**.

2. Where are the endpoints of the line segment you made?

3. Imagine that the line segment went on forever in both directions. Then it would be called a **line**.

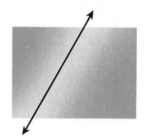

4. Draw a dot anywhere on the line. A **ray** is part of a line. It goes on forever in one direction.

5. Fold the paper in the other direction. Open it. Place a dot where the folds meet.

Two rays with the same endpoint form an **angle**.

6. How many angles did you form? Compare your angles to those of others.

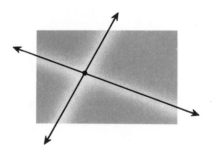

SHARING IDEAS

7. Can two rays form a line? Why or why not?

8. Can you measure the length of a line? Why or why not?

PRACTICE

Tell if the figure is a *line*, *line segment*, *ray*, or *angle*.

9.

10.

11.

12.

Tell how many segments are in the figure.
Tell how many angles.

13.

14.

15.

16.

17.

18.

19.

20.

Mixed Applications

21. Marta photographed part of an airport. Her picture shows a runway. The edge of the runway is an example of which geometric figure?

22. Tell another student about one of the geometric figures. Have that student name the figure.

23. Marc bought a roll of color film for $3.78 and a roll of black-and-white film for $2.99. How much more did the color film cost than the black-and-white film?

24. Marta hung her photographs in the hallway. There were 3 rows with 8 photos in a row. How many photographs were shown in all?

Mixed Review

Find the answer. Which method did you use?

> **MENTAL MATH**
> **CALCULATOR**
> **PAPER/PENCIL**

25. $1.98 + $3.76 = ▆

26. $72 \div 8 =$ ▆

27. $750 - 120 =$ ▆

28. $575 + 246 =$ ▆

29. $8.05 − $4.89 = ▆

ACTIVITY Plane Figures

Tony and Gloria are designing birdhouses. They use different plane figures.

WORKING TOGETHER

You can draw the figures on dot paper.

1. Make a figure with 3 sides that has
   a. no equal sides.   **b.** 2 equal sides.
   c. 3 equal sides.
   How many angles does each figure have?

2. Make a figure with 4 sides that has
   a. no equal sides.   **b.** 2 equal sides.
   c. 4 equal sides.
   How many angles does each figure have?

3. Make figures with 5 sides and 6 sides.
   How many angles do they have?

A closed figure that is made up of line segments is called a **polygon**.   open   closed

4. Complete the table.

Polygon	Number of Sides	Number of Angles
Triangle	■	■
Rectangle	■	■
Square	■	■
Pentagon	■	■
Hexagon	■	■

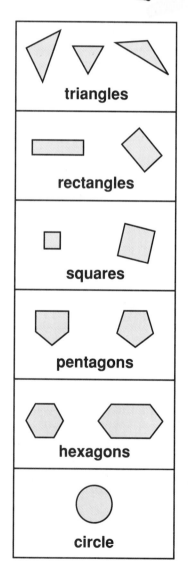

triangles

rectangles

squares

pentagons

hexagons

circle

5. Tell about the number of sides and angles of polygons. Do you see a pattern?

6. How are squares like other rectangles? How are they different from other rectangles?

7. Is a circle a polygon? Why or why not?

PRACTICE

Write *yes* or *no* to tell whether the figure is a polygon.
If it is a polygon, name it.

8.  9.  10.   11.

12.   13.   14.   15.

16. a closed figure that has 5 sides and 5 angles

17. a closed figure that has 3 sides and 3 angles

Mixed Applications

18. Luiz bought a can of paint for $3.98. He paid with a $5.00 bill. What was his change?

19. One wall of a birdhouse has 4 equal sides and 4 angles. What is the shape of the wall?

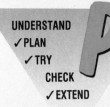
PROBLEM SOLVING

Strategy: Making a Table

Tom, Stacey, and Eric each collect a different kind of model. Tom collects car models. Stacey does not collect plane models. Who collects boat models?

You can solve the problem by making a table.

You know Tom collects car models. Write *Yes* in the box for Tom under Cars.

1. Why can you now write *No* in the other boxes for Tom?

2. Why can you now also write *No* in the boxes under Cars?

	Cars	Boats	Planes
Tom	Yes	No	No
Stacey	No		
Eric	No		

You know that Stacey does not collect planes.

Write *No* under Planes for Stacey.

3. Why can you write *Yes* in the box under Boats for Stacey?

4. Complete the rest of the table. Who collects plane models?

5. How does making a table help you solve the problem?

	Cars	Boats	Planes
Tom	Yes	No	No
Stacey	No	Yes	No
Eric	No		

PRACTICE

Make a table to help you solve the problem.

6. Reggie, Hank, and Nate collect photographs of different kinds of people. Hank does not collect photographs of sports stars. Nate collects dancers' photographs. Who collects photographs of musicians?

7. Connie, Akeem, and Carlos collect different kinds of comic books. Neither Connie nor Carlos collects mystery comics. Connie does not collect adventure comics. Who collects adventure comics?

8. Denzel, Jill, Martha, and Luke collect different kinds of postcards. Denzel does not collect postcards of things that move. Jill collects postcards of jets. Martha does not collect ship postcards. Luke does not collect house postcards. Who collects train postcards?

9. Risha, Cory, and Joan each collect dolls from a different country. Risha collects English dolls. Cory does not collect Dutch dolls. Who collects American dolls?

Strategies and Skills Review

Solve. Use mental math, a calculator, or paper and pencil.

10. Trish had 39 baseball cards. She traded some with her friend Lou. She gave him 12 cards and got 9 cards from Lou. How many cards did she have then?

11. Dante, Sophie, and Kate collect different kinds of puzzles. Kate does not collect picture puzzles. Dante collects crossword puzzles. Who collects number puzzles?

12. Marlon is setting up his model train. The black car is between the yellow car and the orange car. The orange car is between the red car and the black car. The yellow car is in front of the black car. Which car is last?

13. *Write a problem* that can be solved by making a table. Solve your problem. Ask others to solve it.

EXTRA **PRACTICE,** page 442

ACTiViTY Slides, Flips, and Turns

Geometric figures can be moved in different ways.
Each blue figure shows a triangle before it is moved.
Each red figure shows the triangle after it is moved.

You can **slide** a figure.

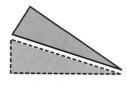
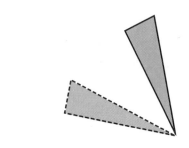

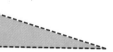

You can **turn** a figure.

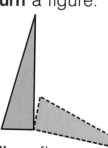

You can **flip** a figure.

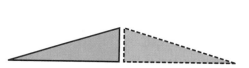

WORKING TOGETHER

Step 1 Trace the triangle. Cut out your tracing.

Step 2 Place your triangle over the blue triangle.
Move your triangle so that it covers the red triangle.

Write *slide*, *flip*, or *turn* to tell how you moved the triangle.

1.

2.
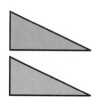

3.
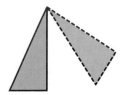

SHARING IDEAS

Tell which movement is described in Problems 4–6.

4. You may move in any direction.

5. You move only clockwise or counterclockwise.

6. It reverses the way the figure looks.

7. Tell how each move changes the position of a figure.

8. Can you always tell how a figure was moved? Why or why not?

PRACTICE

The red figure shows how the blue figure was moved.
Write *slide*, *flip*, or *turn*. Tell how the figure was moved.

9.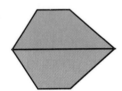

10.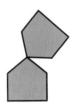

11.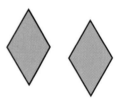

12.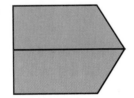

13.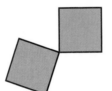

14.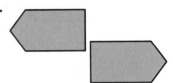

Ellie is making a rug for a dollhouse. She wants the rug to be the same shape and size as the floor.

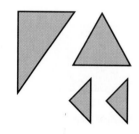

WORKING TOGETHER

Trace the figures on this page. Cut out your figures. Use them to explore shape and size.

1. Form groups of figures that have the same number of sides. How many groups can you form?

2. Try to match the sides and corners of the figures in each group. How are the figures in each group the same? How are they different?

3. Now group together the figures that have the same shape and size. How many groups can you form? Describe the types of groups.

Figures that have the same shape and size are called **congruent figures**.

4. ***Write a list*** of classroom objects that have congruent shapes. Compare your list with those of other students.

SHARING IDEAS

5. Two figures have the same shape. Must they be congruent? Why or why not?

6. Two figures are congruent. Must they be in the same position? Why or why not?

7. Are the pages in your math book congruent? Why or why not? Name other things that are congruent. Talk about why they are congruent.

Tell whether the two figures are congruent.

8.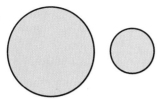

9.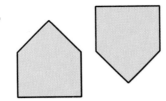

10.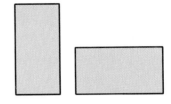

11.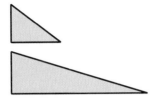

12.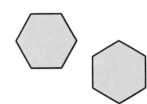

13.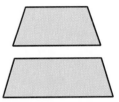

Critical Thinking

14. How are these figures alike?
How are they different?

Mixed Applications

15. Ellie made a rug for the dollhouse bedroom. It has
the same shape as the floor, but it is smaller.
Are the rug and the floor congruent?

16. The gym floor is a rectangle that measures 30 cm
by 20 cm by 30 cm by 20 cm. What is the
perimeter of the floor?

17. All of the dollhouse windows are shaped alike. Are
the windows congruent?

18. Ellie bought a lamp for $8.95. She gave the clerk
$9.00. What was Ellie's change?

LOGICAL REASONING

Show how you can remove 4 toothpicks to leave
4 congruent triangles.

MORE SHAPES
than meet the
EYE

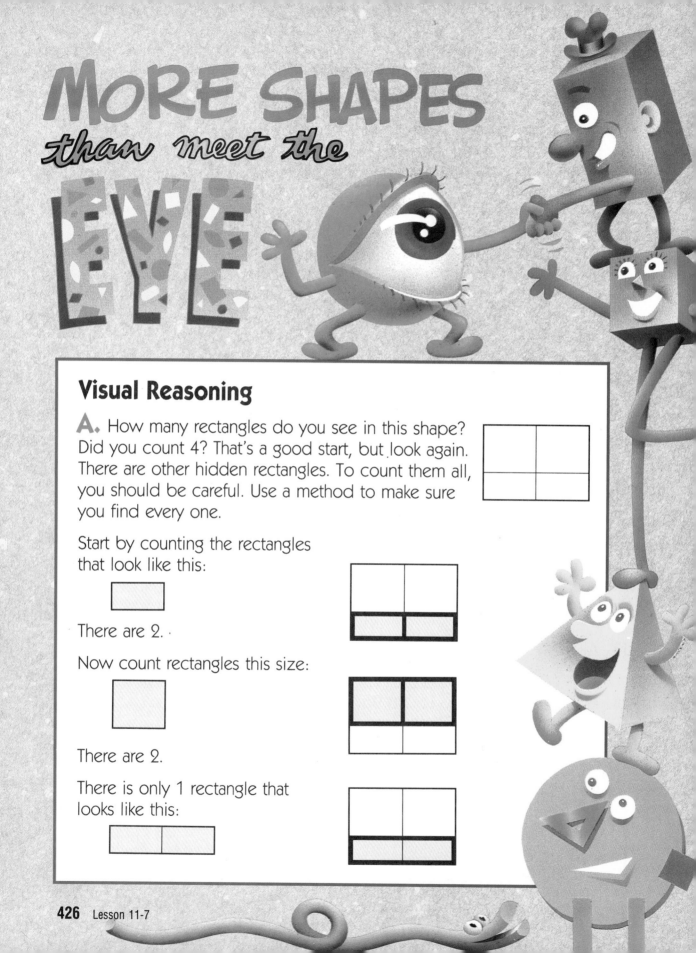

Visual Reasoning

A. How many rectangles do you see in this shape? Did you count 4? That's a good start, but look again. There are other hidden rectangles. To count them all, you should be careful. Use a method to make sure you find every one.

Start by counting the rectangles that look like this:

There are 2.

Now count rectangles this size:

There are 2.

There is only 1 rectangle that looks like this:

1. There are 3 other rectangle shapes. This is how they look:

How many of each shape can you find?

2. Now add the number of each shape you found. Did you get 9? If not, look again.

B. Now look at the picture at the right. How many triangles can you find? Count them carefully. You can use a chart to be sure you count them all. Copy and complete the chart.

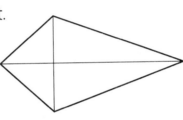

Triangle	Number in Drawing		Triangle	Number in Drawing
◿	2			

C. Now count the rectangles in this shape. Make a chart to help you count them all.

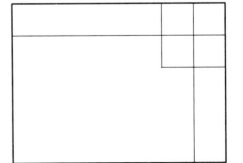

427

 **L**ines of **Symmetry**

Mike is making designs by folding and cutting paper. The designs are alike in a special way.

WORKING TOGETHER

Step 1 Trace these figures. Cut out your figures.

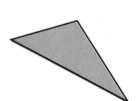 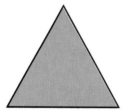  

Step 2 Fold each figure in two. Try to fold each figure to get two matching parts.

1. Which figures were you able to fold into two matching parts?

A figure that can be folded so that its two parts match exactly is a **symmetric** figure. This fold line is a **line of symmetry**.

Step 3 Try to fold the figures in different ways to get two matching parts.

2. Were you able to fold in more than one way to get matching parts?

SHARING IDEAS

3. Does changing the size or position of a figure change the number of lines of symmetry it has? Why or why not?

4. When you fold and cut paper the way Mike is doing, will you always get a symmetric figure? Why or why not?

PRACTICE

Tell whether the line is a line of symmetry.

5.   **6.** 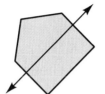 **7.**   **8.**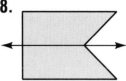

Tell how many lines of symmetry the figure has.

9.   **10.** 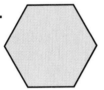 **11.**  **12.**

13. Complete the figure so that it is symmetrical. Draw any other lines of symmetry you see. Repeat with other figures.

14. *Write a list* of things that are symmetrical.

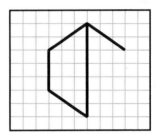

Critical Thinking

Tell whether the statement is *true* or *false*. If you think it is false, give an example.

15. All polygons are symmetrical.

16. Some triangles are symmetrical.

17. No pentagons are symmetrical.

Mixed Review

Find the answer. Which method did you use?

18. $6 + 3 + 5 + 4 =$ ▦   **19.** $608 - 324 =$ ▦

20. $867 + 355 =$ ▦   **21.** $6 \times 8 =$ ▦   **22.** $219 - 70 =$ ▦

MENTAL MATH
CALCULATOR
PAPER/PENCIL

Informal Algebra: Ordered Pairs

Tammy used a grid to plan a model of her neighborhood.

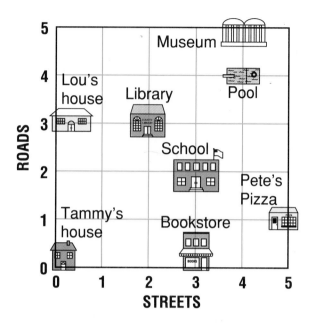

WORKING TOGETHER

1. What are some of the ways you can tell where the school is on the map?

You can write this as an **ordered pair** of numbers. The school is at (3, 2).

The first number tells you how many spaces to go to the right from 0.

The second number then tells you how many spaces to go up.

2. What is at (2, 3)?

3. What ordered pair tells where the bookstore is? How do you know?

4. What is at (0, 3)? at (0, 0)? at (4, 5)?

SHARING IDEAS

5. Why is order important in these pairs of numbers?

6. How are all the ordered pairs on Street 3 alike?

7. How are all the ordered pairs on Road 4 alike?

PRACTICE

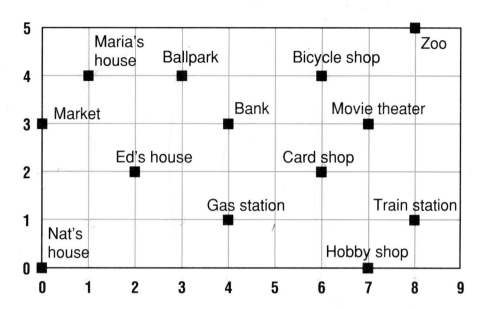

Write the ordered pair that tells the location of the building.

8. bicycle shop

9. Maria's house

10. hobby shop

11. gas station

12. train station

13. Nat's house

Tell what is at the point on the map.

14. (2, 2)

15. (8, 5)

16. (0, 3)

17. (7, 3)

18. (3, 4)

19. (6, 2)

Mixed Applications

Solve. You may need to use the Databank on page 522.

20. The post office in New Town is at the corner of Avenue C and Lane 3. Where is the supermarket?

21. What is at the corner of Avenue A and Lane 4? What is the ordered pair that names this point?

22. There are 9 houses on each block. If Roger walks 5 blocks, how many houses will he pass?

23. *Write a problem* about location or distance in New Town. Have other students solve your problem.

✓ UNDERSTAND
✓ PLAN
✓ TRY
✓ CHECK
✓ EXTEND

PROBLEM SOLVING

Strategy: Using Different Strategies

Judy sold an equal number of adult tickets and student tickets to the school fair. Adult tickets cost $2, and student tickets cost $1 each. She collected $15. How many of each kind of ticket did she sell?

You can often use different strategies to solve the same problem.

Chad is solving the problem using the Guess, Test, and Revise strategy.

First guess: 4 tickets
Test: 4 × $1 = $ 4
       4 × $2 = +$ 8
       Total = $12

His first guess was too low. So he revised his guess higher.

Revised guess: 5 tickets
Test: 5 × $1 = $■
       5 × $2 = +$■
       Total = $■

1. Is his second guess correct? How can you tell?

Sally is checking Chad's answer by using a different strategy. She makes a table.

Number of Tickets	Cost of Tickets		
	$1	$2	Total
1	$1	$2	$3
2	$2	$4	$6
3	$3	$6	$9
4	$4	$8	$12
5	■	■	$15

2. Continue the table until the total cost is $15.

3. Does your answer match Chad's?

4. Which strategy do you prefer? Why?

PRACTICE

Solve the problem. Then use a different strategy to check your answer. Tell which strategies you used. Use mental math, a calculator, or paper and pencil.

5. The students are putting the prize table, the refreshment table, and the crafts table in one row. In how many ways can they arrange the tables?

6. The treasurer is the oldest. Fred is older than Phil and younger than Gregg. Phil's age is between Susan's and Fred's. Who is the treasurer?

7. The bottom row of Rose's stand has 8 blocks. It has twice as many blocks as the middle row. How many blocks are in the top row if it has 1 less block than the middle row?

8. The students had $50.00 to hire workers for the fair. They planned to pay them $24.50 to set up the fair and $24.50 to take it down. Did they have enough money?

Strategies and Skills Review

9. Admission to the puppet show is $1 for children and $2 for adults. There were 58 children and 31 adults at the show. How much did they pay in all?

10. The school sold $326 worth of refreshments at the fair. It cost $172 to buy the refreshments. How much money did the school make?

11. Mrs. Golab's class put on a play. There were twice as many girls as boys in the play. If 18 students were in the play, how many were boys and how many were girls?

12. *Write a problem* that can be solved by more than one strategy. Solve the problem. Use a different strategy to check your answer. Ask others to solve your problem.

STUDENT TICKET

SCHOOL FAIR $1.00

ACTIVITY Space Figures

The students in Tracy's class used containers to make a model of a town.

WORKING TOGETHER

The containers they used are shaped like these space figures.

1. Which figures have curved faces? Which have only flat faces?

2. Which figures have curved edges? Which figures have straight edges?

3. Complete the table.

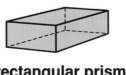

rectangular prism

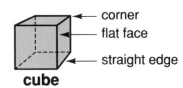

corner
flat face
straight edge

cube

pyramid

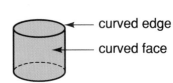

curved edge
curved face

cylinder

cone

sphere

Space Figure	Number of Curved Faces	Number of Flat Faces	Number of Edges	Number of Corners
Rectangular prism	■	■	■	■
Cube	■	■	■	■
Pyramid	■	■	■	■
Cylinder	■	■	■	■
Cone	■	■	■	■
Sphere	■	■	■	■

SHARING IDEAS

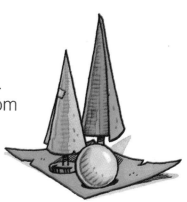

4. Look at real-world examples of space figures. Draw what you see when you look at them from the top, the bottom, and the sides.

5. What plane figures did you see when you looked at the space figures?

6. Can you tell which space figure you are looking at when you can only see one side? Why or why not?

PRACTICE

Write the name of the space figure.

7.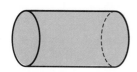

8.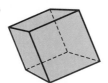

9.

10.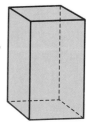

11. It has 2 faces, 1 edge, and 1 corner.

12. It has 5 faces, 8 edges, and 5 corners.

13. It has 6 square faces.

14. It has 2 faces like circles.

15. Pick a space figure. Tell another student what it looks like. Have that student name the figure.

16. *Write a list* of things in the classroom, outdoors, and at home that have the shapes of space figures.

Mixed Applications

17. Mark made a model of a building that had 4 triangular faces and 1 square face. What kind of space figure did he make?

18. Lani used one and one-fourth jars of paint to paint her buildings. Write a number for the amount of paint she used.

EXTRA PRACTICE, page 445; **PRACTICE PLUS**, page 447

ACTIVITY **Volume**

The **volume** of a figure is the number of cubic units it takes to fill the figure.

WORKING TOGETHER

1. Use unused crayons as units. Estimate and find the number of crayons it takes to fill a crayon box.

2. Find other small boxes and cans. Estimate and find the number of crayons it takes to fill them.

3. Use cubes as units. Estimate and find the number of cubes it takes to fill the same containers.

4. Which containers were easier to fill with crayons? Which were easier to fill with cubes?

5. Which units completely filled the containers? Why?

1 cubic unit

6. Use cubes to build each shape below. Then count the cubes to find the volume of each shape.

a. 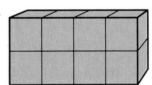 b. 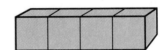 c.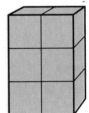

SHARING IDEAS

7. Why are boxes easier to measure with cubes than cylinders?

8. Two boxes have the same volume. Must they have the same shape? Why or why not?

Find the volume. Remember to count the cubes that
you cannot see.

9.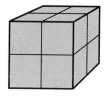

10.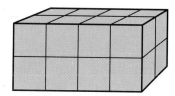

11.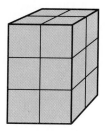

12.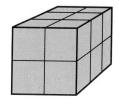

13. Use your cubes to find different rectangular prisms
with volumes of 12 cubic units. Compare your prisms
with those of other students. How many different
prisms can you make?

14. Use cubes as units. Estimate
and find the volumes of
boxes. Make a table.

Object	Estimated Volume	Actual Volume
Crayon box	■	■
Lunch box	■	■
Chalk box	■	■

15. *Write a list* of times when
you need to measure
the volume of something.

DECISION MAKING

Problem Solving: Designing a Clubhouse

SITUATION

The members of the Carpenters' Club want to build a clubhouse. They have three plans of what they think a clubhouse should look like.

PROBLEM

What should the clubhouse look like?

DATA

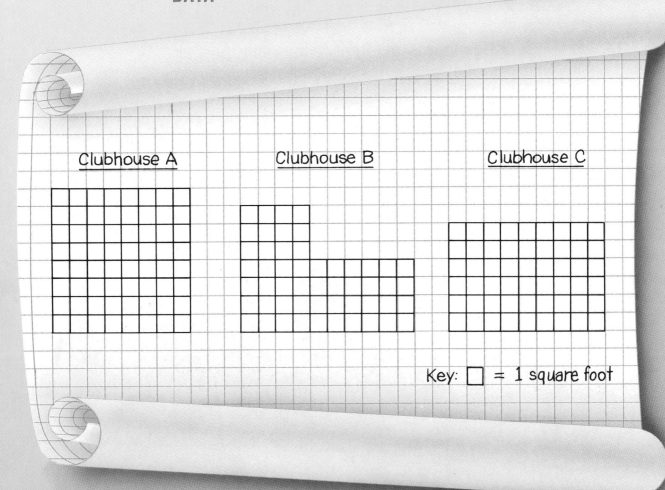

Clubhouse A   Clubhouse B   Clubhouse C

Key: ☐ = 1 square foot

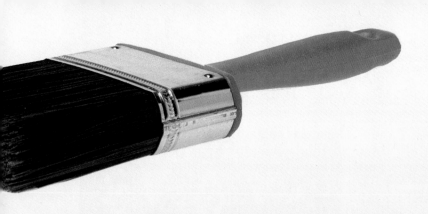

USING THE DATA

1. What different shapes have the club members used to design the clubhouses?

What is the perimeter of:

2. clubhouse A?   3. clubhouse B?   4. clubhouse C?

What is the area of:

5. clubhouse A?   6. clubhouse B?   7. clubhouse C?

MAKING DECISIONS

8. What are some things the club members should consider before designing a clubhouse?

9. What are some materials needed to build a clubhouse?

Which clubhouse should the members build if they want:

10. to have the greatest amount of wall space? Why?

11. to have the greatest amount of floor space? Why?

12. **What if** small groups of club members need to work at the same time in the clubhouse? What could be done to allow each group to work alone?

13. Which clubhouse would you build? Why?

14. **Draw a plan** for a clubhouse of your own. Pick any shape you like. You may wish to use more than one shape. Show your design to others. Give reasons for your decisions.

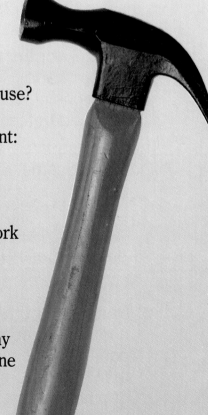

Math and Art

Navajo weavers use dyes to decorate their blankets and rugs. These designs make useful items beautiful. Many of the designs use squares, rectangles, triangles, and other basic geometric shapes. These shapes are combined to form larger figures and patterns.

In some designs more realistic figures are used. These designs may include people, birds, and plants.

What if you were asked to describe the geometric shapes in the rug on this page? Tell what shapes you see.

Think: Look for the basic geometric shapes. Then look for combinations of shapes and shapes inside other shapes.

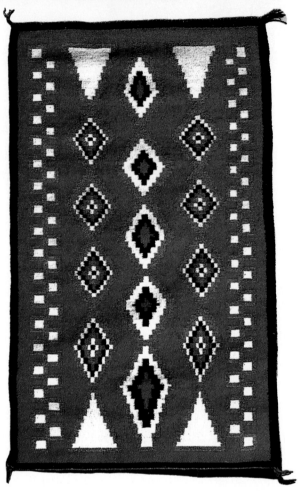

There are squares, triangles, rectangles, and other geometric figures in the rug.

ACTIVITIES

1. Design a pattern for a belt using two geometric shapes. Draw your design on a strip of paper long enough to reach around your waist.

2. Design and draw a pattern for a blanket. Use any number of geometric shapes. Remember that you can use shapes that are a combination of more than one shape. Compare your design with those of other students.

Computer: Symmetric Figures

You can use Logo commands to explore and draw symmetric figures.

AT THE COMPUTER

Enter all the first commands to draw part of a figure. Then ask a partner to enter all the second commands to draw the other part. Talk about how the turtle moves after each command.

First Commands	Second Commands
LT 53 FD 50	RT 53 FD 50
RT 53 FD 20	LT 53 FD 20
RT 90 FD 20	LT 90 FD 20
LT 90 FD 20	RT 90 FD 20
RT 90 FD 20	LT 90 FD 20
PU HOME PD	

1. Compare each line of the first commands to those in the second commands. How are they alike? How are they different?

2. Are all the turns the same size?

3. Are the two parts of the figure congruent?

4. Use the commands left turn (LT) and forward (FD) to draw the line of symmetry. What did you enter?

5. Enter Logo commands to draw your own symmetric figures. Draw part of the figure and have your partner draw the other part. Then draw the line of symmetry. Take turns.

EXTRA PRACTICE

Tell if the figure is a *line, line segment, ray,* or *angle.*

1.

2.

3.

4.

Tell how many segments are in the figure. Tell how many angles.

5.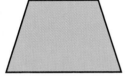

6.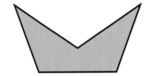

7.

Plane Figures, page 419 ....

Write *yes* or *no* to tell whether the figure is a polygon. If it is a polygon, name it.

1.

2.

3.

4.

Problem Solving Strategy: Making a Table, page 421 ....

Make a table to help you solve the problem.

1. In Mrs. Kane's third-grade class, Bob, Sidney, and Kit have pets. The pets are a dog, a fish, and a turtle. Bob does not like dogs. Sidney has fish. What kind of pet does Kit have?

2. The Oak Hill School is holding tryouts for the soccer, swimming, and baseball teams. Jay, Su, and Shelly will each try out for a different team. Shelly is a good pitcher. Jay does not swim. What team will Su try out for?

Slides, Flips, and Turns, page 423..

The red figure shows how the blue figure was moved.
Write *slide, flip, turn,* or two of the words to tell how
the figure was moved.

1.

2.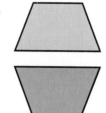

3.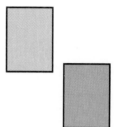

4.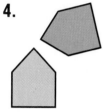

5.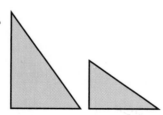

6.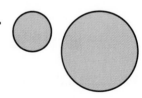

Congruence, page 425 ....

Tell whether the two figures are congruent.

1.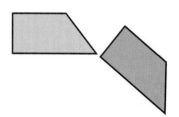

2.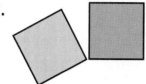

3.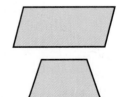

4.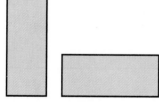

5.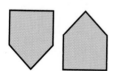

6.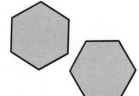

EXTRA PRACTICE

Lines of Symmetry, page 429..

Tell whether the line is a line of symmetry.

1.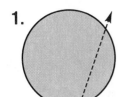

2.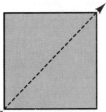

3.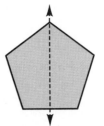

4.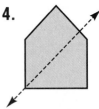

Tell how many lines of symmetry the figure has.

5.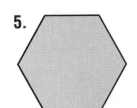

6.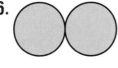

7.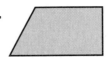

8.

Ordered Pairs, page 431..

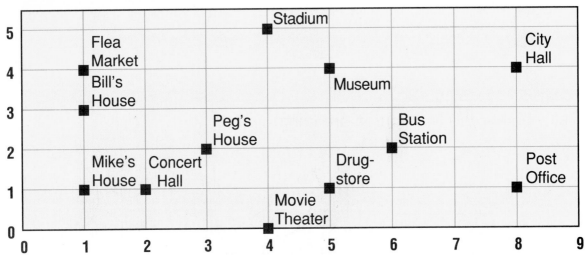

Write the ordered pair that tells the location of each building.

1. Concert Hall

2. Mike's House

3. Bus Station

4. Flea Market

5. Peg's House

6. Museum

Tell what is at the point on the map.

7. (2, 1)   **8.** (4, 5)   **9.** (8, 1)   **10.** (8, 4)   **11.** (3, 2)   **12.** (4, 0)

Problem Solving Strategy: Using Different Strategies, page 433 ....

Solve the problem. Then use a different strategy to
check your answer. Tell which strategies you used.

1. Bill and Pamela are setting up
an information booth, a ticket
booth, and a refreshment booth
for the school fair. In how many
ways can they arrange the
booths?

2. Four friends are holding a
birthday party for the oldest.
Amanda is older than Lupe
and younger than Steven.
Lupe's age is between Kerin's
and Amanda's. Whose birthday
is it?

3. The bottom row of the sculpture
Kyle is building has 9 blocks
of marble. It has 3 times as
many blocks as the middle
row. How many blocks of
marble are in the top row if it
has 2 less blocks than the
middle row?

4. Gretchen has $30 to hire
workers to work in her yard.
She plans to pay them $14.50
to mow the lawn and $14.50
to pull the weeds in the flower
garden. Does she have enough
money?

Space Figures, page 435 ....

Write the name of the space figure.

1.

2.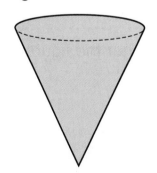

3.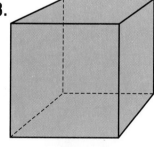

4.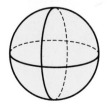

5.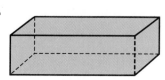

6.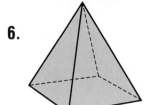

Practice PLUS

KEY SKILL: Plane Figures (Use after page 419.)

Level A

Write *yes* or *no* to tell whether the figure is a polygon.
If it is a polygon, name it.

1.

2.

3.

4.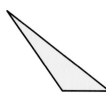

Level B

Write *yes* or *no* to tell whether the figure is a polygon. If
it is a polygon, name it.

5.

6.

7.

8.

Level C

Write *yes* or *no* to tell whether the figure is a polygon. If
it is a polygon, name it.

9.

10.

11.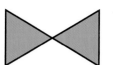

12.

KEY SKILL: Space Figures (Use after page 435.)

Level A

Write *cone, cylinder, cube,* or *sphere* for the space figures.

1.   **2.**   **3.**   **4.**

Level B

Write the name of the space figure.

5. 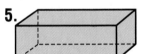   **6.**   **7.**   **8.**

9. a figure that only has a curved face

Level C

Complete the table.

	Space Figure	Number of Curved Faces	Number of Flat Faces	Number of Edges	Number of Corners
10.	Cylinder	■	■	■	■
11.	Cone	■	■	■	■
12.	Sphere	■	■	■	■
13.	Cube	■	■	■	■
14.	Pyramid	■	■	■	■

CHAPTER REVIEW/TEST

LANGUAGE AND MATHEMATICS

Complete the sentences. Use the words in the chart.

1. A ▪ is a closed figure made up of line segments.

2. A ▪ goes on forever in two directions.

3. A figure whose halves match exactly is ▪.

VOCABULARY
symmetrical
sphere
polygon
line

CONCEPTS AND SKILLS

Name the figure.

4.

5.

6.

7.

8.

9.

10.

11.

The red figure shows how the blue figure was moved.
Write *slide, flip,* or *turn.*

12.

13.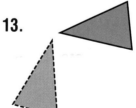

14.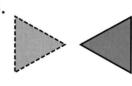

Tell whether the figures are *congruent*.
Tell whether the line is a *line of symmetry*.

15.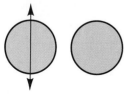

16.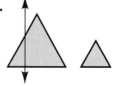

17.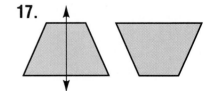

Name the ordered pair or the point.

18. Point *A*

19. (4, 2)

20. Point *B*

21. (3, 1)

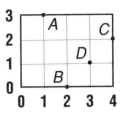

Critical Thinking

Write *true* or *false*. Tell how you decided.

22. The symmetrical parts of a polygon are congruent.

23. None of the faces of a cube are congruent.

Mixed Applications

24. Will is taller than Jan but shorter than Bo. Lynn is shorter than Will. Who is the tallest? What strategy did you use?

25. Jack, Ruth, and Pat each collect a coin: pennies, nickels, or dimes. Jack collects pennies. Ruth does not collect dimes. Who collects nickels?

PERFORMANCE ASSESSMENT

PERFORMANCE ASSESSMENT

Work with your group to solve the problem.

Using dot paper, draw these closed shapes.

a. a shape with 6 line segments

b. a shape with 8 line segments

c. a shape with 3 angles

d. a space figure

e. a shape with at least 2 sides of equal length

Label your drawings a to e. Compare each drawing, one at a time, with the drawings of others.

1. *Think about:*
- how the drawings are alike and different

2. Choose two drawings made by your group. Write at least 2 sentences about the drawings.

CUMULATIVE REVIEW

Choose the letter of the correct answer.

1. What is this figure?

  a. square   **c.** triangle
  b. sphere   **d.** pentagon

2. How was Figure 1 moved to Figure 2?

   Figure 1   Figure 2

  a. slide   **c.** flip
  b. turn   **d.** not given

3. Which figure is symmetrical?

  a.   **b.**   **c.**

  d. not given

4. Which letter is at (3, 0)?

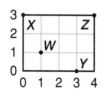

  a. W   **b.** X   **c.** Y   **d.** Z

5. Which is a ray?

  a.   **b.**   **c.**   **d.**
  •—• •—→ ←—→   <

6. Compare: $1\frac{1}{3}$ ● $1\frac{2}{3}$

  a. >   **c.** =
  b. <   **d.** not given

7. $54 \div 9 =$

  a. 6   **c.** 8
  b. 7   **d.** 9

8. The temperature on a spring day is closest to ___

  a. ⁻10°F   **c.** 200°F
  b. 32°F   **d.** not given

9. There are 2 yellow, 6 blue, 4 red, and 3 green buttons in a bag. In one pick, which color is most likely?

  a. blue   **c.** red
  b. green   **d.** not given

10. Compare: 0.30 ● $\frac{29}{100}$

  a. >   **c.** =
  b. <   **d.** not given

11. Compare: 3.55 ● 3.5

  a. >   **c.** =
  b. <   **d.** not given

12. Choose the fraction for 0.75.

  a. $\frac{75}{100}$ **c.** $7\frac{50}{100}$
  b. $7\frac{75}{100}$ **d.** $75\frac{5}{7}$

13. Compare: $\frac{1}{2}$ ● $\frac{2}{4}$

  a. >   **c.** =
  b. <   **d.** not given

14. The capacity of a gasoline truck is about 9,000 ___.

  a. cups   **c.** quarts
  b. pints   **d.** gallons

TESSELLATIONS

The patterns below are examples of **tessellations**.

They repeat a shape to completely cover
a flat surface.

A.    **B.** 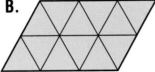   **C.**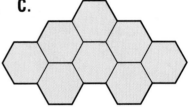

1. Where have you seen other examples of tessellations?

2. What polygon is repeated to make tessellation A? B? C?

3. What do you notice about each of the polygons in the tessellations?

4. Can each of these polygons be tessellated? Use a drawing to help you explain why or why not.

a. 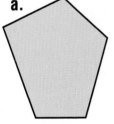   **b.** 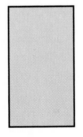   **c.** 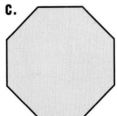   **d.**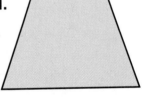

5. The letter *S* can be tessellated. Can you think of other letters that can be tessellated? Use drawings to show how the patterns will look.

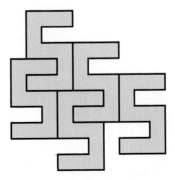

YORUBA

COUNTING

AFRICA

Nigeria

In a busy Nigerian market, a woman buys a bolt of *adire* (ah-DEE-ray) cloth, which is cloth that has been decorated with vegetable paste and then dyed. The seller tells her in the Yoruba (YOR-uh-buh) language, "It costs 45 *naira* (NYE-rah)." When the seller says the number 45, she says "five from ten from three twenties."

In the Yoruba number system, 14 is expressed as 10 plus 4. Numbers 15 and higher are based on 20. A Yoruba person figures how many groups of 20 are in a number and how much is added or subtracted beyond that. Here are some examples:

15 = one group of 20 minus 5
24 = one group of 20 plus 4
31 = two groups of 20, minus 10, plus 1
45 = three groups of 20, minus 10, minus 5

1. What mental math skills would help you to understand the Yoruba way of expressing numbers?

2. What patterns do you see in the Yoruba number system?

3. When do you think of numbers in a way that is similar to the way Yoruba people express numbers?

Multiplying 10s and 100s

Ken is printing tickets to a Save the Forest rally. He prints different amounts of each type of ticket.

SAVE THE FOREST TICKETS

Type	Tickets on Sheet	Number of Sheets
Deluxe	5	100
Special	6	300
Regular	8	500

1. Use a calculator to find the products.

$5 \times 1 = 5$ $6 \times 3 = 18$ $8 \times 5 = 40$

$5 \times 10 = $  $6 \times 30 = $ $8 \times 50 = $

$5 \times 100 = $ $6 \times 300 = $ $8 \times 500 = $

How many tickets can Ken print?

2. Look at the first group of numbers. Compare the number of zeros in each product to the number of zeros in each factor. What pattern do you see?

3. Compare the numbers in the other two groups. Do they all follow the same pattern? Why or why not?

4. Use the pattern to find these products mentally. Then use a calculator to check your answer.

a. $3 \times 900 = $

b. $7 \times 60 = $

c. $8 \times 400 = $

TRY OUT Multiply mentally.

5. $8 \times 10 = $ **6.** $4 \times 300 = $ **7.** $5 \times 700 = $

PRACTICE

Multiply mentally.

8.   10
      × 4

9.   100
      × 7

10.   40
       × 2

11.   50
       × 6

12.   400
       × 9

13. 3 × 10 =

14. 5 × 10 =

15. 7 × 10 =

16. 2 × 100 =

17. 6 × 100 =

18. 4 × 100 =

19. 1 × 60 =

20. 5 × 30 =

21. 6 × 20 =

22. 4 × 300 =

23. 3 × 300 =

24. 7 × 200 =

25. 4 × 60 =

26. 4 × 200 =

27. 8 × 20 =

28. 30 × 2 =

29. 500 × 3 =

30. 3 × 600 =

31. 7 × 100 =

32. 800 × 1 =

33. 500 × 4 =

Critical Thinking

34. How would you find the product of 5 × 8,000? What is the product?

Mixed Applications

35. Tia orders 5 boxes of buttons for the rally. Each box has 500 buttons. How many buttons are there in all?

36. Ida sold 750 tickets. Ned sold 1,025 tickets. Celia sold 939 tickets. How many tickets did they sell all together?

37. Cheryl prints 1,000 fliers for the rally. She hands out 750 fliers. How many does she have left?

38. Dave makes 11 phone calls on Monday. He makes 13 calls on Tuesday. On Friday he makes 12 calls. How many phone calls does he make?

Estimating Products

The Southbend Drama Club has 87 members. Each member is expected to sell at least 4 tickets to the spring play. About how many tickets will the members sell?

Estimate: 4 × 87. Here are two ways to estimate.

Rounding		Front-End Estimation	
Round to the nearest 10.		**Use the front digits.**	

$$
\begin{array}{r} 87 \\ \times\ 4 \\ \end{array}
\qquad \textit{Think:}\qquad
\begin{array}{r} 90 \\ \times\ 4 \\ \hline 360 \end{array}
\qquad\qquad
\begin{array}{r} 87 \\ \times\ 4 \\ \end{array}
\qquad \textit{Think:}\qquad
\begin{array}{r} 80 \\ \times\ 4 \\ \hline 320 \end{array}
$$

They will sell about 320 to 360 tickets.

1. Which method results in an estimate that is greater than the exact answer? Why?

2. Which method results in an estimate that is less than the exact answer? Why?

3. Estimate 7 × 235 using both methods. How do the estimates compare?

4. How would you use these methods to estimate 3 × $3.23? How do these estimates compare?

TRY OUT   Write the letter of the correct answer.

Estimate. Use rounding.

5. 3 × 54   **a.** 15   **b.** 150   **c.** 500   **d.** 1,500

6. 6 × 762   **a.** 48   **b.** 148   **c.** 480   **d.** 4,800

Estimate. Use the front digits.

7. 2 × 98   **a.** 18   **b.** 100   **c.** 180   **d.** 2,000

8. 4 × $6.47   **a.** $24   **b.** $240   **c.** $1,000   **d.** $2,400

PRACTICE

Estimate. Use rounding.

9.	81	**10.**	54	**11.**	79	**12.**	63	**13.**	21
	× 5		× 3		× 7		× 2		× 9

14.	234	**15.**	683	**16.**	461	**17.**	$3.19	**18.**	$1.90
	× 6		× 4		× 8		× 2		× 8

19. $5 \times 37 =$ ■ **20.** $8 \times 358 =$ ■ **21.** $8 \times \$1.25 =$ ■

22. $6 \times \$2.87 =$ ■ **23.** $3 \times 85 =$ ■ **24.** $5 \times 701 =$ ■

Estimate. Use the front digits.

25.	93	**26.**	56	**27.**	72	**28.**	64	**29.**	23
	× 3		× 2		× 6		× 5		× 4

30.	342	**31.**	382	**32.**	641	**33.**	$2.19	**34.**	$4.50
	× 3		× 5		× 7		× 8		× 3

35. $3 \times 46 =$ ■ **36.** $5 \times 58 =$ ■ **37.** $8 \times \$2.50 =$ ■

38. $6 \times 27 =$ ■ **39.** $2 \times 285 =$ ■ **40.** $2 \times \$4.50 =$ ■

Mixed Applications

41. Val spent 17 hours painting sets for the play. Brad spent 12 hours. How many more hours did Val spend painting sets than Brad?

42. The Drama Playhouse has 9 sections with 38 seats in each section. About how many seats are there in all?

Mixed Review

> **MENTAL MATH**
> **CALCULATOR**
> **PAPER/PENCIL**

Find the answer. Which method did you use?

43. $4 \times 60 =$ ■ **44.** $476 - 89 =$ ■ **45.** $10 \times 3 =$ ■

Multiplying Larger Numbers

Dan is using shapes to design place mats. He uses 3 large triangles and 2 rows of 10 small triangles for each place mat. How many triangles does he use for 3 place mats?

WORKING TOGETHER

Step 1 Use place-value models to show how many triangles Dan uses for 3 place mats.

1. Write a multiplication sentence to show how you can find the number of large triangles.

2. Write a multiplication sentence to show how you can find the number of small triangles.

3. Write an addition sentence to show how many triangles there are in all.

Step 2 Use place-value models to show how many triangles Dan would use for 4 place mats.

4. Write a multiplication sentence to show how you can find the number of large triangles.

5. Write a multiplication sentence to show how you can find the number of small triangles.

6. Write an addition sentence to show how many triangles there are in all.

You can show the three steps in one problem.

$$
\begin{array}{r}
23 \\
\times\ 4 \\
\hline
12 \leftarrow (4 \times 3) \\
80 \leftarrow (4 \times 20) \\
\hline
92
\end{array}
$$

7. How does this compare to what you did with models?

8. Use models and write multiplication problems to find these products.

a. $\begin{array}{r} 12 \\ \times\ 4 \\ \hline \end{array}$
b. $\begin{array}{r} 22 \\ \times\ 5 \\ \hline \end{array}$
c. $\begin{array}{r} 45 \\ \times\ 3 \\ \hline \end{array}$
d. $\begin{array}{r} 61 \\ \times\ 2 \\ \hline \end{array}$
e. $\begin{array}{r} 23 \\ \times\ 2 \\ \hline \end{array}$

SHARING IDEAS

9. How do you know when to regroup in multiplication?

10. Tell how you would use models and write multiplication problems for multiplying a 3-digit number by a 1-digit number.

11. Can you use this method to multiply a money amount by a 1-digit number? How?

ON YOUR OWN

Solve. Use models if needed.

12. Dan paid $.39 for a jar of paste. How much did 3 jars cost?

13. Dan sold 4 place mats for $2.20 each. How much money did he get?

14. The Kitchen Shop wants to buy 24 place mats a month. If they buy the same number each month, how many place mats will the Kitchen Shop buy in 9 months?

15. *Write a problem* that asks for a product. Ask others to solve your problem.

Multiplying 2-Digit Numbers: Regrouping Once

A. Carla is sorting her stamps. She puts 28 stamps on each page. How many stamps will go on 2 pages?

She estimates: $2 \times 30 = 60$.

Carla uses place-value models to find the exact answer.

Multiply: 2×28

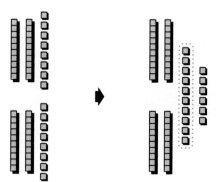

1. How many equal groups did Carla make? How many are in each group?

2. After Carla combined the ones, how many ones did she have? How did she regroup them?

3. After she combined the tens and added the new ten, how many tens did she have in all?

4. What number does her model show? How many stamps are there?

B. Here is a way to multiply without models.

Step 1	Multiply the ones. Regroup.		Step 2	Multiply the tens. Add any tens.

	$\begin{array}{r} 1 \\ 28 \\ \times\ 2 \\ \hline 6 \end{array}$	*Think:* 16 ones = 1 ten 6 ones	$\begin{array}{r} 1 \\ 28 \\ \times\ 2 \\ \hline 56 \end{array}$	*Think:* 2×2 tens = 4 tens 4 tens + 1 ten = 5 tens
$\begin{array}{r} 28 \\ \times\ 2 \\ \hline \end{array}$				

5. Compare the method in A with the method in B. What do you notice?

6. How does regrouping save a step in the problem?

7. Why is 56 a reasonable answer?

PRACTICE

Multiply.

8. 13 × 7	**9.** 15 × 6	**10.** 37 × 2	**11.** 23 × 4	**12.** 17 × 5
13. 51 × 3	**14.** 22 × 4	**15.** 71 × 9	**16.** 51 × 7	**17.** 83 × 2

18. $4 \times 18 =$ ▬

19. $2 \times 35 =$ ▬

20. $3 \times 29 =$ ▬

21. eight times twenty-one

22. seven times sixty

Mixed Applications

23. Len sold 4 sets of coins. Each set had 16 coins. How many coins did Len sell?

24. Leah bought a bracelet for $3.89. She paid with a 5-dollar bill. What was her change?

MENTAL MATH

Sometimes you can multiply three numbers mentally. Look for 10s or 100s.

$5 \times 7 \times 6 = 210$ *Think:* $5 \times 6 = 30$, $7 \times 30 = 210$

Multiply mentally.

1. $8 \times 5 \times 3 =$ ▬   **2.** $4 \times 9 \times 5 =$ ▬   **3.** $5 \times 4 \times 5 =$ ▬

PROBLEM SOLVING

Strategy: Choosing the Operation

The students in Mr. Winter's class are planning a bake sale to raise money for the school. Andrea baked 8 trays of cookies. Each tray has 12 cookies. How many cookies did she bake?

1. What information does Andrea know?

2. What does she need to find out?

Since each tray has the same number of cookies, Andrea plans to use multiplication to solve the problem. $8 \times 12 = \underline{\blacksquare}$

3. How many cookies did she bake?

4. **What if** she baked 2 trays, one tray with 24 cookies and the other tray with 16 cookies? How would you find how many cookies she baked? How many cookies is that in all?

5. Which operation should you use when you combine groups that have the same number of objects in each group?

6. Which operation should you use when you combine groups with different numbers of objects in the groups?

PRACTICE

Decide which operation to use to solve the problem.
Use mental math, a calculator, or paper and pencil.

7. On the first day of the sale, the students sold 32 loaves of bread. On the second day, they sold 9 loaves. How many loaves did they sell on the two days?

8. The students in the third grade sold 38 books at the book fair. There are 8 books left. How many books did they have when the fair started?

9. There are 6 large tables with 15 loaves of bread on each table. How many loaves are there in all?

10. There are 12 artists at the art fair. Each artist is selling 6 paintings. How many paintings are for sale?

Strategies and Skills Review

11. Cindy's father buys 36 tickets at the art sale. The tickets come in books of 4. How many books does he buy?

12. The bake sale raised $262, and the art sale raised $356. Did the students raise at least $600 from the sales?

13. At the PTA rummage sale, there are twice as many tables with clothes as with shoes. There is 1 more table with dishes than with shoes. There are 9 tables in all. How many of each kind of table are there?

14. Janet uses 180 buttons to make a picture. She uses 27 red buttons and 76 yellow buttons. She uses pink buttons for the rest of the picture. How many pink buttons does she use?

15. Glenn wants to buy a book of maps for $4.95, a nature book for $3.98, and a dictionary for $2.98. Is $10.00 enough?

16. *Write a problem* to solve by addition or multiplication. Solve the problem. Ask others to solve your problem.

LOGIC in BOXES

Logical Reasoning

A. Len, Julia, and Rosie eat lunch.
One eats a peanut butter sandwich.
One eats macaroni and cheese.
One eats a ham and cheese sandwich.

What did each student eat?
Use these clues.

CLUES

1. Julia eats a meal made from peanuts.

2. Rosie does not have a sandwich for lunch.

Copy the chart at the right. You can use it to help you find the answer.

	Peanut Butter	Macaroni and Cheese	Ham and Cheese
Len			
Julia			
Rosie			

Look at the first clue. Which meal is made from peanuts?
Julia eats a peanut butter sandwich. Put a ✔ for *"yes"* in the box where *Julia* and *peanut butter* meet.

No one else eats peanut butter. You can put an **X** for *"no"* in the other boxes below peanut butter. You also know that Julia did not eat any other meal. Put an **X** in the other boxes across from Julia.

	Peanut Butter	Macaroni and Cheese	Ham and Cheese
Len	X		
Julia	✔	X	X
Rosie	X		

Clue 1

Look at the other clue.
Which meal is NOT a sandwich?
Put a ✔ in the box where *that meal* and *Rosie* meet.
What two other boxes can you now put **X**s in?
Why? There is one box left.
What does it tell you?

B. The Rockets, the Racers, and the Raiders are teams.
One plays basketball.
One plays baseball.
One swims.

Which team plays which sport?

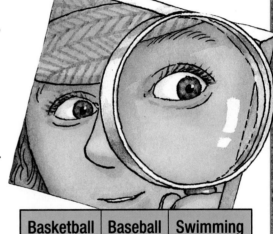

CLUES

1. The Rockets use bats for their games.

2. None of the Raiders knows how to swim.

Copy the chart at the right.
Use ✔s and Xs to help you find the answers.

	Basketball	Baseball	Swimming
Rockets			
Racers			
Raiders			

C. Paula, Roger, and Julio took trips. One went to a lake. One went to a mountain. One went to the ocean.

Which trip did each student take?

CLUES

1. Julio enjoyed the waves and salt water.

2. Roger has never been to a mountain.

Make a chart to help you find an answer.

PROBLEM SOLVING

Strategies Review

Use these problem-solving strategies to solve the following problems. Remember that some problems can be solved using more than one strategy.

- Using Number Sense
- Choosing the Operation
- Drawing a Picture
- Solving a Two-Step Problem
- Using Estimation
- Making an Organized List
- Conducting an Experiment

- Finding a Pattern
- Solving a Multistep Problem
- Working Backward
- Guess, Test, and Revise
- Solving a Simpler Problem
- Making a Table

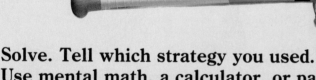

**Solve. Tell which strategy you used.
Use mental math, a calculator, or paper and pencil.**

1. Rex, Martina, and Andy each played one game. Rex played volleyball. Andy did not play soccer. Who played baseball?

2. Carl has $3. He buys a hot dog for $1.50 and juice for $.85. Does he have enough money left to buy an apple for $.50?

3. Sally cuts a large hero sandwich into 2 equal pieces. She cuts 2 feet off one piece to make a 1-foot long piece. How long was the sandwich she started with?

4. Mr. Sims is taking his 3 children to the pony rides. One child does not ride. The other two children each go on a ride 3 times. A ride costs 75¢. How much does Mr. Sims spend?

5. Mickey and Willie are sailing their boats in the pond. Mickey quits after 25 minutes. Willie stays 10 minutes longer. How long does Willie sail his boat?

6. It takes 2 students to move a picnic bench. Marcia, Fred, Doug, and Corey are moving 2 benches. In how many different ways can the students be paired?

7. May made up a jumping game. She drew a polygon made up of 5 squares on the ground. The length of a side of each square is 1 foot. The polygon has 6 sides. What is the perimeter of the polygon?

8. The Martens are having a skip-and-jump race. Each racer must make 2 jumps after 3 skips, 4 jumps after 6 skips, and 6 jumps after 9 skips. How many jumps must they make after 15 skips?

9. Val buys 2 cans of apple juice for 75¢ each and 3 cans of pineapple juice for 60¢ each. How much does she spend for the juice?

10. Lisa and Karen are tossing a disc back and forth. They toss it back and forth 18 times. Lisa drops it 3 times. How many times does she catch it?

11. Kevin is tossing 6 balls at two buckets. He scores 2 points if the ball goes into the red bucket and 9 points if it goes into the blue bucket. He must score exactly 40 points to win a prize. How many balls must he throw into each bucket?

12. *Write a problem* that can be solved by using one of the strategies. Solve the problem. Ask others to solve your problem.

Regrouping Twice

A. There are 3 prize tables at the fair. There are 56 prizes on each table. How many prizes are there in all?

Multiply 3 × 56.

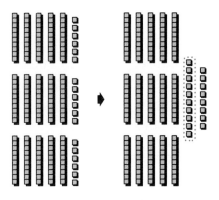

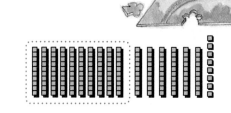

	Step 1	**Step 2**
	Multiply the ones. Regroup if necessary.	Multiply the tens. Add any new tens. Regroup if necessary.

$$\begin{array}{r} 56 \\ \times\ 3 \\ \hline \end{array}$$
$$\begin{array}{r} \overset{1}{5}6 \\ \times\ 3 \\ \hline 8 \end{array}$$
$$\begin{array}{r} \overset{1}{5}6 \\ \times\ \ 3 \\ \hline 168 \end{array}$$

Think:
3 × 5 tens = 15 tens
15 tens + 1 ten = 16 tens

1. What is 56 × 3? How do you know?

B. You can multiply money amounts the same way you multiply whole numbers.

Step 1	**Step 2**
Multiply as you would multiply whole numbers.	Place the dollar sign and decimal point in the product.

$$\begin{array}{r} \overset{6}{\$.48} \\ \times\ \ 8 \\ \hline 384 \end{array}$$
$$\begin{array}{r} \overset{6}{\$.48} \\ \times\ \ 8 \\ \hline \$3.84 \end{array}$$

Write the letter of the correct answer.
Multiply.

2. $6 \times 47 =$ ▇   **a.** 242   **b.** 264   **c.** 282   **d.** 482

3. $5 \times 72 =$ ▇   **a.** 350   **b.** 351   **c.** 360   **d.** 400

4. $3 \times 58 =$ ▇   **a.** 61   **b.** 174   **c.** 214   **d.** 272

5. $5 \times 68 =$ ▇   **a.** 73   **b.** 304   **c.** 340   **d.** 500

PRACTICE

Multiply.

6.
$$\begin{array}{r} 15 \\ \times\ 7 \\ \hline \end{array}$$

7.
$$\begin{array}{r} 27 \\ \times\ 4 \\ \hline \end{array}$$

8.
$$\begin{array}{r} 23 \\ \times\ 7 \\ \hline \end{array}$$

9.
$$\begin{array}{r} 65 \\ \times\ 4 \\ \hline \end{array}$$

10.
$$\begin{array}{r} 89 \\ \times\ 2 \\ \hline \end{array}$$

11.
$$\begin{array}{r} 77 \\ \times\ 3 \\ \hline \end{array}$$

12.
$$\begin{array}{r} 32 \\ \times\ 9 \\ \hline \end{array}$$

13.
$$\begin{array}{r} 29 \\ \times\ 4 \\ \hline \end{array}$$

14.
$$\begin{array}{r} 94 \\ \times\ 3 \\ \hline \end{array}$$

15.
$$\begin{array}{r} 75 \\ \times\ 6 \\ \hline \end{array}$$

16.
$$\begin{array}{r} \$.98 \\ \times\ 5 \\ \hline \end{array}$$

17.
$$\begin{array}{r} \$.44 \\ \times\ 7 \\ \hline \end{array}$$

18.
$$\begin{array}{r} \$.55 \\ \times\ 5 \\ \hline \end{array}$$

19.
$$\begin{array}{r} \$.48 \\ \times\ 8 \\ \hline \end{array}$$

20.
$$\begin{array}{r} \$.93 \\ \times\ 4 \\ \hline \end{array}$$

21. $7 \times 65 =$ ▇   **22.** $3 \times 66 =$ ▇   **23.** $2 \times 56 =$ ▇

24. $37 \times 3 =$ ▇   **25.** $58 \times 7 =$ ▇   **26.** $55 \times 8 =$ ▇

Mixed Applications

Solve. You may need to use the Databank on page 522.

27. There are 17 booths at the fair. There are 2 people working in each booth. How many people are working in all the booths?

28. Tina brought $5.00 to the fair. She bought 3 hard cover books and 2 puzzle books. How much money did she have left over?

29. Jay, Bill, and Eva each sold 75 tickets. How many tickets did they sell in all?

30. Mia bought 9 puzzle books. How much money did she spend?

DECISION MAKING

Problem Solving: Planning a Bake Sale

SITUATION

Lilly's and Otto's class is planning a bake sale to raise money for the zoo's new Monkey House. Their goal is to earn $50 and donate it to the zoo.

PROBLEM

Which items should they include in the bake sale?

DATA

Cookies

RECIPES
Oatmeal Cookies
325.°

oven to
mix 2
sugar
flour.

Possible Items for Lilly and Otto's Bake Sale

Item	Cost to Make	Sale Price	Profit
Apple Pie	$1.50 each	$3.00	$1.50
Peach Pie	$2.00 each	$4.00	$2.00
Cherry Pie	$2.50 each	$5.00	$2.50
Corn Bread	$ .75 per loaf	$1.50	$ .75
Banana Bread	$1.00 per loaf	$2.00	$1.00
Pumpkin Bread	$2.00 per loaf	$4.00	$2.00
Corn Muffins	$ .25 each	$ .50	$ .25
Bran Muffins	$ .30 each	$ .60	$ .30
Blueberry Muffins	$ .40 each	$ .80	$ .40
Oatmeal Cookies	$ .10 each	$ .20	$ .10
Granola Cookies	$ .20 each	$ .40	$ .20
Peanut Butter Cookies	$ .25 each	$ .50	$ .25

USING THE DATA

What is the total cost of making these items?

1. 2 apple pies

2. 9 blueberry muffins

3. 3 pumpkin breads

4. 7 oatmeal cookies

How much profit will the class make
if they sell these items?

5. 5 peach pies

6. 8 bran muffins

7. 6 corn breads

8. 4 pumpkin breads

9. What do you notice about the cost of making an item
and its sale price? its profit?

10. Which group of items earn the most profit?
the least profit?

MAKING DECISIONS

11. *Write a list* of things the class should consider before
holding a bake sale.

12. *What if* they can only bake one item from each group
of baked goods? Which item should they bake? Why?

13. Which items would you bake for the sale? Why?

14. What other ways can you raise money for a good
cause? What things should you consider when planning
a fund-raising event?

Math and Science

Firefighters use a special fire engine, called a pumper, to help them put out fires. A hose from a pumper is attached to a nearby fire hydrant. Two firefighters hold onto another hose coming from the pumper. When everyone is ready, the hydrant is opened and *whoosh!* Here comes the water—over 750 gallons in one minute!

What if it takes 8 minutes to put out a fire? How much water is used to put out the fire?

Think: For every minute, 750 gallons of water are used. To find how much water is used in 8 minutes, multiply by 8.

$8 \times 750 = 6,000$

So 6,000 gallons of water are used to put out the fire.

ACTIVITY

1. Make a poster that shows firefighters using a pumper to put out a fire. Write how long the fire lasted and how many gallons of water were used to put out the fire.

Computer Spreadsheet: Aquarium Supplies

The students at Johnson School are buying new items for their classroom aquarium. They already have a tank, a filter, a heater, and a light. They must decide which fish and which supplies to buy. They must buy either a regular thermometer or a digital thermometer. They have $100 to spend.

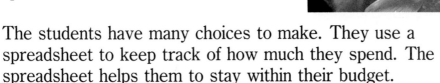

The students have many choices to make. They use a spreadsheet to keep track of how much they spend. The spreadsheet helps them to stay within their budget.

AT THE COMPUTER

Run the computer spreadsheet program called AQUARIUM. Look at the data shown on the screen.

1. The first column shows the items the class can buy. How are the second, third, and fourth columns related?

2. Help the students choose what to buy. Enter a number in the second column for the quantity of each item. Try to spend as close to $100 as you can without going over.

3. **What if** the students decide they want 4 plants, 25 fish, a digital thermometer, and no other supplies? Enter the items in the second column. Try to spend as close to $100 as you can without going over.

4. **What if** they only have $75 to spend? What would you buy? You may pick any combination of items you wish. How close to $75 can you get?

EXTRA PRACTICE

Mental Math: Multiplying 10s and 100s, page 455 ....

Multiply mentally.

| **1.** $\begin{array}{r} 10 \\ \times\ 2 \\ \hline \end{array}$ | **2.** $\begin{array}{r} 10 \\ \times\ 4 \\ \hline \end{array}$ | **3.** $\begin{array}{r} 10 \\ \times\ 8 \\ \hline \end{array}$ | **4.** $\begin{array}{r} 100 \\ \times\ 3 \\ \hline \end{array}$ | **5.** $\begin{array}{r} 100 \\ \times\ 7 \\ \hline \end{array}$ |

6. $2 \times 50 = $ ■

7. $1 \times 30 = $ ■

8. $4 \times 20 = $ ■

9. $3 \times 400 = $ ■

10. $2 \times 200 = $ ■

11. $6 \times 300 = $ ■

12. $4 \times 50 = $ ■

13. $5 \times 300 = $ ■

14. $3 \times 40 = $ ■

15. $40 \times 2 = $ ■

16. $400 \times 4 = $ ■

17. $5 \times 500 = $ ■

Estimating Products, page 457 ....

Estimate. Use rounding.

| **1.** $\begin{array}{r} 72 \\ \times\ 4 \\ \hline \end{array}$ | **2.** $\begin{array}{r} 63 \\ \times\ 3 \\ \hline \end{array}$ | **3.** $\begin{array}{r} 89 \\ \times\ 7 \\ \hline \end{array}$ | **4.** $\begin{array}{r} 51 \\ \times\ 2 \\ \hline \end{array}$ | **5.** $\begin{array}{r} 17 \\ \times\ 8 \\ \hline \end{array}$ |

| **6.** $\begin{array}{r} 312 \\ \times\ 4 \\ \hline \end{array}$ | **7.** $\begin{array}{r} 561 \\ \times\ 3 \\ \hline \end{array}$ | **8.** $\begin{array}{r} 487 \\ \times\ 7 \\ \hline \end{array}$ | **9.** $\begin{array}{r} \$2.07 \\ \times\ 3 \\ \hline \end{array}$ | **10.** $\begin{array}{r} \$2.80 \\ \times\ 6 \\ \hline \end{array}$ |

11. $4 \times 26 = $ ■

12. $7 \times 228 = $ ■

13. $6 \times \$2.25 = $ ■

14. $2 \times \$1.63 = $ ■

15. $5 \times 569 = $ ■

16. $3 \times 802 = $ ■

Estimate. Use the front digits.

| **17.** $\begin{array}{r} 62 \\ \times\ 4 \\ \hline \end{array}$ | **18.** $\begin{array}{r} 41 \\ \times\ 3 \\ \hline \end{array}$ | **19.** $\begin{array}{r} 56 \\ \times\ 7 \\ \hline \end{array}$ | **20.** $\begin{array}{r} 39 \\ \times\ 5 \\ \hline \end{array}$ | **21.** $\begin{array}{r} 12 \\ \times\ 7 \\ \hline \end{array}$ |

| **22.** $\begin{array}{r} 423 \\ \times\ 2 \\ \hline \end{array}$ | **23.** $\begin{array}{r} 371 \\ \times\ 6 \\ \hline \end{array}$ | **24.** $\begin{array}{r} 539 \\ \times\ 3 \\ \hline \end{array}$ | **25.** $\begin{array}{r} \$4.07 \\ \times\ 9 \\ \hline \end{array}$ | **26.** $\begin{array}{r} \$3.80 \\ \times\ 4 \\ \hline \end{array}$ |

27. $3 \times 25 = $ ■

28. $4 \times 38 = $ ■

29. $6 \times \$3.20 = $ ■

30. $5 \times 17 = $ ■

31. $2 \times 193 = $ ■

32. $4 \times \$5.50 = $ ■

Multiplying 2-Digit Numbers: Regrouping Once, page 461 ....
Multiply.

1. 17 × 2 **2.** 12 × 8 **3.** 28 × 3 **4.** 19 × 4 **5.** 14 × 5

6. 51 × 4 **7.** 18 × 2 **8.** 16 × 3 **9.** 19 × 5 **10.** 24 × 3

11. 3 × 16 = ■ **12.** 2 × 45 = ■ **13.** 5 × 19 = ■

14. 2 × 15 = ■ **15.** 4 × 15 = ■ **16.** 3 × 26 = ■

17. three times fourteen **18.** five times seventeen

19. two times twenty-five **20.** four times twelve

Problem Solving Strategy: Choosing the Operation, page 463 ....
Decide which operation to use.
Then solve the problem.

1. Dana's class sold 26 muffins at the school bake sale on Thursday and 19 muffins on Friday. How many muffins did they sell in two days?

2. There are 8 booths at the carnival with 3 adults in charge of each booth. How many adults will they need to work in the booths at the carnival?

3. The boys' soccer team sold 44 tickets to the game last week and 59 tickets this week. How many tickets did they sell for both games?

4. There are 17 cartoonists at the fair. Each cartoonist is selling 5 cartoons. How many cartoons are for sale?

EXTRA PRACTICE

Problem Solving: Strategies Review, page 467 . . . .

Solve. Tell which strategy you used.

1. Cindy used 70 ribbons to decorate baskets for the fair. She used 19 yellow ribbons and 22 brown ribbons. How many other ribbons did she use?

2. Greg wants to buy a sports poster for $5.95, a racing car poster for $4.25, and a movie poster for $5.50. Is $15 enough money to buy the posters?

3. Candy's grandmother bought 12 boxes of greeting cards. Each box has 8 cards in it. How many cards does she have in all?

4. Bob sold 46 magazines one week and 53 the next week. He needs to sell 100 magazines to win a prize. Did he sell enough to win a prize?

5. Of the tourists going to the ski resort, 35 are traveling in vans. Each van has the same number of tourists. There are 5 vans. How many people are riding in each van?

6. It takes 2 students to play chess. Patrick, Jim, Leslie, and Glenda are playing in the chess tournament. In how many different ways can they be paired to play in the tournament?

7. Jessie is stacking cans in a display at the grocery store. There are 9 cans in the first row, 15 cans in the second row, and 21 cans in the third row. How many cans are in the sixth row?

8. Kevin buys 4 apples for 30¢ each and 6 avocados for 69¢ each. How much does he spend for the apples and avocados?

Regrouping Twice, page 469..

Multiply.

| 1. 32 × 8 | 2. 64 × 3 | 3. 16 × 7 | 4. 86 × 2 | 5. 23 × 5 |

| 6. $.33 × 5 | 7. $.67 × 3 | 8. $.54 × 7 | 9. $.94 × 3 | 10. $.68 × 8 |

| 11. 35 × 4 | 12. 84 × 3 | 13. 67 × 5 | 14. 49 × 6 | 15. 72 × 8 |

| 16. $.19 × 9 | 17. $.57 × 8 | 18. $.89 × 4 | 19. $.65 × 5 | 20. $.78 × 7 |

| 21. 33 × 5 | 22. 75 × 3 | 23. 86 × 7 | 24. 77 × 8 | 25. 98 × 6 |

| 26. $.54 × 8 | 27. $.35 × 7 | 28. $.76 × 6 | 29. $.98 × 5 | 30. $.46 × 5 |

31. $4 \times 39 = $ ■

32. $7 \times 53 = $ ■

33. $3 \times 44 = $ ■

34. $4 \times 65 = $ ■

35. $3 \times 88 = $ ■

36. $5 \times 39 = $ ■

37. $2 \times 76 = $ ■

38. $6 \times 89 = $ ■

39. $9 \times 56 = $ ■

40. $7 \times 54 = $ ■

41. $9 \times 49 = $ ■

42. $7 \times 32 = $ ■

43. $2 \times 59 = $ ■

44. $3 \times \$99 = $ ■

45. $6 \times 35 = $ ■

46. $5 \times 25 = $ ■

47. $7 \times 59 = $ ■

48. $3 \times \$45 = $ ■

49. $9 \times 27 = $ ■

50. $3 \times \$79 = $ ■

51. $7 \times 29 = $ ■

PRACTICE PLUS

KEY SKILL: Multiplying 2-Digit Numbers: Regrouping Once
(Use after page 461.)

Level A ....

Multiply.

1. 12
    × 5

2. 17
    × 3

3. 25
    × 2

4. 17
    × 4

5. 41
    × 5

6. 2 × 27 = ▪___

7. 6 × 16 = ▪___

8. 3 × 25 = ▪___

9. John has 5 boxes. There are 15 comics in each box. How many comics does John have?

Level B ....

Multiply.

10. 21
     × 6

11. 31
     × 7

12. 41
     × 8

13. 53
     × 3

14. 42
     × 3

15. 5 × 81 = ▪___

16. 3 × 64 = ▪___

17. 8 × 21 = ▪___

18. Dennis has 7 boxes of toy cars. Each box has 31 cars. How many cars does Dennis have?

Level C ....

Multiply.

19. 51
     × 7

20. 82
     × 4

21. 71
     × 9

22. 41
     × 6

23. 61
     × 7

24. nine times thirty-seven

25. eight times fifty-three

26. Toyland has 9 boxes of toys. Each box has 71 toys. How many toys are there?

KEY SKILL: Regrouping Twice (Use after page 469.)

Level A
Multiply.

1.	36 $\times\ 7$	**2.**	22 $\times\ 8$	**3.**	12 $\times\ 9$	**4.**	26 $\times\ 5$	**5.**	62 $\times\ 7$

6. $5 \times 23 =$ ▬

7. $6 \times \$.32 =$ ▬

8. $3 \times 44 =$ ▬

9. A stable has 37 horses. There are 3 saddles for each horse. How many saddles are there in all?

Level B
Multiply.

10.	82 $\times\ 6$	**11.**	\$.47 $\times\ \ \ 8$	**12.**	53 $\times\ 5$	**13.**	\$.36 $\times\ \ \ 7$	**14.**	63 $\times\ 9$

15. $6 \times 56 =$ ▬

16. $4 \times 63 =$ ▬

17. $2 \times 55 =$ ▬

18. There were 78 people at the fair. Each person bought 8 tickets. How many tickets were sold?

Level C
Multiply.

19.	58 $\times\ 8$	**20.**	85 $\times\ 7$	**21.**	78 $\times\ 5$	**22.**	\$.63 $\times\ \ \ 9$	**23.**	\$.48 $\times\ \ \ 6$

24. seven times eighty-nine

25. six times sixty-seven

26. There were 89 people at each rodeo show. There were 7 shows. How many people attended the shows?

CHAPTER REVIEW/TEST

LANGUAGE AND MATHEMATICS

Complete the sentences. Use the words in the chart.

1. In 4 x 5 = 20, 4 and 5 are ▪ .

2. If you multiply 40 x 5 to estimate the product of 46 x 5, you are using ▪ estimation.

3. If you multiply 60 x 3 to estimate the product of 57 x 3, you are ▪ to estimate.

> **VOCABULARY**
> rounding
> product
> factors
> front-end

CONCEPTS AND SKILLS

Multiply mentally.

4. 4 x 10 = ▪

5. 7 x 80 = ▪

6. 5 x 50 = ▪

7. 9 x 700 = ▪

Estimate. Use rounding.

8.
$$\begin{array}{r} 87 \\ \times\ 3 \\ \hline \end{array}$$

9.
$$\begin{array}{r} 42 \\ \times\ 2 \\ \hline \end{array}$$

10.
$$\begin{array}{r} 412 \\ \times\ 8 \\ \hline \end{array}$$

11.
$$\begin{array}{r} \$4.61 \\ \times\ 4 \\ \hline \end{array}$$

Estimate. Use the front digits.

12.
$$\begin{array}{r} 64 \\ \times\ 7 \\ \hline \end{array}$$

13.
$$\begin{array}{r} 81 \\ \times\ 8 \\ \hline \end{array}$$

14.
$$\begin{array}{r} 329 \\ \times\ 4 \\ \hline \end{array}$$

15.
$$\begin{array}{r} \$3.50 \\ \times\ 3 \\ \hline \end{array}$$

Multiply.

16.
$$\begin{array}{r} 81 \\ \times\ 8 \\ \hline \end{array}$$

17.
$$\begin{array}{r} 24 \\ \times\ 4 \\ \hline \end{array}$$

18.
$$\begin{array}{r} 43 \\ \times\ 7 \\ \hline \end{array}$$

19.
$$\begin{array}{r} \$.85 \\ \times\ 6 \\ \hline \end{array}$$

20. 3 x 38 = ▪

21. 8 x 24 = ▪

22. 5 x $.66 = ▪

Critical Thinking

23. How would you compute 6 x 31,000?
What is the product?

Mixed Applications

24. Andy buys a book for $4.49 and a shirt for $7.98.
He gives the clerk $15.00. How much change
does he get?

25. Leon has 5 puzzles. There are 75 pieces in each
puzzle. How many puzzle pieces are there?

PERFORMANCE ASSESSMENT

Work with your group to solve this problem.

Suppose you are planning a Recycling Awareness
Week. You want to show people the importance of
recycling. You choose the DeCosta family in the
neighborhood and find that in one week they recycled:
32 cans or bottles, 11 pounds of newspapers or
magazines, and 48 sheets of junk mail. Make a poster
that shows how much the DeCosta family may recycle
in 2 months, 4 months, and 6 months.

1. *Think about:*
   - how to set up the poster so that people can
     see how much one family can recycle
   - how to find out how much may be recycled
     in 2 months, 4 months, and 6 months

2. Estimate how much the DeCosta family
may recycle in 1 year. Explain how you found
the estimate.

CUMULATIVE REVIEW

Choose the letter of the correct answer.

1. Multiply mentally: 7 × 600
   a. 42　　　c. 4,200
   b. 420　　d. not given

2. Estimate by rounding: 8 × 68
   a. 48　　　c. 480
   b. 56　　　d. 560

3. Estimate using front-end estimation: 6 × 37
   a. 18　　　c. 180
   b. 24　　　d. 240

4. 9 × 38 = ▇
   a. 272　　c. 342
   b. 287　　d. not given

5. $1.43 + $2.79 = ▇
   a. $3.12　c. $4.22
   b. $3.21　d. not given

6. $\frac{1}{3}$ of 18
   a. 3　　　c. 6
   b. 54　　　d. not given

7. Compare: 0.5 ● $\frac{5}{10}$
   a. >　　　c. =
   b. <　　　d. not given

8. Which is the best estimate for the distance across a lake?
   a. 10 inches　c. 10 miles
   b. 10 yards　d. not given

9.
   $$\begin{array}{r} 93 \\ \times\ 3 \\ \hline \end{array}$$
   a. 99　　　c. 79
   b. 277　　d. not given

10. Which is the best estimate for the weight of a pencil?
    a. 1 ounce　c. 1 liter
    b. 1 pound　d. not given

11. Compare: $\frac{8}{4}$ ● 1
    a. >　　　c. =
    b. <　　　d. not given

12.
    $$\begin{array}{r} 25 \\ \times\ 5 \\ \hline \end{array}$$
    a. 1,250　c. 125
    b. 25　　　d. not given

13. Compare: $\frac{3}{9}$ ● $\frac{1}{3}$
    a. >　　　c. =
    b. <　　　d. not given

14. Which is the best estimate for the height of a flagpole?
    a. 15 inches　c. 15 miles
    b. 15 feet　　d. not given

USING A SHORTCUT

You can use a shortcut to find the sum of all the numbers from 1 to 10.

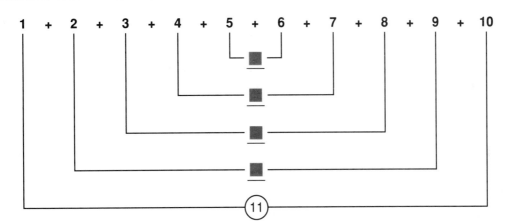

What is the sum of each pair of numbers?

How many pairs are there?

What multiplication sentence shows the sum of all the numbers from 1 to 10?

What is the sum of all the numbers from 1 to 10?

Find the sum using the shortcut.

1. 8 + 9 + 10 + 11 + 12 + 13 + 14 + 15

2. 12 + 15 + 18 + 21 + 24 + 27 + 30 + 33

3. 54 + 55 + 56 + 57 + 58 + 59 + 60 + 61 + 62 + 63

4. How would you find the sum of all the numbers from 1 to 100?

THE
HAIDA STICK GAME

CANADA
Queen
Charlotte
Islands

UNITED STATES

Many of the Native Americans known as the Haida (HY-dah) live on Canada's Queen Charlotte Islands. Their homes stand between tall, thick forests and the Pacific Ocean. The Haida are famous for their detailed carvings of tall totem poles, canoes, boxes, and dishes. Their weavings are also well-known. They combine wool and bark-fiber thread into cloth with striking designs.

The Haida played a guessing game using carved sticks. Each stick had a different carved design, such as a raven or bear. One player divided a set of 18 sticks into two equal groups. The other player guessed which group contained a stick with a

DIVIDING WHOLE NUMBERS

1. There are several ways to divide 18 sticks into equal groups. Name one of the ways the sticks can be divided. How many sticks would be in each equal group?

2. What stick games have you played? How did you play the game?

ACTIVITY

Dividing With Remainders

A. Ray has 14 pears. He puts 3 pears in each bag. How many bags does he use? How many pears are left?

1. Use counters to model the problem. Place 14 counters on your desk. Divide the counters into as many equal groups of 3 as you can. The number of objects left is called the **remainder**.

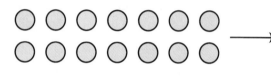

2. How many equal groups of 3 do you have? How many counters are left?

3. How many bags does Ray use? How many pears are left?

4. What would the quotient and remainder be if Ray had 12 pears? 13 pears? 15 pears? 16 pears?

B. You can divide to solve the problem.

Divide: 14 ÷ 3

Step 1

Think: How many threes are in 14?

2 × 3 = 6   6 < 14
3 × 3 = 9   9 < 14
4 × 3 = 12   12 < 14
5 × 3 = 15   15 > 14
There are 4 threes in 14.

Step 2

Divide.

Write 4 in the quotient.
Multiply: 4 × 3 = 12
Subtract: 14 − 12 = 2
Compare: 2 < 3
Write the remainder.

$$
\begin{array}{r}
4\text{ R2} \\
3\overline{)14} \\
-12 \\
\hline
2
\end{array}
$$

5. Can the remainder ever be larger than the number you are dividing by? Why or why not?

6. How can you use multiplication and subtraction to answer a division problem?

PRACTICE

Find the quotient and remainder. Use counters if needed.

7. $3\overline{)5}$ **8.** $4\overline{)7}$ **9.** $2\overline{)9}$ **10.** $5\overline{)23}$ **11.** $8\overline{)25}$

12. $6\overline{)20}$ **13.** $9\overline{)30}$ **14.** $4\overline{)26}$ **15.** $6\overline{)19}$ **16.** $3\overline{)13}$

17. $7\overline{)32}$ **18.** $6\overline{)15}$ **19.** $9\overline{)27}$ **20.** $6\overline{)50}$ **21.** $4\overline{)13}$

22. $75 \div 9 = $ ■   **23.** $54 \div 6 = $ ■   **24.** $15 \div 2 = $ ■

25. $67 \div 7 = $ ■   **26.** $45 \div 8 = $ ■   **27.** $44 \div 5 = $ ■

Solve.

28. Ray puts 4 plums in each bag. He has 34 plums. How many bags does he use? How many plums does he have left?

29. *Write a problem* that asks for a quotient and a remainder. Ask others to solve your problem.

CALCULATOR

You can use a calculator to check division.

Multiply. Then add the remainder.

38 ÷ 7 = 5 R3      38.

Use your calculator to check the division. If it is incorrect, give the correct answer.

1. $17 \div 3 = 5\text{ R}2$ **2.** $25 \div 4 = 6\text{ R}2$ **3.** $60 \div 8 = 8\text{ R}4$

Dividing 10s and 100s

Gregg and his father bake cakes and muffins for 4 local stores. Each week they bake 800 cakes and 2,000 muffins. They send the same number of cakes and muffins to each store.

Use a calculator to find quotients.

$8 \div 4 = 2$ $20 \div 4 = 5$
$80 \div 4 = $ ▊ $200 \div 4 = $ ▊
$800 \div 4 = $ ▊ $2,000 \div 4 = $ ▊

How many cakes and muffins does each store get?

1. Look at the two groups of numbers. Compare the number of zeros in each quotient to the number of zeros in the dividend. What pattern do you see? Do they all follow the same pattern? Why or why not?

2. Use the pattern to find these quotients mentally. Then use a calculator to check your answer.

a. $240 \div 8 = $ ▊   **b.** $5,000 \div 7 = $ ▊

c. $4,000 \div 8 = $ ▊   **d.** $360 \div 4 = $ ▊

TRY OUT Write the letter of the correct answer. Divide mentally.

3. $480 \div 6 = $ ▊   **a.** 40   **b.** 60   **c.** 80   **d.** 800

4. $810 \div 9 = $ ▊   **a.** 9   **b.** 70   **c.** 90   **d.** 900

5. $3,000 \div 5 = $ ▊   **a.** 50   **b.** 60   **c.** 600   **d.** 6,000

PRACTICE

Divide mentally.

6. $6\overline{)60}$ **7.** $6\overline{)30}$ **8.** $7\overline{)70}$ **9.** $9\overline{)90}$ **10.** $2\overline{)20}$

11. $8\overline{)40}$ **12.** $5\overline{)50}$ **13.** $2\overline{)80}$ **14.** $6\overline{)36}$ **15.** $3\overline{)90}$

16. $5\overline{)50}$ **17.** $7\overline{)630}$ **18.** $9\overline{)900}$ **19.** $6\overline{)420}$ **20.** $5\overline{)100}$

21. $7\overline{)350}$ **22.** $4\overline{)280}$ **23.** $7\overline{)700}$ **24.** $9\overline{)810}$ **25.** $9\overline{)900}$

26. $5\overline{)20}$ **27.** $4\overline{)200}$ **28.** $8\overline{)400}$ **29.** $4\overline{)40}$ **30.** $2\overline{)100}$

31. $6\overline{)600}$ **32.** $4\overline{)80}$ **33.** $2\overline{)60}$ **34.** $8\overline{)800}$ **35.** $9\overline{)540}$

36. $600 \div 3 = \blacksquare$ **37.** $300 \div 6 = \blacksquare$ **38.** $50 \div 5 = \blacksquare$

39. $40 \div 4 = \blacksquare$ **40.** $350 \div 7 = \blacksquare$ **41.** $40 \div 8 = \blacksquare$

Write the missing dividend.

42. $\blacksquare \div 8 = 10$ **43.** $\blacksquare \div 6 = 50$ **44.** $\blacksquare \div 4 = 500$

45. $\blacksquare \div 2 = 40$ **46.** $\blacksquare \div 3 = 20$ **47.** $\blacksquare \div 5 = 70$

Mixed Applications

48. Gregg works 6 hours on Friday.
He works 7 hours on Saturday.
On Sunday he works 3 hours.
How many hours does he work in all?

49. A crew of 3 helpers packs 150 cakes in
1 hour. Each helper packs the same number.
How many cakes does each helper pack?

Mixed Review

Find the answer. Which method did you use?

| MENTAL MATH |
| CALCULATOR |
| PAPER/PENCIL |

50. $10 \times 7 = \blacksquare$ **51.** $321 - 16 = \blacksquare$ **52.** $500 \div 10 = \blacksquare$

Estimating Quotients

Sandra, Andrew, Debbie, and Jeff buy 237 baseball cards at a tag sale. They plan to share the cards equally. About how many cards will each person keep?

You can estimate to find the quotient.

Estimate: $237 \div 4$
Here are two methods you can use.

Rounding
Round the dividend to its greatest place.

Think: 237 rounds to 200.
$$200 \div 4 = 50$$

Compatible Numbers
Use a basic fact.

Think: 237 is close to 240.
$$240 \div 4 = 60$$

Each person will keep about 50 or 60 cards.

1. Which estimate is greater than the exact answer? Why?

2. Which estimate is less than the exact answer? Why?

TRY OUT Write the letter of the correct answer.

Estimate by rounding.

3. $3\overline{)58}$ **a.** 2   **b.** 20   **c.** 180   **d.** 200

4. $8\overline{)429}$ **a.** 50   **b.** 60   **c.** 100   **d.** 500

Estimate. Use compatible numbers.

5. $5\overline{)261}$ **a.** 5   **b.** 50   **c.** 70   **d.** 500

6. $7\overline{)272}$ **a.** 3   **b.** 4   **c.** 30   **d.** 40

PRACTICE

Estimate by rounding.

7. $3\overline{)64}$ **8.** $5\overline{)53}$ **9.** $3\overline{)58}$ **10.** $3\overline{)93}$ **11.** $5\overline{)49}$

12. $4\overline{)191}$ **13.** $2\overline{)43}$ **14.** $8\overline{)761}$ **15.** $2\overline{)431}$ **16.** $9\overline{)873}$

17. $346 \div 6 = $ ■   **18.** $543 \div 5 = $ ■   **19.** $78 \div 8 = $ ■

20. $389 \div 4 = $ ■   **21.** $846 \div 2 = $ ■   **22.** $64 \div 3 = $ ■

Estimate. Use compatible numbers.

23. $4\overline{)73}$ **24.** $6\overline{)176}$ **25.** $5\overline{)147}$ **26.** $9\overline{)256}$ **27.** $7\overline{)270}$

28. $6\overline{)321}$ **29.** $3\overline{)266}$ **30.** $6\overline{)432}$ **31.** $3\overline{)121}$ **32.** $8\overline{)645}$

33. $622 \div 7 = $ ■   **34.** $53 \div 3 = $ ■   **35.** $419 \div 7 = $ ■

36. $361 \div 5 = $ ■   **37.** $116 \div 5 = $ ■   **38.** $196 \div 5 = $ ■

Mixed Applications

Solve. Which method did you use?

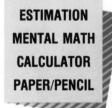

ESTIMATION
MENTAL MATH
CALCULATOR
PAPER/PENCIL

39. Bill's father has 97 baseball cards. Bill gives his father 8 more. How many baseball cards does his father have now?

40. Rudy has 363 stamps in his stamp collection. He sells his stamps to 9 people. Each person buys the same number of stamps. About how many stamps does each buy?

41. Deb puts 19 coins on each page of her coin collecting album. The album has 28 pages. How many coins will there be in the album when it is full?

42. There were 176 adults at the tag sale and 251 people in all. How many children were at the tag sale?

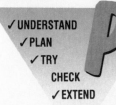

✓ UNDERSTAND
✓ PLAN
✓ TRY
CHECK
✓ EXTEND

PROBLEM SOLVING

Interpreting the Quotient and Remainder

Scott works at the Best Clothes Department Store. He puts 26 sweaters on shelves. Each shelf holds 6 sweaters. On how many shelves will Scott put 6 sweaters?

Scott knows that there are 26 sweaters and that each shelf holds 6 sweaters. He plans to use division to solve the problem.

1. On how many shelves will Scott put 6 sweaters?

$$
\begin{array}{r}
4 \text{ R2} \\
6{\overline{\smash{)}26}} \\
-24 \\
\hline
02
\end{array}
$$

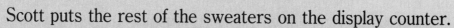

Scott puts the rest of the sweaters on the display counter.

2. How many sweaters does he put on the counter?

3. **What if** Scott puts all the sweaters on shelves? How many shelves will he need? Why?

Scott sees that there are three ways to interpret the quotient and the remainder to answer division problems.

- The quotient answers problems like Problem 1.
- The remainder answers problems like Problem 2.
- A number that is one greater than the quotient answers problems like Problem 3.

4. How can you tell which type of answer is needed?

PRACTICE

Solve the problem. Tell how you interpreted the remainder. Use mental math, a calculator, or paper and pencil.

5. Steve puts 59 cans of juice into cartons. Each carton holds 8 cans. How many full cartons will he have?

6. Joanne is putting 76 oranges into bags. Each bag holds 8 oranges. How many bags does she need?

7. A window display has 30 boxes of sneakers. There are 4 equal rows of closed boxes. The rest of the boxes are open. How many boxes are open?

8. Daniel has 45¢. He wants to buy some stickers that cost 7¢ each. How many stickers can he buy?

Skills and Strategies Review

9. The pet store has 24 fish. There are 4 more fish in the large tank than in the small tank. How many fish are there in the large tank?

10. Sal bought 12 strips of wood to make picture frames. Some strips cost 25¢. Others cost 50¢. If he spent $4, how many of each kind of strip did he buy?

11. The manager of the Nut Hutch has 47 pounds of peanuts to pack into 5-pound bags. She puts the leftover peanuts in a bowl. How many pounds of peanuts does she put in the bowl?

12. Judy wants to store 35 cassette tapes in cases. She buys storage cases that hold 8 tapes each. A case costs $3. How much does she spend?

13. Jane is buying 2 pairs of pants. Each pair costs $34. How much does she spend?

14. *Write a problem* that can be solved by interpreting the quotient and remainder. Solve the problem. Ask others to solve your problem.

Visual Reasoning

A. Copy this chart on a sheet of paper. Look at it carefully. Soon you will see how to complete it.

All of the shapes in row 1 are red. All of the shapes in column 1 are circles. The shape in the box where row 1 and column 1 meet is a red circle.

	Column 1 Circles	Column 2 Squares	Column 3 Triangles
Row 1 Red	○	□	△
Row 2 Half Red Half Blue	◐	▥	△
Row 3 Blue	●	■	▲

1. What will the shapes in row 2 have in common? What will the shapes in column 2 have in common? What shape will you put in the box where row 2 and column 2 meet? Complete the rest of the chart.

2. Now copy and complete this chart. Think about the shapes in each row. Think about the shapes in each column.

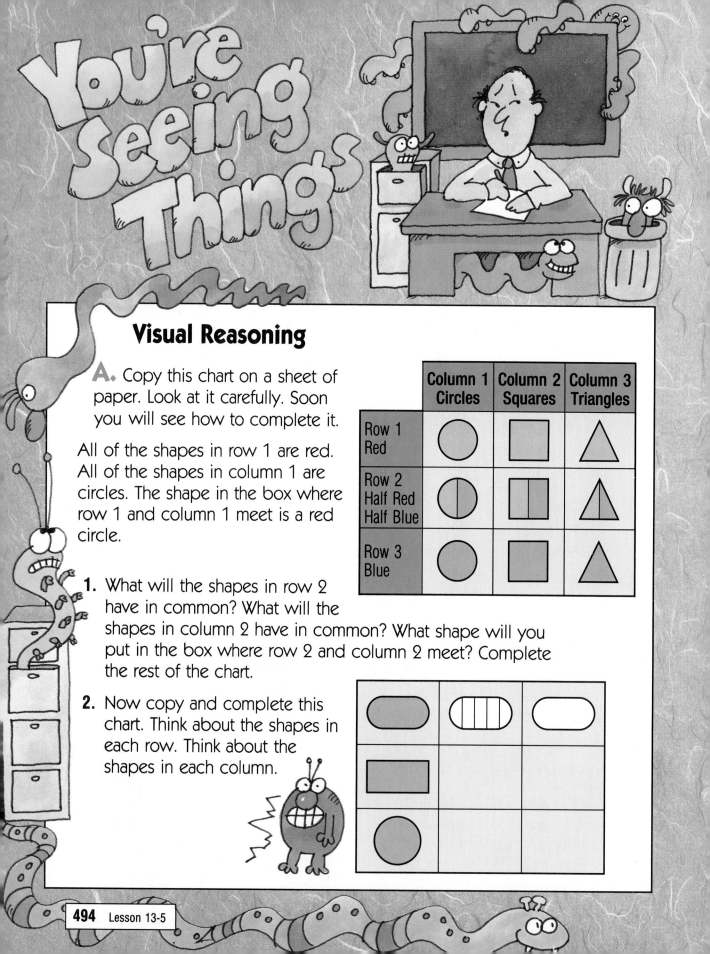

B. How would you complete this puzzle?

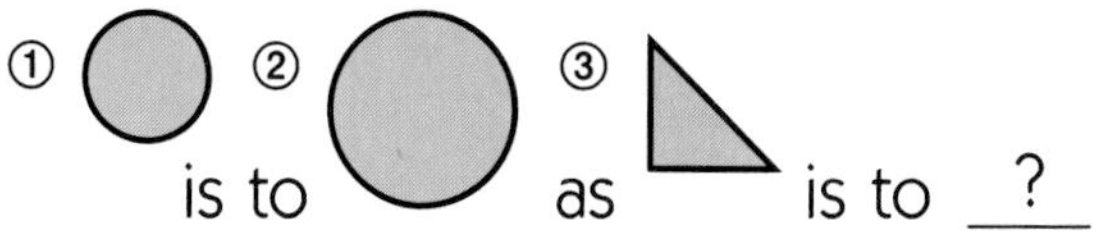

① ⭕ ② ⭕ ③ ◺ is to _?_

is to   as   is to

To complete the puzzle, you must think about how the pictures are related. How is ① related to ②?
It is the same shape, but it is smaller.
The missing picture must be related to ③ in the same way.
The missing picture should be
the same shape as ③ but larger.

Find the shape in the box that
completes the puzzle. Copy
the figure you choose. Label it ④.

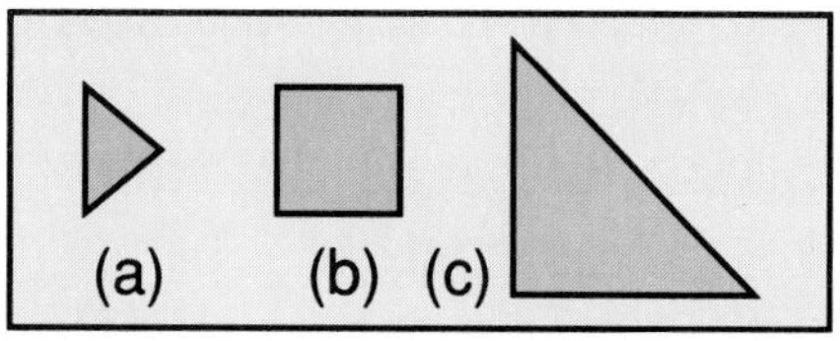

(a) (b) (c)

Now try these puzzles. Write the letter of the correct
shape.

3. 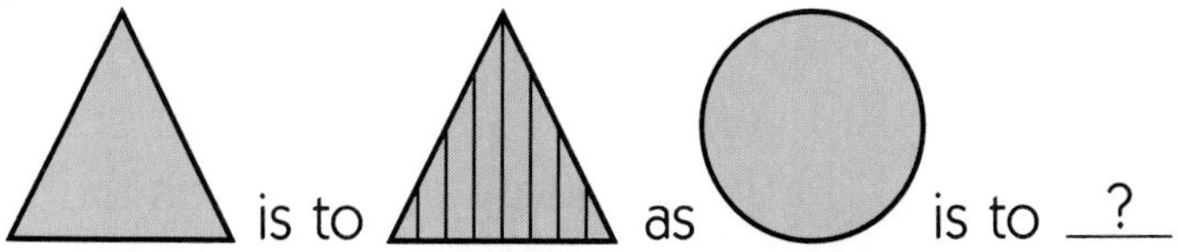 △ is to △ as ⭕ is to _?_

(a) ⭕ (b) ⭕ (c) ▯▯▯

4. 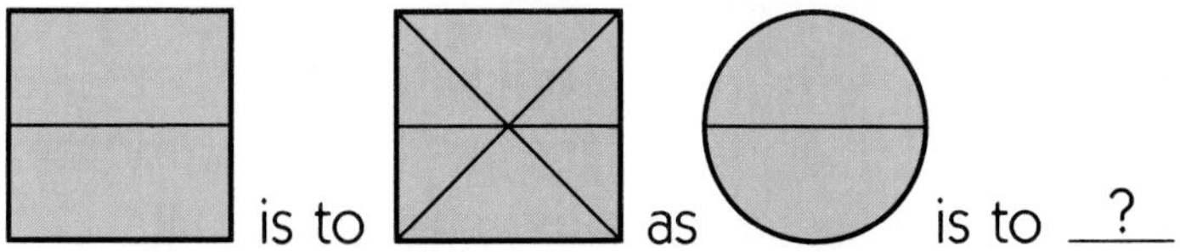 ▭ is to ▨ as ⊖ is to _?_

(a) ⊗ (b) △ (c) ⊕

5. 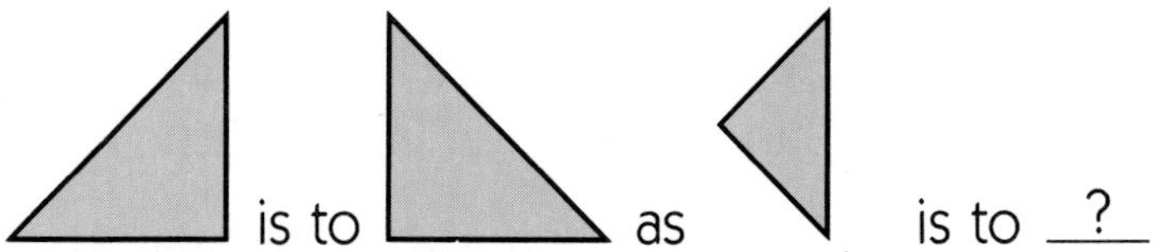 ◺ is to ◹ as ◁ is to _?_

(a) ▷ (b) ◁ (c) △

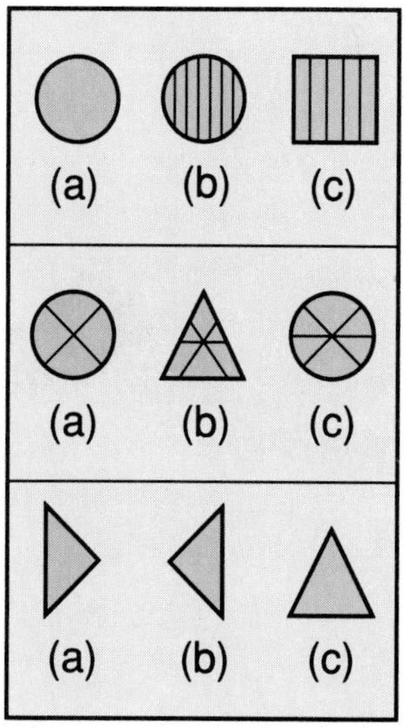

6. Make up a relationship puzzle of your own.
Exchange your puzzle with another student.

PROBLEM SOLVING

Strategy: Choosing the Operation

You have to understand what is happening in the problem to be able to choose the operation to solve it.

Addition: Combine unequal groups.

Subtraction: Separate into unequal groups.

Multiplication: Combine equal groups.

Division: Separate into equal groups.

Mrs. Liu makes and sells candles. She packs them 4 to a box. Yesterday she made 32 candles. How many boxes of candles did she make?

1. Which operation can you use to solve the problem? How many boxes of candles did she make?

Mrs. Liu sells the candles for $3 a box. How much do 5 boxes cost?

2. Which operation can you use to solve the problem? How much do 5 boxes cost?

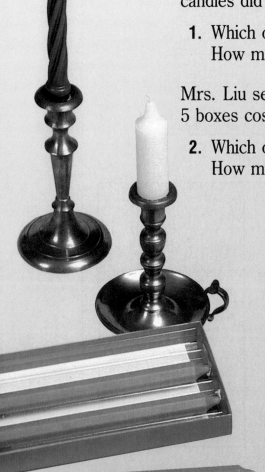

Last month Mrs. Liu sold 28 boxes of candles. This month she sold 39 boxes. How many boxes did she sell in all?

3. Which operation can you use to solve the problem? How many boxes did she sell in all?

How many more boxes did she sell this month than last month?

4. Which operation can you use to solve the problem? How many more boxes did she sell this month than last month?

PRACTICE

Decide which operation to use. Then solve the problem. Use mental math, a calculator, or paper and pencil.

5. The mass of a box of oat bran is 383 grams. The mass of a box of cornflakes is 295 grams. How much greater is the mass of the box of oat bran?

6. Last week Ned's Hardware Store sold 176 boxes of long nails and 142 boxes of short nails. How many boxes of nails did the store sell in all?

7. The contents of a can of soup weigh 24 ounces. Each recommended serving is 8 ounces. How many servings are in the can?

8. It costs 25¢ an hour to park at the meter. How much will it cost to park for 5 hours?

Strategies and Skills Review

9. Jake's Sports Store sold 577 baseball gloves last month and 315 gloves this month. How many baseball gloves did it sell in the two months?

10. Dan earned 46 points one week and 68 points the next week. He needs 100 points to win a prize. Has he earned enough points to win a prize?

11. The regular bus fare from Seneca to Mount Pleasant is $49.50. What other information do you need to know to find how much you save if you buy the discount fare?

12. Mrs. Gordon is making curtains for her house. She uses 4 yards of material to make each curtain. How many curtains can she make with 22 yards of material?

13. The regular price of 6 cans of dog food is $1.08. On sale 6 cans cost $.79. How much do you save if you buy 6 cans on sale?

14. *Write a problem* to solve by addition, subtraction, multiplication, or division. Solve the problem. Ask others to solve your problem.

ActiVity

Dividing Larger Numbers

Sid has 46 lamps to pack. He packs them into 3 boxes. He puts the same number in each box. How many lamps does he put into each box? How many extra lamps does he have?

You can divide to find the number of lamps in each box.

WORKING TOGETHER

Estimate. Then solve the problem by using place-value models.

1. How did you model the 46 lamps?

2. Did you separate the ones or the tens model first?

3. How many tens did you put into each group? How many tens were left? What did you do with the tens that were left? Why?

4. How many ones did you put into each of the 3 groups? How many ones were left?

5. How many lamps does Sid put into each box? How many extra lamps does he have?

Use models to find each quotient and remainder.

6. $72 \div 3 = $ ___   **7.** $53 \div 4 = $ ___   **8.** $88 \div 5 = $ ___   **9.** $412 \div 3 = $ ___

SHARING IDEAS

10. How do your models compare with those of others?

11. Why do you start with the largest place in the dividend when dividing?

ON YOUR OWN

Solve. Use counters if needed.

12. Bev has 27 plums. She gives an equal number of plums to 4 friends. How many plums does each friend get? How many plums does Bev have left over?

13. Ned collects 79 cans. He puts an equal number of cans into 6 boxes. How many cans does he put into each box? How many cans does he have left?

14. Vic has 98 baseball cards. He puts 8 cards on each page of his album. How many pages of his album are filled? How many extra baseball cards does he have?

15. Pat has 323 pennies. She puts an equal number of pennies into 2 piggy banks. How many pennies does she put into each bank? How many pennies are left?

Dividing 2-Digit Numbers

A. Jeb has 47 marbles. He gives an equal number of marbles to 3 friends. How many marbles does each friend get? How many marbles are left over?

He estimates 45 ÷ 3 = 15.

Jeb uses place-value models to find the exact answer.

Divide: 47 ÷ 3

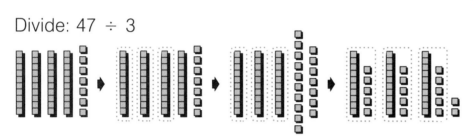

1. How many groups did Jeb make? How many tens are in each group? how many ones? Did he regroup? Why?

2. Are any models not in a group? Which ones?

3. How many marbles did Jeb give to each friend? How many does he have left over?

B. Here is a way to divide without models.

Step 1	Step 2	Step 3
Decide where to place the first digit of the quotient.	Divide the tens.	Bring down the ones. Divide the ones.

Step 1

■
3)47 **Think:** 3 < 4
There are enough tens to divide.

Step 2

 1
3)47 **Think:** 3)4̄
−3   Multiply: 1 × 3 = 3
 1   Subtract: 4 − 3 = 1
        Compare: 1 < 3

Step 3

 15 R2
3)47
 3↓
 17   **Think:** 3)17
−15   Multiply: 5 × 3 = 15
 2   Subtract: 17 − 15 = 2
         Compare: 2 < 3
         Write the remainder.

4. Compare the two methods. How are they the same? How are they different?

5. Is the answer reasonable? How do you know?

PRACTICE

Find the quotient and the remainder.

6. $2\overline{)39}$ **7.** $3\overline{)42}$ **8.** $4\overline{)45}$ **9.** $6\overline{)73}$ **10.** $5\overline{)75}$

11. $3\overline{)63}$ **12.** $2\overline{)72}$ **13.** $5\overline{)77}$ **14.** $4\overline{)62}$ **15.** $7\overline{)85}$

16. $5\overline{)52}$ **17.** $3\overline{)93}$ **18.** $6\overline{)91}$ **19.** $4\overline{)88}$ **20.** $2\overline{)87}$

21. $72 \div 4 = \blacksquare$ **22.** $61 \div 3 = \blacksquare$ **23.** $56 \div 5 = \blacksquare$

24. $83 \div 4 = \blacksquare$ **25.** $99 \div 9 = \blacksquare$ **26.** $87 \div 3 = \blacksquare$

Mixed Applications

Solve. You may need to use the Databank on page 522.

27. Sara has 24 pens. She puts the same number of pens in each of 3 boxes. How many pens are in each box?

28. Max has 4 boxes of pencils. There are 12 pencils in each box. How many pencils does Max have in all?

29. Peter buys 4 folders. He pays with a dollar bill. How much change does he get?

30. *Write a problem* about the price of another item at Sean's store. Have others solve your problem.

CALCULATOR

Solve. You can use mental math, paper and pencil, or a calculator. Tell why you used the method you chose.

1. $47 + 7 = \blacksquare$ **2.** $382 \times 3 = \blacksquare$ **3.** $500 \div 5 = \blacksquare$

DECISION MAKING

Problem Solving: Finding the Best Bargain

SITUATION

Tina's school is having a food drive. She wants to find the best buy so she reads the advertisement carefully. She knows that **unit price** is the amount you pay for one item.

PROBLEM

What should they buy?

DATA

TEX'S GROCERY STORE

TEX'S *Special* CACTUS FRUIT JUICE

Special #1
The Mighty Big Gulp
$16
Large box with 8 1-quart cans

Special #2
Super Sip
$9
Small box with 3 1-quart cans

Special #3
Thirst Buster
$3.⁵⁰
1 quart can

COWBOYS AND COWGIRLS COME AND GET IT! LOOK WHAT WE HAVE ON SALE HERE AT TEX'S GROCERY STORE.

USING THE DATA

What is the cost of the juice?

1. large box

2. small box

3. single can

4. What is the unit price for each can of juice in the large box? the small box?

5. What is the difference between the unit price of a can of juice in the large box of juice and the unit price of a can of juice in the small box?

6. What is the difference in the unit price of a can of juice from the small box and a single can?

7. How much will Tina save if she buys 1 small box instead of 3 single cans?

MAKING DECISIONS

8. **Write a list** of what you should think about when buying foods that come in different amounts.

9. Which special is the best buy?

10. Buying the largest size of an item may not always be the best idea. Why?

11. **What if** Tina has a coupon which takes $1.50 off the price of Special #2? What is the new unit price for Special #2?

12. Which one of Tex's specials would you buy? Why?

13. Talk about how using unit price can help you find the best buy.

Math and Science

Foresters are people who plant trees in forests. Can you guess where they get the trees to plant in the forests?

Many times, baby trees are grown on tree farms. When the young trees are about 1 foot high, they are ready to leave the farm. Foresters plant the little trees in a field or on a hill where other trees have been cut down for timber.

Using a special hand tool, one forester can plant 500 baby trees in one day.

What if a tree farm has 20,000 trees to plant in one day? How many foresters will it take to plant all the trees?

Think: Divide 20,000 by 500.
$$20,000 \div 500 = 40$$

So it will take 40 foresters to plant 20,000 trees in one day.

ACTIVITY

1. Make a chart showing the height and ages of different trees. Share your findings with others.

Calculator: A Guessing Game

How good are you at estimating quotients?
You can play a game with other students to find out. You
will need a calculator and a sheet of paper for scoring.

To Play: You will be given a number to divide and a
range of quotients. You need to choose a 1-digit
number by which to divide the "start number" in
order to get a quotient within the given range. If
you guess correctly on the first try, you get 5 points.
A correct guess on the second try is worth 1 point.

Example → Start Number: 57   Range of Quotient: 6–9

Kevin guesses 8.

He enters 5 7 ÷ 8 = .

The display shows *7.125*.

Since 7.125 is between 6 and 9,
Kevin's guess is correct. He
scores 5 points.

USING THE CALCULATOR

1. Play a game. Each start number and
quotient range is given. See how many
points you can score.

Start Number	Quotient Range
52	7–10
67	8–11
115	15–20
134	15–20
154	17–20
141	14–16

2. Play another game. This time you make up the start
numbers and the ranges.

EXTRA PRACTICE

Dividing with Remainders, page 487..

Find the quotient and remainder.

1. $2\overline{)7}$ **2.** $3\overline{)8}$ **3.** $2\overline{)3}$ **4.** $5\overline{)21}$ **5.** $6\overline{)19}$

6. $8\overline{)27}$ **7.** $4\overline{)17}$ **8.** $9\overline{)44}$ **9.** $8\overline{)19}$ **10.** $3\overline{)11}$

11. $6\overline{)35}$ **12.** $4\overline{)15}$ **13.** $8\overline{)29}$ **14.** $7\overline{)40}$ **15.** $3\overline{)23}$

16. $62 \div 7 = \blacksquare$ **17.** $38 \div 7 = \blacksquare$ **18.** $13 \div 3 = \blacksquare$

19. $29 \div 5 = \blacksquare$ **20.** $41 \div 6 = \blacksquare$ **21.** $31 \div 4 = \blacksquare$

Mental Math: Dividing 10s and 100s, page 489................................

Divide mentally.

1. $5\overline{)50}$ **2.** $8\overline{)40}$ **3.** $4\overline{)40}$ **4.** $8\overline{)80}$ **5.** $2\overline{)40}$

6. $2\overline{)80}$ **7.** $6\overline{)60}$ **8.** $2\overline{)60}$ **9.** $7\overline{)70}$ **10.** $3\overline{)30}$

11. $6\overline{)420}$ **12.** $5\overline{)250}$ **13.** $2\overline{)200}$ **14.** $10\overline{)800}$ **15.** $6\overline{)360}$

16. $6\overline{)300}$ **17.** $5\overline{)200}$ **18.** $5\overline{)500}$ **19.** $6\overline{)600}$ **20.** $7\overline{)420}$

21. $8\overline{)400}$ **22.** $7\overline{)490}$ **23.** $3\overline{)900}$ **24.** $7\overline{)700}$ **25.** $8\overline{)640}$

26. $500 \div 5 = \blacksquare$ **27.** $200 \div 4 = \blacksquare$ **28.** $60 \div 3 = \blacksquare$

29. $300 \div 5 = \blacksquare$ **30.** $480 \div 6 = \blacksquare$ **31.** $630 \div 9 = \blacksquare$

32. $540 \div 9 = \blacksquare$ **33.** $640 \div 8 = \blacksquare$ **34.** $80 \div 4 = \blacksquare$

Write the missing dividend.

35. $\blacksquare \div 7 = 10$ **36.** $\blacksquare \div 5 = 70$ **37.** $\blacksquare \div 3 = 90$

38. $\blacksquare \div 2 = 30$ **39.** $\blacksquare \div 4 = 30$ **40.** $\blacksquare \div 7 = 60$

41. $\blacksquare \div 3 = 600$ **42.** $\blacksquare \div 5 = 400$ **43.** $\blacksquare \div 4 = 20$

Estimating Quotients, page 491

Estimate by rounding.

1. $4\overline{)39}$ **2.** $2\overline{)76}$ **3.** $6\overline{)64}$ **4.** $3\overline{)93}$ **5.** $2\overline{)97}$

6. $5\overline{)185}$ **7.** $6\overline{)587}$ **8.** $8\overline{)419}$ **9.** $3\overline{)261}$ **10.** $2\overline{)372}$

11. $77 \div 4 = \blacksquare$ **12.** $617 \div 3 = \blacksquare$ **13.** $323 \div 5 = \blacksquare$

14. $95 \div 5 = \blacksquare$ **15.** $444 \div 4 = \blacksquare$ **16.** $787 \div 2 = \blacksquare$

Estimate by using compatible numbers.

17. $6\overline{)67}$ **18.** $3\overline{)84}$ **19.** $4\overline{)74}$ **20.** $7\overline{)93}$ **21.** $3\overline{)55}$

22. $3\overline{)124}$ **23.** $2\overline{)162}$ **24.** $6\overline{)349}$ **25.** $8\overline{)492}$ **26.** $7\overline{)621}$

27. $63 \div 3 = \blacksquare$ **28.** $128 \div 4 = \blacksquare$ **29.** $689 \div 7 = \blacksquare$

30. $362 \div 5 = \blacksquare$ **31.** $553 \div 9 = \blacksquare$ **32.** $112 \div 5 = \blacksquare$

Problem Solving Strategy: Interpreting the Quotient and Remainder, page 493

Solve the problem. Tell how you interpreted the remainder.

1. Anthony puts 64 cans of soup into cartons. Each carton holds 10 cans. How many cartons will he need?

2. Maude has 82¢. She wants to buy some stamps that cost 25¢ each. How many stamps can she buy?

3. Rebecca's mom has 25 boxes of shoes in her closet. There are 3 rows of closed boxes with the same number of boxes in each row. The rest of the boxes are open. How many boxes are open?

4. Carl is putting 59 rosebushes into bundles. Each bundle holds 6 rosebushes. How many rosebush bundles can he make?

EXTRA PRACTICE

Problem Solving Strategy: Choosing the Operation, page 497 ....

Decide which operation to use. Then solve the problem.

1. Tom picks 140 gallons of strawberries. David picks 225 gallons. How many more gallons does David pick than Tom?

2. The contents of a can of chili weighs 28 ounces. Each serving is 4 ounces. How many servings are in a can?

3. Last week the Farmer's Market sold 164 boxes of sweet potatoes and 142 boxes of Irish potatoes. How many boxes of potatoes did they sell in all?

4. While working at the refreshment stand, Rose sold 156 cups of hot chocolate and 189 cups of juice. How many refreshments did she sell in all?

5. It costs 75¢ an hour to rent a stroller at the fair. How much will it cost to rent a stroller for 6 hours?

6. Ernie collects 36 ride coupons at the fair. If he puts an equal amount of coupons into 4 stacks, how many coupons are in each stack?

7. A total of 476 reservations were made for the comedy show at the Fair. Only 387 people attended the show. How many people did not attend?

8. It costs 65¢ an hour for parking at the Fair. Tim parked his car for 4 hours. How much did he pay in parking fees?

9. James buys 3 buttons at the fair. Each button costs $.75. How much does James spend on buttons?

10. There are 27 people waiting to go on the Whirl-n-Twirl ride. Each car holds 5 people. How many cars will be full? How many people will be in the last car?

Dividing 2-Digit Numbers, page 501 ....

Find the quotient and remainder.

1. 2)38   **2.** 3)45   **3.** 4)53   **4.** 6)75   **5.** 7)83

6. 5)61   **7.** 2)25   **8.** 6)71   **9.** 5)63   **10.** 4)57

11. 2)67   **12.** 8)93   **13.** 3)69   **14.** 3)47   **15.** 3)81

16. 7)93   **17.** 3)66   **18.** 5)57   **19.** 4)53   **20.** 3)62

21. 6)77   **22.** 5)99   **23.** 3)83   **24.** 4)61   **25.** 7)86

26. 3)46   **27.** 6)82   **28.** 5)93   **29.** 4)51   **30.** 2)92

31. 8)88   **32.** 3)74   **33.** 4)53   **34.** 2)31   **35.** 5)62

36. 5)84   **37.** 8)93   **38.** 7)85   **39.** 3)46   **40.** 6)78

41. $67 \div 5 = \blacksquare$ **42.** $79 \div 6 = \blacksquare$ **43.** $55 \div 4 = \blacksquare$

44. $49 \div 3 = \blacksquare$ **45.** $95 \div 3 = \blacksquare$ **46.** $34 \div 2 = \blacksquare$

47. $92 \div 4 = \blacksquare$ **48.** $57 \div 5 = \blacksquare$ **49.** $89 \div 7 = \blacksquare$

50. $95 \div 2 = \blacksquare$ **51.** $49 \div 3 = \blacksquare$ **52.** $84 \div 6 = \blacksquare$

53. $77 \div 3 = \blacksquare$ **54.** $91 \div 5 = \blacksquare$ **55.** $53 \div 7 = \blacksquare$

56. $51 \div 2 = \blacksquare$ **57.** $83 \div 9 = \blacksquare$ **58.** $55 \div 5 = \blacksquare$

59. $28 \div 3 = \blacksquare$ **60.** $66 \div 7 = \blacksquare$ **61.** $43 \div 8 = \blacksquare$

Practice *PLUS*

KEY SKILL: Dividing with Remainders (Use after page 487.)

Level A ....

Find the quotient and the remainder.

1. $2\overline{)7}$ **2.** $3\overline{)4}$ **3.** $4\overline{)9}$ **4.** $5\overline{)21}$ **5.** $6\overline{)13}$

6. $4\overline{)15}$ **7.** $2\overline{)9}$ **8.** $6\overline{)14}$ **9.** $9\overline{)22}$ **10.** $5\overline{)16}$

11. $15 \div 4 =$ ■   **12.** $14 \div 6 =$ ■   **13.** $16 \div 5 =$ ■

14. Ed has 15 apples to give equally to 4 friends. How many apples does each friend get? How many are left?

Level B ....

Find the quotient and the remainder.

15. $3\overline{)16}$ **16.** $5\overline{)27}$ **17.** $8\overline{)33}$ **18.** $7\overline{)41}$ **19.** $6\overline{)17}$

20. $4\overline{)21}$ **21.** $2\overline{)17}$ **22.** $6\overline{)37}$ **23.** $8\overline{)67}$ **24.** $3\overline{)26}$

25. $29 \div 4 =$ ■   **26.** $23 \div 3 =$ ■   **27.** $55 \div 9 =$ ■

28. There are 26 pens for 4 children to share equally. How many pens should each child get? How many pens will be left?

Level C ....

Find the quotient and the remainder.

29. $4\overline{)31}$ **30.** $3\overline{)23}$ **31.** $5\overline{)48}$ **32.** $6\overline{)38}$ **33.** $9\overline{)57}$

34. $8\overline{)49}$ **35.** $6\overline{)59}$ **36.** $7\overline{)40}$ **37.** $5\overline{)43}$ **38.** $4\overline{)18}$

39. $74 \div 8 =$ ■   **40.** $69 \div 7 =$ ■   **41.** $45 \div 7 =$ ■

42. Joy puts 8 plums in each bag. She has 73 plums. How many bags does she use? How many plums are left?

KEY SKILL: Dividing 2-Digit Numbers (Use after page 501.)

Level A ....

Find the quotient and the remainder.

1. $2\overline{)33}$ 2. $4\overline{)55}$ 3. $6\overline{)68}$ 4. $3\overline{)49}$ 5. $8\overline{)89}$

6. $3\overline{)55}$ 7. $2\overline{)47}$ 8. $5\overline{)58}$ 9. $3\overline{)31}$ 10. $3\overline{)38}$

11. $55 \div 3 =$ ▆   12. $58 \div 5 =$ ▆   13. $38 \div 3 =$ ▆

14. Bob has 58 pens. He puts an equal number of pens into 9 cases. How many pens are in each case? How many are left?

Level B ....

Find the quotient and the remainder.

15. $4\overline{)57}$ 16. $3\overline{)67}$ 17. $5\overline{)62}$ 18. $7\overline{)85}$ 19. $5\overline{)68}$

20. $3\overline{)49}$ 21. $4\overline{)58}$ 22. $6\overline{)79}$ 23. $5\overline{)63}$ 24. $2\overline{)39}$

25. $59 \div 3 =$ ▆   26. $69 \div 6 =$ ▆   27. $75 \div 6 =$ ▆

28. Dee has 50 books. She puts an equal number of books on 4 shelves. How many are on each shelf? How many are left?

Level C ....

Find the quotient and the remainder.

29. $7\overline{)87}$ 30. $4\overline{)74}$ 31. $8\overline{)97}$ 32. $5\overline{)67}$ 33. $2\overline{)79}$

34. $7\overline{)81}$ 35. $8\overline{)93}$ 36. $3\overline{)74}$ 37. $4\overline{)86}$ 38. $6\overline{)91}$

39. $46 \div 3 =$ ▆   40. $77 \div 6 =$ ▆   41. $81 \div 6 =$ ▆

42. Doug has 73 marbles. He puts an equal number of marbles into 6 bags. How many marbles are in each bag? How many are left?

CHAPTER REVIEW/TEST

LANGUAGE AND MATHEMATICS

Complete the sentences. Use the words in the chart.

1. 5 is the ■ when you divide 20 by 4.

2. The number of objects left over when dividing is called the ■.

3. A compatible number uses a ■ to help find an estimate.

VOCABULARY
rounding
remainder
quotient
basic fact
sum

CONCEPTS AND SKILLS

Divide mentally.

4. 6)‾6‾0‾

5. 2)‾8‾0‾

6. 6)‾6‾0‾0‾

Estimate by rounding.

7. 7)‾7‾2‾

8. 6)‾2‾9‾5‾

9. 5)‾4‾2‾2‾

Estimate. Use compatible numbers.

10. 4)‾7‾3‾

11. 4)‾2‾9‾0‾

12. 5)‾3‾1‾1‾

Find the quotient and the remainder.

13. 3)‾5‾

14. 9)‾2‾9‾

15. 4)‾6‾2‾

16. 7)‾4‾5‾

17. $87 \div 3 =$ ■

18. $61 \div 8 =$ ■

Critical Thinking

Check the division. If incorrect, give the correct answer.

19. $47 \div 5 = 9 \text{ R}2$

20. $67 \div 4 = 15 \text{ R}7$

21. $720 \div 9 = 80$

Mixed Applications

22. Rob puts 47 pumpkins onto tables. Each table holds 8 pumpkins. To display all the pumpkins, how many tables will Rob need?

23. Kim picks 5 baskets of apples. There are 24 apples in each basket. How many apples does Kim pick?

24. Donald bought 175 daisies and 258 roses for his shop. How many flowers did he buy?

25. There are 29 plums for 9 children to share. How many plums will each child get? How many plums will be left?

PERFORMANCE ASSESSMENT

Work with your group to solve this problem.

Suppose your class is going to a magic show. Each row in the theater has 9 seats. How many rows will be completely filled by your class? How many rows are needed to seat all the students? Find the answer using 2 different methods.

1. *Think about:*
    - the number of students in your class
    - the number of completely filled rows
    - the total number of rows needed
    - what 2 methods to use

2. Write a paragraph to explain how you found your answer.

CUMULATIVE REVIEW

Choose the letter of the correct answer.

1. Estimate by rounding:
   $319 \div 8$
   a. 4   c. 400
   b. 40   d. 4,000

2. Estimate by using compatible numbers: $353 \div 7$
   a. 21   c. 60
   b. 50   d. 70

3. Divide mentally: $500 \div 5$
   a. 10   c. 1,000
   b. 100   d. not given

4. $8\overline{)78}$
   a. 9 R6   c. 11 R6
   b. 10 R2   d. not given

5. $7\overline{)84}$
   a. 14   c. 10 R4
   b. 11   d. not given

6. Nan bought 3 shirts for $4.98 each. About how much money did she spend?
   a. $15.00   c. $24.00
   b. $20.00   d. $30.00

7.   500
         $\times$ 30
   a. 150   c. 15,000
   b. 1,500   d. not given

8. $16 \times 6 = \underline{\blacksquare}$
   a. 56   c. 96
   b. 72   d. not given

9. Which is the best estimate for the capacity of a fish tank?
   a. 6 pints   c. 6 gallons
   b. 6 cups   d. not given

10.   123
          $\times$ 8
   a. 894   c. 8,164
   b. 984   d. not given

11. $29 \div 4 = \underline{\blacksquare}$
    a. 3   c. 7 R1
    b. 4 R3   d. not given

12. Which has two endpoints?
    a. ray   c. line segment
    b. line   d. not given

13. Which number sentence is true?
    a. $\frac{3}{4} < \frac{1}{8}$ c. $1\frac{2}{3} > 2\frac{4}{6}$
    b. $2\frac{1}{5} < 2\frac{7}{10}$ d. not given

14. $\frac{1}{4}$ of 12
    a. 3   c. 12
    b. 4   d. 48

DIVISIBILITY RULES FOR 5 AND 10

A number is **divisible** by another number when the remainder is zero. You can tell if a number is divisible by 5 or 10 without dividing.

You can write your own rules to check for divisibility. Divide each of these numbers by 5. Then divide them by 10.

10   12   15   20   24   25   30   35   36   40

1. Which numbers are divisible by 5? by 10?

2. Look at the digits in the ones place of the numbers divisible by 5. What do you notice?

3. What do you notice about the digits in the ones place of the numbers divisible by 10?

4. Use what you have noticed to write a rule about numbers that are divisible by 5. Test your rule on other numbers.

5. Use what you have noticed to write a rule about numbers that are divisible by 10. Test your rule on other numbers.

Is the number divisible by 5? Write *yes* or *no*.

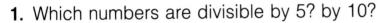

6. 29	**7.** 35	**8.** 68	**9.** 50	**10.** 77
11. 138	**12.** 100	**13.** 272	**14.** 1,180	**15.** 2,165

Is the number divisible by 10? Write *yes* or *no*.

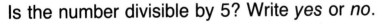

16. 90	**17.** 46	**18.** 75	**19.** 50	**20.** 78
21. 110	**22.** 412	**23.** 395	**24.** 1,050	**25.** 2,750

DATABANK

The Databank contains statistics and data similar to what can be found in outside reference books. The charts, graphs, menus, and maps contained here provide the real-world information needed to solve problems throughout the Pupil's Edition.

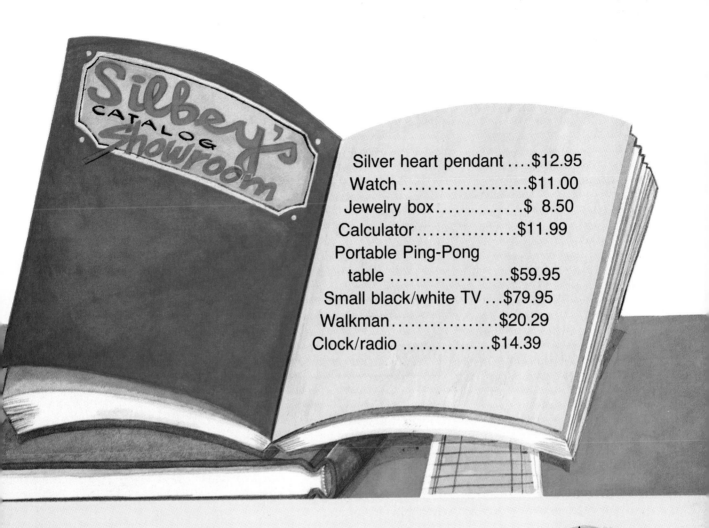

Silver heart pendant $12.95
Watch $11.00
Jewelry box.............$ 8.50
Calculator................$11.99
Portable Ping-Pong
   table $59.95
Small black/white TV ...$79.95
Walkman................$20.29
Clock/radio $14.39

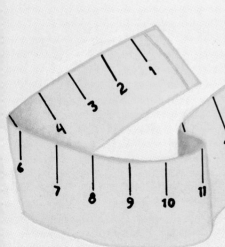

HEIGHT OF CHILDREN	
Name	Height in centimeters
Charles	124
Amy	117
Gene	119
Juan	120
Billy	129
Maria	128

REFRESHMENTS AND SOUVENIRS

Item	Price
cap	$2.75
banner	$3.25
juice	$ .75
pencil	$ .50
pretzel	$ .75
calendar	$5.25

RED CANYON CAMPGROUND

Nature Trails Start Here

TRAIL	DISTANCE
Little Mountain	1 KM
Sunset Path	5 KM
Happy Trail	9 KM
Adventure Walk	13 KM

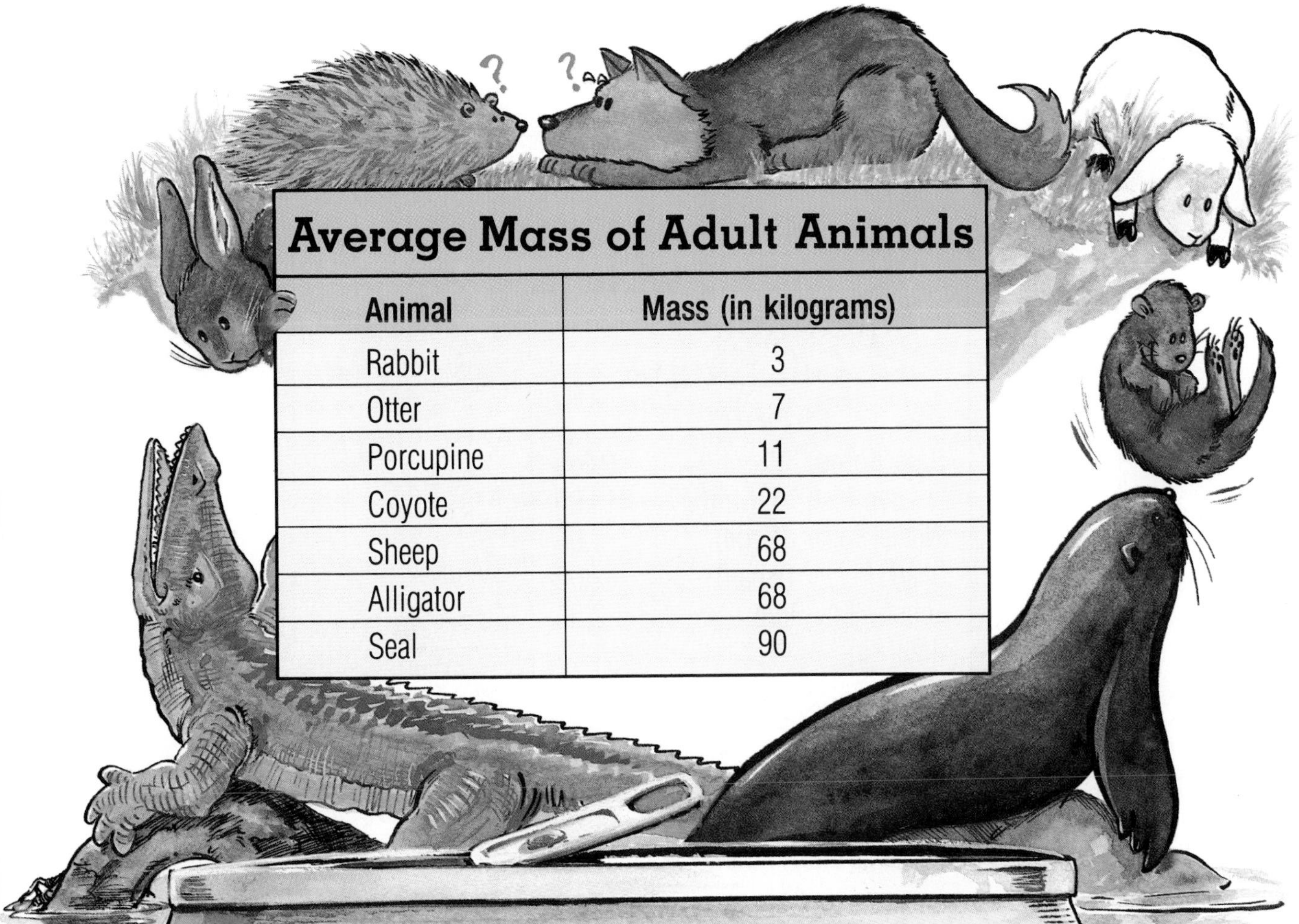

Average Mass of Adult Animals

Animal	Mass (in kilograms)
Rabbit	3
Otter	7
Porcupine	11
Coyote	22
Sheep	68
Alligator	68
Seal	90

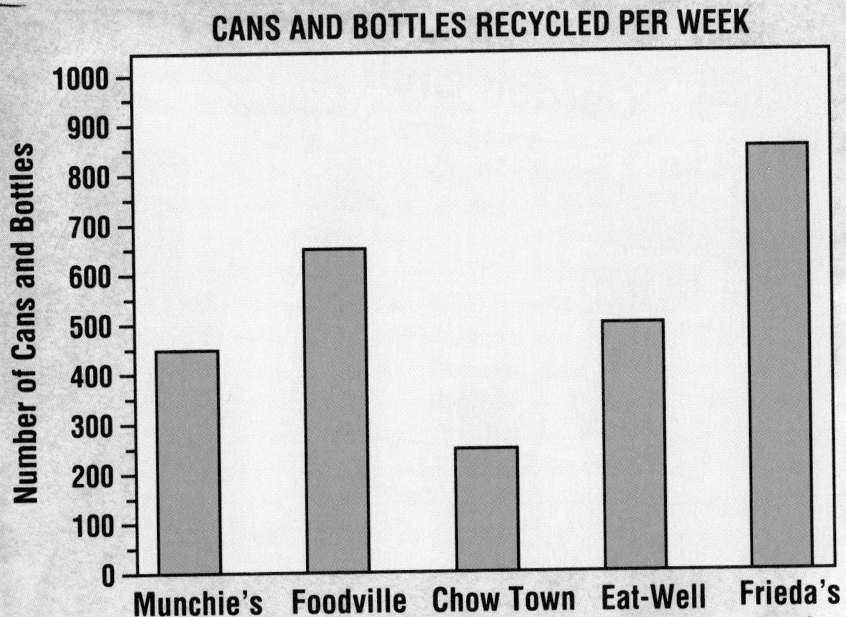

CANS AND BOTTLES RECYCLED PER WEEK

Number of Cans and Bottles

1000
900
800
700
600
500
400
300
200
100
0

Munchie's Market   Foodville   Chow Town   Eat-Well Foods   Frieda's Foods

Aquarium Gift Shop Sale

Sale Items	Price
"I Love Fish" T-Shirt	$10.00
Whale Poster (large)	5.00
Shark Poster (small)	2.00
Lobster Key Ring	2.50
Crab Pin	1.00

Evergreen Garden Club

Seeds Planted	Height in Week 1	Height in Week 2
Beans	$\frac{1}{2}$ inch	$\frac{3}{4}$ inch
Carrots	$\frac{1}{2}$ inch	1 inch
Tomatoes	$\frac{1}{4}$ inch	$\frac{3}{4}$ inch

AVERAGE LENGTH OF BIRDS
(from tip of bill to tip of tail)

Bird	Average Length (inches)
American Crow	$17\frac{1}{2}$
Fish Crow	$15\frac{1}{2}$
Mexican Crow	$14\frac{1}{2}$
Northwestern Crow	16
Blue Jay	11
Brown Jay	$16\frac{1}{2}$
Gray Jay	$11\frac{1}{2}$
Green Jay	$10\frac{1}{2}$

PLUM HEALTH FOOD BAR

Item	Price
Granola	$1.75
Organic apples	3 for $1.85
Health salad	$3.95
Carrot juice	$0.95
Milk	$0.60

NORMAL MONTHLY TEMPERATURES IN DEGREES FAHRENHEIT

Location	March	June	September	December
Fairbanks, Alaska	9	59	45	−10
Boston, Massachusetts	38	68	65	34
Chicago, Illinois	36	69	65	28
Duluth, Minnesota	23	59	54	14
Houston, Texas	61	81	78	54
Miami, Florida	72	81	82	69

521

DATABANK

NEW TOWN

Lanes / Avenues grid:

- TV Tower — A, 4
- Post. Office — C, 3
- Music Center — D, 5
- Duck pond — G, 5
- Supermarket — F, 3
- Animal Park — D, 1

Lanes (vertical axis): 1 2 3 4 5 6
Avenues (horizontal axis): A B C D E F G H

Price List for Used Books
Paperbacks 5¢
Hardcovers 25¢
Puzzlebooks 50¢

5 pens
85¢ Special

non-toxic
3 markers
81¢ Bargain

6 covers
90¢ Cheap!

4 folders
68¢

GLOSSARY

A

addend A number to be added to another number.
Example: 9 + 6 = 15
The addends are 9 and 6.

addition An operation that tells how many in all when you put together two or more numbers.

angle A figure formed when two rays meet at the same endpoint.
Example:

A.M. A way to indicate the time from 12 midnight to 12 noon.

area The number of square units needed to cover a surface.

B

bar graph A graph that shows information by using bars of different lengths.

C

capacity The amount a container can hold.

centimeter (cm) A unit of length in the metric system. 100 cm = 1 m
(*See* Table of Measures.)

circle A closed curved figure. All the points of the circle are the same distance from the center.
Example:

cone A space figure whose base is a circle.
Example:

congruent figures Figures that have the same shape and size.
Example:

cube A space figure with six square sides all the same size.
Example:

cup (c) A unit for measuring liquids.
(*See* Table of Measures.)

customary system A system of measurement. (*See* Table of Measures.)

cylinder A space figure with two faces that are circles.
Example:

D

data Information.

databank A place where data is stored.

decimal A number that uses place value and a decimal point to show tenths and hundredths.
Examples:
0.8, 1.7, 23.04
↑   ↑   ↑ decimal point

decimeter (dm) A unit of length in the metric system. 1 dm = 10 cm (*See* Table of Measures.)

degree Celsius (°C) A metric unit for measuring temperature.

degree Fahrenheit (°F) A customary unit for measuring temperature.

denominator The number below the bar in a fraction. It tells the number of parts in all.
Example: $\frac{2}{5}$ ← denominator

difference The number obtained by subtracting one number from another.
Example: $7 - 2 = 5$ ← difference

digit Symbol used to write numbers.
Examples: 0, 1, 2, 3, 4, 5, 6, 7, 8, and 9

dividend A number to be divided.

divisible A number is divisible by another number if the remainder is zero after dividing.

division An operation on two numbers that tells how many sets or how many in each set.
Example: 3 ← quotient
divisor → 3)9 ← dividend

divisor The number by which the dividend is divided.

E

equal (=) Symbol meaning "has the same value as."

equivalent fractions Different fractions that name the same amount.
Examples: $\frac{1}{2}$ and $\frac{2}{4}$; $\frac{1}{3}$ and $\frac{3}{9}$; $\frac{1}{4}$ and $\frac{4}{16}$

estimate To find an answer that is close to the exact answer.

even number A number that ends in 0, 2, 4, 6, or 8.

expanded form A way to express a number.
Example: 364 can be written as $300 + 60 + 4$.

F

fact family Related facts using the same numbers.
Example: $2 + 3 = 5$; $3 + 2 = 5$; $5 - 3 = 2$; $5 - 2 = 3$

factors Numbers that are multiplied to give a product.
Example: $4 \times 6 = 24$
The factors are 4 and 6.

flip To move a figure over a line.
Example:

foot (ft) A unit for measuring length. (*See* Table of Measures.)

fraction A number that names part of a whole or a set.
Examples: $\frac{3}{4}$, $\frac{4}{5}$, $\frac{1}{3}$

G

gram (g) A metric unit of mass. (*See* Table of Measures.)

graph A drawing used to show information by using lines, bars, or pictures.

greater than (>) Symbol to show that the first number is greater than the second.
Example: 9 > 6

I

inch (in.) A unit for measuring length. (*See* Table of Measures.)

K

kilogram (kg) A metric unit of mass. (*See* Table of Measures.)

L

less than (<) Symbol to show that the first number is less than the second.
Example: 13 < 64

line A straight path that goes in two directions without end.
Example:

line segment A straight path that has two endpoints.
Example:

line of symmetry
line of symmetry A line on which a figure can be folded so that both sides match.
Example:

M

mass A measurement that indicates how much of something there is. It is measured by kilograms and grams.

median When a set of numbers is arranged from least to greatest, the median is the middle number.
Example: 2, 4, 7, 9, 12. The median is 7.

metric system A system of measurement.
(*See* Table of Measures.)

mile Unit for measuring length.
1 mile = 5,280 feet
(*See* Table of Measures.)

mixed number A number that has a whole number and a fraction.
Example: $5\frac{3}{4}$

multiplication Combination of two numbers (factors) to give one number (product).
Example: $3 \times 7 = 21 \leftarrow$ product
factors

N

numerator The number above the bar in a fraction. It tells the number of parts.
Example: $\frac{2}{5} \leftarrow$ numerator

O

odd number A number that ends in 1, 3, 5, 7, or 9.

order property When adding or multiplying, the order of the numbers does not affect the result.

ordered pair A pair of numbers that gives the location of a point on a map or graph.

ordinal number A number used to tell order or position.
Example: second

ounce (oz) A unit for measuring weight. (*See* Table of Measures.)

P

perimeter The distance around a closed figure.

pictograph A graph that shows information by using picture symbols.

pint (pt) A unit for measuring liquid. (*See* Table of Measures.)

place value The value given to the place a digit occupies in a number.

plane figure A figure that lies on a flat surface.
Examples:

square

circle

P.M. A name for time between 12 noon and 12 midnight.

polygon A closed figure with straight sides. For example, a *pentagon* has five sides, a *hexagon* has six sides.

pound (lb) A unit for measuring weight. (*See* Table of Measures.)

probability The chance of something happening.

product The result of multiplication.
Example: $3 \times 4 = 12 \leftarrow$ product

pyramid A space figure that is shaped by triangles on a base.
Example:

Q

quart (qt) A unit for measuring amounts of liquid. (*See* Table of Measures.)

quotient The result of division.
Example: $28 \div 4 = 7 \leftarrow$ quotient.

R

range The difference between the greatest and least numbers in a set of numbers.

ray A plane figure with one endpoint that goes forever in one direction.
Example: •——•→

rectangle A plane figure with four sides and four equal angles. The opposite sides are the same length.
Example:

remainder The number left over after dividing.
Example: $64 \div 7 = 9 \text{ R1} \leftarrow$ remainder

right angle An angle that forms a square corner.
Example:

rounding Finding the nearest ten, hundred, thousand, and so on.
Example: 53 rounded to the nearest 10 is 50.

S

skip-count Counting by twos, threes, fours, and so on.
Examples: 2, 4, 6, 8, 10, . . . 3, 6, 9, 12, . . . or 4, 8, 12, 16, . . .

slide To move a figure along a line.
Example:

space figure A figure that is not flat but has volume, like a *rectangular prism.*
Example:

sphere A space figure that has the shape of a round ball.
Example:

square A plane figure that has four equal sides and four square corners.
Example:

subtraction An operation on two numbers to find the difference.
Example: $13 - 2 = 11$

sum The result of addition.
Example: $5 + 2 = 7 \leftarrow$ sum

T

triangle A plane figure with three sides and three corners.
Example:

turn To move a figure in a curved path.
Example:

U

unit An amount or quantity used as a standard of measurement.

V

volume Number of cubic units that fit inside a space figure.
Example:

W

weight A measurement that tells how heavy an object is.

whole number Any number, such as 0, 1, 2, 3, 4, 5, 6, 7, . . .

Y

yard (yd) A unit for measuring length. 1 yd = 3 ft (*See* Table of Measures.)

Z

zero property When adding zero to or subtracting zero from a number, the result is the number. When multiplying by zero, the result is zero. You cannot divide by zero.

TABLE OF MEASURES

TIME

60 minutes (min)	= 1 hour (h)
24 hours	= 1 day (d)
7 days	= 1 week (wk)
12 months (mo)	= 1 year (y)
about 52 weeks	= 1 year
365 days	= 1 year
366 days	= 1 leap year

METRIC UNITS

LENGTH
- 10 centimeters (cm) = 1 decimeter (dm)
- 10 decimeters = 1 meter (m)
- 1,000 meters = 1 kilometer (km)

MASS
- 1 kilogram (kg) = 1,000 grams (g)

CAPACITY
- 1 liter (L) = 1,000 milliliters (mL)

TEMPERATURE
- 0° Celsius (°C) . . . Water freezes
- 100° Celsius . . . Water boils

CUSTOMARY UNITS

LENGTH
- 1 foot (ft) = 12 inches (in.)
- 1 yard (yd) = 36 inches
- 1 yard = 3 feet
- 1 mile (mi) = 5,280 feet
- 1 mile = 1,760 yards

WEIGHT
- 1 pound (lb) = 16 ounces (oz)

CAPACITY
- 1 pint (pt) = 2 cups
- 1 quart (qt) = 2 pints
- 1 gallon (gal) = 4 quarts

TEMPERATURE
- 32° Fahrenheit (°F) . . . Water freezes
- 212° Fahrenheit . . . Water boils

SYMBOLS

<	is less than
>	is greater than
=	is equal to
°	degree
↔	line AB
•—•	line segment AB
•→	ray AB
∠	angle
(5, 3)	ordered pair 5, 3